The Office of Prime Minister

The
Office of Prime Minister

by

BYRUM E. CARTER

1956

PRINCETON UNIVERSITY PRESS

PRINCETON   NEW JERSEY

To my

Mother and Father

Contents

Contents

Preface

The late Professor Laski once described the American President as 'both more and less than a prime minister.' The American President has been a frequent object of study and a number of works have been published which attempted to portray this office in all of its aspects. It is surprising, however, that no comparable work has been written upon the British Prime Minister. There have been many studies of the Cabinet, the Parliament, and the Constitution, which have included consideration of the place of the Prime Minister within a broader context, but no study has concentrated specifically upon the office of the Prime Minister in all of its ramifications, institutional, and extra-institutional. It is the author's hope that this book may serve as a temporarily adequate first attempt to paint a total picture of the modern office of the Prime Minister.

It must be admitted that many of the elements which make political studies exciting and appealing are absent from this work. The great issues of policy, which catch the attention and focus the emotions, are incidental, not central, to the objective with which this study was pursued. No effort is made to assess the adequacy of the policies pursued by such controversial figures as Lloyd George, Baldwin, MacDonald, or Churchill. Instead, attention is concentrated upon the policy making process. This, of necessity, sometimes leads to a concern with technicalities and minute differentiations, but a technicality is not necessarily unimportant, nor a small distinction of little significance.

The intent of the author is to present an objective statement of what the Prime Minister does, and what is done to him. More than that, it is a description of the office within a certain rather definite historical period. Although a brief historical

---

[1] Harold J. Laski, *The American Presidency* (New York, Harpers, 1940), p. 11.

9

sketch of the rise of the office is provided, the basic concern is with the Prime Minister in this century. This is not to say that no attention is given to the practices and uses of the office under Peel, Gladstone, Disraeli, or other nineteenth-century Premiers, but, upon the whole, the examples selected to clarify the statements of general principles are chosen from the actions of twentieth-century political leaders.

This delimitation would seem to be necessary for two reasons. Limitations of space make a general study of the office since Sir Robert Walpole impossible. In addition, the office has changed substantially since the extensions of the suffrage in 1867 and 1884. To treat the pre-democratic and the post-democratic office as if it were actually the same position would be to confuse more than to clarify.

The basic source materials upon which this study is based are not government documents or papers. Public papers have been used, but it is nevertheless true that the study deals with many matters, and those frequently the most important, which are not of such a kind as to be capable of expression in public documents. The basic materials have been memoirs and biographies. Professor Jennings has pointed out the dangers inherent in the use of such materials.[1] It is not necessary to repeat all of the factors he mentions, but it is obvious that memoirs and official biographies do not necessarily present all of the facts. Statesmen are as human as the ordinary mortal; they too dislike being revealed in a bad light. It is to be expected, therefore, that such materials are likely to omit instances in which the individual writing, or whose biography is being presented by a friend, acted 'foolishly'. Captain Harry Butcher reports a conversation with Winston Churchill in which 'The Prime Minister said that it was foolish to keep a day-by-day diary because it would simply reflect the change of opinion or decision of the writer, which, when and if published, makes one appear indecisive. . . . For his part, the Prime Minister said, he would prefer to wait until the war is over and then write impressions, so that, if necessary, he could correct or bury his mistakes.'[2] Unfortunately it may be the case that such 'mistakes' deserve serious con-

[1] W. I. Jennings, *Cabinet Government* (Cambridge, Cambridge University Press, 1936), pp. 10–12.

[2] Captain Harry Butcher, *My Three Years with Eisenhower* (New York, Simon and Schuster, 1946), p. 319.

sideration, but it is not always possible to run them to ground. Fortunately, a study which is concerned with procedure is less frequently involved in this difficulty than one which is concerned with the content of the decisions reached.

It is also obvious that the materials available for the last half of the twentieth century are far less adequate than those for the first half. There are a smaller number of available memoirs, and most of those which do exist are inferior in quality when compared to those available through the First World War. This is of some importance, for two reasons. First, it means that it is more frequently necessary to use examples chosen from the earlier period. It also means that the student has greater confidence in his ability to comprehend what actually did occur in the earlier period. This follows from the fact that the greater number of memoirs enables him to cross-check references to the same situation, and thus attempt to balance them and discover what actually did occur. The same measure of evidence does not exist for the later period, for too frequently it was necessary to rely upon a single source. No individual, however meritorious he may be, can be depended upon to reach a high-level of objectivity in evaluation of his own actions, but through cross-checks made on memoirs and biographies of other participants it becomes possible to arrive at a somewhat closer approximation to the truth of the situation.

Even in those cases in which there is a considerable mass of material, it is also necessary to realize that the author himself, in evaluating them, may have 'inarticulate major premises' which result in undue selectivity among the materials, or which may lead him to weigh the statements of one individual somewhat more heavily than they might deserve.

When all of these factors are added together, it is obvious that no one can hope precisely to describe the office of the Prime Minister as it actually is. As Stanley Baldwin said, in speaking of the Constitution, 'The historian can tell you probably perfectly clearly what the constitutional practice was at any given period in the past, but it would be very difficult for a living writer to tell you at any given period in his lifetime what the Constitution of the country is in all respects, and for this reason, that almost at any given moment . . . there may be one practice called "constitutional" which is falling into desuetude and there may be another practice which is creeping into use but is not yet constitutional.'[1] The same statement may be applied with equal justification to the position of the Prime Minister.

The author has obvious obligations to many persons who have given him assistance either directly or indirectly. Some of these may be noted by the footnote references to the works of those who have pioneered in the study of twentieth-century British politics. Certainly this work would never have been possible had not Professor W. I. Jennings and Professor A. B. Keith produced monumental studies in British constitutional law and practice. Much of this work is built upon the solid foundations which they have provided.

Other persons have contributed more directly, and more personally, to whatever merit this study may have. Professor Leslie Lipson assisted in the formulation of the scope of the study. Professor John Gaus, formerly of Wisconsin, now of Harvard, did much to turn my interest to this subject by his emphasis upon the values and insights to be derived from the study of the memoirs and letters of British Cabinet members. Professor William Ebenstein of Princeton did more than any other individual to develop my interest in the field of comparative government. Professor David Fellman of Wisconsin read the entire manuscript in its early stages and contributed many suggestions of great value. To him the author owes an almost unlimited debt. Harry Lease assisted in checking some of the footnotes, while Betty Goldberg, Fred Horrigan and Victor Hoffman helped with proof-reading. Mr. Hoffman and Mr. Horrigan also worked on the index. My wife contributed both patience and assistance. Acknowledgment should also be made of a grant from the Graduate School of Indiana University which facilitated completion of the study. To these persons must go a great deal of whatever credit this book may have. All errors are, of course, the responsibility of the author.

Bloomington, Indiana, 1955.

[1] 261 *H.C. Deb.* 5s., 531; Jennings, *op. cit.*, p. 12.

I

The Historical Development of the Office of Prime Minister

The contemporary Prime Minister is one of the strongest elective officers in the world. In time of war his powers often expand to such an extent as to challenge those exercised by modern dictators, although he is always subject to the eventual check of colleagues, legislature and public. Nevertheless, the exigencies of war frequently require a concentration of authority and decision in one man as a necessary basis for the effective prosecution of military matters. In such circumstances it is the Prime Minister who serves as the locus of that concentration of authority.[1]

This situation is the product of over two centuries of growth, often rapid, sometimes slow, interspersed with periods of regression, as during those years between the administration of Walpole and the younger Pitt or between Pitt and 1834. The office has developed with the growth of the Cabinet and the gradual change whereby the control of political power slipped from King to Parliament, and to a large extent from Parliament to Cabinet, has inevitably resulted in an increase in the authority of the Prime Minister in that powerful committee of the Parliament. Naturally, the growth of political institutions *per se* has been affected by many external forces: the growth of science, changes in the economy of Britain occasioned by technological innovation; changes in class structure, class relationships and class expectations; the growth of egalitarian concepts of government and economic organization; changes in Britain's world

[1] *Post.*, Chapter VIII. Cf. Clinton L. Rossiter, *Constitutional Dictatorship* (Princeton, Princeton University Press, 1948), chaps. 10–13.

position; and war, which has frequently accelerated an already existing tendency or given impetus in a new direction.[1]

There had frequently been chief ministers in the history of England prior to the eighteenth century,[2] but they were not comparable to the modern Prime Minister for their power was based upon the royal favour, or upon extra-institutional influences, rather than upon the control of a working parliamentary majority to which they would be responsible should they take action unacceptable to the members of the legislative body. For purposes of convenience it is best to start the discussion with the Restoration of 1660.

Charles II returned to England as the rightful King to exercise his authority over a people tired of civil war and political and social experimentation. The English had experimented with a republic, a protectorate, had had their only written constitution, and had considered even further experiments in social organization. They had been subjected to the rule of censorial and dogmatic religious revolutionaries. It is safe to say that they were tired of experimentation, tired of the restrictive moral code elaborated for them by their governors. They turned to the restored King and the illusions of the past.

In fact, it was impossible to return to the royal pretensions of the past in their entirety. The Civil War had made it clear that the King could not possibly hope to exercise the authority claimed by James I in his *Trew Law of Free Monarchies*.[3] It is probable that there was no precise knowledge of how the institutional arrangements between King and Parliament were to be worked out. Such matters were left to the essentially pragmatic test of experience. Charles II could not hope to rule as an absolute King. His powers might be very substantial, but it was clear that Parliament stood as a restraint upon capricious

---

[1] Since the beginning of the eighteenth century the British have fought a multiplicity of minor wars and a number of major ones. Among the more important major conflicts are the War of the Spanish Succession, the imperial wars with France, the wars with the French Republic and Napoleon and two world wars in this century. It is obvious that such events inevitably impinge upon the characteristics of important political office.

[2] Cf. Clive Bigham, *The Chief Ministers of England, 920–1720* (New York, Dutton, 1923).

[3] James argued that kings ruled by divine right and said of kings, 'even by God himself they are called Gods.' *The Political Works of James I* (Cambridge, Mass., Harvard University Press, 1918), p. 307.

authority. The Restoration marked a return to the past idea of a balance between King, Lords, and Commons in which none could act without consideration of the interests and approval of the others.[1] This system of balances, however, applied to the relation between the King and Parliament, not to the relations between the King and his ministers.

The executive power was still firmly concentrated in the hands of the King. What had been decided, in an admittedly imprecise fashion, was that the King could not act in some areas without the consent of the Parliament. The ministers in these circumstances were his ministers. They were appointed by him and they were responsible to him alone. They did not depend upon Parliament for the maintenance of their position, nor were they chosen as representatives of the Parliament. In fact, the Parliament looked upon the ministers with considerable suspicion. Although some of them sat in the legislative chambers, they were considered the agents of the Crown. They were enemies, not friends. They represented the King in any conflict over policy which he might have with the Parliament.[2]

The ministers themselves did not form a ministry for they were not united. There were a number of ministers, but no one minister had the specific obligation of forming a ministry. There was no one minister who could control and direct the activities of his ministerial colleagues, nor did the ministers as a body attempt to present a united front to King and Parliament. All were appointed by the King, all owed direct loyalty to him, and all were responsible to him alone.[3] Some ministers were more influential than others, and thus might be able to influence the King to accept their personal policy, but the final decision in such matters rested with the King. Lord Clarendon was

[1] Sir Roger L'Estrange, prior to the restoration, stated the merits of this system as follows: 'This was that triple cord, . . . this was our gold, seven times refined, for every bill, being thrice read, debated and agreed, in either House, was at last brought to the King, for his royal assent, the mint of our laws: a trial so exact, that surely no dross could escape it; since all interests must thereto concur (as truly, it was but fit they should, in the establishment of that, which must bind them all) . . .' Quoted in Francis D. Wormuth, *The Origins of Modern Constitutionalism* (New York, Harper and Brothers, 1949), p. 57.

[2] Mary Taylor Blauvelt, *The Development of Cabinet Government in England* (New York, Macmillan, 1902), p. 35.

[3] *Ibid.*, p. 38.

frequently recognized as the first minister, but he was not the chief of the government for the King was both *de jure* and *de facto* the holder of that position. Clarendon's position depended upon his personal ability to persuade the King to accept his point of view, for there were no institutional weapons of any magnitude at his disposal.[1]

Clarendon did not protest against this procedure for he seems to have believed that it was the most desirable system. It was his conviction that Englishmen would not tolerate a Prime Minister. He believed that they would prefer to be ruled by an absolute monarch rather than by 'a lawful monarch who ruled through a prime minister.'[2] His personal predilections seem to have been in favour of an absolutism such as that exercised by Elizabeth, an absolutism tempered by the existence of reserve parliamentary power.[3] At the same time he was opposed to the divine right conceptions which were prominent in France at the time. In Clarendon's view ministers might legitimately attempt to influence the King, but it was the latter who made the decision, and an obligation rested upon the ministers to assist him in the execution of his decision whatever it might be.[4] He was not concerned either to expand or limit the existing power of King or Parliament.[5]

Clarendon's influence was unquestionably large, but he was still the King's choice and his position depended upon the maintenance of royal favour.[6] One development under Clarendon,

---

[1] As an example it might be noted that Clarendon was forced on occasion to accept the appointment of ministers whom he disliked. In the case of Sir Henry Bennett he was obligated to accept a man he thought incompetent. Mark A. Thompson, *A Constitutional History of England* (London, Methuen, 1938), iv, 109–10; Blauvelt, *op. cit.*, pp. 39–40.

[2] Clarendon, *Autobiography* (Oxford, Clarendon Printing House, 1759), i, 89.

[3] Blauvelt, *op, cit.*, p. 28.

[4] However, Clarendon did take his opposition to Charles's Declaration of Indulgence to the floor of the Parliament.

[5] For example, when the first Parliament after the restoration offered to vote larger supplies than had been requested, Clarendon did not accept the offer as he did not desire to make the King independent of Parliament. Blauvelt, *op. cit.*, p. 35.

[6] Clarendon fell from office, however, as a result of parliamentary rather than royal action. He was ousted in 1667 as a result of parliamentary disapproval. The Parliament expressed the view that he was responsible for all of the events of the preceding seven years; a view which amounted to the

however, had important long-run consequences. Clarendon recognized that it was no longer possible for the King to consult with the Privy Council as a whole and therefore proposed the establishment of committees with which the King could consult. At least one of those committees, the Committee on Foreign Affairs, was established. Since that time the Council has not governed England and the chief responsibility has passed into the hands of a smaller body. At the same time they were controlled by the King, but the committee constituted a step towards a cabinet in the modern sense.[1]

The attitude of James II towards his ministers was the same as that of Charles. He too thought that the ministers were his personal representatives and held office only at his discretion and confidence. James' statement, 'I will have unanimity among my ministers', meant only that they should be unanimous in their loyalty to the King.[2] Like Charles, James appointed ministers of divergent views for their disagreements were matters of little moment when the final decision would be his personally. The treatment of the ministers as his personal servants did not involve any public disapproval for it was the customary and expected treatment reserved for ministers.

William of Orange knew that he was not an absolute King when he ascended the throne of England, for the acceptance of the Declaration of Rights was a prerequisite to his acquisition of the throne. The express provisions of the Declaration did not assert the principle of parliamentary supremacy, but the effect of the limitations set forth and the historical context within which it was enunciated made it clear that no pretensions of absolutism could be held by a future English King. It had been

belief that he was 'essentially the king's prime minister'. W. T. Morgan, *English Political Parties and Leaders in the Reign of Queen Anne* (New Haven, Yale University Press, 1920), pp. 14–15. The assertion itself was incorrect. The two main charges levied against him were responsibility for the Dutch War and the division of the fleet. Actually he had suggested neither and had opposed the former. It is questionable as to whether the Parliament actually thought him responsible, for it is more likely that they chose to act against Clarendon in order to embarrass the King who was beyond their reach.

[1] Blauvelt, *op. cit.*, pp. 29–32.
[2] *Ibid.*, pp. 69–70.

the Parliament which made him King; he did not rule by divine right.[1]

William continued in the belief that the ministers were responsible to him and not to Parliament. He exercised direct control over the government himself, attending all of the sessions of the cabinet, making ministerial appointments and determining the final position to be taken by the ministry as a body. William 'made a beginning, however, through practical experience upon the lesson which was more fully learned in the next reign, that the easiest way to accomplish what he desired, the line of least resistance in carrying out his policy, was to choose his chief ministers from those political leaders who were best able to secure the support of Parliament.'[2] The King continued to serve as his own Prime Minister. He controlled the ministerial appointments, and in some instances, even appointed individuals to subordinate departmental positions, in some cases without the prior knowledge of the head of the department.[3] The initiative in policy and execution was his.

[1] It is frequently said that the Glorious Revolution established the sovereignty of the Parliament. Thus Professors Sabine and Shepard, in the introduction to their translation of Hugo Krabbe's *The Modern Idea of the State* (The Hague, M. Nijhoff, 1922), p. xxi, write, 'In point of fact, the net outcome of the Revolution of 1688 was to transfer the sovereign power from king to Parliament, leaving the conception of sovereign power itself largely unchanged. Similarly, Professor Keith has written, 'The Bill of Rights, 1689, proved the supreme authority of Parliament as represented by the two houses. They had met under a summons legally without value, for it did not emanate from the King, and had assumed the right to declare the throne vacant, and to constitute a new sovereignty.' A. B. Keith, *The Constitution of England from Queen Victoria to George VI* (London, Macmillan, 1940), i, 3. While this probably expresses the final legal relationship between Parliament and King after 1688, it must be recognized that it is not particularly helpful in explaining the relationship which existed in the eighteenth century. This cannot be dealt with in terms of absolute dominance versus absolute submission. In fact, the relations of King and Parliament could not be precisely defined but had to be left to actual events for delineation. Neither Blackstone nor Montesquieu were so far from British political realities as is ordinarily assumed, for executive and legislative authority were frequently differentiated in practice, and the British still thought that substantial powers inhered in the King. The public support of the King is evidenced by George III's successful reassertion of that authority in the first twenty years of his reign.

[2] George B. Adams, *The Origin of the English Constitution* (New Haven, Yale University Press, 1931), p. 360; Blauvelt, *op. cit.*, pp. 75–76.

[3] Blauvelt, *op. cit.*, p. 81.

Queen Anne's attitude towards the ministers was no different from that of her predecessors. She considered them as her personal servants[1] and on occasion she made selections which did not reflect the majority view of the House of Commons. Her first ministry was predominantly High Church Tory at a time when the Parliament was predominantly Whig.[2] She thought that such ministers were responsible to her personally and not to the Parliament; she continued to attend the meetings of the cabinet.[3] Anne was weaker, however, than William had been and although she wished to head her own government she tended to let authority drift into other hands on occasion. Godolphin was unquestionably the first minister for some time and exercised substantial control over patronage and the direction of the activity of the cabinet council. At the same time it was still necessary to consult the Queen on matters of foreign policy and important domestic issues.[4] Although Godolphin's power was substantial he was never a Prime Minister, for he owed no obligation to the Parliament specifically nor did he exercise complete control in the cabinet, sharing it first with Marlborough and later with both Harley and the duke.[5]

Harley, who succeeded Godolphin, was described as a 'prime minister' by his contemporary, Jonathan Swift.[6] It is true that he had some of the attributes of that office. He was more specifically accountable for appointments than his predecessors, and he also accepted personal responsibility for governmental action in some instances, although in many cases the actual initiative had come from the Queen. In his relationships with the Parliament and with his colleagues in the ministry, however, his

[1] For an example of Anne's attitude see her letter dismissing Godolphin in which she wrote, 'The many unkind returns which I have received from you, and especially what you said to me personally before the Lords, make it impossible for me to continue you any longer in my service.' *Ibid.*, p. 110.

[2] Morgan, *op. cit.*, p. 73.

[3] *Ibid.*, pp. 61–84; Blauvelt, *op. cit.*, pp. 104–5.

[4] Morgan, *op. cit.*, pp. 239–40.

[5] *Ibid.*, p. 397. Evidence of his strength may be seen in his success in appointing Sunderland to the ministry in 1706 over the objections of the Queen. This is the first instance of its kind and marks a step toward the development of the principle that the chief minister has the right to select his own ministerial colleagues. John Morley, *Walpole* (New York, Macmillan, 1889), p. 143; Blauvelt, *op. cit.*, p. 107.

[6] Marcel Sibert, *Étude sur le Premier Ministre en Angleterre* (Paris, A. Rousseau, 1909), p. 37.

position was not so well defined. The idea of responsibility towards the Parliament had not developed and although he governed through the Parliament in part, he was still more clearly the servant of the Queen. Nor was he able to exercise control over his colleagues and there is no indication that they felt themselves accountable to him for their actions in any strict sense.[1]

While it is safe to say that the modern office of the Prime Minister had not yet emerged, it is true that Anne's reign was of basic constitutional importance in that the movement towards cabinet government was accelerated. Ministerial meetings were held regularly, usually at least once a week. At the same time it was not always clear as to exactly who should be called to such meetings. The Queen seems to have thought it was in her discretion to decide this question. Nor were all public affairs discussed in full ministerial meetings. The Queen, on occasion, took full responsibility for actions herself; in other instances she consulted some of the ministers, but not all. In addition the individual ministers exercised considerable discretion in deciding whether an issue should or should not be presented to the cabinet meeting.[2] Some clarification as to the relative importance of the members of the ministry was achieved, however, through the informal dinners which Harley held on Saturdays. The dinners enabled the ministers to meet together without the presence of the Queen who always presided over the formal sessions of her ministers. In addition it also enabled Harley to exercise some selectivity in determining who would be invited and some ministers were excluded. All of these events were making it clearer, than had previously been the case, that there existed an inner group in which the real power of the whole ministry lay.[3]

Anne's ministers were not always unified on the basis of one party rule. She herself did not hesitate to attempt to include both Whigs and Tories in the same ministry, but on occasion she was forced to accept the principle of one party composition. In 1710, the Whigs refused to enter a cabinet with the Tories and she was compelled to form a ministry which was entirely Tory in composition.[4] In part her success in maintaining two-party ministries was the result of the fact that some of the

---

[1] Blauvelt, *op. cit.*, pp. 127 ff.   [2] *Ibid.*, pp. 128–30..
[3] *Ibid.*, pp. 130–1.   [4] *Ibid.*, p. 135.

leaders of the parties themselves, such as Marlborough, Godolphin, Somerset, and Argyle, were opposed to one-party ministries. Nevertheless, the latter years of her reign revealed a tendency towards party consolidation expressed overtly by the Whig action in 1710. The Whigs were developing a coherent unified organization and, simultaneously, Bolingbroke was leading the Tories down the same path. It was a trend of enormous importance in enlarging the authority of the cabinet and changing the locus of executive authority, and eventually even basic legislative initiative, in the British system.[1] The concomitant increase in the authority of the House of Commons was also leading to the acceptance of the principle that the ministry served the Parliament rather than the monarch.

Anne's death led to an intensification of the movement towards responsible government. The question of succession had been a matter of some controversy in England and the decision to call the Hanoverians to the throne was a victory for the Whigs over the Tories. This fact was in itself of fundamental importance, for it meant that the King found himself allied with one party and dependent upon it both morally and practically for his position. It is anomalous that it should have been the Whigs rather than the Tories who benefited from royal favour, for the latter had been the supporters of the monarchical principle to a greater extent than the Whigs. This led to a diminution in the authority of the King, a diminution which was 'due to the transitory circumstances: to the alien character of the new royal house, its obligations to the Whig party, the complete supremacy of that party in political life owing to the suspected Jacobite tendencies of the Tories, and to the monopoly of political power in the hands of a few great families.'[2]

George I had some interest in English politics, but he was more often inclined to concern himself with the problems of Hanover rather than those of England.[3] Additionally he did not have an adequate grasp of English and in consequence neglected attending the Cabinet Council.[4] On several occasions

[1] Morgan, *op. cit.*, p. 243.

[2] A. Mervine Davies, *The Influence of George III on the Development of the Constitution* (London, Oxford University Press, 1921), pp. 5–6.

[3] Morley, *op. cit.*, p. 49; Blauvelt, *op. cit.*, p. 145.

[4] C. Grant Robertson, *England Under the Hanoverians* (New York, Putnam, 1927), p. 186. George II continued the practice of absenting himself from meetings of the cabinet council.

he returned to Hanover and in his absence left the control of domestic affairs in the hands of his ministers.[1] There were individual instances in which he attempted to exercise his prerogative, such as in the selection of Lord Townshend as first minister, or his later dismissal of that individual in the face of public disapproval, but on the whole his reign led to an enormous increase in the power of the ministry.[2]

Under the reign of the first two Hanoverians the first prototype of the modern Prime Minister emerged in the person of Sir Robert Walpole. Walpole first divided authority with Townshend, the latter controlling foreign affairs while Walpole handled finances,[3] but this division of authority was unworkable. It proved to be impossible to keep the areas completely segregated, and the struggle for power between the two men became evident in a dispute arising out of the terms of the Treaty of Hanover. Although the treaty had been negotiated by Townshend, Walpole was forced to bear the brunt of the defence of the treaty in the House of Commons. Similarly the treaty required financial means for its execution and this too fell within the purview of Walpole's functions. Walpole was dissatisfied with both of these responsibilities, in particular because he disliked the treaty and recognized that it was unpopular with the public.[4] Such internal friction obviously made the operation of the ministry difficult and the issue between the two men was joined. 'Cabinet unity and efficiency required, as the logic of its development slowly proved, that Ministers must agree on political principles, which in practice must come to mean the principles of the most important chief.'[5] Townshend lost his last support—court favour—shortly after the accession of George II, and Walpole was left with full control of the Cabinet following Townshend's resignation in 1729. It is from this date that we may say the office of Prime Minister came into existence, although it must be realized that many of Walpole's successors were far weaker than he.[6] Walpole 'virtually created the office of Prime Minister and made possible the evolution of the modern system of ministerial responsibility.'[7]

---

[1] Morley, *op. cit.*, p. 49.   [2] Blauvelt, *op. cit.*, pp. 149–52.
[3] Robertson, *op. cit.*, p. 44.   [4] *Ibid.*, p. 51.
[5] *Loc. cit.*   [6] *Ibid.*, p. 64; Blauvelt, *op. cit.*, p. 223.
[7] A. B. Keith, *The King and the Imperial Crown* (New York, Longmans, Green and Co., 1936), p. 64; J. A. R. Marriott, *English Political Institutions* (Oxford, Clarendon Press, 1925), p. 87.

Walpole's power was based upon a multiplicity of factors. First, court favour had made possible his victory over Townshend and he continued to hold that favour until the last years of his administration. His power, however, rested more firmly upon parliamentary support and a strong party organization. Again, his administration emphasized the importance of combining the office of First Lord of the Treasury with that of chief minister. While no longer of such importance as in the eighteenth century, the offices are now combined by law.[1] In a very large part Walpole maintained his position because his control of the Treasury meant control over fiscal policy and thus control of all aspects of government.[2] He was also remarkably effective in developing techniques for controlling the Parliament and the ministry. He demanded and obtained cabinet unity, insisting that if disagreement existed between ministers it must be kept private; the cabinet was to present a united front to the public. In those instances in which a minister publicly opposed his policy, he exerted himself to remove him, frequently with success.[3] Within the cabinet he was the master of all his colleagues; within the Parliament he was the leader of the House of Commons.[4] He continued the use of the inner cabinet and invited small numbers of his colleagues to confer with him either at dinner or in the privacy of his home.[5] He was involved in all cabinet decisions of major importance, but through the use of the inner cabinet, he was sometimes able to prevent the cabinet as a whole from critically considering an issue which he thought to be of fundamental importance.

Walpole also concentrated attention on the party organization for he realized that party strength provided the basis for parliamentary strength. Through party organization he was able to maintain control of the Parliament and thus the control of the development of policy. He had a clear knowledge of the fact that his power was based upon party power and that cabinet government rested indirectly upon the party system.

[1] *Ministers of the Crown Act of 1937*, 1 Edw. 8, 1 Geo. 6, c. 38.

[2] A. B. Keith, *The British Cabinet System, 1830–1938* (London, Stevens and Son, 1939), p. 17.

[3] Blauvelt, *op. cit.*, p. 236; Robertson, *op. cit.*, p. 188; Adams, *op. cit.*, p. 391.

[4] Marriott, *op. cit.*, p. 87.

[5] Morley, *op. cit.*, pp. 150–1.

Walpole therefore put pressure on Whig nobles and landed gentry to contribute to the party coffers. He exercised control over the corruption funds, thus enabling himself to play a predominant role in the selection of Whig candidates. Even his policies were often so conceived as to gain the support of the well-to-do and thus to increase the financial resources of his party.[1] Through this process he built a strong, relatively unified organization, although it had split by the end of his administration and his defeat in 1742 was the result of a combination of Tories and disaffected Whigs.[2]

Even in resignation Walpole established a constitutional precedent. He resigned because he had lost a vote of confidence in the House of Commons; thus he acted upon the basis of the rule that the Prime Minister must resign in case he is defeated in that chamber.[3]

His term of office was also influential in strengthening the political position of the House of Commons for his presence in that house for twenty-one years had increased its prestige. After Walpole it proved to be impossible to form a ministry which did not include representatives from the Commons. In 1756 Newcastle was obliged to give up office simply because he was unable to find a man to lead the lower house. 'There was no particular objection to him as Prime Minister. The trouble was that when the Prime Minister is a peer, two men are necessary. When he is a commoner, one is sufficient.'[4]

The first man to be called 'prime minister' without prejudicial connotations was Henry Pelham. Walpole had indignantly denied that he was Prime Minister when the Protest of Dissentient Peers had demanded his removal, charging he was Prime Minister and that no such office existed under the British constitution.[5] Pelham and his colleagues were successful

---

[1] Blauvelt, *op. cit.*, pp. 199–202.   [2] *Ibid.*, p. 157.

[3] Robertson, *op. cit.*, pp. 83–4; Blauvelt, *op. cit.*, pp. 157–8. While Walpole's action clearly foreshadowed the practice of later British constitutional development it must not be assumed that it was considered binding by his more immediate successors. For example, the younger Pitt was defeated on several occasions in the first months of his government, but neither resigned nor sought dissolution, preferring to wait until he was more confident of public support before pursuing the latter course.

[4] Blauvelt, *op. cit.*, pp. 194–5.

[5] Coxe, *Walpole* (London, 1798), iii, 564. The Protest stated in part, 'a sole or even a first minister is an officer unknown to the law of Britain,

in resisting the King in 1746 when the King had displeased them. The entire ministry, including subordinates, resigned *en masse*. The King attempted to form another government but the individuals appointed discovered that they could not carry out the government in the face of a hostile Parliament and in consequence they resigned and Pelham and his colleagues were restored to power.[1] Generally speaking, however, although Pelham was referred to as Prime Minister, he exercised no authority comparable to that which had been concentrated in the person of Walpole. The power in the cabinet under Pelham was triangularly divided with Newcastle and Harwicke. Pelham had a slight pre-eminence over the others, but he neither controlled all of their actions nor controlled the party apparatus in the fashion in which Walpole had been successful.[2]

The period from the fall of Walpole until the administration of the younger Pitt is one in which the progress made towards responsible government and the trend towards a chief of the cabinet were halted. The British constitution was turned back towards the past. This was the case primarily because of internal party division between 1742 and 1770 which made impossible any such control as that exercised by Walpole and by reason of the fact that the third of the Hanoverian kings, George III, had no intention of allowing the reality of authority to pass from his hands into those of his ministers. Even the presence of William Pitt in the office of Prime Minister did not result in any substantial accretion to the office itself. Pitt's power was a personal power, not an institutional power, he 'was first of the long line of popular politicians.'[3] He was not given to the nation by the King, nor was he given to the King by the

---

inconsistent with the constitution of this country and destructive of liberty in any government whatever.' Walpole in replying stated, 'I do not pretend to be a great master of foreign affairs; in that post it is not my business to meddle; and as one of his Majesty's council I have only one voice.' Marriott, *op. cit.*, p. 88. It is true that Walpole had but one voice, but it was frequently louder and stronger than the combined voices of his ministers. Whatever may be the merits of the allegations contained in the Protest concerning the destructive characteristics of such an office, there is little doubt but that it was correct in asserting that Walpole was a Prime Minister.

[1] Blauvelt, *op. cit.*, pp. 166–7.
[2] *Ibid.*, p. 229.
[3] J. A. Spender, *The Public Life* (New York, Frederick A. Stokes, 1925), i, 9.

Parliament; instead he was given to them by the people.[1] It is also striking that he was not a party man in any strict sense of the term. Pitt believed that men in office should 'be properly adapted to the employments they are appointed to.'[2] Party considerations were secondary to ability.[3] The ministry which Pitt formed in 1766 reflected this attitude as it included Whigs and King's Friends. It was internally divided and hence weak.[4] It is obvious given such actions that Pitt's administration provided little permanent impetus in the direction of ministerial control of politics.

The trend toward the replacement of the King by the Prime Minister in the cabinet was halted by George III who aimed at the restoration of the royal prerogative to his own hands. George was determined that 'the country should be governed by his personal friends, not by Whigs nor Tories; ministers should be selected from either side, so that government might be based on what was called a "broad bottom".'[5] The King thus struck at the roots of cabinet government by striking at political parties and party government. This meant more specifically that he had to strike most directly at the Whigs for they had dominated the government since the accession of the Hanoverians. For the first ten years of his reign he worked at this endeavour making effective use of the funds at his disposal to engage in political bribery. This practice was made easier by the existence of a large number of patronage constituencies.[6] The failure of the Whigs to concern themselves with parliament-

[1] George II is reported to have said to him, 'Sir, you have taught me to look for the sense of my people in another place than the House of Commons.' Quoted in Blauvelt, *op. cit.*, p. 216.

[2] Basil Williams, *The Life of William Pitt* (London, Longmans, Green, 1913), ii, 205.

[3] George III wrote to Pitt on the 29th of June 1766, stating, 'I know that the Earl of Chatham will zealously give aid toward destroying all party distinctions and restoring that subordination to government which alone can preserve that inestimable benefit, liberty, from degenerating into licentiousness.' *Correspondence of William Pitt, Earl of Chatham* (London, J. Murray, 1838–40), ii, 21.

[4] Blauvelt, *op. cit.*, p. 262.

[5] James A. Farrer, *The Monarchy in Politics* (London, T. F. Unwin, 1917), p. 1.

[6] Throughout the eighteenth century there were 558 seats in the House of Commons; 234 of these were under patronage. L. B. Namier, *The Structure of Politics at the Accession of George III* (London, Macmillan, 1929), i, 182.

ary reform in times of plenty led to dire results from their standpoint when the drouth struck. They began to agitate for parliamentary reform, but it was too late and the King now turned to his advantage the constituencies which had earlier paved the way for Whig control of the government. The King built up a body of supporters to whom Edmund Burke applied the name, 'King's Friends',[1] and through this procedure carried out an attack on the party system itself until he had finally conquered the Whigs and gained the initiative in policy for himself.[2]

By 1770 George III had succeeded in establishing his own person as the centre of political loyalty. The Whigs had been pushed from power and with that development there came a diminution in the prestige of the cabinet and of the individual ministers who sat in that body, primarily a resultant of the fact that George III 'tried to be his own Prime Minister and to control and direct his cabinet personally.'[3] The zenith of this royal authority came with the administration of Lord North, who would not allow anyone to call him 'prime minister' insisting that 'there was no such thing in the British constitution.'[4] In truth, he was right with respect to himself for he was not a prime minister; the King exercised the directing function himself although he did not participate in the sessions of the cabinet. Such participation was unnecessary and his submission to the now traditional absence of the monarch from such meetings did not hide the reality of his control. Personal participation was unnecessary for the ministers owed their political life to him. He continued to intervene in every aspect of the cabinet from details of patronage to control of governmental actions in the Parliament.[5] The political opposition recognized the dominant position of the King as may be seen from Charles Fox's statement that 'his Majesty was his own unadvised minister'.[6]

---

[1] Edmund Burke, 'Thoughts on the Present Discontent', in *The Works* (Boston, Little, Brown, 1881), i, 446.

[2] Robert, *op. cit*, pp. 217–50. See William L. Mathieson, *England in Transition, 1789–1832* (New York, Longmans, Green, 1920), pp. 2–3, for a concise statement of this thesis.

[3] Davies, *op. cit.*, p. 20.   [4] *Loc. cit.*

[5] *Ibid.*, p. 26; Robertson, *op. cit.*, pp. 251–2.

[6] Charles Fox, *Memoirs* (London, R. Bentley, 1853), i. 203.

Lord North was forced from office on the 20th of March 1782, as a consequence of military disaster in America.[1] Lord Rockingham came into office although George III considered Rockingham and the personnel he proposed as undesirable. Additionally, Rockingham insisted upon terms, all of which had the effect of reducing the influence of the Crown.[2] The King followed tactics in this instance much like that in the period from 1760 to 1770. He stirred up dissension among his already divided enemies. He was aided in this by the fact that he was able to retain Thurlow as Chancellor and as Lord Campbell has said, 'During the Rockingham administration the Chancellor was really the leader of his Majesty's opposition in the House of Lords'.[3] The Whigs themselves were divided between Rockingham and Chatham Whigs, the former standing for party organization and government, the latter for breaking down party lines. The death of Rockingham led to the resignation of Charles Fox and Shelburne became First Lord of the Treasury. Shelburne's power was based upon royal favour, although it was not great, for he was even bitterly disliked within the cabinet itself. To the political opponents of the King Shelburne was one of the King's Friends and they coalesced against him to drive him from office. Shelburne was succeeded, after considerable delay on the part of the King, by the coalition ministry of North and Fox.[4] Even the coalition could not last for the moral position of Fox was destroyed by the presence of North in the cabinet.[5] Instability characterized this government as it had the governments of Rockingham and Shelburne.

The King had not given up in his hopes of regaining control of policy himself and the opportunity came rather quickly. In the last month of 1783, George named William Pitt chief minister and asked him to form a government. Pitt was the youngest man ever to hold the office—he was twenty-five when he proceeded to the formation of his ministry. His initial position was not a happy one. The Parliament was against him and the opposition could always manage to muster a

---

[1] Blauvelt, *op. cit.*, p. 271. [2] *Ibid.*, p. 272.

[3] Lord Campbell, *Lives of the Chancellors* (Philadelphia, Blanchard and Lea, 1854), v, 434.

[4] Blauvelt, *op, cit.*, pp. 275–7.

[5] A. B. Keith, *The King and the Imperial Crown* (New York, Longmans, Green, 1936), p. 64.

plurality of from forty to fifty votes in any important division. In addition all of the great men of the House, with the exception of Pitt and Dundas, were in the opposition. On the first day of the Parliament he was twice beaten by decisive majorities. A modern Prime Minister would have either resigned or requested an immediate dissolution. Pitt did neither. It was his intention that the public should first be given an opportunity to assess the character and policy of the government before putting it to the test of a public vote. At the same time he prepared for a dissolution at the favourable moment and when it came obtained both Whig and Royalist support.[1]

George III chose Pitt hoping to control him, but it has been said that 'in ridding himself of the tyranny of the Whigs, with the assistance of Pitt, he only exchanged one bondage for another.'[2] This statement is reflective of the fact that Pitt strengthened the office of the Prime Minister, but it is not too accurate a portrayal of the relations of Pitt and the King. In fact, the evidence indicates that there was no sharp conflict of policy or will between Pitt and the King. They seem to have been in rather substantial agreement upon most matters and thus no serious differences of opinion arose to create opposition between them. The authority of the Prime Minister was at the same time expanded, however, since it was unnecessary for George III to attempt to exercise direct control in such circumstances.[3] It was the Prime Minister's authority *vis-a-vis* his ministerial colleagues which expanded most noticeably, not his independence of the King.

Pitt concentrated authority in his own hands in much the same fashion that Walpole had done. His own view of the functions of the office of the Prime Minister are worth repeating in part. Melville describes a conversation with Pitt in which '[Pitt] stated his sentiments with regard to the absolute necessity there is in the conduct of the affairs of this country that there should be an avowed and real Minister, possessing the chief weight in council and the principal place in the confidence of the King. In that respect there can be no rivalry or

---

[1] Lord Rosebery, *Pitt* (New York, Macmillan, 1895), pp. 53-4; Adams, *op. cit.*, pp. 498-9.

[2] Rosebery, *op. cit.*, p. 62.

[3] For a statement of the relations of George III and Pitt see D. G. Barnes, *Pitt and George III* (London, Oxford University Press, 1939).

division of power. That power must rest in the person generally called First Minister; and that minister ought . . . to be the person at the head of the finances. He knows to his own comfortable experience that notwithstanding the abstract truth of that proposition, it is no ways incompatible with the most cordial concert and mutual exchange of advice and intercourse among the different branches of the executive branch; but still, if it should come unfortunately to such a radical difference of opinion that no spirit of conciliation or concession can reconcile, the sentiments of the Minister must be allowed and understood to prevail, leaving the other members of administration to act as they may conceive themselves conscientiously called upon to act under such circumstances.'[1]

The long ministry of Pitt and his own clear recognition of his personal position did much to establish a precedent for the office of the Prime Minister. His relations with the King were handled tactfully. The cabinet followed him as a unit and the King was thus limited in his ability to interfere with the internal operation of the cabinet. The King's relations with individual ministers were usually carried on through Pitt himself.[2] Nevertheless, it must be emphasized that these developments were made possible only by reason of the mutual confidence which existed between Pitt and George III. At the same time the assertion of the authority did have the effect of diminishing the royal authority and transferring it to the cabinet and the Prime Minister. The King actually had no real alternative to Pitt through his seventeen years for the political alternative was Fox and for George III that was no alternative at all.

The immediate successors to Pitt were not able to exercise any control or influence comparable to his. Between 1806 and 1834 there was a struggle between King and ministers which eventually culminated in the clear recognition of the political supremacy of the ministers and placed the monarch in a position roughly corresponding to that which he now occupies. The Reform Act of 1832 was unquestionably instrumental in accelerating the trend towards a clear-cut conception of cabinet responsibility to the Parliament. The Reform Act cut away some of the rotten boroughs, although some were left. It

[1] H. Pellew, *Life of Viscount Sidmouth* (London, J. Murray, 1847), ii, 116.
[2] Adams, *op. cit.*, pp. 428–9.

expanded the suffrage upon the basis of a property qualification which reflected a compromise between the extremes taken in the initial discussions. As a compromise it was a failure for economic advance came so rapidly that the intent of the compromise was vitiated almost as soon as it had been agreed to.[1] It brought an active middle class into British politics which was not satisfied with a secondary political role, but demanded instead that it, through its representatives, should be able to determine policy and participate in its execution. The Reform Act thus involved a change in the balance of social power in Great Britain and further led to an acceleration of the movement towards parliamentary supremacy and the primacy of the House of Commons.[2] Almost immediately the control of the Parliament over ministery and King was made evident.

The first clear test came in 1834 when the King dismissed the Whig ministry of Lord Melbourne and invited Sir Robert Peel to form a government. The action was clearly based upon royal favouritism for it was obvious that Peel could not command a majority in the House of Commons while Melbourne could. Peel proceeded to the formation of his government and appealed to the country, recognizing that it was essential to have a new House of Commons if he was to govern. The House returned was also hostile to him and Peel therefore resigned and Melbourne was restored to office. 'Thus it was proved that in the reformed Parliament not only must the minister have a majority, but the mere fact that he was minister would not be sufficient to insure that victory.'[3]

[1] 'The Reform Bill added 217,000 to an existing electorate of 500,000, but within the next generation the qualifications prescribed added 600,000 more. So great was the rate of economic change that the compromise of 1832 could not acquire the force of custom long unchanged.' K. B. Smellie, *A Hundred Years of English Government* (New York, Macmillan, 1937), pp. 48–9.

[2] 'The foundation of the modern constitution of England was laid when the Reform Act of 1832 created for the first time an electorate which could not be controlled by the King and the oligarchy, by whose co-operation the destinies of the country had been guided. . . .' A. B. Keith, *The Constitution of England from Queen Victoria to George VI* (London, Macmillan, 1940), i, vii.

[3] Blauvelt, *op. cit.*, p. 290. Technically the King did not dismiss Melbourne, 'but his veiled offer of resignation was accepted by the King as something he had a right to ask.' Smellie, *op. cit.*, pp. 63–4. Peel, in the campaign, appealed to the electorate upon the grounds that they were voting their confidence in the royal prerogative.

Another clash between monarch and ministers came in the early years of the reign of Victoria and although outwardly trivial it did much to emphasize the passing of authority from monarch to cabinet. When Victoria ascended the throne she found Lord Melbourne in office and she gave him her complete confidence. The ladies of the bedchamber who surrounded her were appointed from the supporters of Melbourne. In May 1839 Melbourne was defeated in the House of Commons and resigned. Sir Robert Peel was asked to form a ministry. In the course of the discussions Peel informed the Queen that it would be necessary to remove the present ladies of the bedchamber as he feared that the Queen was surrounded by Melbourne's supporters and would be influenced in her attitude by them.[1] The Queen refused to do so insisting that his control over appointments did not extend to the ladies, a position which was supported by Melbourne when she requested his advice. Peel refused to continue with the formation of a ministry under those circumstances and the Queen recalled Melbourne who formed a new ministry. For two years Melbourne managed to maintain his government but in 1841 he was defeated. A dissolution followed and Melbourne was rejected by the electorate. Sir Robert Peel was again called upon to form a new ministry and again he insisted that he must have the power to appoint new ladies of the bedchamber. In this instance the Queen gave in without difficulty and seems to have recognized that she had been in error in 1839. The whole dispute emphasized the growing power of the Prime Minister at the expense of the Crown. The Prime Minister had even been able to control appointments to the inner circle of the monarch.[2] Although the Queen frequently intervened in individual appointments, and although she frequently raised objections and tried to persuade the Prime Minister to make selections more congenial to her own outlook,[3] it was now recognized that in the last resort the Prime

[1] Peel was in the minority in the Commons and did not believe it would be possible for him to rule successfully without some overt evidence of the Queen's confidence in his ministry. Such confidence would have been indicated had she been willing to replace the ladies.

[2] Smellie, *op. cit.*, pp. 65–7; Blauvelt, *op. cit.*, p. 290; A. B. Keith *The King and the Imperial Crown* (New York, Longmans, Green, 1936), pp. 86–7.

[3] Some instances of the Queen's concern with appointments may be found in W. I. Jennings, *Cabinet Government* (Cambridge, Cambridge University Press, 1936), pp. 49–53.

Minister would have his way. He might even insist upon the right to appoint minor court officers to ensure himself that the monarch's most intimate circle would not be antagonistic to his ministry.

Sir Robert Peel placed his stamp upon the office of Prime Minister. Under his administration the Prime Minister was able to exercise a more detailed supervision over the administrative actions of the subordinate departments than had been the case of any of his predecessors and even more than could be exercised by his successors. He carefully supervised the work of his subordinates and his fellow cabinet members. In this respect he differed remarkably from his predecessor, Melbourne. Melbourne's cabinet has been described as a 'complete republic' in which Melbourne had 'no overruling authority'.[1] Peel was of an entirely different temperament for he attempted to exercise full control over his departments, going so far in 1842 as to personally introduce the budget although that task would normally fall to the Chancellor of the Exchequer. Where most Prime Ministers confined their attention to the more important departments, he extended his supervision to all departments. Peel 'frankly claimed the duty to deal with these departments, and added that of exercising the then wide and unrestricted royal patronage, the whole of the communications with the sovereign, correspondence with persons of station on public business, the reception of deputations, and attendance for six or seven hours a day for five or six days a week when Parliament was sitting.'[2] Gladstone reported that in the cabinet of Sir Robert Peel a minister wishing to bring a measure forward always consulted Peel before bringing the issue before the cabinet.[3] It is for these reasons that Lord Rosebery described him as 'the model of all Prime Ministers'.[4]

What was possible for Peel was not possible for his successors. The most evident explanation of the detailed control and supervision exercised by Peel is found in the fact that the limits of

[1] Charles Greville, *Journals* (New York, D. Appleton, 1885), August 24th, 1840.

[2] A. B. Keith, *The British Cabinet System, 1830–1938* (London, Stevens and Sons, 1939), p. 75.

[3] John Morley, *Life of Gladstone* (New York, Macmillan, 1903), ii, 35.

[4] Lord Rosebery, *Miscellanies* (London, Hodder and Stoughton, 1921), i, 197.

administrative action by the State were quite narrowly defined during his administration. Later Prime Ministers, even men of such strength as Gladstone, Disraeli or Lloyd George, could not hope to exercise such supervision. Even should they desire to do so the characteristic scope of State action under which Peel had operated no longer existed. Therefore, the Prime Ministers were forced to concentrate their attention on the more important departments and the problem of general correlation rather than wasting energy in admittedly less significant aspects of governmental action. Even the conduct of foreign affairs in the time of Peel was a relatively leisurely matter handled through the exchange of dispatches which took some days in transmission. Telegraphy destroyed this characteristic of foreign relations and messages which would previously have been exchanged over a period of weeks were transmitted in days. In such circumstances if the Prime Minister hoped to be informed of the process of such negotiations he had to apply himself to that department in strict fashion and at the sacrifice of attention to other departments.

In another respect Peel had an advantage over his successors in office. He held office prior to the greater expansions of the suffrage and the consequent personalization of the campaigns. In consequence, Peel never had to fight an election on the national level. He was able to return to his home constituency, a safe one, and conduct his campaign there.[1] No Prime Minister at this time made national tours and appealed to the electorate as such through direct public appearances. Peel never had to worry about the tribulations of such a major electoral fight.[2] This more leisurely and gentlemanly characteristic of politics meant that it was also less necessary to spend time on party affairs and the cementing of organized relationships with the public than was the case with Gladstone or Disraeli. The time gained due to the absence of such necessities could be spent in the supervision of administrative details.

Gladstone's statement with relation to Peel and his ministers

---

[1] W. I. Jennings, *Cabinet Government* (Cambridge, Cambridge University Press, 1936), p. 150.

[2] After 1841 it was true that the people's verdict came to be considered a more important factor in the choice of a ministry. C. S. Emden, *The People and the Constitution* (Oxford, Clarendon Press, 1933), p. 162. Nevertheless, the appeals made to the public were still restricted in scope.

clearly indicates the strength with which he dominated his cabinet. This was not, of course, characteristic of all his successors. At the same time that Gladstone emphasized the prior consultation with the Prime Minister which was a characteristic of Peel's cabinet, he added, 'Nobody thought of consulting Palmerston first, but brought his measure at once to the Cabinet.'[1] Palmerston lacked the confidence of his ministers and he did not personally receive the kind of loyalty received by Peel. It may be added in justice to Palmerston, however, that he dealt with stronger ministers—for example, Gladstone was his Chancellor of the Exchequer in 1860 and was able to carry his views against the opposition of the Prime Minister. Lord John Russell also failed to extend his authority so widely although he was capable of taking overt and sometimes unjustified individual action which bound his colleagues without their knowledge or prior consent.[2]

A basic change was developing in the British political system. It was clear that the Prime Minister and his cabinet were absorbing the power which had been claimed by the earlier kings, but at the same time the cabinet was merely a committee of the Parliament and was responsible to it for its actions. The consequence was that the British were rapidly travelling down the road to the clear cut supremacy of the Parliament, in practice, as well as in legal theory. Within the cabinet, however, the relationships between ministers were not always so clear-cut. There was no precise way to define the powers of the Prime Minister *vis-a-vis* his ministers and it depended, as it still does, upon his own abilities, inclinations, the external circumstances, and the attitudes and abilities of his colleagues. It is safe to say that as a general rule the Prime Ministers of the middle nineteenth century did not stand in a power relation to their colleagues quite comparable to that of the prime ministers of this century, although the coming of Gladstone and Disraeli introduced a new element of strength into the office. There were occasions when the actions of the prime ministers had the effect of binding their colleagues to a policy which they had not previously approved, as in the case

---

[1] John Morley, *Life of Gladstone* (New York, Macmillan, 1903), ii, 35.
[2] His statement on the Corn Laws while leader of the opposition was made without the prior knowledge of his colleagues, but bound all of them to the course of action he had elaborated should they obtain office.

of Lord John Russell's letter denouncing the Catholic hierarchy in 1850.[1] Although not so dramatic, the cabinet of Peel had found itself forced to proceed with the repeal of the Corn Laws because Peel had concluded that such action was necessary. The alternative was his resignation and their fall.[2]

Although the precise relationship between Prime Minister and colleagues has not yet been spelled out and, in fact, is likely never to achieve any absolute specificity, three factors of basic importance did much to increase the potential power quotient of that officer in the last half of the nineteenth century. These factors were (1) the rise to political leadership of Gladstone and Disraeli; (2) the suffrage extension of 1867 followed inevitably by a further expansion of the electorate in 1884; and (3) the centralization of party organization.

Disraeli and Gladstone rose to positions of pre-eminence in their parties at approximately the same time. Both were extremely able parliamentarians, both were strong party men.[3] In personality they provided a peculiar contrast considering their party affiliations for 'Disraeli's sympathy with the masses, his understanding of the inner meaning of the democratic movement and the new forces of society, might have qualified him for the leadership of a progressive party; Gladstone with his ecclesiastical and forensic temper, his reverence for the formalism of the past, never quite shook off his earlier conservatism.'[4] Nevertheless, Disraeli became the leader of the Conservatives and hinged his appeal upon 'Empire', while Gladstone led the Liberals and concentrated his attention upon domestic affairs. Both were extremely able and both were the recipients and great public adulation and support.

The Reform Act of 1867 gave 'to the working man a preponderance of voting power'.[5] It was a logical continuation of the principles of 1832 and it was further elaborated upon in the

---

[1] Lord John Russell, *Later Correspondence of Lord John Russell* (New York, Longmans, Green, 1925), i, 46.

[2] The repeal of the Corn Laws was, of course, of considerably more importance than Russell's letter, but it is described as less dramatic since it actually took place over a period of months.

[3] Sir Sidney Low and Lloyd C. Sanders, *The History of England during the Reign of Victoria* (New York, Longmans, Green, 1907), pp. 221–2. The statement as to their party loyalty refers to their later period. Disraeli entered the Commons as a Radical, while Gladstone first took his seat as a Tory.

[4] *Ibid.*, p. 222.   [5] Smellie, *op. cit.*, p. 189.

act of 1884 which extended the suffrage to householders of the counties. 'The enlarged electorate led to the development of an entirely new technique of political leadership. The Constitution required a Prime Minister and a Leader of the Opposition who could touch the springs of action in the common man. Persuasion and propaganda were to replace patronage and corruption.'[1] It was rapidly becoming impossible for a party leader to confine his attentions to his own constituency; he now had to campaign for national support. The effect of the suffrage extension was to personalize elections in such a way that they were to a large degree personality contests between party leaders.[2] In such instances the necessary characteristics for political leadership might be expected to change and it is noticeable that to some extent this has followed.[3]

Although it seems quite likely that the suffrage reforms would have led to the personalization of politics whatever the character of the immediate political leaders had been, it is evident that the presence of Gladstone and Disraeli, both men of magnetic personality, did much to hasten the change in the character of British politics. Gladstone's popularity may be seen from a story Walter Bagehot mentions in respect to the election

---

[1] *Ibid.*, p. 193.

[2] Lord Bryce in the course of a discussion of the election of the American President in which he stipulates that it is first a choice of personalities, but also involves a referendum on policy as well, adds, 'a curious parallel may be drawn between it and a general election of the House of Commons in England. A general election is in form a choice of representatives, with reference primarily to their views upon various current questions. In substance it is often a national vote . . . committing executive power to some one prominent statesman. Thus the elections of 1868, 1874, 1880 were practically votes of the nation to place Mr. Disraeli at the head of the government.' *The American Commonwealth* (New York, Macmillan, 1891), p. 69.

[3] There were, of course, Prime Ministers whose power was based on the public prior to this act, but they were political sports. The position of Chatham has been discussed earlier, but it should be noted that Earl Grey's position in 1832 was also based upon overwhelming popular support. 'Grey's position was unique in the constitutional history of his time, and ranks him as, in a sense, the earliest of modern Prime Ministers. He was not the King's choice, like Pitt, whose triumph at the polls in 1784 the late election recalled, nor was he that of Parliament on Bagehot's principle; he stood henceforth directly on the support of the people, who had returned him to power as representing the Reform Bill.' J. R. M. Butler, *The Passing of the Great Reform Bill* (London, Longmans, Green, 1914), p. 228.

of 1868. 'A bad speaker is said to have been asked how he got on as a candidate. "Oh," he answered, "when I do not know what to say, I say 'Gladstone', and then they are sure to cheer and I have time to think".'[1] Gladstone caught the meaning of the change almost immediately for he made a stumping tour of the country which caused the Conservatives considerable displeasure.[2] By 1874 Gladstone had actually propounded a budget in the midst of his election campaign,[3] and in 1880 the Queen was displeased at the character of the campaign conducted by the Liberals. She was even more displeased at a later time when Rosebery developed a policy in a public address without previously informing her of either his intent or the policy itself.[4]

It was becoming evident that it was the public which was behind the government and the public was willing to give governments substantial majorities with which to work, a position far different from the slim margins by which previous governments had controlled the House of Commons.[5] The effect of public opinion may be seen in the case of Disraeli's resignation, prior to meeting the Parliament, after electoral defeat in 1868, and the similar action of Gladstone in 1874.[6]

[1] Walter Bagehot, *The English Constitution* (New York, World's Classics, 1942), p. 268.

[2] Smellie, *op. cit.*, p. 193.

[3] Lord Selborne, *Memorials* (New York, Macmillan, 1896), i, 330.

[4] George Buckle (ed.), *Letters of Queen Victoria*, 3s. (London, J. Murray, 1931), ii, 437–8.

[5] 'Before 1867 Cabinets had been dependent upon the subtle calculations of groups and were defeated or successful by very small margins. Peel, in 1841, had turned out the Whigs by one; Russell, in 1852, was displaced by nine; Derby in the same year by nineteen. In 1866 the second reading of the Finance Bill had been carried by five and Ministers were afterwards defeated by eleven. In 1868 Gladstone carried the Irish Church Bill by 118 and this majority was the sign of a new political era. Governments could now look to majorities of a hundred or more. The number of constituencies which were contested at a General Election was greatly increased. Before 1867 it was common for half the seats to be uncontested. In 1859, 101 constituencies had been fought; in 1865, 204; in 1868, 277; in 1880, 352.' Smellie, *op. cit.*, p. 194.

[6] Emden, *op. cit.*, p. 164. Emden notes, however, 'The precedent set in 1868 has been followed by both parties on every occasion in which the two-party system has been in plain operation. But some few years elapsed before it was freely admitted that it was the decision of the people, and not merely convenience, which dictated this course.'

The expansion of the electorate and the necessity of making national appeals led to advance in another area as well—this was the province of party organization. The initiative in this was taken by the Liberals under the direction of Joseph Chamberlain and the National Liberal Federation came into existence in 1877. The Federation began to draw up party principles and stood fair to exercise a substantial control over the party. This was vitiated, however, by the virtual fusion of the Federation with the Central Office of the party in 1887, for through this procedure the party leaders were able to make certain that the Federation did not avow any principles of which they did not approve. Although it took some time to work out the precise relationship between the Central Office and the local associations, the former gradually gained authority over the latter and the party leaders were thus placed in a position to exercise control over policy and the major activities of the local bodies.[1] A similar trend towards centralization also took place in the Conservative Party.[2]

All of these developments affected the power of the Prime Minister both in Parliament and in the cabinet. The political parties became more highly disciplined organizations and the electorate could choose between them with some success in differentiating the policy for which they stood. At the apex of the party, however, was the Prime Minister who was recognized as the party leader. In such circumstances the Prime Minister was able to draw upon the organized power of the party in the House of Commons. The members of the party were pledged to a general acceptance of the party programme; therefore, he could depend upon his party's support in the Parliament for the effective prosecution of his policy. Secondly, his own position as head of the party had consequences which tended to further cement his power over the party. The party in appealing to the electorate appealed most often through its greatest men, of whom the greatest was obviously the party leader. This meant that to some extent the electorate thought of the party in terms of its leaders and more particularly in terms of the number one figure in the party. In such circumstances the position of a successful party leader was strengthened by the evidence of public support for him personally. This meant that no member of the party would lightly disagree with

[1] *Ibid.*, pp. 134–6.   [2] *Ibid.*, pp. 136–7.

him or vote against a measure which he thought of substantial importance, for to do so was to run the risk of losing party support, or at least the possible gain which might come through even a letter from the party leader in support of his candidacy. All of these developments had done much to increase the number and the potency of the weapons in the hands of the Prime Minister in his relations to others.

To these institutional developments must always be added the impact of the personalities of Gladstone and Disraeli for they did much to cause the parties to think in terms of dynamic leadership. Both of these great leaders were able to impose their policies upon their followers, although even a Gladstone could not carry the policy of Home Rule and retain the unity of the Liberal Party. Disraeli, on the other hand, was successful in holding his party together while often acting without consideration of the viewpoints of others, for his position was so strong with Crown and public as to make no alternative to him possible for the Conservatives.

The modern office of Prime Minister had actually come into existence by the end of the nineteenth century. There have been minor changes in the characteristics of the office since that time, but the general constitutional position was settled by the end of the reign of Victoria. At the same time, as will be noted, the potentialities in that position have been more often used in the twentieth century because of the existence of situations which called for more complete use of all facets of its latent powers. Nevertheless, it was clear by the end of the century that the Prime Minister and his colleagues, the cabinet, exercised their authority upon the basis of the control of the House of Commons. It was evident as well that if he and his colleagues should be defeated in the lower house they would either resign or request a dissolution by the King. The Prime Minister, at the same time, stood in a more powerful relationship to the Commons because of his strong public and party support. In fact, a Prime Minister with deep-rooted support in the electorate was virtually unassailable in the House of Commons. These same factors also did much to make him more than *primus inter pares* in the cabinet, although it is evident that the precise relationship depended upon the ability of the Prime Minister and the degree of public support and party control which he had gained. He was clearly the chairman of the cabinet; he determined the agenda and served as the chief individual locus for the corelation of inter-departmental relations.[1] The power of the King in relation to his first minister had declined. Ministers were no longer appointed at the pleasure of the monarch for the appointing power was lodged in the hands of the Prime Minister who determined the membership of cabinet and the subordinate ministerial posts, and exercised control of patronage. Bagehot defined the power of the King as being confined to 'the right to be consulted, the right to encourage, the right to warn'.[2] Although this was not an adequate description of what Victoria had done in fact and under-estimated her political influence, it was nevertheless true that Bagehot's statement was becoming generally accepted and that no future monarch could hope to intervene as the Queen had. It is even probable that the public of her time would not have tolerated her interferences in the internal politics of the Liberal Party in 1880 and 1886, but the public did not know,[3] and her successors seem to have realized that her actions were clearly contrary to the constitutional rule as to the place of the monarch.

[1] Gladstone stated, 'The head of the British Government is not a Grand Vizier. He has no powers, properly so called, over his colleagues: on the rare occasions, when a Cabinet determines its course by the votes of its members, his vote counts only as one of theirs. But they are appointed and dismissed by the Sovereign on his advice. In a perfectly organized administration, such for example as that of Sir Robert Peel in 1841–6, nothing of great importance is matured, or would even be projected in any department without his personal cognizance; and any weighty business would commonly go to him before being submitted to the Cabinet.' Gladstone, *Gleanings of Past Years* (New York, Scribner, no date), i, 242–3.

[2] Bagehot, *op. cit.*, p. 67.

[3] Gladstone's own respect for the monarchy led him to keep his difficulties with the Queen private. Kingsley Martin, *The Magic of Monarchy* (New York, Knopf, 1937), pp. 57–8.

II

The Selection of the
Prime Minister

I. THE ROLE OF THE KING

The formal selection of the Prime Minister is made by the King, thus preserving the fiction that he is the King's minister. In actuality this power is formal rather than real for the King must exercise his choice within the bounds of rules which effectively limit the exercise of his discretion.

In the first place, his appointee must be able to command the support of a majority of the House of Commons. This means that in normal circumstances he will have no discretion, but will be required to select the one person who is able to command that support. This is clearly the case when one party controls the Commons and has a recognized leader. 'Where the wishes of a party are unmistakable, and the political circumstances normal, convention now requires that the King shall act upon the wishes of the party.'[1] Thus whatever the King's opinion might have been as to the respective merits of Attlee, Bevin or Morrison in 1945 he had no alternative but to select Attlee for he was the recognized leader of the party.

There is, of course, no legal stipulation which requires that the person appointed to the office of Prime Minister shall be able to command the support of the Commons. At the same time there is a conventional rule, the violation of which would lead to serious consequences for the monarch. Should he select

[1] Harold J. Laski, *Parliamentary Government in England* (New York, Viking Press, 1938), p. 191. The procedural mechanisms for the selection of the party leaders are examined in Chapter IV.

an individual who cannot obtain the acquiescence of the legislators, that individual would face the necessity of choosing between two alternatives almost immediately, for he would suffer defeat in the House of Commons as a matter of course. His alternatives would be (1) to resign, thus leaving the King face to face with the necessity of selecting the individual who should have been chosen in the first place, or (2) to request the King to dissolve the Parliament, thus placing the issue before the electorate. In the hypothetical case under consideration it is obvious that the King would have realized the existence of these alternatives and would therefore have already recognized that a dissolution would be required. The King's appointee, in such a case, might succeed in winning the electoral contest as Pitt did in 1784, but even in doing so the King would have gained little and lost much. This is the case for the party which should have been in office would realize that the King was not neutral, and the office and person of the King would become matters of political controversy. The strength of the monarchy is found in its reputation for political neutrality; it serves as a focus of loyalty for persons of all political persuasions. Should the monarch so act as to support one party against another the whole concept of political neutrality would be undermined and it is possible that the existence of the monarchial principle itself might very well become a matter of intense political controversy again in Great Britain. In such circumstances no King is likely to act in such a fashion; it is academic to visualize an action of this character in the foreseeable future.

A second limitation is found in another conventional rule; the Prime Minister must be a member of the House of Commons. This rule seems to have been definitely established in 1923 when Stanley Baldwin was chosen over Lord Curzon following the resignation of Bonar Law. Overtly the public reason, and the reason given Lord Curzon, was that since the Labour Party was the chief party of opposition, and since that party had no strength in the House of Lords, it was essential that the Prime Minister should be in the Lower House.[1]

[1] Harold Nicolson, *Curzon: The Last Phase* (New York, Houghton, 1934), p. 355; Earl of Ronaldshay, *The Life of Lord Curzon* (New York, Boni and Liveright, n.d.), iii, 352. It is reported that Curzon had told Sir G. Cunningham in September 1917 that he doubted whether a member of the peerage could be Prime Minister with Labour so strongly represented in the House of Commons.

Leopold Amery, however, states, 'As a matter of fact Lord
Curzon's appointment was practically settled when two junior
members of the Cabinet, the late Lord Bridgeman and myself,
intervened with Lord Stamfordham and urged reconsideration
in favour of Mr. Baldwin as likely to be more acceptable to his
colleagues and to the rank and file of the party. Lord Balfour,
who was called up from the country, agreed and suggested
Lord Curzon's peerage as a sound reason for passing him over.
The final decision was, to the best of my belief, made mainly
on the issue of the personal acceptability of the two candidates.
If a constitutional precedent was created, it was largely as the
ex post facto cover for a decision taken on other grounds.'[1] Whatever may have been the actual reasons for the decision, it seems
evident that in fact a constitutional precedent was established
although it may have been established *ex post facto*.[2] No Prime
Minister since 1902 has been from the House of Lords. Since
that time there has been a progressive decline in the power of
that House for the Parliament Act of 1911 and the growth of
the Labour Party effectively removed it from the main arena
of political controversy. It is the House of Commons which
makes and unmakes governments; it is to the House that the
government is responsible; the whole machinery of government
revolves around the Lower House. It is now impossible for a
man to sit in the House of Lords and have real contact with
parliamentary affairs.[3]

[1] Leopold Amery, *Thoughts on the Constitution* (New York, Oxford University Press, 1948), pp. 21–2. Nicolson's study substantiates this position. He
indicates that 'In the interval between Monday night and Tuesday morning
many forces had mobilized. The Labour Party had indicated that it would
be irksome for them, as His Majesty's Opposition, were the Prime Minister
to be a member of the Upper House. Balfour had intervened to suggest that
Curzon was temperamentally unsuited to guide the destinies of the country
in a democratic age. Certain leading conservatives—Lord Long, Lord
Salisbury, Mr. Amery and others—had also conveyed to Buckingham
Palace their serious misgivings. The cumulative effect of these representa-
tions was to reverse the previous decision.' Nicolson, *op. cit.*, p. 355.

[2] It is reported, however, that Chamberlain seriously considered recommending Lord Halifax as his successor in 1940, but Halifax himself thought
his absence from the Commons made such a course undesirable. Keith
Feiling, *The Life of Neville Chamberlain* (London, Macmillan, 1946), p. 441;
Winston Churchill, *The Gathering Storm* (Boston, Houghton Mifflin, 1948),
p. 663.

[3] Sir William Harcourt recorded that Lord Rosebery in 1894 told him
'that the whole machinery of Government was in the House of Commons;

There are, however, some circumstances in which the King may be able to exercise some discretion in carrying out the appointment of the Prime Minister. This may occur when there are three parties, none of which has a majority in the House of Commons; in case there is a split of serious proportions in the ranks of the governing party; or, as in the case of 1916, when there is a split within the ranks of a coalition Cabinet.

The presence of three parties, none of which commands a majority, does not automatically mean that the King will be able to exercise his discretion in whatever way he sees fit. In fact, although such a situation has existed on two occasions, in neither did the King have any actual choice. In 1924 the Parliament contained three parties, none of which had a majority; the Conservatives won 255 seats, Labour 191, and the Liberals, 158. Stanley Baldwin, the incumbent Prime Minister and a Conservative, met the Parliament where he was immediately defeated; he therefore resigned. In such circumstances it might seem at first glance that there were two alternatives open to the King, to select either Labour or the Liberals, seeking in the last case for information as to whether the Conservatives would support a Liberal government. In fact, this was made difficult by the fact that the Labour Party was considered to be the official Opposition in the House since it was the second largest party.[1] It was, therefore, difficult to pass over the Labour Party leader. In addition, Asquith, the leader of the Liberal Party, had made a statement in December of 1923, in which he had made it clear that while the Liberals would not support a Conservative government they were willing to allow Labour to form a ministry.[2] In consequence of

and that it was next door to an absurdity to conduct it from the House of Lords.' A. G. Gardiner, *The Life of Sir William Harcourt* (New York, Constable, n.d.), ii, 271. If this was true in 1894 it is obviously even more true today. Lord Rosebery did make the effort to govern from the House of Lords, but the difficulties foreshadowed by his comment became realities.

[1] 'The practice of the present century has created an official "Opposition" whose leader is the "leader of the Opposition".' W. I. Jennings, *Cabinet Government* (Cambridge, Cambridge University Press, 1936), p. 23.

[2] Asquith made his statement to the National Club Liberal on the 18th of December 1923, shortly following the general election. Cf. Lord Oxford and Asquith, *Memories and Reflections* (Boston, Little, Brown and Co., 1928), ii, 249.

these conditions the King sent for Ramsay MacDonald, the leader of the Labour Party, and he became Prime Minister. The situation in 1929 was almost identical with that of 1924, save that Labour was the largest party in the newly elected Parliament and Baldwin's resignation occurred before he met the Parliament. In this case no alternative to Labour existed for it was clear that the Conservatives had been repudiated by the electorate and could not expect to receive Liberal support. On the other hand the Liberal Party was far too weak in the Parliament to take the leadership in forming a government.[1]

The clearest instance of the exercise of actual discretionary power in the selection of the Prime Minister took place in 1894 upon the heels of the resignation of Gladstone. Gladstone resigned ostensibly for reasons of health, actually in consequence of a division over naval estimates within the Cabinet.[2] In this instance there was no clear-cut agreement within the party itself as to who should replace Gladstone as their leader. Two men stood in the forefront, Lord Rosebery and Sir William Harcourt. Both were men of considerable popularity within the ranks of the party. Gladstone, on the other hand, was prepared to recommend Lord Spencer as his successor, but the Queen did not call upon him for advice.[3] The Cabinet was internally divided between the two men although the indications are that Rosebery was the more popular of the two as Harcourt had antagonized many of his colleagues, including John Morley.[4] The Queen, however, did not seek the advice of the other Cabinet members; instead she acted upon her own initiative and named Lord Rosebery to the position.[5] It is very clear in this instance that the Sovereign was so able to act only because

[1] Philip Viscount Snowden, *An Autobiography* (London, J. Nicholson and Watson, 1934), ii, 755–7. The House elected contained 289 Labourites, 260 Conservatives and 58 Liberals.

[2] Gardiner, *op. cit.*, ii, 252–3.

[3] John Morley, *Works* (London, Macmillan, 1921), i, 36. Gardiner states 'Gladstone's mind wavered between Kimberly and Spencer. He was entirely hostile to a Rosebery leadership. He had been in disagreement with some of his tendencies on foreign politics.' Gardiner, *op. cit.*, ii, 264, n. 2.

[4] Morley, *op. cit.*, i, 362–3; Gardiner, *op. cit.*, ii, 264–5.

[5] At least there is no direct evidence which indicates that she consulted any of the leading members of the Liberal Party prior to the appointment. It is probable that she was conscious of the attitude of many of the Cabinet members, however.

the party had abdicated its function of choosing its own leader. Its internal division had made it possible for the Queen to choose her own favourite and thus to name the party's leader for them. Had the party been united behind Sir William Harcourt she could not have taken such action, but in the absence of party action she was successful in exercising her own initiative. As it happened, the largest bloc of the Cabinet approved of her selection.

The incidents of 1916, to the contrary, clearly indicate that the King had no alternative but to appoint Lloyd George. Asquith's position within the Cabinet had become impossible by the last of the year as a result of a growing dissatisfaction among some of its principal members, particularly Bonar Law and Lloyd George. The charges were frequently made that Asquith was not capable of effectively directing the prosecution of the war. As time passed Lloyd George and Law were drawn into a rather close union in their efforts to obtain internal Cabinet reform and they issued Asquith an ultimatum which he found it impossible to accept. Asquith submitted his resignation to the King, although there is some reason to believe that he did so in order to break the rebellion by proving that no one else could successfully form a government.[1] He suggested that Bonar Law should be asked to form a government.[2] Law asked if Asquith would serve in the Cabinet under him and Asquith refused. After this development, Law, in accordance with a previous understanding made with Lloyd George, returned to the King and advised him to send for Lloyd George. This was done and Lloyd George became Prime Minister.[3] In these circumstances it is evident that the King had no real discretion. He first approached Law, acting upon the advice of

[1] Lord Beaverbrook, *Politicians and the War, 1914–1916* (London, T. Butterworth, 1932), ii, 237–8. Asquith followed this course only after consultation with McKenna, Harcourt, Runciman, Samuel and Grey. Herbert Viscount Samuel, *Memoirs* (London, Cresset Press, 1945), pp. 120–2.

[2] Oxford and Asquith, *op. cit.*, ii, 159. This section of the book was written by Lord Crewe, rather than by Asquith himself.

[3] Beaverbrook, *op. cit.*, ii, 285–99; Oxford and Asquith, *op. cit.*, ii, 159. Beaverbrook states that after Asquith's resignation Law had told Lloyd George that he would put George's name to the King for 'by now Bonar Law believed sincerely that while his judgement might be better than Lloyd George's, Lloyd George had more drive—and that drive was wanted to win the war.' Beaverbrook, *op. cit.*, ii, 282.

Asquith. When Law proved unable to gain the support of Asquith, but made it evident that he himself would serve under Lloyd George, and proposed the latter's name to the King, the Sovereign had no choice but to approach the fiery Welsh leader and offer him the office of Premier.

The crisis of 1931 is clouded by an absence of adequate objective information. A multiplicity of articles and books have dealt with the events of August 1931, but they have too frequently been based upon hearsay rather than accurate information. Of the major participants in the events which led to Ramsay MacDonald's becoming the head of the National Government only Herbert Samuel has written memoirs. His memoirs do much to disprove earlier allegations, particularly allegations as to the King's role in the events. Final judgment must await the opening of the papers of MacDonald, Baldwin, and George V.

Two constitutional questions arose as a result of the remarkable events which led to a Labour Premier's ditching of his colleagues and his acceptance of the position of head of a National Government. The first question revolves around the role of the King. Did the King act constitutionally in the crisis? The second issue concerns the Prime Minister specifically, and raises the question of whether it was within his constitutional power to accept the office of Prime Minister of a National Government without the authorization of his party.

The background of the crisis may be stated briefly.[1] The Labour Government was a minority government. It depended upon Liberal support for the retention of power. The economic crisis of 1931 led to a split within the Cabinet. The Prime Minister and the Chancellor of the Exchequer insisted that cuts in unemployment compensation were essential. A majority of the Cabinet opposed such action.[2] The Trade Union Congress also insisted that such cuts should not be ordered. On the other hand, the Liberal Party insisted upon further economies and threatened to withdraw their parliamentary support unless such cuts were forthcoming. The division in the Labour Cabinet made action impossible.

---

[1] Cf. Snowden, *op. cit.*, ii, 929–50.

[2] *Ibid.*, ii, 948. It is reported in another source that a majority had accepted the necessity of the cuts. J. H. Thomas, *My Story* (London, Hutchinson, 1937), p. 195.

On the 23rd of August 1931 the Cabinet empowered the Prime Minister to tender his resignation to the King.[1] The resignation of the Prime Minister always brings with it the automatic resignation of the rest of the Cabinet. The Prime Minister did so and then informed his Cabinet that he had advised the King to send for Baldwin and Samuel.[2] The other members of the Labour Cabinet took it for granted that Baldwin would become the Prime Minister.[3] MacDonald, however, attended the meeting of the King with Baldwin and Samuel. Sidney Webb reported the currently accepted story of what took place as follows:[4]

'What is said is that the King with whom the Prime Minister had been in constant communication but who never went outside his constitutional position, made a strong appeal to him to stand by the nation in this financial crisis, and to seek the support of leading members of the Conservative and Liberal Parties in forming, in conjunction with such members of his own Party as would come in, a united National Government. The King is believed to have made a correspondingly strong appeal to the Liberal and Conservative leaders.'

The next day MacDonald reported to the Labour Cabinet that it had been decided to form a government of individuals, and that he would serve as the Prime Minister. None of the members of the Cabinet had been previously informed of his intention to take this action.[5]

MacDonald's action was startling and it caused an immediate public furore. The newspapers almost universally lined up on the side of MacDonald and insisted that he was a man of great patriotism.[6] Faced with the responsibility for the financial crisis he had not shirked his burden, but had even broken with his party to fulfil his obligations as a patriot. The only papers which questioned the action with any severity were the *Manchester Guardian* and the *Daily Herald*, the latter the organ of the Labour Party.[7] It might have been expected that debates on

---

[1] Sidney Webb, 'What Happened in 1931', *Political Quarterly*, iii, 8. Snowden, *op. cit.*, ii, 940.

[2] *Ibid.*, ii, 950–1.   [3] Webb, *op. cit.*, p. 9.   [4] *Loc. cit.*

[5] Snowden, *op. cit.*, ii, 951; Thomas, *op. cit.*, p. 195.

[6] See in particular *The Times*, 25 August 1931.

[7] The *New Statesman and Nation* did not criticize MacDonald. It attempted to occupy a middle position, and it contended that the wild charges emanating from both sides were equally erroneous. See the issue for 29 August 1931, p. 244.

the constitutionality of the action would take place in the Commons and the Lords, but they did not. It is probable that the reason for the failure of the Parliament to consider the action was that the King was involved. The later 'agreement to disagree' received a full-scale constitutional debate in both Houses.

The late Professor Laski was highly critical of the action of the King in the crisis. Thus he wrote, 'It is notable that, in the formation of the National Government, no attempt was made by the King to elicit the views of the great bulk of the Labour Party who had transferred their allegiance from Mr MacDonald to Mr. Arthur Henderson. It appears certain that the impetus to the peculiar form of the new administration came wholly from the King[1].' He also insists that, 'It has never been suggested that the idea of a MacDonald Premiership in the National Government emanated from Mr. Baldwin or from Sir Herbert Samuel[2].' Professor Jennings does not find this procedure unconstitutional. As he puts it, 'the rule which is enshrined in the precedents and which is desirable so long as we have a monarchy is that while the Cabinet remains in office the Prime Minister should be loyally supported, but that when the Cabinet decides to resign the King should consult what party leaders he pleases in order to determine what Government Parliamentary exigencies demand[3].' To this he adds the comment, 'It is irrelevant (except as evidence of Mr. Mac-Donald's good faith or otherwise) to ask at whose suggestion the National Government was formed[4].'

The clash of constitutional principles between Professors Laski and Jennings is obvious. Laski is concerned because he is of the opinion that MacDonald was the King's personal appointee. Professor Jennings is willing to admit that this may be true, but insists that upon the basis of constitutional precedents the King has such power if the appointee can command

[1] Laski, *op. cit.*, p. 340. See *The Crisis and the Constitution: 1931 and After* (London, Hogarth, 1932), p. 34. where he describes the formation of the National Government as being derived from 'a Palace Revolution'.

[2] Harold J. Laski, *Parliamentary Government in England* (New York, Viking Press, 1938), p. 195.

[3] W. I. Jennings, 'The Constitution under Strain', *Political Quarterly*, iii, 196.

[4] W. I. Jennings, *Cabinet Government* (Cambridge, Cambridge University Press, 1936), p. 40.

the support of a majority in the Commons. It must be remembered that even if Professor Laski's conception of the events were true the leaders of the Conservative and Liberal Parties could have stifled the action by refusing to participate. Actually, however, the King does not seem to have played a significant part in the formation of the National Government although he may have been sympathetic to the action.

Viscount Samuel reports that it was he who proposed the establishment of a broad-based National Government. He further says that it was he who suggested that such a government would be stronger if there was no change of Premier. MacDonald is reported to have fallen in with the argument, and 'the King acted on the advice unanimously tendered to him'.[1] There would have been no reason to consult Arthur Henderson in these circumstances for the advice had been tendered to the King by a combination of individuals who could command the support of the House of Commons. Samuel emphasizes the insignificance of the role of the King by commenting, 'So far as I was myself concerned, neither directly nor indirectly did any expression reach me of any personal opinion or wish of His Majesty. In every particular the principles and practices of our democratic constitution were scrupulously followed.'[2] This, of course, completely removes the King from any constitutional responsibility for the events of 1931. Instead of taking the initiative he merely followed the advice of all three party leaders.

Samuel does not mention any previous conversations with MacDonald in which the possibility of a National Government under MacDonald's leadership had been mentioned. It is, of course, possible that the King might have approached MacDonald with such a suggestion earlier, but no evidence exists which indicates such action. The contacts between Baldwin and MacDonald have not been reported in any detail. Neville Chamberlain, who participated in conversations between Baldwin and MacDonald, does not mention any approach made by MacDonald along this line. On the contrary, Chamberlain himself seems to have suggested the possibility of a National Government to MacDonald.[3] MacDonald does not seem to have been at all unsympathetic to such approaches, but

[1] Samuel, *op. cit.*, p. 204. [2] *Ibid.*, pp. 221-2.
[3] Feiling, *op. cit.*, p. 193.

in justice to him he does not seem to have taken the initiative in the action.

A second constitutional question exists, however. That is whether MacDonald had the right to become the head of a National Government without the authorization of his party. He agreed to take this place, 'without a word of previous consultation with any of his Labour colleagues. He knew that he would have the great majority of the Labour Cabinet against him, and practically the whole of the Parliamentary Labour Party.'[1] MacDonald's relationship with his party continued to be peculiar. Both Baldwin and Samuel immediately called meetings of their respective parties to obtain authorization for their action.[2] MacDonald did not do so. Two days after the formation of the National Government he sent a private letter to each member of the Parliamentary Labour Party in which he defended his action. On the 28th of August 1931, four days later, the Parliamentary Labour Party met, but MacDonald did not appear nor did he send any message appealing for support. It is possible, however, that he did not know of the meeting. Snowden says, 'I do not know if Mr. MacDonald had any invitation to attend this meeting. I was not aware of it until after it had been held.'[3]

Snowden is himself of the opinion that MacDonald may have wished to form an association with political colleagues whom he found more congenial. He reports that MacDonald no longer liked to associate with trade union leaders.[4] When Snowden told MacDonald that he would now be popular in strange quarters, MacDonald replied, 'gleefully rubbing his hands: "Yes, tomorrow every Duchess in London will be wanting to kiss me".'[5]

Whatever the reasons for MacDonald's action may have been, the question still remains as to whether he was entitled to act without party authorization. He was, after all, the leader of a party, but he had acted without the authorization of the party and without making any serious efforts to gain their support, he knew that substantial portions of the party were opposed, although he may have deluded himself about his ability to carry a majority with him. As Professor Jennings says, the Prime Minister 'holds office only because of and so long as he possesses the confidence of the party. It is for the party to

[1] Snowden, *op. cit.*, ii, 952.   [2] *Ibid.*, ii, 953.   [3] *Ibid.*, ii, 953.
[4] *Ibid.*, ii, 954.   [5] *Ibid.*, ii, 957.

say when it is no longer prepared to support the Cabinet, and for the leaders of the party in the Cabinet to say when they can no longer control Parliament through the party organization.'[1] This raises an issue of considerable magnitude. Its implications are present in the question raised by Professor Jennings, 'Can a conservative Prime Minister inform the King that he has turned socialist and proposes to substitute socialist members for his conservative colleagues?'[2] Of course, MacDonald's action was not quite this extreme, and it may be the case that he though most of the party would follow him. MacDonald seems to have been somewhat vainglorious and it is not difficult for a man of that temperament to persuade himself that he will receive support, even when it is obvious to others that he will not.[3]

No constitutional precedents may be cited to decide the merits of this controversy. Nothing like it had ever happened before. It stands alone. Unquestionably the Prime Minister had a moral obligation to his party. It had made him what he was. He had assisted it too, but in the last resort he held his position because the party had selected him as its leader. MacDonald's action may not have been unconstitutional, but it is obvious that he betrayed his party. It must be remembered that one course was open to the Prime Minister which was quite clearly

[1] W. I. Jennings, 'The Constitution under Strain', *Political Quarterly*, iii, 198. Cf. Harold J. Laski, *The Crisis and the Constitution: 1931 and After* (London, Hogarth, 1932), p. 16. Professor Laski puts the case succinctly in the following words: 'In modern times, no man has become Prime Minister merely as a person; it is to his position as a party leader that he owes his Premiership. His autocracy is limited by the degree to which he can carry his colleagues and the party with him; which is to say, in other words, that he can be autocratic only by consent.'

This statement, it should be added, is not entirely correct. Lloyd George was not a party leader when he became Prime Minister. Eight years after Professor Laski wrote these words Winston Churchill took the Premiership although he was not his party's leader. In both cases the individuals appointed were chosen as persons rather than as party leaders. In both cases, however, Great Britain was at war and normal political practice was not necessarily to be expected in such circumstances. It would be difficult to point to either of these examples as extenuating the MacDonald appointment in 1931.

[2] W. I. Jennings, 'The Constitution under Strain', *Political Quarterly*, iii, 199.

[3] Cf. Clement Attlee, *The Labour Party in Perspective—and Twelve Years Later* (London, V. Gollancz, 1949), p. 56.

constitutional. He could have resigned. Everyone expected him to, and everyone expected Baldwin to become Prime Minister. If the party system is to operate effectively it would seem to be essential that the Prime Minister should always resign in such circumstances. If MacDonald thought of his action in terms of personal honour, it still remains true that he had great moral obligations to the party. Unless he thought himself indispensable, and he had no business thinking he was, the only justifiable course of action he could have taken was resignation.

No problem existed in the case of Stanley Baldwin's succession of Ramsay MacDonald, an action taken primarily in order to fight the election more effectively, for Baldwin had obviously been the chief power in the Cabinet even while MacDonald served as Prime Minister.[1] Similarly, it was equally obvious that Neville Chamberlain would have to be selected to succeed Baldwin upon the latter's resignation. The events of 1940, on the other hand, probably require a brief statement. Chamberlain had lost the confidence of the House of Commons although he had won a formal vote: thirty-three Conservatives voted against him while sixty more abstained.[2] Chamberlain had attempted to form a National Government, but Labour had been unwilling to enter a government under his leadership.[3] Chamberlain called Churchill to see him and explained that the question he now had in mind was as to whom he should recommend as his successor. It is reported that he preferred to recommend Lord Halifax, but that Halifax thought it unwise because he was not in the Lower House.[4] It was clear, therefore, that Churchill would be the person recommended. Chamberlain so recommended to the King and the King appointed Churchill to the office. Churchill stipulates that he had said earlier that he 'would have no communication with either of the Opposition Parties until I had the King's commission to form a government.'[5] It is noticeable that Churchill agreed to form the government without any stipulation being made as to its being

---

[1] For comments on MacDonald's position in the National Government see Feiling, *op. cit.*, p. 228; Samuel, *op. cit.*, pp. 214–15; L. M. Weir, *The Tragedy of Ramsay MacDonald* (Plymouth, Secker and Warburg, 1938), p. 452.

[2] Feiling, *op. cit.*, pp. 439–40; Churchill, *op. cit.*, p. 660.

[3] Feiling, *op. cit.*, p. 441; Churchill, *op. cit.*, p. 662.

[4] Feiling, *op. cit.*, p. 441; Churchill, *op. cit.*, p. 663.

[5] Churchill, *op. cit.*, p. 663.

national in composition.[1] At the same time it was evident that the other parties would serve under him for, as Churchill himself said, 'During the eleven years before the outbreak of the war, I had in my more or less independent position come far more often into collision with the Conservative and National Governments than with the Labour and Liberal Oppositions.'[2]

It is evident from the foregoing material that the King can exercise authority only in those instances in which the party has clearly failed to indicate its leader, or when there is a balance of party strength among three parties, none of them holding a majority of the seats in the Commons. Even in the latter case he has no discretion if one of the three parties has already publicly stated its support of one of the other parties. Present indications as to the future of the British party system clearly indicate that it is unlikely that the Liberals or any other 'third party' will be able to hold the balance of power between Labour and Conservatives in the House of Commons. It is very difficult to visualize a House divided more closely than the Parliament elected in 1950, but even in that case the Liberals did not hold the balance of power. It is thus very likely that the King's discretion will not exist in ordinary circumstances for it is improbable that the parties will be caught in a situation in which they have no leader. The Parliamentary Labour Party can solve any such problem by the simple course of meeting in caucus to select its leader as he is so chosen at present.[3] The Conservatives might also take advantage of the same institutional procedure in the absence of a clearly recognizable party leader.[4]

In selecting a Prime Minister the King must, on occasion, seek advice in order to be certain that he is acting correctly. It is of some importance to know what the limitations of consultation may be in such circumstances. In the more normal cases there is no real problem and hence no need for consultation.

[1] *Ibid.*, p. 665.   [2] *Ibid.*, p. 666.

[3] Control by caucus has also become an essential aspect of the process of selecting the Premier in New Zealand. In this way the decisions of the majority of the members of the party prevent the exercise of any discretion by the Governor-General. Leslie Lipson, *The Politics of Equality* (Chicago, University of Chicago Press, 1948), pp. 287–9.

[4] The events of 1923, however, indicate how easily the attitude of the party can be discovered even without the existence of a formalized institutional procedure such as the caucus.

Normally, if a government is defeated the King will call upon the Leader of the Opposition immediately, whether that government is defeated in the House of Commons or in a general election. In fact, the former is now an unusual occurrence and the only resignation in this century as a result of such a defeat took place in 1924.[1] In 1895, 1905, 1922, 1924, 1929, 1945, and 1951, the King immediately sent for the Leader of the Opposition. Given the effective operation of a two-party system the King is restricted to consultation with the Leader of the Opposition, and no one else in such circumstances. In all of these instances it is likely that the outgoing Prime Minister advised the Sovereign to follow that course of action. Normally the resigning Premier is consulted, but this is not always the case as the events of 1894, 1908, and 1923 indicate. The King is not obliged to act upon his advice for in this case there is no way to hold the adviser responsible for the consequences. Responsibility in this case rests upon the new Prime Minister.[2]

There are some circumstances in which the scope of possible consultation becomes considerably wider. If the Prime Minister either dies or resigns as a result of ill-health, it must be expected that the King will seek advice from various quarters in the party in power. This is not always the case, for in some instances the succession is evident. In 1908, the King did not seek information from Liberal Party leaders; instead he sent for Asquith on his own initiative. No problem existed since Asquith was clearly recognized to be the second-ranking figure in the Party.[3] No evidence is available in respect to Chamberlain's appointment to the office although it is probable that Baldwin recommended his successor. The events of 1923, however, indicate that the King may seek advice from many sources. In 1908 the King had not sought Campbell-Bannerman's advice and the evidence tends to indicate that he did not seek Bonar

---

[1] Balfour's resignation in 1905 was not the result of an adverse vote. In 1924, Ramsay MacDonald was defeated in the House of Commons but sought and obtained a dissolution.

[2] A. B. Keith, *The British Cabinet System, 1830–1938* (London, Stevens and Sons, Ltd., 1939), p. 365.

[3] Reginald Viscount Esher, *Journals and Letters* (London, J. Nicholson and Watson, 1934), ii, 256. The King had seen Asquith earlier, prior to Campbell-Bannerman's resignation but during his illness. J. A. Spender and Cyril Asquith, *Life of Oxford and Asquith* (London, Hutchinson and Co., 1932), i, 194.

Law's advice as to his successor in 1923. Law wrote to Curzon at the time stating, 'I am sorry to say that I find it necessary to resign. . . . I understand that it is not customary for the King to ask the Prime Minister to recommend his successor in circumstances like the present and I presume that he will not do do; but if, as I hope, he accepts my resignation at once, he will have to take immediate steps about my successor.'[1] The King did see several of the leaders of the Conservative Party including Arthur Balfour, Lord Long, Lord Salisbury and Mr. Amery. It is obvious, however, that in situations of this sort the King is not free to consult with persons representing any other party. In both 1908 and 1923 there was no question of the fall of the government as a whole and the King was, of necessity, restricted to consultations with government party members.

Such limitations do not necessarily apply in case the Prime Minister resigns as a result of internal dissension in the Cabinet itself. In such circumstances it is necessary to weigh the factors present before taking action to contact persons outside the government party. In 1894 the Queen could not have legitimately consulted anyone outside the Liberal Party following Gladstone's resignation for although there was a dispute within the Cabinet it was not serious enough to bring the entire government to the ground. In fact, she did not consult any of the party leaders. In the crisis leading to the fall of the Asquith coalition in which all the parties were joined it was obviously within the limits of possible action for the King to see the representatives of all parties. In this case he did see Asquith, Balfour, Lloyd George, Bonar Law, and Arthur Henderson, the

[1] Nicolson, *op. cit.*, pp. 353–4. It has been reported that the King did ask Law's opinion as to whom he should send for but that the two gentlemen who had brought Law's resignation stated that he was too ill to take such responsibility. The King is then reported to have asked that Law should 'merely advise him to which other Minister in the Cabinet he should have recourse.' Law proposed to send Lord Salisbury's name but in the meantime the King entered into consultation with other representatives of the Conservative Party. Winston Churchill, *Great Contemporaries* (New York, G. P. Putnam's Sons, 1937), p. 246.

[2] Nicolson, *op. cit.*, p. 355; Blanche Dugdale, *Arthur James Balfour* (New York, G. P. Putnam's Sons, 1937), pp. 266 ff.

[3] In fact, Gladstone found that his views on the naval estimates were supported by only one other member of the Cabinet. Gardiner, *op. cit.*, ii, 252–3.

latter representing the Labour Party.[1] The internal division which led to the fall of Ramsay MacDonald's Cabinet in 1931 also led to consultations of a more far-reaching nature. In this instance it is necessary to remember that the government was a minority government and faced inevitable defeat in the House of Commons should it pursue the course insisted upon by the majority bloc in the Cabinet.[2] In consequence the King saw Baldwin and Samuel, although he took this action only after being advised to do so by the Prime Minister.[3] On the other hand, it is noticeable that he did not see Arthur Henderson, who led the vast majority of the Labour Party members of Parliament.

The situations described immediately above are on the whole out of the ordinary, but in such circumstances it seems inevitable that the King must be able to exercise some discretion in seeking out persons for consultation. 'Except when the Government resigns after a defeat, he has a choice which he must exercise in such a way as to secure the strongest Government in the minimum time. To do this, he must secure the best information available. The best information as to coherent parties can be obtained from the party leaders. The best information as to parties in dissolution can be obtained from the leaders of the respective groups. Sometimes, on the other hand, the "elder statesmen" who have retired from the political contest can best see the situation as a whole. The King may consult any of these, and he needs no formal advice from a Prime Minister.'[4]

II. THE BACKGROUND OF THE PRIME MINISTERS

Between the resignation of Gladstone in 1894 and 1953, twelve individuals have held the office of Prime Minister of

[1] Spender and Asquith, *op. cit.*, ii, 273–5; Beaverbrook, *op. cit.*, ii, 285–99; Oxford and Asquith, *op. cit.*, ii, 160; Dugdale, *op. cit.*, ii, 126–7.

[2] Snowden, *op. cit.*, ii, 929–50.

[3] *Ibid.*, ii, 950; Samuel, *op. cit.*, p. 204. Professor Jennings has pointed out that the King had the right to see Baldwin and Samuel upon his own initiative. Jennings, 'The Constitution under Strain', *Political Quarterly*, iii, 196.

[4] W. I. Jennings, *Cabinet Government* (Cambridge, Cambridge University Press, 1936), p. 40.

Great Britain. Of these, one, Lord Salisbury, had held that office prior to 1894. Of the Premiers of this period only three, Ramsay MacDonald, Stanley Baldwin, and Winston Churchill, held the office on more than one occasion. Although the background of many of the Prime Ministers of this period reveal a rather remarkable similarity, it is noticeable that there are more differences between them than existed in the case of those persons who served as Prime Minister between 1832 and 1894.

The Premiers of the years 1832 to 1894 were uniformly well educated men. Of the ten men who held the office during this time only Disraeli lacked a university education. It is also noticeable that that education was normally received at the two great British universities, Oxford and Cambridge. Only one of the nine persons receiving a university education graduated from another university: Lord John Russell took his degree at Edinburgh University. Oxford and Cambridge divided the other eight Premiers equally. The pattern of privileged class education is also revealed by the fact that eight of the ten Prime Ministers received their preparatory training in Harrow or Eton, the most exclusive of the British public schools. In this case Eton held the advantage with five Prime Ministers to three for Harrow. The similarities in educational background reflect a basic similarity in social background as well, for the Premiers of the nineteenth century were uniformly men of independent means who were able to devote their full time to the pursuit of political objectives without fear of the financial consequences.

Most of the British Prime Ministers of the years 1894 to 1950 also received the advantage of higher education. Excluding Lord Salisbury, seven of the eleven Prime Ministers since Gladstone's resignation completed a university education. One, Chamberlain, attended college for two years.[1] Two received secondary education, and one, Ramsay MacDonald, received only an elementary education, although it was supplemented by a rigorous self-education which made him the superior of many who had received greater formal educational advantages.

[1] Chamberlain attended Mason College where he studied engineering but did not graduate. His status at the end of the second session explains his failure to complete his college work. He stood at the bottom of the list in metallurgy, mathematics and engineering design, Feiling. *op. cit.*, p. 12.

Again Oxford and Cambridge divided the honours in the production of Premiers, each having three. Of these men, only Asquith won high academic honours taking a First in *Literae Humaniores*.[1] Attlee received a Second in Modern History. Eton and Harrow continued to produce a disproportionate number of Prime Ministers, each producing two, but it is quite noticeable that while still high, this ratio is extremely low when compared with the previous period.

The development of political democracy is probably primarily responsible for the change in the educational background of political leaders. Democracy threw up new leaders from hitherto untapped sources in the body politic. In particular, the rise of the Labour Party and the increasing importance of the trade union movement have given rise to new men, often men without the advantage of formal academic training, who have gained their education through the practical experience gained in the day-to-day struggle to exist and improve their status and that of their class. Neither Herbert Morrison nor Ernest Bevin, who were, at one time, the chief contenders for Attlee's position as party leader, received a university education, nor, for that matter, even a complete secondary school training.

The Premiers of the twentieth century have more frequently had to depend upon skills of various kinds for making their own living than was the case with their nineteenth-century predecessors. Neither Herbert Asquith nor Lloyd George found themselves in a position to enter politics without concern for the financial disadvantages entailed. Asquith found it necessary to continue his practice as a barrister after the Liberal Government fell in 1895. Ramsay MacDonald obviously was not able to depend upon inherited wealth being an illegitimate child of poor Scottish agricultural labourers.

Others have engaged in work of various sorts, some out of financial interest as with Bonar Law, others out of interest, combined with some need, as with Winston Churchill. Three of the Premiers, Attlee, Asquith, and Lloyd George, entered the legal profession, the first two as barristers, the latter as a solicitor. Attlee also taught at the University of London. Stanley Baldwin, Bonar Law, and Neville Chamberlain all made

---

[1] Both Sir Robert Peel and Gladstone won double firsts in the earlier era. It should be noted, however, that Balfour gained some reputation as a philosopher.

careers for themselves in business. Ramsay MacDonald held various jobs, most of them in the party organization proper, but he also did literary work and free-lance journalism. Winston Churchill served for a time in the Army and followed this with a career as a journalist.

Few men can hope to obtain the office of Prime Minister at an early age. Excluding Lord Salisbury, the average age for the Premiers at the time when they first took office was fifty-nine. This is almost precisely the same average as for those who held the office between 1832 and 1894. Since Gladstone's resignation only one man, Lord Rosebery, has taken the office while under fifty. Five were between fifty and sixty, while five were over sixty.[1]

TABLE ONE

Age of Prime Ministers (1894–1953) on first taking Office.

Name	Age
Rosebery	43
Balfour	54
Campbell-Bannerman	69
Asquith	55
Lloyd George	53
Law	64
Baldwin	55
MacDonald	57
Chamberlain	67
Churchill	65
Attlee	62

It is not difficult to find the reason for late accession to the position. It is implicit in Churchill's statement, 'I am a child of the House of Commons.' The road to political leadership in Great Britain is normally a long and difficult one, interspersed with stumbling blocks of considerable magnitude. It is in the House of Commons that a man must first make his reputation

[1] Gladstone thought that sixty should be the maximum age for Premiers. It was his opinion that neither Russell nor Palmerston contributed anything of value after their sixtieth birthday. Gladstone himself, however, took office in 1892 when he was over eighty.

as a political leader. Normally a long apprenticeship is required before he is ready to step into the limelight of Cabinet membership and perhaps the future prospect of holding the office of Prime Minister.

Since the executive is chosen out of the membership of the legislature in Great Britain it is first necessary to make a mark in the Parliament. Forensic ability, of a peculiar kind, is one of the requisites for political leadership. The ability to influence the legislature and to persuade it to accept your point of view, or at least to provide through your statements an effective basis for an appeal to the public, constitutes an essential requirement of the politician's art.

In the case of most of the Premiers it has been necessary to spend some years in the Commons before the party leaders recognized their merits. There are not many British political figures of whom it may be said, as it was of Asquith, 'that he was never a member of the rank and file. From the start he assumed the manner of a front bencher and the House accepted him at his own valuation.'[1] The length of time spent in the House is naturally affected by some forces which are beyond the control of the individual. If his party loses elections with some frequency it is obvious that he cannot hope to move into a ministerial position as quickly as more fortunate men of comparable ability. On the other hand, it is always possible to make an impression while in opposition and be accepted in the ranks of the leaders of the opposition.

No man can expect to hold the office of Prime Minister in normal circumstances unless he has spent considerable time in the House of Commons. Even in the case of those Prime Ministers who have been peers it is noticeable that they have sometimes spent time in the House of Commons prior to inheriting or being granted their titles. Excluding Lord Salisbury and Lord Rosebery, the Prime Ministers between 1894 and 1953 had served an average of over twenty-three years in the Lower House before first acquiring the top position. Ramsay MacDonald served the shortest time—fourteen years; Winston Churchill was at the other extreme, with thirty-eight years of parliamentary experiences behind him.

The road to the Premiership runs over more than long parliamentary experience. The hopeful must also go through the

[1] Spender and Asquith, *op. cit.*, i, 56.

test of his administrative abilities, first, in all probability in a
junior ministerial position, later within the ranks of the Cabinet
itself. Ramsay MacDonald constitutes the one outstanding
exception to the rule. MacDonald had never held a position in
any ministry prior to forming his Cabinet in 1924. In his case,
however, factors which were far from ordinary were operative.
His party had almost miraculously developed from minor importance in 1914 to the second largest in the country by the fall
of 1923. The only previous opportunity for administrative

TABLE TWO

Number of Years in the House of Commons prior to first taking Office
as Prime Minister (1894–1953)

Name	Years in Commons
Balfour	28
Campbell-Bannerman	37
Asquith	22
Lloyd George	26
Law	21
Baldwin	15
MacDonald	14
Chamberlain	19
Churchill	38
Attlee	23

experience had been during the war when Labour participated
in both the Asquith and Lloyd George coalitions. MacDonald,
however, had been one of the leaders of the anti-war bloc of the
Labour Party and hence had not participated in the government. Arthur Henderson was the only member of the party who
had had actual experience at the Cabinet level, but he clearly
could not be chosen for the office as MacDonald was the party
leader.

Stanley Baldwin[1] also had a limited amount of administrative experience, but he had held minor posts for four years

[1] Sir Charles A. Petrie, *The Life and Letters of the Right Hon. Sir Austen
Chamberlain* (Toronto, Cassell and Co., 1940), ii, 213; D. C. Somervell, *The
Reign of King George the Fifth* (New York, Harcourt, Brace and Co., 1935),
p. 310.

and important offices for two prior to first becoming Prime Minister. Again, in his case, the circumstances were peculiar. Had Sir Austen Chamberlain followed Bonar Law out of the Lloyd George Coalition it is likely that he would have become Prime Minister in 1923 rather than Baldwin. The problem of Lord Curzon has already been noted, although one aspect of it will be discussed later.

The rest of the Premiers, with the exception of Asquith, went through a more or less long period of administrative apprenticeship. Asquith never served in a junior ministerial position, holding the office of Home Secretary between 1892 and 1895 without previous ministerial experience. He also served for over two years between 1905 and 1908 as Chancellor of the Exchequer and frequently as deputy leader of the party. At the other extreme is Churchill, who held ten different ministerial offices, holding one of them on two separate occasions, prior to first becoming Prime Minister.[1]

It is often said that the man who holds the office of Chancellor of the Exchequer is next in line for the leadership of the party. Often this is true and there can be little question that in normal times this official is one of the key figures in the Cabinet and is frequently in line for the top position. Thus Asquith, Baldwin, and Neville Chamberlain all held this office immediately prior to taking office as Prime Minister.

There are, of course, circumstances in which other departments are more important. In times of war the war departments, as would be expected, are frequently more productive of major political leaders. This is to be expected, for the outstanding figures gravitate toward the more immediately important offices. Lloyd George was at the War Office before becoming Prime Minister in 1916. Winston Churchill was First Lord of the Admiralty when he was called by the King. It is noteworthy, however, that prior to the outbreak of hostilities Lloyd George was Chancellor of the Exchequer.

The Foreign Office is also frequently productive of the Premier. Both Lord Salisbury and Lord Rosebery held that office immediately prior to taking the position of Prime Minister. At the present time it is generally recognized that Anthony Eden is next in line for the Premiership.

[1] See Appendix One for a complete list of the ministerial posts held by each of the Premiers prior to their acquisition of the chief office.

In the United States most of the Presidents have gained a great deal of their political experience as governors of one of the States of the Union. Local success leads to national success. Professor Lipson has also noted that in the case of the Premiers of New Zealand in the modern era, 'many have started in the sphere of local government, acting as councillors or mayors, or else doing duty on school committees, harbour boards, or road boards. Thus gaining experience and attracting attention in their own local bailiwick, they could secure a party's nomination and win an election to Parliament.'[1]

This can not be applied with much success to the British Prime Ministers although it is more characteristic of the Premiers since 1894 than for those prior to that date. Local government experience was of no importance prior to this century, and it remains of little importance today. Normally, the political experience of Conservative Party leaders in particular has been confined to the Parliament. Only Neville Chamberlain, who followed the Chamberlain tradition in Birmingham, participated to any substantial degree in local politics. On the other hand, both of the Labour Premiers have had some local government experience, although in each case such experience came quite early in their political careers.

The Labour Party has always placed more stress upon local politics than the Conservatives. This is indicated when one notes that Herbert Morrison, for example, added substantially to his national reputation through his activities as Chairman of the London County Council.[2] There is some question, however, as to whether this concern with local government proper is likely to continue, although in the case of London, it is obviously a road to political prestige and opportunity. Historically, the Labour Party at its inception could not hope for much success when fighting elections on a national level. In consequence it concentrated a considerable amount of its attention on local elections, both because it might take some positive action in the municipalities, and because it enabled them to create a more effective party apparatus for more important elections. Since Labour has become one of the two great parties, however, it is

---

[1] Lipson, *op. cit.*, p. 293.

[2] J. T. Murphy, *Labour's Big Three* (London, Bodley Head, 1948), pp. 146–61; Francis Williams, *Socialist Britain* (New York, Viking Press, 1949), pp. 77–8.

at least possible that much of the attention earlier given to local politics will disappear and the party will concentrate its predominant interests, as with the Conservatives, upon the national level. If this is the case, local political experience is not likely to count for a great deal in the way of political advancement. It is, of course, possible that a man may still impress his abilities upon the party through efforts in the local area and thus gain its endorsement as a parliamentary candidate. It will still be in the Parliament, however, that British political hopefuls must expect to make their mark if they hope for high success.

The American student is familiar with the fact that some areas of the United States are more likely to produce presidential candidates than others. The peculiar character of the Electoral College contributes to the selection of individuals from States which are both large and politically doubtful. There is no indication that geographical considerations play a comparable role in the selection of the party leader in Great Britain. The public never votes directly for the Prime Minister, although it votes indirectly for him in electing the members of the House of Commons. There are no doubtful areas with disproportionate voice in the selection of the government.

On some occasions the particular national background of a party leader may be emphasized. Stanley Baldwin's 'Englishness' was emphasized. But only in England. The inhabitants of England have not shown any tendency in this century to vote for a party with an Englishman at its head rather than a party led by a Welshman or Scotsman. The Scots do not seem to have reflected nationalistic bias although MacDonald may have gained a few votes in consequence of being Scotch by birth. Lloyd George's popularity in Wales was phenomenal, but he is the only Welshman who has held the Premiership.

A breakdown of the geographical background of the Prime Ministers since 1894, excluding Lord Salisbury, reveals that six were English, three were Scottish, one was Welsh, and one, Bonar Law, came from Canada. If the analysis is carried a little further it will be found that there is no indication that any one area is more likely to produce a leader of a particular party than some other area. Of the three Scots, one was a Conservative, one a Liberal, and the other was a Labour Prime Minister. The fact that more of the party leaders have been English does not indicate anything of significance for the English are the most numerous portion of the population of the United Kingdom.

It seems safe to say that geographical, or national, considerations are not of importance in the selection of party leaders. No evidence can be discovered in the memoirs of British statesmen which indicates that such a consideration entered the minds of party leaders in the various selections of the official party leader.

As with geography, there is little indication that religion is of any importance in the selection of party leaders. It may be that a Roman Catholic might not be acceptable as Prime Minister,[1] but this is not the case with any other religious body. Among the various branches of protestantism no major significance can be attached to the faith professed by the party leader.

It is even difficult to ascertain the precise religious beliefs of the men who have held the Premiership in the last fifty-nine years. *Who's Who* does not mention religious affiliations in most cases, nor do the biographies or memoirs of the British statesmen usually consider this matter. Occasionally reference is made to the religious attitude of the subject while a child, but it is sometimes impossible to trace his attitudes into maturity.[2]

A specific breakdown of the religious affiliations of those for whom it has been possible to discover acceptable evidence shows that four have been Anglicans, two took communion in the Church of Scotland, and four have been Nonconformists. Actually even these figures arc misleading, for Balfour is included in both the Anglican and Scottish Church figures. He accepted communion in both and had little sympathy for those who criticized him upon the grounds of doctrinaire religious considerations.[3] The only Premier whose religious attachments led him into serious political controversy was Lloyd George. Lord Rosebery described him quite aptly as 'the great protagonist of nonconformity.'[4] This religious protagonism, however, took

[1] This point is, of course, difficult to substantiate. It is probable that anti-popery no longer carries much political weight in Great Britain. Even so, no Catholic has ever held the office of Prime Minister.

[2] The relative insignificance of religion as an issue in British politics may also be noted in the difficulty of obtaining information on the religious affiliations of parliamentary candidates. Cf. H. G. Nicholas, *The British General Election of 1950* (London, Macmillan, 1951), pp. 57–8.

[3] Dugdale, *op. cit.*, i, 30.

[4] J. Hugh Edwards, *David Lloyd George* (New York, J. H. Sears and Co., Inc.), i, 31.

place in his early career. It might conceivably have affected his selection as Prime Minister in normal times, for he did antagonize many Anglicans, but in the peculiar circumstances of the crisis of 1916 it was not even considered.

This attitude towards religion does provide a contrast with the nineteenth century. Membership in either the Anglican or the Scottish Church was of some importance, although it is difficult to assess it with any degree of accuracy. The Liberal Party had its roots sunk into religious dissent, but at the same time Gladstone himself was an ardent Anglican. Religious controversy was more important in the nineteenth century and it might have been the case that the Liberals would have faced more difficulty if they had been led by a dissenter. Today, however, there is no indication that it is of any importance with the possible exception that a Catholic may face rather serious difficulties.

Family has always been of considerable importance in British politics. However, indications are that it is becoming increasingly less important than in the past, although it still plays a relatively minor role in the selection of party candidates. The scions of members of the nobility have certain initial advantages in making a political career, but they are not as substantial as they were in the past. The extensions of the suffrage have resulted in a decline in the relative importance of questions of family descent.

This provides a substantial contrast with the Prime Ministers of the period 1832–94. The old emphasis upon aristocratic lineage remained of considerable importance during that time. Disraeli, Peel, and Gladstone, were the only Premiers of the period who were not descendants of aristocrats. Sir Robert Peel's father was, however, a baronet. The remaining Prime Ministers were uniformly of aristocratic descent, and in all cases their fathers were not the first of the family to hold title. The fact that Disraeli and Gladstone were of middle-class origin is itself of some importance, for neither became Prime Minister until after the passage of the suffrage act of 1867.

The Prime Ministers of the period since 1894 have most frequently been of middle-class origin. Excluding Lord Salisbury, seven Premiers came from the middle class, three were of aristocratic lineage, and one came from the lower class. Ramsay MacDonald, the illegitimate son of Scottish agricultural workers, is the only Premier who can definitely be placed as of lower class origin. Lloyd George and Bonar Law might be described as of lower middle-class extraction. The three Premiers who had definite and close attachments to the aristocracy were Rosebery, Balfour, and Churchill. Lord Rosebery, of course, held a peerage in his own right when he became Prime Minister. Balfour traced his lineage back to Robert the Bruce on his father's side. His mother was a Cecil, and the sister of Lord Salisbury. Churchill's father held a title, and the family patents of nobility trace back at least as far as the illustrious Duke of Marlborough, the great English hero of the War of the Spanish Succession. The only one of these three to hold the office of Prime Minister in the last forty years was Churchill, but it is obvious that his ancestry was of no significance as a determining factor in his appointment.

All three of these men, and Neville Chamberlain as well, did gain initial political advantage from their family background. Rosebery's title, when added to his wealth, enabled him to enter politics at an early age. Since the House of Lords was still of importance at the time he was able to make his mark relatively early. Balfour gained a substantial advantage from his relationship to Lord Salisbury, for he very early received a safe Conservative constituency.[1] Unquestionably this gave him an advantage over the ordinary political hopeful. Winston Churchill too gained political advantage from the fact that his father, Lord Randolph Churchill, was a major political figure in his own right. The basic fact in this situation was not so much that he was of aristocratic lineage as that his father had already made the name Churchill something to be conjured with.

Neville Chamberlain, although not a member of the aristocracy, gained a comparable advantage. Joseph Chamberlain was more than a politician in Birmingham; he was a legend. Neville Chamberlain and his brother, Austen, were both able to take advantage of their father's reputation in advancing their political careers. It may be questioned whether Neville Chamberlain would have been elected in any constituency originally other than Birmingham. In Birmingham the name Chamberlain was enough to ensure election. It was not enough, however, to make him Premier. He had to have ability as well. But his name brought him initial opportunities; it made it possible for

[1] Dugdale, *op. cit.*, i, 31.

him to reveal his abilities. It also enabled him to move into the society of the political leaders of Great Britain even before he had made a personal reputation.[1]

The indications are that family lineage is no longer of the importance it occupied in the past. It would not be safe to completely neglect such considerations for they may bring opportunities that might not otherwise be available, but they are not of basic importance. They open the road, but they do not guarantee the achievement of its objective.

The Prime Minister is the leader of a party. This is the case in nearly all instances, although it is not always true that he has been formally selected as the party leader prior to being appointed Prime Minister. In time of war, of course, it is possible that an individual who is not the party leader may become Premier. Lloyd George was not the leader of the Liberal Party, and his accession to the Premiership resulted in a split within the ranks of his party. Winston Churchill was not the leader of the Conservative Party in 1940, and he did not become the leader until six months after he had become Prime Minister.

Normally, however, the Prime Minister is the leader of the party. The recognition of his status may be derived either from formal action or from a tacit recognition that he is the pre-eminent figure in the party.[2] The important point, however, is not merely that he is a party man; he must be a loyal party man. The man who crosses the aisles with any frequency is not likely to become Prime Minister. The man who publicly opposes the party's line is not likely to become its leader. He may be a man of ability, but party loyalty is one of the first prerequisites for selection as party leader.

The only Prime Minister of this century who crossed party lines with any frequency was Winston Churchill. Churchill started his political career as a Conservative. He was first elected to the House of Commons as a Conservative. He very quickly crossed the lines, however, and became a Liberal. As a Liberal he became a member of the Cabinet. After the First World War he withdrew from the Liberal Party and was elected to the Parliament as a Constitutionalist. Some months

[1] Feiling, *op. cit.*, p. 83.
[2] The formal method of selecting the party leaders is treated in Chapter IV.

later he went back into the Conservative Party. It is probable that this rather unorthodox political background caused him considerable difficulty. Many of the long-time orthodox Tories were suspicious of this man who did not seem to be politically stable. Even as late as 1945 charges were sometimes heard that he was an 'unreconstructed Liberal'. It is improbable that he would ever have become Prime Minister in normal times. The war crisis made possible what otherwise was impossible.

The attitude of major, and even minor, figures in the party must inevitably have an important effect upon the selection of the party leader. A man's temperament may adversely affect his colleagues. That is, they themselves may think it undesirable to have to associate with him when he is in a position of power. Or they may think his temperament likely to cost the party votes. As noted earlier Leopold Amery has said that the selection of Baldwin over Curzon was made upon the grounds that the former was 'likely to be more acceptable to his colleagues and to the rank and file of the party'.[1] Lord Curzon, whether intentionally or not, gave the impression that he felt himself superior to others. He did not work well with his colleagues in the Cabinet. He was considered pontifical and boring. Even his personal carriage, necessitated by a back injury, grated upon his colleagues and tended to antagonize part of the public. He was unpopular with the press, both the 'popular' and the 'responsible' press looking at him with some distaste. His unpopularity with the press was inevitably reflected in public unpopularity. In this case it is not at all surprising that the party leaders should have felt that he was not the most desirable selection as party leader. After all, it was necessary to appeal to the public in order to maintain control of the government. It was felt that his personality would repel rather than attract votes. In such circumstances his personality made him impossible as a democratic leader.[2]

Where fear of public reaction to Curzon's personality was one of the chief operative factors in the conclusion that Baldwin should receive preference over Curzon, it was personal experience with Sir William Harcourt in the Cabinet itself which led so many of his colleagues to consider him undesirable as the

[1] Amery, *op. cit.*, p. 22.
[2] Nicolson, *op. cit.*, pp. 352-5. See Chapter I of Nicolson's study for a brilliant analysis of Curzon's personality.

head of the government. Harcourt had unquestioned intellectual power, parliamentary experience, ministerial experience, and a substantial degree of public support. These were not enough, however, for his personal traits had made him important enemies among the highest figures in the party, as is indicated by the following statement:[1]

'Yet his disqualifications were felt by the great majority of his colleagues to be crippling. They arose mainly from temper, in the comprehensive as well as the narrow sense of that term. It was impossible to foresee from hour to hour what would and would not unseal the inexhaustible vials of his wrath and discharge their blistering contents on the heads of foes, friends, and colleagues. While his choler endured, he assailed its object with a vehemence and variety of invective which declined no medium, rejected no weapon, spared no sensitive spot. As soon as it had subsided he was prepared to laugh hugely, to shake hands, and forget. Not so, always his victims.'

In particular, John Morley was bitterly opposed to Harcourt's ambition to be Prime Minister. 'Harcourt was rough, and Mr. Morley was sensitive. Harcourt hit hard and thoughtlessly, and forgot all about it; Mr. Morley winced and remembered.'[2] Since Morley was one of the most important men in the Cabinet his antagonism was destructive of Harcourt's ambition.

The inclusion of all sections of the populace in the electorate has done much to change the necessary qualifications for the Premiership. To the intellectual, administrative, and parliamentary ability required of the nineteenth-century Prime Minister has been added the necessity of personal characteristics which appeal to the electorate. There is no way of stating what these characteristics are, however. It is not always true that a dynamic individual like Lloyd George is preferred over the judiciously inclined Asquith. Even the admitted public admiration for Churchill as a war leader was insufficient to enable him to carry his party to power in 1945. Clement Attlee, far from a dynamic figure, led his party to victory against the redoubtable Prime Minister.

Some considerations, however, would seem to be operative upon all men who aspire to this high place. A man must be of unimpeachable moral character. British moral standards are

[1] Spender and Asquith, *op. cit.*, i, 90.   [2] Gardiner, *op. cit.*, ii, 265.

still essentially puritanical in content. A man who likes the gaming tables, or has an interest in women of 'the wrong sort' is not likely to rise to high post. Even a man who has made an unsuccessful marriage is likely to find his road to the Premiership blocked forever. No Prime Minister has been divorced. It is possible that this informal rule may be tested in the future. Anthony Eden, the Crown Prince of the Conservative Party, divorced his first wife. The facts of the case were such, however, as to create public sympathy for Eden, and it may be the case that he may some day become the first Prime Minister to have been divorced.[1]

The British people also expect their political leaders to have a high degree of public integrity. The use of public office for private advantage is a serious violation of the customary standards of British public life. This may be seen in the fact that members of Boards of Directors of 'public 'concerns must relinquish those posts before joining the ministry.[2] Similarly, trade union leaders must resign their posts in comparable circumstances.[3]

Two men who have held the office of Prime Minister in this century were subjected to criticism for alleged violations of these rules. They were Lloyd George and Neville Chamberlain. In both cases the charges preceded their elevation to the Premiership by several years.

Lloyd George's personal reputation was involved in the controversy over the Marconi Co., of America and its relations with the Marconi Co. of Great Britain.[4] The British government proposed to establish a wireless system which would tie Great Britain to the dominions and to the United States. Bids were accepted and the Marconi Co. of Great Britain was awarded the contract. It was later discovered that Lloyd George and two other ministers held stocks in the Marconi Co. of America. They had bought the stocks upon the advice, received indirectly, of the principal representatives of the British company. The British and American companies had entered into a private agreement which it was realized would have the effect of increasing the value of the stocks of the American company. Lloyd George was informed of this by the brother of the British company's representative. He therefore

---

[1] See Appendix Two. [2] 154 *Hansard (Commons)*, 4s., 234.
[3] 169 *H.C. Deb.*, 5s., 735. [4] 54 *H.C. Deb.*, 5s., 391–514, 346–664.

purchased stock in the American company and was able to reap a substantial profit when the agreement was publicized. He was informed, as his critics in the Commons admitted, that the American company had no concern with the contract sought by the British company.[1] Actually the continuation of the level of profit did depend upon the British company's attaining the contract. After their agreement the two companies were so closely united that the withdrawal of the contract from the British concern would have affected the American company adversely. There was, of course, some question of whether Lloyd George, and the other two ministers involved, did not feel a personal obligation to the representative of the British company who had tipped them off to the profits to be obtained from investment in the American concern.

Actually, although the House of Commons debated the issue for two full days, no definite decision was taken and a critical motion moved by the Conservatives was defeated on a strict party vote.[2] This experience does not seem to have hindered Lloyd George in his future career. It is, of course, possible that it might have been more difficult for him to become Premier in normal times as a consequence of this action, but it does not seem probable. In the dark months of the war in 1916 it does not seem to have been an issue in his selection at all.

Neville Chamberlain's experience was considerably less serious. Chamberlain as Minister of Health admitted that he retained a directorship in a family firm. He insisted that he did not take an active part in its administration, and asserted that he had no knowledge of whether the firm did or did not have government contracts.[3] Actually, as Arthur Henderson was able to show, the company had fourteen contracts with the government.[4] Henderson also pointed out in addition that Chamberlain held 2,395 shares in the company out of a total of 5,000.[5] Again, no adverse effects seem to have followed the revelation of Chamberlain's interest in the firm.

The man who stands for something, and stands for it through adversity, is sometimes the recipient of later public support. Campbell-Bannerman stood for what he thought was right

---

[1] *Ibid.*, 397. [2] *Ibid.*, 662–3.
[3] 197 *H.C. Deb.*, 5s., 2278–80. [4] 198 *H.C. Deb.*, 5s., 90.
[5] *Ibid.*, 88. This incident is not mentioned in Feiling's biography of Chamberlain which probably indicates its relative insignificance.

during the Boer War. Firmly convinced of the rectitude of his course he accepted public abuse and censure. The very integrity of his position eventually created public respect and support. He was obviously a man who could be trusted. He did not opportunistically change his course because it was unpopular. He was not a good speaker, he did not have a dynamic personality, but he had integrity, and it brought him respect.[1] Ramsay MacDonald's anti-war attitude did not damage his later political career. Again, there seems to have been considerable respect for a man who had the courage of his convictions. When the period of post-war doubt came, when the people were no longer convinced of the rightness of the war, and when the treaty had been subjected to serious criticism, MacDonald fell heir to the support of those who admired his strength in taking a position when it was unpopular.

A multiplicity of other factors may affect some portions of the electorate. Stanley Baldwin affected the attire and attitude of the country squire. To some this may have been an important fact in the dictation of their choice of Premiers. To others it may have seemed undesirable, but it seems more likely that the myth which he attempted to create was upon the whole effective. Pictures of political leaders with their families are frequent enough in appearance to justify an assertion that there is at least a belief among politicians that the family man has an initial advantage over the man without a family. The family man, it is well known, can be trusted, while there is some question about the man who does not have a family. With the exception of Arthur Balfour, who was a bachelor, and Sir Henry Campbell-Bannerman, all of the Premiers since Lord Salisbury have had children. Other non-rational considerations may also affect voters, even extending down to such unimportant matters as the smoking habits of political leaders. The large number of pipe-smoking political leaders might be explainable in terms of an individual preference for pipes, but it might also be explained by the fact that the pipe has more emotional appeal than the cigarette or the cigar.

Lord Bryce, in 1891, noted that it was a rather surprising fact that the men who held the office of the American Presidency

[1] See Lloyd George's comment on Campbell-Bannerman in Lord Riddell's *Intimate Diary of the Peace Conference and After* (New York, Reynal and Hitchcock, 1934), p. 51.

were upon the whole second-raters. He himself provided an explanation of this which need not immediately concern us here, but it is noteworthy that he stressed the fact that the British Premiers were uniformly men of superior ability to those who held the office of the President. 'It would seem', he wrote, 'that the natural selection of the English parliamentary system, even as modified by the aristocratic habits of that country, has more tendency to bring the highest gifts to the highest place than the more artificial selection of America.'[1]

It is unquestionably true that the institutional patterns of British politics make impossible the choice of persons merely because they can command the support of doubtful areas or the choice of obscure men because they are less likely to have a large number of enemies in important places. The British political leader cannot be obscure; he must have made his reputation in the midst of political controversy. This does not mean that all British Premiers are uniformly of high calibre. Stanley Baldwin cannot be classified as a man of great ability.[2] Perhaps we might justifiably say that Baldwin was a British Calvin Coolidge. Similarly abilities of one kind do not necessarily involve general understanding or comprehension. Neville Chamberlain's ability as an administrator is not subject to serious question nor is his ability as chairman of the Cabinet. At the same time one might say that his comprehension of the realities of modern politics was generally inadequate; he was a British model Herbert Hoover.

While Bryce's remarks as to the relative merits of Premiers and Presidents was generally true for the period following the American Civil War, it is no longer valid as a generalization. The period since 1900 does not indicate that the abilities of the British Premiers have been noticeably greater than those of the American Presidents of the same period. Theodore Roosevelt, Woodrow Wilson, and Franklin D. Roosevelt can stand comparison with comparable British political figures of the same era. It must be said, however, that the British system is such that is hardly likely that anyone of the calibre of Senator Harding could achieve the position of Prime Minister.

[1] Lord Bryce, *The American Commonwealth* (London, Macmillan, 1891), i, 80.

[2] Cf. A. L. Rowse, 'Reflections on Lord Baldwin', *Political Quarterly*, xii, 305–17.

III

The Prime Minister
and the Public

I. INTRODUCTION

'Force,' wrote David Hume, 'is always on the side of the governed, the governors have nothing to support them but opinion.'[1] While the rise of modern technology and the development of weapons of mass destruction may require that some exception be taken to the first portion of this statement, it is obvious that all government, if it is to endure, must have the support, either active or tacit, of the public. Even dictatorships are based upon public support, although the reasons for, and the nature of, that support may not be the same as in the constitutional state.

There is a distinction between a government which recognizes that it is limited by some few principles and institutions which have widespread public support, and the idea that government policy should itself reflect the opinion of the public. In Great Britain there is 'a close relation between the policies followed by the Government and the general ideas of the majority of the electorate'.[2] There is little question but that Professor Jennings' statement is correct, but it must not be assumed that the majority always approves everything which the government does. In fact, it is really difficult to be precise about what we mean when we speak of the public. 'This

[1] 'Of the First Principles of Government', in Henry D. Aiken (ed.), *Hume's Moral and Political Philosophy* (New York, Hafner, 1948), p. 307.
[2] W. I. Jennings, *The British Constitution* (Cambridge, Cambridge University Press, 1944), p. 209.

public,' it has been said, 'is a mere phantom. It is an abstraction. The public in respect to a railroad strike may be the farmers whom the railroad serves; the public in respect to an agricultural tariff may include the very railroad men who were on a strike. The public is not . . . a fixed body of individuals. It is merely those persons who are interested in an affair and can affect it only by supporting or opposing the actors.'[1]

The theory of the mandate[2] expresses most directly the thesis that the public must sanction a policy before it can be put into execution. Under the theory of the mandate a government is obligated not to take action, except in time of crisis, unless that action had received public support in the last election. This means that it must have been at issue in the last election. It is then assumed that since the government obtained sufficient support to control the House of Commons it has received a mandate, and is entitled to proceed with the enactment of the programme which has been approved.

Realistically speaking, it is obvious that no one can ever tell whether a precise policy has or has not received a mandate from the public. The only thing which can be known with such assurance is that one party has received a sufficient number of votes to control the House of Commons. The actual reasons for which they received those votes may, and do, differ widely. One person may vote for one party because he favours its foreign policy over that of the other party. At the same time he may think the domestic programme of the latter party is better, but that foreign policy issues are of greater importance than domestic issues. His vote, however, is weighed upon the side of the domestic as well as the foreign policy programmes of the party.

Did the British people vote for socialism in 1945, or did they vote for the Labour Party because they were displeased with the pre-war record of the Conservatives? Was socialism a basic issue, or were they more concerned with foreign policy, housing, social security, etc.? Public opinion polls indicated that the most important single issue in the election was hous-

---

[1] Walter Lippmann, *The Phantom Public* (New York, Harcourt, Brace, 1925), p. 77.

[2] For the relationship between the theory of the mandate and the obligation to dissolve the Parliament, see Chapter VII.

ing.[1] Perhaps some of these issues were of fundamental importance while the socialist proposals were not weighed heavily one way or the other. Public opinion polls in late 1949 indicated public opposition to the nationalization of steel, but this did not prevent the Labour Party from again winning control of the House of Commons in February 1950. It may even be asked whether there was a mandate for any portion of the Labour Party's programme in 1945? The party received only forty-eight per cent of the total vote cast. This was more than any other party received, but it is still true that over half of the votes cast were against Labour.[2] The indications are thus clear that it is never possible to know precisely why the public voted one way or another, or even what it did vote for, other than one party or another, one party leader in preference to the other.

Furthermore, it must be recognized that there are varying degrees of political interest among the citizenry. In some persons it takes the form of acute interest in almost all areas of controversy, but in the case of others, perhaps equal in number or even larger, it takes the form of no interest whatsoever. It is probably safe to say that the majority of persons are interested but not to a particularly intense degree. Even should they have the interest most persons do not have the time to devote to the study of contemporary problems which must serve as a prelude to action, although it is true that they may consider the 'slogans' thrown up for public consumption by the parties as the equivalent of knowledge.[3] R. H. Tawney has said, 'The fact is, that in all large communities the majority of men are not thinking about public questions. But, on the other hand, the majority of men trust the ballot and elect persons who are thinking about those things; and what you have to consider is the judgment of that minority who command the confidence of their fellows.'[4] Tawney's statement would seem to be basically correct, but

[1] R. B. MacCallum and Alison Readman, *The British General Election of 1945* (New York, Oxford University Press, 1947), p. 237. Forty-one per cent of those sampled selected housing as the most important issue. Full employment followed with fifteen per cent.

[2] *Ibid.*, p. 282.

[3] Even the most acutely interested citizen, of course, can never know all of the problems, or enough about the facts to make intelligent decisions in all areas of governmental activity.

[4] Quoted in John M. Gaus, *Great Britain: A Study in Civic Loyalty* (Chicago, University of Chicago Press, 1929), p. 21.

even so it is sometimes extremely difficult to determine the membership in that influential minority.

The task of the statesman is made easier by the existence of a large number of voters who can be depended upon to stick by the party through its most extreme trials and tribulations. Even in 1931, the low-water year of the Labour Party, it received over six and a half million votes.[1] The Prime Minister and his colleagues, and, on the other side, the opposition leader and his friends, are able to concentrate their attention upon the 'floating vote'. It is this group which actually determines the outcome of elections. Professor Jennings has estimated that there are approximately two and a half million persons in Britain who do not have an overweening allegiance to either of the two major parties.[2] It is to them that the parties address their appeals, for it is upon their support that any accession to power depends. One effect of this, it might be noted, is to pull the programmes of the parties closer together than might otherwise be the case, for both depend upon the same source for power.

Before 1867 there were a few indications that public opinion had to be recognized as the basis of political authority, but they tended to be sporadic in character. Chatham had risen to power as a result of his popularity with the public, but he was a political sport for the eighteenth century. Earl Grey had achieved high public favour in 1832. Even the Reform Act of 1832, however, did not bring with it popular rule. The suffrage extensions brought the middle class into the throne room, but their pressure was felt directly through the election of representatives to the House of Commons. The rest of the public was still cut off from the effective exercise of political authority. Occasionally declarations, such as the Tamsworth Manifesto, seemed to recognize the importance of public opinion, but even Peel was to state later that it was not essential for the minister to state his policy views to the public prior to taking office.[3]

---

[1] Jennings, *op. cit.*, p. 43.

[2] *Ibid.*, p. 43. Later (p. 47) he speaks as follows: 'Both parties are trying to catch about 750,000 votes to be cast by the more prosperous workers . . . and the clerks and other white-collar workers in places like Hammersmith and Fulham.' There is no necessary conflict here. Those portions of the floating vote which are located in doubtful constituencies obviously carry more weight than those which are lost amidst predominantly Conservative or Labour voters.

[3] C. S. Emden, *The People and the Constitution* (Oxford, Clarendon Press, 1933), pp. 206–7.

The electorate prior to 1867 was also rather similar in background. At least it could be expected that the voters read the principal political papers, although perhaps only those of their own party, and that they had formed decisions or ideas upon the basis of what they had read. They were a relatively well-informed electorate as compared with that which came to power after 1867. They had an understanding of the issues, often seen through the eyeglasses of prejudice and class interest, but at least they knew what the controversy was about. They could be reached through the printed page and direct personal campaigning was not required. Peel never found it necessary to carry on a national campaign, or even to appeal to the nation as a whole, although the Tamsworth Manifesto inclined in that direction.

The extension of the suffrage in 1867 changed the character of the electorate and hence of British politics. 'The enlarged electorate led to the development of an entirely new technique of political leadership. The Constitution required a Prime Minister and a Leader of the Opposition who could touch the springs of action in the common man. Persuasion and propaganda were to replace patronage and corruption.'[1] The change introduced was to be drastic in character and the change in technique may be seen in the following description.[2]

'From 1868 onwards the public man was in the open, and a faithful Press followed him to the platform whence he now made appeals which were at least equal in importance to those which he had made from his place in Parliament . . . we pass to a new kind of public life in which political campaigning is as important a part of a leader's activities as administering or criticizing from his place in Parliament. The star performer no longer keeps to his constituency or saves himself to election times, but is all over the country at all times obeying the call of whips and party managers.'

Gladstone seems to have been the first major political figure to grasp the implications of the change in the composition of the electorate. His Midlothian campaign of 1880 provided an example of the new democratic statesman in action. His

[1] K. B. Smellie, *One Hundred Years of English Government* (New York, Macmillan, 1937), p. 193.

[2] J. A. Spender, *The Public Life* (New York, Frederick Stokes, 1925), i, 37–8.

campaign was conducted in the form of a series of addresses to his own constituents, but the issues upon which he touched amounted to appeals over the head of Parliament, 'and beyond the range of his constituents, for a personal plebiscite, or mandate to rule the country'.[1] In 1885 he carried this a step further by campaigning outside his constituency. In this case his action was nearly as important as the campaign of 1880, for he was now the Prime Minister, whereas in 1880 he had been out of power. The conclusive step towards the modern technique was taken by Lord Salisbury. In 1892 he issued a manifesto, addressed to the 'Electors of the United Kingdom'.[2] It was, of course, impossible for him to address constituents directly, since he had none. Nevertheless, his action established the practice which was to be followed by his successors. Stanley Baldwin, it is true, did not issue such an appeal until 1929, but even he was forced to recognize its necessity.

The Prime Minister may reach the public in several ways. At the immediate moment the intention is not to elaborate on them but to state them. Later a closer look is taken at each of the methods, either in this chapter or in one of the ensuing chapters.

One of the most important methods of influencing the public is through speeches in the Parliament.[3] The content of any speech delivered by the Prime Minister will receive wide circulation throughout Great Britain by both the newspapers and the radio. Similarly, answers to questions in the House of Commons will also receive similar treatment if they are of importance.

In addition to speeches in the House of Commons the Prime Minister may also address public meetings with the knowledge that his comments will be carried far beyond the bounds of the meeting hall. Further, he may in some cases address formal dinners or speak on ceremonial occasions. In addition to the knowledge that they will be distributed by other media, such occasions provide an opportunity of direct access to men who help mould opinion.

The newspapers themselves provide the principal means of circulating the statements and views of the Prime Minister. In

---

[1] D. C. Somervell, *Disraeli and Gladstone* (London, Jarrolds, 1925), pp. 212–13.

[2] Emden, *op. cit.*, p. 290.   [3] *Post*, Chapter VII.

addition to the direct reporting of speeches which he makes elsewhere, he may, on occasion, deal directly with the newspapers and their editors in attempts to influence them. Or he may, on other occasions, reply to questions asked by the press. During the war Winston Churchill had periodic conferences with newspaper editors.[1]

The radio provides another means of contacting the public. Through the radio he is able to speak directly to the nation as a whole. The radio, however, is subjected to strict regulations which make it less effective as a means of influencing the public than is the case in the United States.

Additionally, the Prime Minister may reach the public through written materials which are distributed by the party and also reported in the press. In particular he is likely to play a major role in the preparation of the party's statement of principles during an election period.[2]

The Prime Minister, or more properly, the government as a whole, is also able to take advantage of the Government Information Services as a means of contacting the public. The government's reports are circulated by the government itself, and also receive synoptic treatment in the press. This is not particularly important for immediate partisan advantage, as an attempt to introduce biased reporting would be likely to backfire against the government. However, if the government reports are favourable in tone, they may, in the long run, have an advantageous effect upon the public support given to the Prime Minister.

The individual citizen is not entirely cut off from the possibility of making his opinion felt other than through the ballot. He may, by writing a letter to his representative in the Parliament, be responsible for raising a question which requires public attention. He may also seek and obtain signatures to a petition, and the petition may be presented to the House of Commons. This latter procedure is now not of basic importance but the letter to the member is still of some importance and may lead to the solution of a private grievance, or even the raising of a public issue.

Associations can reach the government more directly. The

[1] Francis Williams, *Press, Parliament and People* (Toronto, W. Heinemann, 1946), p. 42.
[2] *Post*, Chapter V.

trade unions, the F.B.I. (Federation of British Industries), agricultural organizations, societies formed for special purposes and others may enter into direct contact with the government. It is now a part of standard British administrative practice to consult interested associations in the formulation of policy.[1] The impact of pressure and interest groups in Great Britain is felt at the executive, rather than at the legislative level. In most cases the contacts made are with specific departments, but when an issue is of particular importance, representatives of such groups may see the Prime Minister himself. He must see them for failure to do so would involve risking the loss of support in the next election.

It is still possible that assemblies of ordinary citizens may also affect governmental policy. The formation of special organizations to oppose the Incitement to Disaffection Bill, and the meetings at which the criticisms of the bill were aired, did much to bring about modifications in the bill itself.[2]

Last, but far from least, the public eventually passes judgment upon the government at the ballot box itself. The Prime Minister knows that eventually he must subject himself and his programme to the vote of the people. This means that throughout his term of office he must take care not to act in such a manner as to antagonize significant portions of the public. The fact that the public eventually has the determining voice in whether he does or does not continue in power inevitably affects the use which he makes of power.

The office which he occupies makes the Prime Minister one of the most newsworthy figures in Great Britain. Only the King and the Royal Family are likely to receive greater news coverage.[3] It might be added that this concern with the Royal Family is advantageous to the Prime Minister in some ways, for many of the duties of the King are social in character, and this leaves the Prime Minister free to spend his time on more important matters.

Still, among the members of the real executive, the Prime

[1] W. I. Jennings, *The Law and the Constitution* (London, University of London Press, 1933), pp. 88–9.

[2] W. I. Jennings, *Parliament* (Cambridge, Cambridge University Press, 1939), pp. 227–8.

[3] Cf. Walter Bagehot, *The English Constitution* (London, Worlds Classics edition, 1928), ch. ii; Kingsley Martin, *The Magic of Monarchy* (New York, Knopf, 1937) ch. i, v.

Minister is normally the most significant figure. The attention of the public is concentrated upon him. This concentration is not limited to his public acts, although they are of primary importance, but may extend to his private life as well. The Prime Minister cannot hope to escape public attention. If he plays golf that is an item of news. If he has a tea party the names of the guests will be reported to the public. He gives up his right to privacy when he becomes the Prime Minister.[1] He may wish for privacy but it is impossible to have it.

'The public man who says that his private life is his own affair has no longer the power of making it so. The picture of him which is formed in the public eye is built up of a thousand little details which may have nothing to do with his political action. He chooses voluntarily the life of publicity and cannot escape its liabilities. . . . Whoever embarks on the public life must make up his mind that it is a highly artificial mode of existence requiring sacrifices of privacy and convenience which no other profession demand, subject to rules and traditions which may be wholly unmerited. The political star-performer leads the actor's life and is liable to the discipline of the clergy. Conformity may be disagreeable but rebellion is generally disastrous.'[2]

Spender's comment emphasizes an aspect of the life of the politician which may not be pleasant, but which must be fulfilled. The private life of the Prime Minister, and other political leaders, must be beyond reproach. He is subject to the same rigorous strictness in morality as the Royal Family. Essentially the moral code by which the British public judges its leader is still puritanical in character.[3] No Prime Minister can afford to have it known that he has a mistress, or that he gambles for large stakes; nor may he afford the luxury of a divorce.[4] Since all of his activities are subject to constant scrutiny by the press and his political opponents, the only certain way to keep the

---

[1] The same focusing of public attention characterizes the American scene. Ex-President Hoover has stated that the one great blessing of his failure to achieve re-election was that it enabled him to regain some of his lost privacy. 'The Personal Memoirs of Herbert Hoover', *Colliers*, 17 February, 1951, p. 13.

[2] Spender, *op. cit.*, i, 148–9.

[3] For examples of such rigid moral concepts see Kingsley Martin, *op. cit.*, ch. iv.

[4] See Appendix Two.

public from knowing of such activities is not to engage in them. Sir Charles Dilke was ruined politically because he was named as a co-respondent in a divorce case. Parnell was destroyed because he lived with a woman without benefit of wedlock. Even Edward VIII lost a throne because he insisted upon marrying a woman who had been twice divorced.

Among other things the Prime Minister must, of course, recognize that he will be subject to abuse. As Lloyd George said, 'You have to be inured to attacks. I have been attacked for thirty years. I don't remember a single year in which I have not been attacked.'[1] Criticism may take the form of direct personal abuse in some cases, although contemporary British criticism of political opponents has never slipped to the low level which has characterized American politics in recent years.

Some men come to occupy positions of minor deities among large portions of the electorate. The same men are usually characterized as emissaries of Satan by their political opponents. Gladstone's position with his followers was certainly at least that of a political saint. George N. Barnes told a little story which exemplifies, in a somewhat exaggerated form, the hold which Gladstone had on a large portion of the British electorate. 'Gladstone was the political god and Jenkins was one of his prophets. Another of the period was a gentleman named Lacaita, who was returned about the same time as one of the Dundee members with the largest majority of any candidate in Great Britain, and his main qualification—so the other side said—was that he was the son of an Italian with whom Gladstone had foregathered while on his Italian travels.'[2]

Lloyd George came to occupy a position of comparable importance in his native Wales. Tom Clarke tells a tale which, although another exaggeration, indicates his status there. 'The other day in Red Wharf Bay, Anglesey, I was looked upon as a heathen by a Welsh newsagent when I asked for the *Daily Mail*.' . . "Nobody in these parts reads that lying rag, look you," said the man, "except a silly old man in Pentraeth, indeed. Stick you to the *Daily News* and Lloyd George." He went on to protest so much about the virtues of Lloyd George that I

[1] Lord Riddell, *Intimate Diary of the Peace Conference and After* (New York, Reynal and Hitchcock, 1934), p. 308.

[2] George N. Barnes, *From Workshop to War Cabinet* (New York, Appleton, 1924), pp. 17–18.

interposed, "But he's not God, you know." "Ah, indeed, no, you are right," was the reply, "but he is young yet, look you!" [1]

Most men cannot, of course, expect to receive this kind of public adulation. It is doubtful that they should wish it, and highly doubtful whether it is desirable in a democratic society, but it has existed infrequently in British history. The party which has a leader who can achieve such public adulation is likely to reap the advantage in long years of power. It is also likely to be dominated by the leader who has such status.

II. THE PRIME MINISTER AND THE PRESS

Reports in the press serve as one of the principal means by which the Prime Minister is able to influence the public. In all probability it is the most important single medium of communication, for the radio is subject to stringent controls which make it less important as a vehicle for political statements. The press, on the other hand, gives full coverage to statements, speeches, and comments made by the Prime Minister. Even in these days of paper shortages the statements of the Prime Minister are still a staple of the press diet, although it is no longer possible to report them in detail, as was true in the past.

The press will include reports of speeches and statements made in the House of Commons. Additionally, in some cases, the Prime Minister may make a direct statement to the press. [2] This is not a frequent occurrence for the British have not developed the practice of the news conference as it is used by the American President. It might be added that it is not as necessary in Britain as in the United States, for the Prime Minister has to face a frequent barrage of questions in the House of Commons which serve to elicit comparable information. The absence of such requirements in the United States makes direct press questioning somewhat more necessary.

Several considerations must arise in treating the relations of the Prime Minister and the press. The character of the British

[1] Tom Clarke, *My Northcliffe Diary* (New York, Cosmopolitan Book Corporation, 1931), p. 108.

[2] See the *Sunday Times*, 14 November 1937, for a report on how Mac-Donald approached the press in September 1931 in seeking support for the abandonment of the gold standard.

press, that is, its organizational structure, and particularly the influence of the London dailies and the extent of concentration of ownership are both of importance. The extent to which the newspapers have attempted to dictate government policy, or to bring one individual to the fore while undermining another, must receive consideration. The actual relations of the Prime Ministers with publishers and editors must be treated. The extent to which the Prime Minister, or some of his representatives, have attempted to influence the handling of the news is also worthy of attention.

The contemporary British press bears little resemblance to its nineteenth-century ancestors. The nineteenth-century press did not direct its appeal to the masses as a whole, but to a restricted portion of the electorate. The style and tone of a paper like the *Times* was not such as to make it a favourite reading matter for the masses who were enfranchised after 1867 and 1884. The old press was more objective and more rational in emphasis than the popular press which developed in the twentieth century. However, it is probably true, as a critic has said, that 'most of the older papers had gone stodgy and formal, still read mainly by people of leisure.'[1]

One consequence of this situation was that the political influence of the press, while not negligible, was still far inferior to that which it was to exercise in the ensuing century. This situation underwent a change in the last decade of the nineteenth century. Under the influence of Alfred Harmsworth, later Lord Northcliffe, the press became popular. Harmsworth sought to create a press which would become the standard reading matter of the people as a whole.[2] The result was a press

[1] Tom Clarke, *Northcliffe in History, An Intimate Study of Press Power* (London, Hutchinson, n.d.), p. 37.

[2] Lord Beaverbrook described Northcliffe in the following terms: 'Lord Northcliffe influenced the course of politics profoundly, but always from the outside. He never had any personal relations with politicians, and rather prided himself on this fact. If he disagreed with them he simply turned on them the heavy artillery of the popular Press. . . . He had no power of exposition or persuasion. He stated his views; when questioned he reiterated it; and in the ultimate resort he simply dogmatised.

'The support of the Northcliffe Press could indeed be secured by politicians. But the appeal had to be addressed to power and conviction. An agreement between the two conflicting influences could never be reached by means of personal subtleties or by the nuances of a detailed argument.' Lord Beaverbrook, *Politicians and the Press* (London, Hutchinson, n.d.), pp. 46-7.

which was more vital, more dynamic, and at the same time qualitatively inferior to that which had preceded it. Nevertheless, the new press was widely read, and it was in consequence of more importance politically. 'W. T. Stead had raised a smile by suggesting that the editor of a London newspaper was on a par with a Cabinet minister; Harmsworth claimed to be the master and superior of most of them and brought some reputed to be powerful to his feet by threatening to suppress their names and speeches or to turn his newspapers on them.'[1] Northcliffe once told Bonar Law that the press could make or ruin a statesman.[2] This was a new conception, although it must be added that Law was more nearly right in his belief that while the press could help to make a statesman, it 'could not drag him down if he were really competent.'[3] The example of Northcliffe's relations with Lloyd George indicates that Law was correct.

The press also changed in another way as well. 'While the old Press was always predominantly radical, or at least progressive, being run by writers and thinkers, the modern Press is almost entirely conservative or reactionary, being controlled by wealthy industrialists.'[4] In the nineteenth century newspapers could be started upon the basis of a limited capital investment. Today, it requires an enormous initial investment and perhaps months of financial loss if one is to establish a newspaper. Further, the operating costs remove it from serving as a possible source of investment except for those who have substantial wealth. Concentration of ownership and control have become the keystone of the modern British press. 'The number of men who actually control the papers through which the great majority of British citizens get their information is phenomenally small. A few names such as Beaverbrook, Camrose, Elias, Rothermere, Astor, Cadbury, all but exhaust the list.'[5]

This does not necessarily involve the existence of a chain of

---

[1] Spender, *op. cit.*, i, 40–1. As Spender adds, 'politics and politicians were raw materials for his newspapers to be used or discarded according as it could be turned into "copy".'

[2] Riddell, *op. cit.*, p. 67.   [3] *Ibid.*, p. 67.

[4] H. R. G. Greaves, *The British Constitution* (London, Allen and Unwin, 1947), 2nd edition, pp. 251–2.

[5] *Ibid.*, p. 252.

newspapers with outlets in every section of Great Britain. Great Britain is a small country. In consequence it is possible to speak of a 'national press' as distinguished from a provincial or regional press. In particular, the great London dailies circulate throughout Great Britain and their influence is far greater than that of the provincial press. There may be some provincial papers which have greater circulations in their restricted area than do the London papers, but the London papers reach the entire country and their influence is thus far greater than that of any of the provincial papers.[1] In the election of 1950 the London dailies were the principal vehicles for carrying electoral news to the electorate. The election period actually reflected greater influence upon the part of the London press than usual, 'owing to the B.B.C.'s abstention from all political news reporting during the election period.'[2] In addition to this domination by the London press, there are also chains which catch up substantial portions of the provincial press.[3] It must be added, however, that the intensity of political partisanship may vary within the chain as a consequence of local dissimilarities.[4]

The change in the character of the press and the greater influence which it came to carry also involved another danger. If ownership of a London daily, or a chain, were concentrated in one individual, the individual who headed the chain had enormous powers, and furthermore, power which was not easily controlled. When Stanley Baldwin was engaged in a controversy with Lord Rothermere and Lord Beaverbrook, he made the statement, 'What the proprietorship of these papers is aiming at is power, but power without responsibility—the prerogative of the harlot through the ages'.[5] A concentration of such 'power without responsibility' endangers the possibility

---

[1] A glance at the circulation figures of the London morning papers is enough to indicate that they must reach wide areas of the country. For example, in February 1950, the *Daily Telegraph* had a circulation of 983,645; the *Daily Express*, 4,099,000; the *Daily Mail*, 2,215,000; the *Daily Herald*, 2,030,401; the *Daily Mirror*, 4,603,123; the *News Chronicle*, 1,525,128. H. G. Nicholas, *The British General Election of 1950* (London, Macmillan, 1951), p. 144.

[2] *Ibid.*, pp. 144–5.

[3] For a breakdown of the chains see Viscount Camrose, *British Newspapers and Their Controllers* (Toronto, Cassell, 1947), ch. iii.

[4] Nicholas, *op. cit.*, pp. 144–5.   [5] *The Times*, 18 March 1931.

of the public receiving such objective reports of the news as to make possible intelligent, discriminating judgment. A chain, or control of one of the great London dailies, enables the proprietor to influence individuals throughout the country, rather than in a restricted area.

The fear of the political consequences of concentration eventually led to the establishment of a Royal Commission on the Press in 1947. The Royal Commission was specifically appointed, 'with the object of furthering the free expression of opinion through the Press and the greatest practicable accuracy in the presentation of news, to inquire into the control, management and ownership of the newspaper and periodical Press and the news agencies, including the financial structure and the monopolistic tendencies in control, and to make recommendations thereon . . .'[1] This was an outgrowth of criticism by Labour M.P.'s that their party was unfairly treated in the press.[2] The extent of concentration was substantial,[3] but it was further noted that 'between 1921 and 1948 there was a marked tendency away from concentration of ownership in the national press.'[4] Further, the Commission contended that the concentration was not so great 'as to prejudice the free expression of opinion or the accurate presentation of news or to be contrary to the best interests of the public'.[5]

This does not obviate the fact that the heads of such chains are in a position to influence or to distort the treatment of news in such a fashion as to deprive their readers of essential information. It seems evident that it is the proprietor who determines the policy of the papers, rather than the editor or editors. Francis Williams has commented that the editor at the present time serves as 'the executive agent of the proprietor'.[6] The head of a chain is able to determine a policy line which will be carried out throughout all of his papers. Lord Rothermere admitted that he determined the general policy line of the *Daily Mail*, the *Evening News*, and the *Sunday Dispatch*.[7] This was

[1] *Report of the Royal Commission on the Press* (1949), Cmd. 7700, p. 1.
[2] 428 *H.C. Deb.* 5s., 452–577,
[3] *Report of the Royal Commission*, p. 175, paras. 664–69.
[4] *Ibid.*, p. 175, para. 670.   [5] *Ibid.*, p. 176, para. 672.
[6] *Minutes of Evidence taken before the Royal Commission on the Press*, 3rd day, Cmd. 7318, p. 3.
[7] *Minutes of Evidence*, 32nd day, Cmd. 7480, p. 5.

done through daily conferences with the editors of the papers. Lord Kemsley, the head of the largest chain in Great Britain,[1] also exercised the same sort of control over his papers upon his own admission.[2] Michael Foot, in his testimony before the Royal Commission, went so far as to assert that the Kemsley chain was the worst in the country so far as misrepresentation was concerned.[3] He even included the *Daily Worker* in the comparison. An indication of the point he was making may be adduced with respect to the coverage of the Gravesend by-election in 1947. The Kemsley chain gave 72 per cent of its coverage to the Conservative Party, and only 18 per cent to the Labour Party. Lord Kemsley admitted this disproportion, but insisted that since his paper was avowedly Conservative, he had the right to make such a division.[4] Evidence was also submitted to show that the Kemsley chain had distorted the extent of public opposition to bread rationing in 1946, and had failed to report instances of action by private groups supporting the government's action.[5]

Lord Beaverbrook testified that he did not try to direct the line taken by the editors of his papers. However, when he was asked what happened if his editors were tempted to take a different line on empire affairs, he replied, 'I talk them out of it'.[6] Similarly, he explained that all of his papers were opposed to the Marshall Plan because he had been able to 'teach' the editors.[7] It seems probable, however, that Beaverbrook's control is not so extensive as it once was. The general manager of the *Daily Express* has said that Beaverbrook no longer plays a very active part in the management of his papers.[8]

The press is able to influence the public in several ways. Editorial policy serves as one of the techniques, but it is probably true that the editorial columns have little significant influence. The editorials of the London *Times* or of the *Manchester Guardian* do exercise influence because both papers are

---

[1] Cf. Camrose, *op. cit.*, p. 15.

[2] *Minutes of Evidence*, 36th day, Cmd. 7503, pp. 14–15.

[3] *Minutes of Evidence*, 7th day, Cmd. 7730, pp. 1–2.

[4] *Minutes of Evidence*, 36th day, Cmd. 7503, pp. 20–1.

[5] *Minutes of Evidence*, 1st and 2nd days, Cmd. 7317, pp. 50–1; for Lord Kemsley's admission that the public opposition had been exaggerated see *Minutes of Evidence*, 36th day, Cmd. 7503, pp. 18–19.

[6] *Minutes of Evidence*, 26th day, Cmd. 7416, p. 7.   [7] *Ibid.*, p. 9.

[8] *Minutes of Evidence*, 16th day, Cmd. 7364, p. 1.

directed towards a selectively chosen reader group, but the more popular press must turn to other techniques. It is obvious, of course, that the press must be allowed to express its editorial views as it wishes. Problems do not arise until editorial and factual materials become confused in such a manner that the public cannot distinguish one from the other.[1]

Significant areas of distortion exist. Political partisanship is to be expected in editorial columns, but its presence in stories, 'heads', or 'leaders', may be so used as to give a picture which is not an accurate reflection of the content of the news stories. Since in many cases the reader does not peruse all of the column he may arrive at a false conception of what occurred as a consequence of the 'head' which does not reflect the story, although it purports to do so.[2] News stories may also be doctored. In some cases this may be done by the omission of significant points. In other instances it may be done by a failure to report a statement by the Prime Minister or some other officer. Papers which support the government may similarly suppress statements by opposition party leaders. If suppression is unusual, it is always possible to place the statement made by your political opponent on page two or somewhere else deep in the paper where it is unlikely to catch the eyes of the reader. In 1950 the *Daily Herald* buried Churchill's Edinburgh statement calling for a Big Three conference on page two.[3] The replies made by

---

[1] For two excellent examples of partisanship in the treatment of political matters see the *Report of the Royal Commission on the Press*, Appendix VII, Part II, section 5, 'The Gravesend By-Election, 1947'. Probably to the mortification of the Labourites the evidence indicates that the *Daily Herald*, the official organ of the Labour Party, was the most partisan in the treatment of both incidents. Where the Kemsley chain exaggerated the public opposition to the bread rationing programme, the *Daily Herald* paid little attention to instances of real public opposition. Similarly, it gave disproportionate attention to the Labour candidate in Gravesend and exercised great selectivity in the choice of 'heads'.

For a study of the same use of selectivity in reporting the election campaign in 1950, see Nicholas, *op. cit.*, pp. 145–89. Similar materials may be found on the 1945 election in McCallum and Readman, *op. cit.*, ch. ii.

[2] Lord Beaverbrook admitted that he paid great attention to the 'leaders' used in his papers, but added that he did not force his writers to prepare a lead contrary to their conscience if they did not wish to do so. Nevertheless, implicit in his comment was the conclusion that he merely selected someone else to write the 'lead' in such circumstances. *Minutes of Evidence*, 26th day, Cmd. 7416, p. 4.

[3] Nicholas, *op. cit.*, p. 161.

Attlee and Bevin naturally received first page emphasis.[1] Normally, of course, statements made by the Prime Minister are not completely suppressed. Other men, however, even men of Cabinet rank may run foul of such action. Michael Foot, in testimony before the Royal Commission, said, 'I think for a period Lord Beaverbrook was on Lord Kemsley's black list; at any rate, it was an extraordinary fact that when Lord Beaverbrook was Minister of Aircraft Production there were no stories about the Ministry of Aircraft Production on Lord Kemsley's front page'.[2] Lord Beaverbrook himself admitted that his papers did have a black list, but added the comment that no political name had ever been placed upon it.[3]

Even the use which is made of pictures in some cases amounts to a deliberate effort at distortion. Northcliffe, for example, upon Asquith's resignation in 1916, ordered his editors to print the 'worst possible picture of him'.[4] At the same time the editors were ordered to get a smiling picture of Lloyd George.[5] A further element of journalistic bias was introduced by the captions placed under the pictures. Under the picture of Lloyd George was placed the phrase, 'DO IT NOW', while under Asquith's picture were the words, 'WAIT AND SEE'.[6] Similarly, an effective partisan slant may be given by publishing only pictures of the leaders of the party which is supported by the paper. It has been said that the pictures in the *Daily Graphic* during the election of 1950, 'were almost invariably of Conservatives, while the mention of Labour candidates or Ministers was almost invariably derogatory. The newspaper seemed to conceive of itself as existing merely to furnish the faithful with pictorial evidence of their party's activities.'[7]

A man faced with a universally hostile press has a difficult task ahead if he is to achieve political advancement. Opposition

---

[1] *Ibid.*, p. 162.

[2] *Minutes of Evidence*, 7th day, Cmd. 7330, p. 11. For Black Lists as a technique of suppression see *Report of the Royal Commission*, paras. 451–67; *Minutes of Evidence*, 1st and 2nd days, Cmd. 7317, p. 8; *Minutes of Evidence*, 3rd day, Cmd. 7318, p. 27.

[3] *Minutes of Evidence*, 26th day, Cmd. 7416, pp. 1–2.

[4] Tom Clarke, *My Northcliffe Diary* (New York, Cosmopolitan Book Corporation, 1931), p. 6. Northcliffe later seems to have been troubled by this action as Asquith was 'a gentleman'.

[5] *Ibid.*, p. 96.   [6] *Ibid.*, p. 96.   [7] Nicholas, *op. cit.*, p. 180.

by all of the press is likely to lead to defeat.[1] This is not the same thing, however, as saying that no man can hope to become Prime Minister if he is opposed by a majority of the press. All of the Labour Party's victories have been won in the face of opposition from the most substantial portion of the press. Ramsay MacDonald had to face press opposition in 1923 and again in 1929, but in both instances he became Prime Minister. He received majority press support only when he crossed the line and became head of the National Government in 1931. Papers which had previously castigated him became his ardent supporters. Again in 1945 and 1950 Attlee was able to lead his party to victory in the face of opposition from the most substantial section of the 'national press'.[2] Even so, if would be easy to exaggerate the extent of the press opposition to the Labour Party in both of the elections since the conclusion of the Second World War. In the election of 1945 it has been estimated that the Labour Party was supported by London dailies with a combined circulation of 6,000,000. At the same time the Conservatives had the support of London papers with a circulation of 6,800,000.[3] It is probable, it should be noted, that the support of Lord Beaverbrook was disadvantageous to Churchill.[4] In the election of 1950 the London morning newspapers supporting the Conservatives had a combined circulation of 8,079,094. The papers supporting Labour had a circulation of 6,644,123.[5] *The Times*, although nominally independent, gave the Conservatives kinder treatment, but the addition of the circulation of that paper would not significantly change the distribution.[6] The Sunday press in London was more predominantly Conservative, but at the same time it was less partisan, since it is primarily an 'amusement press'.[7] The provincial press was more likely to be Conservative in politics, but at the same time it did not take as partisan a position.[8]

---

[1] For a contrary example, see *Minutes of Evidence*, 1st and 2nd days, Cmd. 7317, p. 15.

[2] It has been said that it is impossible to reduce the provincial press to politically meaningful totals in attempting to assess the circulation of papers according to their political alignments. Nicholas, *op. cit.*, pp. 144–5.

[3] McCallum and Readman, *op. cit.*, p. 181.

[4] *Ibid.*, pp. 199–201.   [5] Nicholas, *op. cit.*, p. 144.

[6] *Ibid.*, pp. 145, 147. As of 15 February 1950, *The Times* had a circulation of 257,803.

[7] *Ibid.*, pp. 182–5.   [8] *Ibid.*, pp. 188–9.

One commentator has said that the fact that the press is controlled primarily by those in the upper social class makes it easier for a Conservative government to take drastic action than for a Labour or Liberal government to do the same. 'This circle controlling both Government and the Press, had no difficulty in dethroning a king, but had Government and Press been divided in control, as under a Lloyd George or Labour Government, there would probably have been patent discord and perhaps even a very different outcome.'[1] There is merit in this comment, but it is rather interesting that the chief protagonist in the abdication crisis has estimated that the majority of the press was upon the side of the King.[2] It must be admitted, however, that the supporters of the King did not take a very vocal line in the controversy. It is obvious that the press, like the House of Lords, serves different purposes when dealing with a Conservative Government than it does when dealing with a Labour Government. As Professor Greaves has said, 'What is the strength of reactionary government may be the weakness of a progressive government.'[3]

Universal press hostility is not likely to be faced by any party leader. There are always some papers which support even the more radical parties. The Labour Party does not have to face a universally hostile press today. It has become socially acceptable to be a Labour Party member, and in consequence the party has some press support, although it must expect that it will be minority support. The Labour Party, of course, has its own paper, the *Daily Herald*. The *Daily Herald* is obliged by its own charter to espouse the programme adopted by the annual conference of the Labour Party, although ownership of the majority stock in the corporation is vested in private hands.[4]

---

[1] Greaves, *op. cit.*, p. 257.

[2] Duke of Windsor, *A King's Story* (New York, Putnam, 1951), p. 372. The Duke estimates that the average circulation of the papers supporting the government was 8,500,000, while the papers supporting him totalled a circulation of approximately 12,500,000.

[3] Greaves, *op. cit.*, p. 257.

[4] Inevitably difficulties have developed out of this situation. See the testimony of Francis Williams, editor of the *Daily Herald* from 1936 till 1940, in *Minutes of Evidence*, 3rd day, Cmd. 7318. Among other comments Williams stated that the commercial owners of the paper were concerned over the paper's pessimistic comments on foreign affairs, holding that they were likely to drive away advertisers.

The remainder of the press is predominantly Conservative in alignment, although the *Daily Mirror*, the paper with the largest circulation in Great Britain, supported Labour in the 1950 election. Since the press is big business, it must be expected that its proprietors will have big business attitudes. It is doubtful that this is of much significance, however. The public seems to be wary of what it reads in newspapers.[1] One journalist has commented as follows: 'The sin of modern newspapers . . . is not so much that they are misleading people; people are not on the whole misled, because they do not take them seriously enough; but that what could and should have been an important public service has deteriorated into a purely amusement enterprise.'[2]

Still any man who wishes to become Prime Minister must have friends in the press. If he cannot expect to have friends in all of the press, he must at least have friends within the ranks of that portion of the press which supports his party. One of the principal reasons for Harcourt's failure to achieve his ambition in 1894 was that he 'had no skill in making terms with the press. So far from flattering it, he habitually derided it, and no public man of his time had fewer friends or more numerous and implacable enemies in the press than he had. When the crisis came he was almost entirely deserted by the Liberal newspapers. . . .'[3] Some Prime Ministers have learned how to deal with this new agency of political influence, others have failed to do so and reaped the consequences.

Of all the Prime Ministers of this century, it is probable that Asquith had the least conception of the necessity of considering the press, and the thought of deliberately trying to influence it does not seem to have entered his mind. Even in his personal habits he did not read newspapers, a practice far different from

[1] One critic has contended that the press has exercised a subtle, and exceedingly harmful influence in the preservation of false values. Speaking of the services rendered to the upper class by the press he says, 'perhaps the most valuable service rendered by the press is to habituate the public, by the attention given to a small wealthy section of society, to the idea that this tiny minority should occupy a special position, that is to say to the idea of inequality.' Greaves, *op. cit.*, pp. 263-4.

[2] *Minutes of Evidence*, 3rd day, Cmd. 7318, p. 15. (Testimony of Francis Williams.)

[3] A. G. Gardiner, *The Life of Sir William Harcourt* (New York, Constable, n.d.), ii, 267.

that of Winston Churchill who devoured all of the London press before going to bed.[1] In the last years of Asquith's administration he faced constant, and increasingly vociferous, newspaper criticism. He never made any effort to approach his press critics personally, nor did he ever send colleagues to attempt to influence them in his favour.

Even further, he never answered them directly. 'His general attitude towards his newspaper critics and the little group which worked hand in glove with them in the Government and in the House of Commons was one of patient endurance.'[2] He would not engage in public controversy with them, preferring to leave them 'to the public judgement'.[3] Unfortunately, from his standpoint, the public was not in a position to judge. Since he did not reply directly to his critics, the public did not know both sides of the controversy, and in consequence, the merits of his position were not known to any significant portion of the public.

He could have attempted to approach and influence Lord Northcliffe, his bitterest critic, but he did not do so. As has been said, 'It would have been as distasteful to his inclinations to invite the editor of a newspaper to luncheon with a view to influencing his leading articles, as it would have been abhorrent to his principles to restrict the freedom of the press'.[4] Asquith's critics, however, felt no such compunction and both the military leaders with whom he disagreed, and his political critics in the administration approached newspapers. They deliberately sought the assistance of the press in creating a public atmosphere which would make Asquith's position untenable.[5] None of these factors may have been immediately responsible for Asquith's fall, but unquestionably the deluge of criticism which showered forth from the press did much to make it acceptable to the public when it finally came. In the last days the Northcliffe papers, the *Morning Post*, the *Chronicle*, the *Express*, and the *Daily Press* all came out in support of Lloyd George's demand

[1] Williams, *op. cit.*, p. 35.

[2] J. A. Spender and Cyril Asquith, *Life of Oxford and Asquith* (London, Hutchinson and Co., 1932), ii, 229.

[3] *Ibid.*, p. 230.

[4] Duff Cooper, *Haig*, (London, Faber and Faber, 1935) i, 341.

[5] Major-General Sir C. E. Callwell, *Field Marshal Sir Henry Wilson, His Life and Diaries* (London, Cassell, 1927); Major-General French, *The Life of Field Marshal Sir John French* (London, Cassell, 1931), pp. 391 ff.

for internal Cabinet reorganization.[1] Lloyd George also had the support of the *Manchester Guardian*.[2]

The attitude of the newspapers had also influenced Asquith's policy earlier. He exercised extreme caution in handling the Fisher–Churchill controversy, because of his fear of press reaction. Fisher was one of the favourites of the Conservative press.[3] The criticisms of the government's shell programme in 1915 also did much to prepare the ground work for the formation of the Asquith coalition, although they were not the principal causes.[4] Similarly, the Northcliffe papers did much to create a public attitude sympathetic to compulsion,[5] although in this instance Asquith was torn by the double problem of the support given by the press, and his fear that the Liberal Party leaders in local areas would not support it.[6]

When all is said, Asquith's failure to attempt to gain press support is the most substantial demerit which must be placed against him in evaluating his effectiveness as a democratic leader. He had failed to understand the importance of the new press, and the extent to which it influenced the public.

If Asquith was clearly unable to recognize the implications of the rise of the new press, this blind spot did not exist for Lloyd George. He recognized its importance and set out to capture it for his own advantage. Lord Esher, in one of his frequent moments of petulance, said that Lloyd George 'lived by the press, and by the press he shall die'.[7] In a sense, this statement was true.

Lloyd George 'intuitively understood the modern Press which was so painful a stumbling-block to his more solemn colleagues. He was in the jargon of the day, the supreme propagandist. His mind leapt with that of Fleet Street; he seemed to deal with public affairs as if he were editing a popular newspaper with its

---

[1] Lord Beaverbrook, *Politicians and the War, 1914–1916* (New York, Doubleday, Doran, 1932), ii, 157, 195–9.

[2] J. L. Hammond, *C. P. Scott of the Manchester Guardian* (New York, G. Bell and Sons, n.d.), pp. 203–9.

[3] Spender and Asquith, *op. cit.*, ii, 164.

[4] Tom Clarke, *My Northcliffe Diary* (New York, Cosmopolitan Book Corporation, 1931), pp. 69–90.

[5] *Ibid.*, pp. 73 ff.

[6] Spender and Asquith, *op. cit.*, ii, 208 ff.

[7] Lord Esher, *The Captains and the Kings Depart: Journals and Letters of Viscount Esher* (New York, C. Scribner's Sons, 1938), ii, 167.

"splash" for every day, its headlines, its pictures. He knew that lights must not be hid under bushels in a democratic age.'[1] He built his ladder to the position of Prime Minister upon the effective use of the press, and he sought out and deliberately tried to create favourable press reactions to himself and his policies. As early as 1909 he turned loose the whole of his dynamic personality upon Lord Northcliffe, and by the expedient of releasing to him full information upon a bill to be introduced the following day, made for himself a friend in the highest ranks of the press.[2] This incident started a friendship which was to be extremely advantageous to both in later years.

Later, in the midst of the shell controversy, he is reported to have inspired Lord Northcliffe to take up the criticism of the government's shell programme. Out of this came Lloyd George's eventual appointment as Minister of Munitions. This was precisely the position which Lloyd George desired at the time, and it was the support of Lord Northcliffe's papers which prepared the way for the creation of the ministry and his appointment.[3]

Although Lloyd George spread his efforts over the whole of the press, it was with Northcliffe that his relations were the most intimate. It was Northcliffe who had carried on the campaign for Lloyd George's succession to the position of Prime Minister. It was Northcliffe who characterized Lloyd George as the saviour of Great Britain, and as the absolutely essential man. At their highest point the relations were extremely cordial, and it was sometimes difficult to know precisely who dominated whom. Northcliffe had direct access to Lloyd George at any time during the first years of his administration. At one time he told Tom Clarke, 'Ring up Lloyd George and ask him. You have his telephone number. Give him my compliments and tell him I told you to. Ring him up any time on vital matters.'[4] Lord Beaverbrook also explains that in his relations with representatives of the foreign press he found that all of them wished to see Lloyd George. After a time, however, the Prime

---

[1] Spender, *op. cit.*, i, 120–1.

[2] Tom Clarke, *Northcliffe in History* (London, Hutchinson, n.d.), pp. 87–8.

[3] Lord Beaverbrook, *Politicians and the War, 1914–1916* (New York, Doubleday Doran, 1928), i, 93–4.

[4] Tom Clarke, *My Northcliffe Diary* (New York, Cosmopolitan Book Corporation, 1931), p. 98.

Minister 'felt he was being pressed too hard and began to decline such demands on his time. I then hit upon the device of sending Lord Northcliffe to the Prime Minister to ask for such interviews—and he invariably succeeded, although I was a member of the Ministry and he was not.'[1]

Lloyd George was always willing to use the press to destroy his opponents. Even before he was Prime Minister he desired to have Haig removed as Commander-in-Chief in France. Northcliffe said, 'The little man (Lloyd George) came to see me some weeks ago and told me that he would like to get rid of Haig, but that he could not do so as he was too popular. He made the proposition to me that I should attack him in my group of newspapers and so render him unpopular enough to be dealt with. "You kill him and I will bury him." Those were his very words.'[2]

Eventually a break came in his relations with Lord Northcliffe. The basic cause of the difficulty may be found in the general principle stated by J. A. Spender, 'The root difficulty of relations between public men and newspaper magnates is that there is nearly always a misunderstanding as to which is master, and this in the end makes trouble'.[3]

That this was the real cause of the split may be seen by Lloyd George's description of the quarrel which led to the break.[4]

'When Northcliffe asked me to put him on the Peace delegation I told him to go to hell. I broke with Northcliffe. I refused absolutely to have him at the Peace Conference. I put up with him for four years. The break had to come—when he wanted to dictate to me. As Prime Minister I could not have it. Northcliffe thought he could run the country. I could not allow that. Northcliffe was a great man—but he could not be allowed to dominate the Prime Minister.'

[1] Lord Beaverbrook, *Politicians and the Press* (London, Hutchinson, n.d.), p. 12.

[2] Tom Clarke, *Northcliffe in History* (London, Hutchinson, n.d.), pp. 111–12.

[3] Spender, *op. cit.*, i, 121.

[4] Tom Clarke, *My Northcliffe Diary* (London, Cosmopolitan Book Corporation, 1931), pp. 106–7. Lord Beaverbrook in his *Politicians and the Press* (London, Hutchinson, n.d.), p. 15, says that the split was caused by Lloyd George's refusal to make Northcliffe Lord President of the Council. This seems to be erroneous, however. Cf. Lord Riddell, *op. cit.*, p. 3.

Lloyd George did not need Northcliffe any longer. The war had been won and he was the saviour of the country. He had authority and prestige beyond challenge, and 'had no need to consider "give and take" with any would-be newspaper dictator'.[1] Northcliffe had had a great deal to do with making him, but he had created a Frankenstein monster which he could not control.

Lloyd George had never confined his attentions to Northcliffe alone. He had attempted to garner the favour of larger parts of the press. It is not possible to discover information which adequately reveals the whole of his relations with the press, but it is rather significant that so many newspaper editors, publishers, and top-ranking journalists were on the Honours Lists.[2] From what we know of Lloyd George's attitude to specific newspaper editors and publishers it does not seem likely that the multiplicity of honours given to newspapermen were accidental, or were given entirely upon the basis of merit. He was also fortunate in receiving the support of C. P. Scott, editor of the *Manchester Guardian*, Britain's leading Liberal newspaper. This support unquestionably assisted Lloyd George in retaining the support of a large portion of the Liberal Party.

After he had lost the support of Northcliffe, he was not entirely without newspaper friends, and he pursued his usual course of seeking press support prior to taking important action. In 1918, he invited Lord Beaverbrook to have dinner with him. Lloyd George's emissary was Churchill, and the latter 'made it quite plain that the idea was to obtain newspaper support for a projected General Election.'[3] Nor did Lloyd George confine his attentions to Lord Beaverbrook in connection with this enterprise. He also had Lord Rothermere and Sir Edward Hulton to dinner, and was able to gain the support of both for the General Election.[4] Later he sought the support of Beaverbrook for his projected Irish settlement and Beaverbrook remained in close contact with the Prime Minister and other ministers through-

[1] Tom Clarke, *My Northcliffe Diary* (London, Cosmopolitan Book Corporation, 1931), p. 107.

[2] 116 *H.C. Deb.* 5s., 1341, 1786; *Post*, ch. vii.

[3] Beaverbrook, *Politicians and the Press* (London, Hutchinson, n.d.), p. 14.

[4] *Ibid.*, p. 16. He was unable to obtain the support of C. P. Scott for the election, however. Hammond, *op. cit.*, p. 246.

out the negotiations.[1] Beaverbrook was also a party to several discussions about the advisability of a General Election on the issue of the Irish settlement.[2]

Lord Beaverbrook has defended the action of the Prime Minister in seeking press support for his Irish programmes in terms which have wider implication. He puts his defence as follows:[3]

'The duty of a Prime Minister is not only to make up his own mind as to the wisest course to pursue but to persuade the nation as a whole to support his policy. In a democratic country wisdom has got to be justified by its popular appeal. A Premier has therefore not only to lead but to induce others to follow him. He must persuade the nation after he has convinced himself. In order to effect his purpose he is clearly quite justified in accepting the assistance of a great popular organ like the *Daily Express*.'

It is not intended here to criticize the argument made by Lord Beaverbrook. It is clear that a Prime Minister who is able to seek and capture press support is in a more advantageous position than one who is not. Not all of Lloyd George's actions can be defended upon moral grounds. His use of honours, and the manner in which he used Northcliffe while it was to his advantage to do so, and then threw him into discard when he was no longer necessary, are not elevating actions. In the latter case, however, it is obvious that Northcliffe tried to use him, but lost the final test of strength. Both were guilty of actions which must strike one as immoral. But in the immediate context of this study it must be said that the use of these techniques enabled Lloyd George to maintain a hold upon public opinion, unique in British history until that moment. They become even more unique when it is remembered that he had no real party of his own.

Stanley Baldwin could always depend upon the support of a majority of the Conservative papers, but his controversy with Lord Beaverbrook and Lord Rothermere is of some interest. Baldwin's relations with Beaverbrook were never particularly cordial. In the first place, Beaverbrook was campaigning for 'Food Taxes' and 'Imperial Preference'. Baldwin never felt

[1] Lord Beaverbrook, *Politicians and the Press* (London, Hutchinson, n.d.) p. 43.
[2] *Ibid.*, p. 45.   [3] *Ibid.*, p. 44.

quite safe in going all the way in this matter. Lord Rothermere, on the other hand, was opposed to some of Beaverbrook's ideas, but criticized Baldwin for his Indian policy and his social legislation.

The controversy became most acute during a period in which Baldwin was Leader of the Opposition. The two newspaper proprietors wished to force a change in the party programme. Beaverbrook's objective seems to have been principally the change in the programme. He does not seem to have desired to remove Baldwin as the party leader. Rothermere, on the other hand, felt little confidence in Baldwin as leader and at the same time abhorred some of his policies. The result of this was a series of attacks in the newspapers owned by the press lords.[1]

An effort was made to settle the disputes, for it naturally injured the prestige of the party to have an open fight between its leader and two of its most powerful press supporters. Lord Beaverbrook, at the behest of the Central Office of the Conservative Party, met with Baldwin and Neville Chamberlain to discuss the issue. An agreement was reached under which Baldwin promised a referendum on the issue of food taxes when he should next come to power. The Central Office, whether with or without Baldwin's knowledge, in publishing the statement, added the words only '*if and when the Dominions ask us.*'[2] Lord Beaverbrook felt he had been tricked, and Baldwin added to this belief by making a speech in which he insisted that the food taxes were not practicable.[3] Lord Beaverbrook, therefore, again became vocal in his criticism.

Baldwin's reaction to the criticism was a demand that he be given a free hand in dealing with fiscal matters. He described the problem of his relations with Beaverbrook and Rothermere as a national question arising out of efforts of Rothermere and Beaverbrook, 'to dictate, to domineer, to blackmail'.[4] He also stressed their 'power of being able to suppress everything that a man says that you do not like, the power of attacking all the time without their being any possibility of being hit back. . . .'[5]

Baldwin was primarily nettled by the fact that both of the

---

[1] Beckhoffer Roberts, *Stanley Baldwin: Man or Miracle?* (New York, Greenburg, 1937), pp. 184–5.

[2] *Ibid.*, p. 187. Original italicized. Keith Feiling, *The Life of Neville Chamberlain*, (London, Macmillan, 1946) p. 177.

[3] Roberts, *op. cit.*, p. 187.   [4] *Ibid.*, p. 189.   [5] *The Times*, 25 June 1930.

Press Lords not only criticized his programme, but sought to bring changes in the party itself which would be favourable to their views. They went so far as to back candidates in by-elections in an effort to embarrass Baldwin. They knew they had supporters in the Shadow Cabinet. Notably, Beaverbrook knew that Neville Chamberlain supported his programme, as, after all, it was originally Joseph Chamberlain's. Beaverbrook, however, seems to have underestimated Chamberlain's loyalty to Baldwin. Chamberlain served as party chairman and took care to put official candidates in the field against those who supported 'Empire Free Trade'.[1] The failure of even such vigorous attacks as those of Beaverbrook and Rothermere to shake Baldwin's position indicates the power which resides in the party leader.

The material available for the treatment of the relations of Neville Chamberlain with the press are severely limited. At the same time one aspect of the relationship deserves mention, for it again shows an attempt by a Prime Minister to influence the direction and policy pursued by newspapers. Mr. Chamberlain was, of course, throughout his administration primarily concerned with the conduct of foreign relations. The policy which he followed was one of appeasement. Throughout the relations between Great Britain and Germany in this period one of the most frequent complaints made by the Germans was the attitude of portions of the British press. In at least one instance a German official made a direct plea for an end to the hostility of the press. Lord Layton of the *News Chronicle* said that Goebbels himself sent him a message 'to say that it was disturbing to international relations to see such personal hostility against the Fuehrer'.[2]

In March of 1938 the German Government sent a specific request to the British Cabinet in which it was said that satisfactory relations between Britain and Germany could not develop if the British papers insisted upon publishing materials which 'were unwelcome to Hitler as the Head of the German State'.[3] The British Government pointed out that it could not restrain the press directly. It is important, however, that the

---

[1] Feiling, *op. cit.*, p. 180.
[2] *Report of the Royal Commission on the Press* (1949), Cmd. 7700, p. 137, para. 506.
[3] Williams, *op. cit.*, p. 141.

Chamberlain government did make a deliberate effort to restrain the press through persuasion. 'Newspapers were asked to moderate leading articles, to be discreet in what they published from their foreign correspondents, to be careful of "offensive" cartoons, of which those by Low and the late Will Dyson then cartoonist to the *Daily Herald* . . . were particularly singled out.'[1] Arthur Mann, the editor of the *Yorkshire Post*, a paper which was critical of Chamberlain's policy, also said that such pressure was applied to him.[2] The editor of the *Glasgow Herald* stated that he and the proprietor of the paper had been invited to see a 'senior member of the cabinet. The Minister made it quite clear that while he and his colleagues realized that our shortcomings were due to lack of information, they were undeniably shortcomings.'[3] He added, however, 'that when the paper adhered to its policy no further approach was made to him'.[4]

Francis Williams has said that 'It is perfectly natural and proper for a Government to do what it can to secure newspaper and public support for its policies. If news which ought to be published, or views which ought to be voiced, are amended as a consequence of such approaches the fault is the newspaper's, but the Cabinet's.'[5] Williams's position is probably basically correct, but the attempt to tone down the reports of foreign correspondents smacks of an attempt to restrain the possible expression of views which were contrary to those of the government. Should such action be successful it would make it impossible for the public to know any position except that taken by the government. It is true, of course, that the newspapers have an obligation not to allow themselves to be coerced in this fashion, but it may be true as well that the Prime Minister and his colleagues have no right to make such a request in the first place.

[1] *Ibid.*, p. 141. Williams was at the time the editor of the *Daily Herald* whose cartoonist had been specially singled out.

[2] *Report of the Royal Commission on the Press* (1949) Cmd. 7700, p. 137, para. 506.

[3] *Ibid.*, p. 137, para. 507. [4] *Ibid.*, p. 137, para. 507.

[5] Williams, *op. cit.*, pp. 143-4, Sir Samuel Hoare served as the liaison man between the government and newspaper editors and proprietors. It seems obvious that Chamberlain knew what Hoare was doing as the latter was one of the four man inner Cabinet. Feiling, *op. cit.*, p. 421. No mention of these incidents, however, appears in Feiling's biography of Chamberlain.

The Prime Minister and the Public

All Prime Ministers have recognized the essential need of publicity and the support of the press. Ramsay MacDonald reportedly was 'eager . . . to get all the advertisement that the Press could give him. . . .'[1] It was MacDonald who first appointed a Press Secretary to the Prime Minister. That individual's principal function was publicizing the activities of the Prime Minister.[2] MacDonald's successors have continued to retain that office, even including Attlee, who is sometimes said to be publicity shy.[3]

The relation between the Prime Minister and the press is one of give and take. Both attempt to influence the other, and this is to be expected. The Prime Minister must realize that if the press is overwhelmingly hostile he is in some danger of losing power in the long run. A friendly press brings advantages. No Prime Minister, of course, can ever hope to have the support of all the press, nor need he fear the hostility of all of the press. A Labour Prime Minister knows that he will face the opposition of most of the newspapers in the United Kingdom. A Conservative Prime Minister knows that he will usually have the support of a majority of those papers, at least during an election period.

It would be easy to exaggerate the influence of the press. The Labour Party has won two elections in recent years in the face of the opposition of the largest portion of the press. It would, however, be easy to underestimate its influence as a result of these developments. Perhaps the influence of the press is felt more directly on specific issues than upon election results *per se*. The press may be able, if it pushes a particular line of criticism or an alternative policy, to force adjustments in the Prime Minister's course of action. This is not always true, and the degree of influence depends upon the situation of the time. Additionally, some papers carry greater weight, not because of their extensive circulation, but because of the persons who buy them. Criticisms found in the *Manchester Guardian*, *The Times*, or a journal such as the *Economist*, are likely to have more effect upon a government in the long run than attacks made by only

---

[1] L. M. Weir, *The Tragedy of Ramsay MacDonald* (Plymouth, Secker and Warburg, 1938), p. 558.

[2] *Ibid.*, p. 558.

[3] Francis Williams, 'Introduction' to Clement Attlee's *The Labour Party in Perspective—and Twelve Years Later* (London, V. Gollancz, 1949), p. 17.

one segment of the popular press. The criticisms of the government's economic policy after 1945, which were developed in the pages of the *Economist*, were probably an important factor in the change in that policy.

It remains true that the Prime Minister must always be concerned with the press. It is one of the principal media for reaching the public. It is one of the chief instrumentalities in moulding public opinion. It can embarrass him, even though it may not always be able to destroy him. A friendly approach to the press may be desirable in one instance. In other instances a direct break and attack may be similarly advantageous, if some sections of the press still maintain their support. There is no 'right' way of dealing with the press. But to completely disregard it is generally a 'wrong' way, as Asquith discovered.

III.
THE GOVERNMENT INFORMATION SERVICES

It is not intended here to examine the role of the Government Information Services as a whole, or to attempt to discuss their place in a free society.[1] The Prime Minister himself is seldom directly concerned in their use. The Information Services are more likely to issue specific reports upon the operations of a particular department. This does touch, indirectly, upon the relations of the Prime Minister and the public. The reports issued by the Information Services will affect public attitudes towards the government. This does not mean that they will be read directly by large numbers of people, or that written materials published by the government itself receive wide distribution. They will, however, be read by some portions of the minority, those persons, who in Tawney's words are 'thinking about things'. The latter group may then use them as one of the bases for judging the effectiveness of the government. If their conclusion is that the government has done either well or badly, this conclusion will reach larger numbers of persons eventually.

Some fear has been expressed 'that an Information Officer would seek to show his department's work in a favourable light

---

[1] For an interesting and amusing account of the duties of a press officer see Howard F. Lancum, *Press Officer, Please!* (London, Lockwood, 1946).

and conceal or gloss over its mistakes'.[1] This is matched by a fear which is common in the government that 'when a newspaper seeks to throw a searchlight on any department's activities, the characteristic reaction is too often that the newspaper is up to no good'.[2]

Both dangers do exist, but the Information Services are less likely to so act than the newspapers. The Information Services need the confidence of the press and should they report falsely, and the press discover that they have done so, they would lose that confidence. Furthermore, any indication that the Information Services were being used for partisan advantage would lead to an expression of criticism upon the floor of the House of Commons. Such criticism might easily prove to be so disadvantageous to the government as to make the first distortion of facts too risky to be worth while. As has been said, 'any attempt by a Government to use its information machinery for this purpose would be apparent and would prove a boomerang'.[3] The Prime Minister would then seem to be limited to the advantage which may be gained from publicizing the effective work of the departments which operate under his general supervision. If his administration has actually done well, the Information Services may add to his public support by the distribution of materials which indicate that it has proved effective. If it has done badly, the same distribution of materials may ultimately affect his position with the public adversely.

IV.

THE PRIME MINISTER AND THE RADIO

The British Broadcasting Corporation is a public corporation. This in itself required the development of certain rules as to the political use which might be made of the radio. Unless there were definite rules the government's position would be far too powerful. The result has been a series of limitations which have

---

[1] *Report of the Royal Commission on the Press* (1949) Cmd. 7700, p. 146, para. 537.

[2] P.E.P., *Report on the British Press* (London, 1938), p. 200.

[3] P.E.P., 'Government Information Services', *Planning*, 2 February 1945, p. 13.

made the radio something of a minor vehicle for the transmission of political information. 'In contrast with the United States, where every major political speech and many minor ones are transmitted, British political broadcasting is still very sparse. Out-and-out party battles have enjoyed only a minor place at the microphone.'[1] The B.B.C. is supposed to be politically neutral. This is further indicated in the assumption that the Board of Governors should be independent and non-political in character, although this has not always been the case.[2]

The Prime Minister does not find himself in an exceptionally advantageous position to use the radio. There are specific rules as to the allocation of time during election periods; these rules attempt to maintain an approximate parity between the Government and the Opposition. Complaints have sometimes been heard about the allocation of time, but in general the approach seems to have worked remarkably well. Practically speaking, the amount of time allowed during elections seems extremely small when compared with American experience. In the General Election of 1935 twelve addresses were distributed, five to the Government, four to the Labour Party, and three to the Liberal Party.[3] In the election of 1945 a greater number of addresses were permitted with the Conservatives being allowed to deliver ten, Labour ten and the Liberal Party four. The time allowed in each case was fifteen minutes.

The allocation of the number of addresses to be given by any one individual rests upon the party's determination. The Prime Minister may play a major role in making electoral addresses over the radio, or he may, on the other hand, play a role of minor importance. Ramsay MacDonald in 1929 carried a considerable share of the burden of radio addresses. Naturally, in 1931, an effort was made to divide time between Baldwin, MacDonald, and Samuel.

The election of 1945 provides the most significant instance of

[1] Lincoln Gordon, *The Public Corporation in Great Britain* (New York, Oxford University Press, 1938), p. 223.

[2] Baldwin appointed the Earl of Clarendon, a member of his own ministry, as the first chairman. The second chairman was a former Speaker of the House, but the next two had been Conservative politicians, one, Viscount Bridgman, an ex-Home Secretary. *Ibid.*, p. 170.

[3] *Ibid.*, p. 226. Terence O'Brien, *British Experiments in Public Ownership and Control* (New York, Norton, 1938), p. 136.

the domination of time by the Prime Minister. Of the ten addresses allowed to Conservatives, Churchill gave four. He gave the first address, the last, and two intermediate speeches. On the other hand, the Labour Party in the elections of 1945 divided its time between ten separate speakers. Attlee, the party leader, led off with a general statement of party principles. Thereafter separate portions of the party programme were dealt with in speeches made by other figures. The concluding speaker was Herbert Morrison. In 1950 both parties were restricted to five addresses. Both Attlee and Churchill gave only one speech, and in each case their statements were the concluding appeals made by their respective parties. Churchill also gave one pre-election broadcast.

The Prime Minister, as the head of the real executive, may have to make some radio addresses which are direct reports to the nation. This is not an ordinary practice, but in some instances a report may be necessary. In this respect the Prime Minister and his party gain a slight advantage over the opposition. In 1931 Ramsay MacDonald was able to make a direct address to the nation on the formation of the National Government. The address was carried as a report to the nation, but it amounted to an appeal for national solidarity behind the coalition. The Opposition criticized this action, but it was not given time to reply.[1]

Neville Chamberlain used the radio to report to the nation at the start of the war with Germany, but the secondary position of the media is indicated by the fact that he did not speak over the radio after returning from Munich. Instead he spoke to the crowds gathered outside No. 10 Downing Street.[2] The radio was frequently used by Winston Churchill in the war years as a method of directly reporting on the military or diplomatic situation of the time. No opposition was to be expected in this instance as he headed a National Government in which all parties were united for the achievement of a common objective.

The government also has another slight advantage in the use of the radio which grows out of the fact that they hold the reins of political power. The Prime Minister and other ministers may be invited to speak at ceremonial occasions. The B.B.C. broadcasts the speeches made at such gatherings as the Lord Mayor's banquet and the Royal Academy banquets. The

[1] Gordon, *op. cit.*, p. 229.   [2] Feiling, *op. cit.*, p. 381.

principal speeches at such events are usually made by persons holding high governmental positions, including the Prime Minister. Since such speeches often involve policy pronouncements, an advantage exists over the Opposition.[1]

It has also become the practice for the Chancellor of the Exchequer to deliver a short speech in which he attempts to popularize the budget. No real advantage is gained by this practice, however. The opposition is always allowed to reply to his statement immediately.[2]

The radio does serve the Prime Minister and his colleagues as one of the effective media of reaching the public. Further, it does contribute to his primacy in the party.[3] But it does not compare in importance with the more direct public speeches or the direct reports of parliamentary speeches. While the government has an advantage in the use of the radio, it is extremely small. Furthermore, the limits placed upon the use of the radio for political purposes tend to make it a secondary rather than a primary medium of political communication as in the United States.

V. THE PRIME MINISTER AND ELECTION CAMPAIGNS

Sixty years ago Lord Bryce, speaking of an English election, wrote, 'A general election is in form a choice of representatives, with reference primarily to their views upon various current questions. In substance it is often a national vote (what the French call a plebiscite), committing executive power to some one prominent statesman.'[4]

More recently Lord Robert Cecil has stated the same thesis.[5] 'I should say that if you really looked into the real principle of our constitution now, it is purely plebiscital, that you have

---

[1] O'Brien, *op. cit.*, pp. 137–8.

[2] P.E.P., 'Government Information Services', *Planning*, 2 February 1945, p. 17.

[3] *Post*, ch. v.

[4] Lord Bryce, *The American Commonwealth* (New York, Macmillan, 1891), p. 69.

[5] Quoted in Herman Finer, *The Theory and Practice of Modern Government* (New York, Henry Holt, 1949), p. 363.

really a plebiscite by which a particular man is selected Prime Minister, he then selects his Ministry himself, and it is pretty much what he likes subject to what affects the rule that he has to consider—namely, that he must not do anything that is very unpopular.'

Since the days of Gladstone there has been an increasing tendency to centre elections around the person of the party leader. This is, of course, less true of the Labour Party than of the Conservatives or the Liberals in their day of power. Even in the case of the Labour Party, however, the election of 1929 was fought largely around the personality of Ramsay Mac-Donald as contrasted with that of Stanley Baldwin.

The emphasis upon the party leader may take several forms. It may take the form of propaganda couched around the merits and abilities of the party leader. Their contact with the common people, their belief in English (or British) principles, their deep religious attachments, all of these may play a part in the appeals made by the parties. The Conservatives frequently emphasized that Baldwin was a representative Englishman, for to be a representative Englishman meant that you captured more votes. The campaign may be characterized by posters in which the party leader's picture is presented with such captions as 'Safety First', 'Honest Stan', 'You Can Trust Him', or 'Help Him Finish the Job'. The latter poster, which was used by the Conservatives in 1945, provided their chief propaganda weapon in the battle of the ballots. Almost the whole of the party's appeal was concentrated around Churchill, as a consequence of the belief that the man who had led Britain to victory in war would not be repudiated. The constructive programme of the party took second place to the emphasis upon the personality of the Prime Minister. This was a far cry from the Labour Party's campaign in which emphasis was placed on issues and principles rather than the personality of their leader. The startling result was that the dry, comparatively unappealing Attlee led his party to victory at the polls.

It is quite doubtful that the election of 1945 can be interpreted in terms of a plebiscite between alternative Prime Ministers. It might be the case that the British people would have liked to have had Churchill as a Labour Prime Minister, but that their personal admiration for Churchill did not extend to the Conservative Party. It is, of course, quite probable that the Conservatives would have been defeated even more overwhelmingly if he had not been their leader. All of the indications of divisions on issues prior to the election indicated that the electorate preferred the Labour Party, and the only hope the Conservatives had was to stick with Churchill in the belief that the great war leader would not be repudiated.

This was not the first election in which the chief appeal to the electorate had been concentrated around the personality of the leader. Gladstone's great campaign of 1880 was an example of the same kind of electoral effort. The coalition in 1918 subordinated its programme to the personality of Lloyd George and won. In 1935 the Conservatives plastered huge posters of Stanley Baldwin throughout the land and exhorted the people to stick with 'Honest Stan', insisting that 'You Can Trust Him'. An earlier appeal around Baldwin and 'Safety First' in 1929 was not enough and the party suffered a serious defeat.[1] It seems evident that the principal reason for the change in Premiers in 1935 was the recognition of MacDonald's unpopularity in the country. It does not seem probable that it was merely an accident that Baldwin became Prime Minister shortly before an election. It is admitted that one of his first considerations after becoming Prime Minister was the date on which an election should be held.[2]

Generally speaking, the Labour Party has not approached campaigns in this fashion. The party tends to emphasize principle rather than personality. This is probably a result of the fact that they are a reformist party whereas the Conservatives, while not 'standing pat' in their attitude, do not propose any radical revision of the social order. In 1929 there was a tendency to emphasize Ramsay MacDonald and his personal merits, but it never went as far as the Conservative emphasis on Baldwin. It is quite possible that since 1931 another reason for this rather anti-personal emphasis in the Labour Party has developed. MacDonald had twice led the party to electoral victory, and he had created for himself a position of public prestige. But in 1931 he broke with the party to the accompaniment of accusations of treason. The selection of first Lansbury, then Attlee, as party leader, may have, in part, been a consequence of a fear of strong leadership arising out of MacDonald's

[1] Roberts, *op. cit.*, pp. 168–9.
[2] Feiling, *op. cit.*, p. 260.

action. The recognition of the importance of the leader in the normal election did manifest itself in demands that Attlee resign as leader in favour of a more dynamic personality.

It is possible that Attlee's personality played a role of some importance in the election in a negative sense. Churchill was a strong, dynamic leader. The British received him with adulation during his tour of the country, but it is possible that they looked with some suspicion upon him as a peace-time leader. He was a great war leader, yes. But was it possible that he liked war? Some sections of the public may have preferred the more mundane Attlee for the tasks of reconstruction. It is even possible, although not probable, that there was some fear that Churchill might get them into international difficulties where Attlee would not. The time for risks and gambles was over, but Churchill's Greek policy looked like a calculated risk. If the desire of the public was to settle down Attlee might have seemed more desirable than Churchill despite the fact that the former headed a reformist party and the latter a conservative party. The Conservative leaders seem to have decided that it had been unwise to couch their appeal around the person of Churchill, for in 1950 they were careful to play down the personal element in the election.[1]

The Prime Minister is not able to limit his participation in a campaign to his own constituency. He is expected to speak in many other areas and to offer his support to the party candidates in those localities. Churchill's tour of the country in 1945 was the longest in British political history. It was a triumphal tour in which he appeared in Wales and Scotland as well as in various portions of England. The effort was to bring the personality of the Prime Minister, and the memory of what he had done, directly to the attention of the electorate. The importance of the leader is made evident by the fact that it was not until he started his tour that predictions of a Conservative victory began to appear.[2] Churchill was received with tremendous ovations and in consequence the *Yorkshire Post* said, 'No one seeing the wild delight of Mr. Churchill's greeting . . . could

---

[1] Nicholas, *op. cit.*, p. 215. Mr. Churchill remained the most newsworthy figure in the campaign, but greater attention was given to other Conservative leaders as well as to the constructive programme of the party.

[2] McCallum and Readman, *op. cit.*, p. 156.

doubt that he has the wholehearted support of the country in seeing this job through to the end.'[1]

Attlee too spoke outside his constituency in 1945, but he made no effort to conduct a campaign equal in length to that of Churchill. He too drew large meetings, but it has been said that they did not come 'to see him, but to hear him'.[2] Where Churchill was received with ovations and where the crowd stayed to see him leave, Attlee received less in the way of ovations and the whole atmosphere of the meetings was less adulatory.

Both candidates made tours in 1950. Churchill's tour was not so extensive as it had been in 1945, but it was nevertheless not inconsiderable in length. Nevertheless, he shared the burden of public meetings throughout the country with his principal colleagues to a greater extent than he had in 1945. Attlee's tour was extensive and involved a rather astounding number of speeches. Churchill's tour caught public attention as he spoke out against rationing, shortages, and taxation. His appearance in Plymouth in support of his son's candidacy also received additional public attention. Attlee's tour lacked the drama and fire of Churchill's, but it had a character of its own which made it difficult for the Conservatives to effectively push their charges that Labour was a radical, destructive party. It has been described in the following words:[3]

'On Wednesday, February 8th, he set off on his 1,000-mile tour. Whether the setting owed anything to the astuteness of the party managers, or whether it was, as it seemed to be, merely the natural expression of the Prime Minister's habits and personality, there can be no doubt that it was a *tour de force* of unassuming advertisement. The family car, pre-war and far from *de luxe*, Mrs. Attlee at the wheel, no entourage beyond the indispensable detective, the roadside stop when ahead of schedule, Mrs. Attlee would catch up on her knitting and Mr. Attlee would do a crossword puzzle—this was the very stuff of honest, uninvidious, unpretentious, non-queue-jumping,

---

[1] *Ibid.*, p. 156. The only paper which raised the question of whether the crowds which came out to see the Prime Minister would also vote for him was the *Manchester Guardian*. See the issue for 28 June 1945.

[2] McCallum and Readman, *op. cit.*, p. 169.

[3] Nicholas, *op. cit.*, pp. 93–4. The *Manchester Guardian* described Attlee as a 'Horatio of the Hustings', a 'master of non-gesture'.

post-war Britain. It was as devoid of drama as Queen Victoria's *Leaves* from her *Highland Journal*, and almost as appealing. However worked upon by hostile critics, it could not be presented as part of a picture of Socialist folly and extravagance, nor as a curtain-raiser to the class war which would proceed via the liquidation of the middle class to the eventual establishment of a Communist State.'

These were, of course, not the first examples of the great tour. Gladstone's campaign in 1885 involved speeches in many areas. Lord Salisbury also made 'stumping' visits to great towns.[1] It was these two political leaders who established the practice of the tour. In 1924 Ramsay MacDonald made a tour which extended from Glasgow to South Wales. He made speeches in practically every town through which his motorcade passed. On one occasion he 'spoke at twenty-seven meetings in one day'.[2] Even Churchill never made an effort of this magnitude and it is worthy of note that Snowden believes that in the long run it did more damage than good, for it left MacDonald in a weakened condition when the campaign reached its peak. The indications are that the tour is now an integral part of the election campaign, although it is not necessary for the party leader to carry it to the outrageous limits which it reached under MacDonald. It seems to be necessary to speak in the principal sections of the country, but it is not necessary to speak in every hamlet and village through which the Prime Minister may happen to pass. Tours may, of course, be made other than at election time. Many of the Prime Ministers have visited constituencies when no election was taking place. Such tours may help to build a basis for later electioneering.

A British election campaign does not last long, but it generates great heat. Many issues may be raised in the course of conducting a campaign and the Prime Minister plays a major role in the determination of what shall be emphasized and what shall not.[3] The party leader usually makes the first statement of the election. What he emphasizes may set the whole tone of the

---

[1] Lady Gwendolin Cecil, *Life of Robert Marquis of Salisbury* (London, Hodder and Stoughton, 1932), iv, 160.

[2] Philip Viscount Snowden, *An Autobiography* (London, J. Nicholson and Watson, 1934), ii, 708.

[3] His role in this respect is examined from a slightly different standpoint in the following chapter.

campaign. Whatever efforts may be made by his colleagues they are not in a position to counteract effectively the statements he makes. They cannot expressly disagree with him, and despite their concentration upon other matters they are faced with the fact that what he says will receive the widest publicity. If he makes a bad choice of issues, they can no nothing about it.

An example of what, in retrospect, seems to have been an extremely unwise choice may be found in the election of 1945. In his opening radio address Churchill said, 'Socialism is in its essence an attack not only upon British enterprise, but upon the right of an ordinary man or woman to breathe freely, without having a harsh, clumsy, tyrannical hand clapped across their mouth and nostrils. A free Parliament—look at that—a free Parliament is odious to the Socialist doctrinaire.'[1] He went on to argue that a Socialist system could not be established without a Gestapo. It is unquestionably true that this had a damaging effect. Churchill was accusing his partners in the prosecution of the war with the intention of establishing a system of tyranny the equivalent of which they had been fighting. The British people did not believe it. Lord Rothermere, always a staunch Conservative supporter, is reported to have said, 'If he continues like that the election is as good as lost'.[2] Unfortunately for the Conservative cause, he did continue in a similar vein, when he raised the picture of the late Professor Laski as the head of a British Gestapo. The incident, however, emphasizes the important role of the Prime Minister, or party leader, in the statement of issues. Nothing could be done by other Conservative speakers to wash away the effects of Churchill's approach.[3]

Other electioneers have been more effective in their choice of issues. In 1918 Lloyd George issued an appeal 'for the subordination of party interests in favour of national unity'. The same appeal was used by the National Government in 1931 and in both instances it paid off in victory at the polls. Other

[1] *The Listener*, 7 June 1945, p. 629.

[2] Virginia Cowles, *No Cause for Alarm* (New York, Harper, 1949), p. 73.

[3] It is reported that after the election Churchill had bronze plaques made and sent to all members of his war-time government. 'Socialists whom he had branded as future Gestapo leaders were surprised to receive these souvenirs with their names inscribed and bearing the words: "Salute the Greatest of all Coalitions. 1940–1945".' Cowles, *op. cit.*, p. 75.

elections have seen other issues of importance raised, 'The People against the Lords' in the elections of 1910, and the 'Red Letter' in the election of 1924. The circumstances give rise to the kind of issue which the party wishes to emphasize, but it is still the case that a party leader can make an unwise choice among the issues on which it will be fought. MacDonald wished to fight the election of 1924 on the trade treaty with the Soviet Union, but it was a disadvantageous issue when the 'Red Letter' entered the election.[1] In 1929, Stanley Baldwin and the Conservatives were satisfied with 'Safety First', and the posting of pictures of 'Stan Boy' in an attempt to take advantage of the popularity of Al Jolson's 'Sonny Boy'.[2] This too resulted in defeat.

Both of the major parties have staples in their propaganda. The Conservative emphasis on King, country and empire appears in each election. Patriotism is always an essential aspect of their programme and it is not unusual to imply that they are the only 'patriotic party'. Sometimes this may be seen in such events as the insistence upon the maintenance of the term 'National Party' long after it has lost meaning.[3] In the elections of 1935 and 1945 the emphasis was on 'National Party' rather than Conservative. In fact, there was no National Labour Party and no real National Liberal Party. It was desirable to hold on to the old name for it was felt that the term 'National' had appeal in and of itself, without consideration of what it stood for. Attlee insisted that it was an impudent claim, and further insisted that the predominance of rich men in the party indicated that it was far from being a National Party. In fact, it was claimed that the Labour Party, since its basic membership was deeper in society, was more national than the Conservative. Attlee's reaction to the Conservative use of the term was probably, in part at least, a result of his recognition that it did carry some weight with portions of the electorate. The Conservative emphasis on patriotism may be further seen from the practice, frequently followed, of using the Union Jack as if it were the party's symbol. This was done at the meetings of the Conservatives in 1945, but this was not an innovation. Ramsay MacDonald, after becoming head of the National

---

[1] Weir, *op. cit.*, p. 187. [2] Roberts, *op. cit.*, p. 169.
[3] Similarly the term 'Unionist' continues to receive Conservative attention although it too has long since lost its meaning.

Government, frequently spoke at meetings in which the Union Jack was prominently in evidence. 'At a great meeting at Derby, the platform was draped with the national flag, and the red, white, and blue banners were fluttering everywhere.'[1]

The Labour Party, on the other hand, always emphasizes the evils of capitalism and the rosy future which lies ahead under socialism. Whatever may be the arguments raised in individual cases, this general position is always maintained. This provides a clear alternative to the Conservatives, but at the same time it distorts the actual degree of disagreement between the two parties. The Conservative Party is always painted as being concerned with the 'privileged few' rather than the general welfare. The socialist character of the Labour Party is further emphasized by the practice of opening meetings with the singing of the 'Red Flag'. The revolutionary song is not always known to the audience, however. On at least one occasion in 1945, after an initial failure to get crowd participation in the 'Red Flag', they ended up singing 'John Brown's Body'.[2]

The Prime Minister and other speakers may also find it necessary to appeal to the prejudices of the crowd. It is wise to start a speech by extolling the merits of the audience and all party leaders do so. Stanley Baldwin, speaking at Leeds in 1931, opened his speech by saying, 'I put my faith in the good sound commonsense of Yorkshire men and women'.[3] Or the party leader may identify himself with the audience with such statements as 'I am not astute . . .'[4] thus implying that he is a common man.

L. Susan Stebbings has described some of the earmarks of a successful political speech as flattery, denunciation of the other side, even extending to an imputation of dishonesty, appeals to patriotic motives, and 'appeal to the mental habits of (the) audience'.[5] All political leaders use such approaches to some extent. The great orator is always at an advantage over those who are less able, so long as he does not make an unwise choice of the issue upon which he wishes to base his case. A reliance upon 'an appeal to the mental habits of (the) audience' does much to solve this problem.

---

[1] Weir, *op. cit.*, p. 443.   [2] McCallum and Readman, *op. cit.*, p. 169.
[3] *Manchester Guardian*, 21 October 1931.   [4] *Ibid.*
[5] L. Susan Stebbings, *Thinking to Some Purpose* (Pelican Books, 1939), p. 101.

An effective leader of a party must normally be a man who can create enthusiasm in his listeners. This is perhaps less true of Britain than of the United States, as witness the victory of the Labour Party under Clement Attlee in 1945 and 1950, but nevertheless it remains basically true. The Labour Party had other speakers who were able and dynamic, and the division of radio time provides an indication that they realized the importance of the gifted orator. Few really poor public speakers have held the office of Prime Minister. Perhaps Campbell-Bannerman was the only one, but as Lord Riddell said, 'He stood for something in the mind of the public'.[1] His honesty, his insistence upon standing upon his principles whatever the immediate public reaction, brought eventual public respect and support. What the public wants may differ, but Lloyd George was probably right when he said, 'The Briton is a fighting man. He likes a fighting speech'.[2] K. B. Smellie has indicated that the most effective campaigns have been those based on direct offensive tactics.[3]

'The most successful campaigns have been destructive offences such as Mr. Lloyd George's campaign against the Peers in 1910 and the blasting by Mr. Snowden's broadcasting of his former colleagues in 1931. If possible a party should secure the initiative, present a programme of little detail, and repeat often a clear and plain tale or lie. The constructive offensive is possible but difficult. It requires careful preparation and constant watchfulness. The least hopeful is the defensive retrospective such as that of the Conservative Government in 1929.'

A note of warning should be added, however. Churchill's campaign in 1945 provided an example of a destructive offensive, but it failed. The Labour Party, on the other hand, managed to work out a constructive offensive in this case.

However powerful, however able, however great an orator a Prime Minister may be, still, in the last resort, his power is derived from the fact that he leads a party. No man, however able he may be, can hope to rise to the position of Prime Minister, except in time of crisis, unless he heads a party. Ramsay MacDonald remained as Prime Minister after 1931, but only because he was a desirable figurehead from the Conservative standpoint. He had no party following in the country.

[1] Riddell, *op. cit.*, p. 51.   [2] *Ibid.*, p. 181.   [3] Smellie, *op. cit.*, p. 352.

The Prime Minister and the Public

His personal position did not enable him to pull any significant number of the Labour Party's members behind the National Government. His future depended upon the whims of the Conservative leaders, for he had no real strength of his own.[1] Even more noteworthy is the fact that Lloyd George, great as his position had been, was never able to regain the seats of power for he had no party behind him until it was too late. He had destroyed his party, but in doing so he destroyed his own future prospects.

[1] By the end of his last term as Prime Minister he was extremely unpopular. A critic states that 'at the cheaper cinemas where the commonalty congregate, the appearance of MacDonald on the screen, which used to be hailed with applause, came to be greeted with cat-calls and derisive laughter.' Weir, *op. cit.*, p. 437. Obviously the National Government could not go to the people with MacDonald as Prime Minister.

IV

The Prime Minister
and the Party

INTRODUCTION

In the words of Professor Jennings, 'A realistic survey of the British Constitution today must begin and end with parties and discuss them at length in the middle.'[1] This chapter involves a direct concentration on the relations of the Prime Minister and the party, or more specifically, on the relations of the leader of the party with the central organization, and the rank and file. Party, however, receives consideration in every other chapter of the study, for to omit it would distort the picture of the operations of all aspects of British political institutions.

The British are acutely conscious of political parties. ' "Party" is inherent in the English political nature—and nothing was ever more truly said than that England hates coalitions.'[2] At first sight the statement that 'England hates coalitions' may be questioned by the observer who can point to the fact that coalitions have frequently governed Britain in the last sixty years. A more intensive examination, however, will lead the student to accept the conclusion reached by Lord Esher. Only the wartime coalitions have not faced opposition. The Unionist coalition of 1894 and the National Government of 1931 involved the combination of two or more parties, but a strong opposition party always remained. Furthermore, it is somewhat doubtful that

[1] W. I. Jennings, *The British Constitution* (Cambridge, Cambridge University Press, 1944), p. 31.
[2] Reginald Viscount Esher, *The Captains and the Kings Depart* (New York, C. Scribner's Sons, 1938), ii, 264.

either of the two combinations was a coalition in any realistic sense of the term. The Liberal Unionists were assimilated into the Conservative Party after 1900. The National Government led a House in which the Conservative Party had a majority by itself. Additionally, the National Labour Party existed only in name.

The continuation of the Lloyd George coalition for four years after the end of hostilities provides the strongest argument against Esher's dictum, but it is of doubtful value. It was held together by personal obligation and loyalty to the Prime Minister. Furthermore, the British bias against coalitions may have been indicated by the increase in strength of the Labour Party during this period. The Labour Party withdrew from the coalition at the conclusion of the hostilities. It suffered an initial defeat in the elections of 1918,[1] but between 1918 and 1922 it seems to have attracted those persons who were displeased with the coalition and saw little hope in the Liberals under Asquith.

The party leader, whether he be Prime Minister or Leader of the Opposition, is the most important single member of the party. It is only upon the most extraordinary occasions that another member of the party reaches a position of higher public status. Joseph Chamberlain in 1900 was probably a greater figure in the eyes of the public than Lord Salisbury. Certainly much of the electoral campaign of 1900 turned around Chamberlain's personality.[2] While the party leader has prestige, he also has responsibilities. He is a great man because he is the party leader and he therefore has obligations to the party. 'A Prime Minister it has been said, has three duties, to his King, his country, and his party; and it is never certain which is the correct order in the scale of value.'[3]

The election of 1931 involved a controversy over Mac-Donald's action which was couched in terms of his patriotism

[1] The Labour Party returned only 57 M.P.s to the House of Commons in 1918. Francis Williams, *Fifty Year's March, The Rise of the Labour Party* (London, Odhams Press, n.d., p. 285. Four years later the party won 140 seats. Philip Viscount Snowden, *An Autobiography* (London, J. Nicholson and Watson, 1934), ii, 571.

[2] K. B. Smellie, *One Hundred Years of English Government* (New York, Macmillan, 1937), p. 222; J. L. Garvin, *The Life of Joseph Chamberlain* (London, Macmillan, 1935), iii, 295.

[3] W. I. Jennings, *Parliament* (Cambridge, Cambridge University Press, 1939), p. 125.

on the one hand, and his treason to the party on the other. The National Government's supporters argued that torn by the choice of party or country, MacDonald had selected his country. The Labour opposition emphasized that it was not possible to secure the welfare of the country except through the party, and that the man who was guilty of treason to his party could not be trusted with high position. Patriotism and the party system were visualized as inseparable.[1]

The attitude taken by the Labour Party towards its former leader was to be expected, but the belief that the party leader has primary obligations toward the party has been stated by others as well. Sir Robert Peel, who twice forced through action which a majority of his party opposed, and who eventually destroyed his party, was subjected to criticism by two later Conservative Prime Ministers, Disraeli and Balfour. Balfour said of him, 'Peel twice committed what seems to me the unforgivable sin. He gave away a principle on which he had come into power—and mind you, neither time had an unforeseen factor come into the case. He simply betrayed his Party.'[2] On one occasion while in opposition Balfour refused the offer of a political truce which might be used to settle outstanding problems. He himself approved of the idea, but his party did not. He told Lloyd George, when refusing, 'I cannot become another Robert Peel in my Party'.[3] Balfour's position was simply that the Prime Minister's first obligation is always to his party. He himself, as Prime Minister, faced a situation in which the strains and stresses occasioned by divergent economic views within his own Cabinet made the maintenance of party unity his principal objective. The internal division in the Cabinet, and the external division in the party, made it impossible to take any definite action on tariffs. Balfour resisted any personal inclination to take a definite stand and tried to straddle an ever-widening gulf in order to hold the party's wings together. The fact that the failure to take immediate constructive action might result in eventual electoral defeat was secondary to the fact that the party had to be held together. The party was more important than a single loss at the polls.[4]

[1] *Ante*, ch. ii.
[2] Blanche Dugdale, *Arthur James Balfour* (New York, G. P. Putnam's Sons, 1937), ii, 49–50.
[3] *Ibid.*, ii, 49.   [4] *Ibid.*, i, 250 ff.

'The whole strength of the Prime Minister . . . rests upon the fact that he is a party Chief, the recognized Leader of a party which has obtained a majority, or at least a larger number of seats than other parties, in the House of Commons—whether he has the support of a majority in the nation or not. If his party loses that, or revolts against his leadership, in an instant all his power melts away.'[1] Of course, his position as party chief enables him to take actions which would be impossible for an ordinary party member, but there is no question but that even a Prime Minister cannot long hold power without a party. Sir Robert Peel was through as a government leader when he destroyed his party. Ramsay MacDonald no longer had any basis for his authority after he failed to carry significant portions of the Labour Party with him. MacDonald was able to secure a Cabinet post as late as 1935 without any party support. But this was primarily a result of the fact that the Conservative Party could have been seriously embarrassed by MacDonald had it refused to grant him office. Even more significant is the fact that Lloyd George, the most powerful Prime Minister in British history, with the exception of Churchill, was never able to regain his earlier power after he had lost his party. In constructing the coalition and maintaining it through the conclusion of the war he destroyed his own party and his own future prospects.

THE TWO PARTY SYSTEM

The power derived from the position of party leader is further accentuated by the fact that the British party system is basically a two-party system. It offers the opportunity of full control of the government to one party or the other. The party leader may then expect that he will some day occupy the position of Prime Minister and lead a government composed of members of his own party. The party leaders in multi-party states seldom have the opportunity of wielding such power. In fact, since governments in multi-party states are nearly always coalitions it is sometimes disadvantageous to be a party leader. The party leader is too closely aligned with the principles of his party, and it is sometimes easier to gain the support of other parties if one

[1] Ramsay Muir, *How Britain is Governed* (New York, R. R. Smith, 1930), p. 83.

of the secondary figures in the major party is selected as Premier.[1]

The British party system developed historically as a two-party system. Today, after a brief interlude in which a third party of considerable strength affected the power relationships in Parliament, it is again a two-party system.[2] Two factors tend to make difficult the rise of a third party which can effectively challenge the major parties. Those two factors are the single-member constituency, and the organization of the House of Commons around the government and an official opposition.

Third parties can never hope to attain representation in the House of Commons even roughly proportionate to the total vote which they receive. For example, in 1945, the Liberal Party received nine per cent of the total vote cast. In return for that substantial portion of the vote they obtained only twelve seats in the House of Commons out of 640. The Labour Party, in the same election, with forty-eight per cent of the popular vote elected 393 members.[3] The Labour Party had one representative for every 30,000 votes. The Liberals had one representative for every 186,666 votes. In such circumstances it is not surprising that the Liberal Party has frequently agitated for proportional representation. Nor is it surprising that neither the Labour nor the Conservative Parties are friendly to such an electoral change. Both of the major parties may now hope to win majority control of the House of Commons. The only party which would gain from proportional representation would be the Liberal Party. In the absence of such reforms the Liberal Party continues to decline in parliamentary strength. In the election of 1950 they were able to win only nine seats in the Commons.[4] In 1951 this was reduced to six. Decline has intensified the acceleration at which decline takes place, until today it is obvious that the Liberal Party has no future prospects of

[1] W. L. Middleton, *The French Political System* (New York, E. P. Dutton, 1933), ch. v.

[2] The most significant result of the elections of 1950–1 was the almost complete destruction of all minor parties. The Liberal Party was reduced to six seats, and the Communists were unable to win a single contest.

[3] R. B. McCallum and Alison Readman, *The British General Election of 1945* (New York, Oxford University Press, 1947), p. 248.

[4] H. G. Nicholas, *The British General Election of 1950* (London, Macmillan, 1951), p. 299. The Liberals ran 475 candidates, of these 319 lost their deposits.

power. The electorate does not vote for a party which is beaten before the election starts. And the only parties which are not are the Labour and Conservative Parties.

The organization of the House of Commons is unquestionably of lesser importance, but it does have a minor effect in cementing the two-party system. There is always an official Opposition in the House of Commons. The principal roles in the determination of the business of the House are played by the leaders of the government and the leaders of the official opposition.[1] Any other party is left somewhat outside the main arena of business. It does not have as great a role in the determination of what portions of supply shall be debated, or in the arrangements by which the opposition agrees to expedite one matter for the government in order to obtain an opportunity to raise another issue. This means that the Official Opposition has some advantage in selecting items which will have an effect upon public opinion. Furthermore, the press is likely to give greater attention and publicity to the criticism which emanates from the Official Opposition, since it is recognized as the alternative government.

In consequence of these considerations the British elections are concerned primarily with the determination of what party shall govern; what man shall be Prime Minister. The emphasis in the British elections is upon the selection of a Prime Minister and a government, not upon achieving some mirror-like reflection of public opinion and wants. Two alternative Prime Ministers stand before the public; two alternative parties with alternative principles are presented. The electorate makes its choice between them. Elections are essentially plebiscites.

The party leader is recognized as the party's nominee for Prime Minister should the party obtain power. The method by which the party leader is selected is therefore of considerable importance. It should be stressed before examining this procedure that the Labour Party does not have an official leader. The National Labour Party has a National Executive Committee, which is the highest administrative authority in the party. The Executive Committee selects its own chairman. The chairman of the party, however, is not the party's nominee for Prime Minister. In fact, the chairman is usually a person of secondary importance, and it is very unusual even to re-elect

[1] *Post*, ch. vii.

him to the post. The position is basically an honorary post, and does not carry with it any significant political power. The nominee for Prime Minister comes from the ranks of the Parliamentary Labour Party, which is separately organized. There are close ties between the Parliamentary Party and the National Party, which will be discussed later, but the National Party does not make the selection of a party leader. Constitutionally speaking, the National Party has no leader.

The method used by the Conservative Party in the selection of its leader has been described as follows:[1]

'The Leader of the Party, who was formerly elected by Conservative Members of Parliament, is now elected at a joint meeting of Members of both Houses, all prospective candidates and the Executive Committee of the National Union. The leader is always recognized as being the Party's nomination as Prime Minister. In a number of instances, notably that of the late Earl Baldwin in 1923, appointment as Prime Minister has preceded election as Leader of the Party.'

The procedure outlined above may be followed in the future, but it must be stressed that the statement of the old procedure is somewhat misleading. It is true that the leader was elected by the Conservative Members of the Parliament, but it distorts the actual events to say that 'The leader is always recognized as being the Party's nomination as Prime Minister'. The only exception noted is the appointment of Stanley Baldwin. In fact, every Conservative Prime Minister, except Law, appointed since Balfour became party leader only after he had become Prime Minister. In a sense, recognizing the influence of political leaders upon the determination, the actual selection of the Conservative Party leader has been made by the King.

Thus in 1922, Bonar Law became Prime Minister on the 19th of October. At the time Sir Austen Chamberlain was the party leader, but Chamberlain had determined that he would stick with Lloyd George. Lloyd George resigned as soon as the news of the Carlton Club's decision to withdraw from the coalition reached him, and Bonar Law succeeded him as Prime Minister.[2] Immediately prior to taking office, he was elected

---

[1] David Clarke, 'The Organisation of Political Parties', *Political Quarterly*, xxi (January–March 1950), 87.

[2] Earl of Ronaldshay, *The Life of Lord Curzon* (New York, Boni and Liveright, n.d.), iii, 321.

party leader at a meeting of the Conservatives. The difficulties involved in the selection of Law's successor, which culminated in the surprising choice of Baldwin, did not receive party ratification until after Baldwin had become Prime Minister. Lord Curzon, who had expected to receive the appointment, nominated Baldwin as party leader.[1]

The appointment of Neville Chamberlain in 1937 followed the usual pattern. He became Prime Minister upon the resignation of Stanley Baldwin, and three days later he was selected as the leader of the party.[2] This is not particularly significant in the case of Chamberlain for it was evident that he was the logical successor to Baldwin, but it is peculiar that the party had taken no formal action prior to his appointment as Prime Minister.

Winston Churchill, who was in the ill-graces of a substantial portion of the Conservative Party because of his opposition to the government's policy, first towards India and later towards Germany and Italy, did not become party leader until some time after he had become Prime Minister. Churchill took office as Prime Minister in May 1940, but it was not until the 4th October 1940 that he became the leader of the Conservative Party. Neville Chamberlain had remained the party leader until that time. Churchill explains that he accepted the position on the grounds that 'I should have found it impossible to conduct the war if I had to procure the agreement in the compulsive days of crisis and during long years of adverse and baffling struggle, not only of the leaders of the two minority parties, but of the leader of the Conservative majority'.[3] There is little question but that Churchill was right in his statement that 'Whoever had been chosen and whatever his self-denying virtues, he would have had the real political power. For me there would have been only the executive responsibility.'[4] To this he added the desirability of not finding it necessary to depend upon the votes of the Labour and Liberal Parties. He emphasizes the importance of the party leadership as a bargaining weapon in the comment, 'Moreover, in dealing with the

---

[1] *Ibid.*, iii, 353.

[2] Keith Feiling, *The Life of Neville Chamberlain* (London, Macmillan, 1946) p. 294.

[3] Winston Churchill, *Their Finest Hour* (Boston, Houghton Mifflin, 1949), p. 496.　　　[4] *Ibid.*, p. 496.

Labour and Liberal Parties in the coalition, it was always an important basic fact that as Prime Minister and at this time leader of the largest party, I did not depend upon their votes and I could in the ultimate issue carry on in Parliament without them'.[1]

The Labour Party follows a more formal procedure. As has been pointed out previously, the National Party has no leader, but the Parliamentary Labour Party does. The leader of the Parliamentary Party is normally recognized as the party's nominee for the position of Prime Minister should it obtain power, although the party formally withholds the power to make a final determination. 'At the beginning of every session a leader, deputy-leader, and whips are elected by vote of the members.'[2] Formal control thus inheres in the members of the party, and there is no absolute guarantee that a leader will be continued in office from one session to the next. Actually, however, this does not adequately explain the realities of the situation, for normally he does remain in power.

In one significant instance, which was to be historically of great importance, a party leader was rejected by the Parliamentary Labour Party and replaced by another. After the defeat of most of the major leaders of the party in the election of 1918, J. R. Clynes became the leader of the Parliamentary Party. In the election of 1922 many of those former leaders returned to seats in the House of Commons. Arthur Henderson, who had earlier led the party, was not in the Parliament, however. The change in the composition of the party led to immediate demands that the question of who should serve as parliamentary leader be raised again. Henderson, although outside, probably had some influence upon the choice made, for he favoured MacDonald. At the election which followed, only two nominations were made—J. R. Clynes and Ramsay MacDonald. MacDonald was elected with the strong support of most 'of the left-wing Clydeside group led by John Wheatley'.[3] The I.L.P. members seemed to think that MacDonald was further left than Clynes, and shared their views.[4] Mac-

---

[1] *Ibid.*, p. 496.

[2] Clement Attlee, *The Labour Party in Perspective—And Twelve Years Later* (London, V. Gollancz, 1949), p. 87.

[3] Williams, *op. cit.*, p. 298.

[4] Fenner Brockway, *Socialism Over Sixty Years, The Life of Jowett of Brad-*

Donald was elected by a margin of sixty-one to fifty-six. Twenty-two members were absent.[1] It was a fateful choice.

Once MacDonald was elected leader he retained that position until he broke with the party to form the National Government in 1931. His leadership was really never seriously challenged with the exception of the controversy which arose at the annual conference of the party in 1930. This will be examined later in dealing with the role of the conferences and the possibility that they may tend to restrict the party leader in his actions. Sir Oswald Mosley, while a Labour M.P., did try to get the Parliamentary Party to pass a vote of censure against MacDonald in 1930, but his own intemperate insistence upon a formal division made his effort ineffectual.[2]

When MacDonald took office as Prime Minister of the National Government, Arthur Henderson was chosen as the leader of the Parliamentary Party. He did not hold the position for very long, as a consequence of the general election of 1931, in which he lost his seat in the House. In fact, all of the party's major figures were swept away by the deluge in which the parliamentary strength of the Labour Party fell from 289 to 46. George Lansbury was the highest ranking figure in the last government left in the House. Consequently he became the leader of the party and held the office from 1931 until 1935.[3] Clement Attlee, the second ranking figure left in the Parliamentary Party, became the deputy leader. Lansbury eventually resigned in 1935 as a consequence of the repudiation of his anti-war views by the annual conference of the party.[4] Attlee was selected temporarily as the leader of the party, and served in that capacity during the election of 1935.[5]

It seems to have been expected that Attlee was filling this position only for the election period. The election results brought other major figures back into the Parliament. When the new House met, however, a surprise awaited those who had expected Attlee's place to be filled by another. Three persons

---

ford (London, Published for the National Labour Press by G. Allen and Unwin, 1946), p. 192; Dean McHenry, *His Majesty's Opposition, Structure and Problems of the Labor Party, 1931–38* (Berkeley, University of California Press, 1940), p. 139; Williams, *op. cit.*, p. 298.

[1] Williams, *op. cit.*, p. 299.   [2] Snowden, *op. cit.*, ii, 877.

[3] McHenry, *op. cit.*, pp. 142–3.   [4] Williams, *op. cit.*, p. 352.

[5] Ibid., p. 353; McHenry, *op. cit.*, p. 147.

were nominated: Attlee, Morrison, and Greenwood. On the first ballot Attlee had fifty-eight votes, Morrison forty-four, and Greenwood thirty-two. Greenwood dropped out and on the following ballot Attlee received eighty-eight votes to Morrison's forty-four. Attlee had picked up thirty votes, Morrison's vote had remained constant.[1] Since that time Attlee has held the position of party leader and was consequently sent for by the King when the election results of 1945 became known.

Various reasons for Attlee's selection have been given. Patricia Strauss, a critic of Attlee's, has said, 'The Labour Party is incurably sentimental. Many Members felt that as Attlee had been Deputy Leader, and he had carried on when Lansbury resigned, his feelings would be hurt if someone else were elected above him.'[2] To this she added the remark that the enactment of a statute providing a salary for the Leader of the Opposition had cemented him in his job. 'If the Party would elect Attlee rather than hurt his feelings, they would not lightly reject him now that it would hurt his pocket.'[3]

Francis Williams has given a different reason. His argument is upon the whole more credible, and derives from a higher opinion of Attlee's abilities.[4]

'Those Labour M.P.'s who had been in Parliament in the difficult days from 1931 had come to appreciate Attlee's qualities as leader. They knew his integrity, his quiet strength, his ability to hold together the varying groups within the Party, and they voted almost solidly for him.'

It is probable that there is some merit in both of the arguments. Mrs. Strauss unquestionably underestimated Attlee's ability as a leader. At least the experience since 1945 indicates that he is, upon the whole, a very able man. It is, however, probable that sentimental feelings of obligation to a man who had taken a job when it was hard, might have led some members to cast their vote for him when he might expect greater rewards. Robert Michels has pointed out that a sense of moral obligation to their leaders frequently develops in a political party or any other kind of organization.[5] An additional factor,

[1] Patricia Strauss, *Bevin and Co.* (New York, G. P. Putnam's Sons, 1941), p. 90; Williams, *op. cit.*, p. 353; McHenry, *op. cit.*, p. 147.

[2] Strauss, *op. cit.*, p. 90.   [3] *Loc. cit.*   [4] Williams, *op. cit.*, p. 353.

[5] Robert Michels, *Political Parties* (Glencoe, Illinois, Free Press, 1949), pp. 60–69.

which neither Williams nor Mrs. Strauss mentioned, also tended to militate against Morrison's selection. He had antagonized the trade unions by his opposition to worker representation in the management of the London Passenger Transport Board. His interest was in efficiency, and he seems to have felt that worker participation in management would hinder efficiency. It is probable that this was the most important single factor in explaining his defeat by Attlee.

The Parliamentary Labour Party may, in some circumstances, change its leader, but it is evident that the practice of re-electing the old leader is hardening into a customary practice. Certainly, once the party leader has held the office of Prime Minister it is almost impossible to shake him from office except in the most unusual circumstances. Lansbury might have been rejected had he remained leader after the election of 1935, as the top leaders had always been suspicious of both his left-wing views and his general ability. But Attlee, a middle-of-the-road man, won over extremely able competition.

The leader of the Conservative Party normally retains that office as long as he wishes. Balfour did resign in 1911, but he did so upon his own initiative, although there was a growing opposition to him as leader. It is probable that he could have mastered his opponents if he had wished to. He seems to have been relieved to get rid of his responsibilities.[1] Bonar Law, his successor, held the position until he himself resigned as a result of ill-health. Sir Austen Chamberlain, it is true, lost the position, but it was a consequence of his refusal to follow the party into opposition to Lloyd George. Once Stanley Baldwin had become party leader he retained the post until his resignation as Prime Minister fourteen years later. Winston Churchill, of course, has retained the position of party leader since 1940, despite undercurrents of opposition among the Young Tories. His personal prestige places him beyond effective challenge.

The security of tenure which the leaders of both parties have gives them substantial advantages in dealing with the rank and file of the party. There are several ways in which their influence may be felt, ranging from their influence on the organization of the party and the selection of national party organization officers to their influence upon the selection of candidates, the use of funds, and the determination of party principles. For the

[1] Dugdale, *op. cit.*, ii, 54–62.

sake of simplicity these will be examined separately whenever possible. In addition, in the case of the Labour Party, it is also necessary to examine more closely the relationship between the leader and the Parliamentary Party, as definite efforts have been made to create a system of inter-relationships between them of a rather unusual character.

The Conservative leader occupies a position of pre-eminence and power with respect to his national party which is considerably superior to that of the Labour Party leader. The latter is the leader of the Parliamentary Party only. The Conservative leader is the leader of both the party in the Parliament and in the country.

The formal procedure adopted in recent years provides, as mentioned earlier, that the participants in the selection of the Conservative leader include not only members of the Parliament who are of the party, but prospective candidates and the executive committee of the National Union. The executive committee, it should be noted, is an appointive rather than an elective body. Its membership is usually selected from the elected 'office-holders of the Party'.[1]

Actually the entire central organization of the party in Great Britain grew up around the leader and his supporters in the Parliament. The Conservative Central Association was initially set up by Disraeli and it was created under his direct control. He appointed the Party Manager.[2] Until 1911 the Central Office was under the control of the Chief Whip, who served as party manager. But the growth in the parliamentary duties of that officer led to the formal selection of a Chairman of the Party Organization.[3] It is obvious that so long as the Chief Whip was in charge, the Prime Minister or party leader, had direct control of the party organization, for it was he who made the selection of the Chief Whip.

In fact, this situation still exists. 'The appointment of the principal officers of the Party Headquarters . . . rests with the Leader of the Party. He appoints the Chairman and Vice-Chairman of the Party Organization, the Treasurers of the Party and the Chairman of the Conservative Research Depart-

[1] Clarke, *op. cit.*, p. 87.
[2] W. I. Jennings, *The British Constitution* (Cambridge, Cambridge University Press, 1944), p. 160.
[3] Clarke, *op. cit.*, p. 87.

ment.'[1] The extent of control derived from this appointing power is obvious. The Chairman of the Party Organization, it should be stressed, is principally responsible for the organization and publicity of the party. One of the vice-chairmen usually has the responsibility of assisting in the selection of candidates. This means that the party leader is in a position to influence organization, and the selection of candidates directly, in consequence of the fact that he appoints the officers who are principally responsible for such activities.

As has been mentioned, he appoints the chairman of the Conservative Research Department. The Research Department is thus made directly responsible to the party leader. It has proved to be a desirable innovation. 'It is responsible for the preparatory work on policy and the general supply of information to all enquirers.'[2] Additionally, it has served the leader quite advantageously when the party is in opposition. It has served as a research centre in which materials and information could be obtained which might enable the opposition to deal with complicated legislation more advantageously than might otherwise have been possible. The government always has some advantage in debate because it has access to the expert knowledge and specific information available in the departments. The Research Centre enables the opposition to secure more adequate bases for its argument. As David Clarke has said, 'The more technical nature of legislation and debate, especially on economic affairs, and the wealth of information available now make a permanent civil service for the Opposition in Parliament indispensable'.[3] Such a body now exists in Research Centre, and is under the control of the party leader, who may direct that research be undertaken into any area which he desires.

The organization of the National Labour Party is one of the most complicated arrangements devised by the mind of man. The intent here is not to examine all of the aspects of the organization, but to note the place of the Parliamentary Labour Party leader within the framework of the national party organization. The relations between the Parliamentary leader and the Parliamentary Party will be examined later.

[1] *Ibid.*, p. 87.   [2] *Ibid.*, p. 88.
[3] *Loc. cit.* The Fabian Society has served as a research group for the Labour Party almost since its inception.

At the top of the hierarchy of party administrative organizations is the National Executive Committee. This Committee has twenty-five members who are elected by the party conference at its annual meetings. The Constitution of the Labour Party provides that they are to be elected 'in such proportions and under such conditions as may be set out in the Standing Orders for the time being in force'.[1] Under the terms of Standing Order Four, adopted at the same conference, provision is made for twelve representatives to be chosen from the Trade Unions, one from the Socialist, Co-operative, and Professional organizations, seven from Federations, Constituency Labour Parties, and Central Labour Parties, and five women who may be chosen from any group. Prior to this time the Executive had been composed of twenty-three persons, twelve of whom were members of the trade union group.[2] In addition, the leader of the Parliamentary Labour Party is an *ex officio* member of the National Executive.[3] The Executive Committee is the highest authority in the party except during the time that the party conference is in session.

The exact position and influence of the Parliamentary Labour Leader inevitably depends upon the circumstances of the time and his own abilities. Certainly, he is in an advantageous position to influence the actions of the National Executive, and in those instances in which the party holds power his authority, derived from the fact that he is Prime Minister, is quite substantial.

The National Executive is quite a potent body. It is empowered to take action which may result in the disaffiliation of 'an organization or expulsion of an individual. . . .'[4] Furthermore it submits resolutions and declarations 'affecting the Programme, Principles and Policy of the Party. . . .'[5] It also serves as one of the means of liaison between the National Party and the Parliamentary Party.[6] In addition, it serves as the highest judicial body in settling disputes between affiliated organizations.[7]

[1] *Party Constitution and Standing Orders* as approved by the Margate Conference (London, 1947). *The Constitution*, clause viii, section 1.

[2] *The Constitution and Standing Orders of the Labour Party*, 1935, Standing Order IV, section 1.

[3] *Constitution of 1947*, clause viii, section 1; *Constitution of 1935*, clause viii, section 1. The party treasurer is also an *ex officio* member.

[4] *Constitution of 1947*, clause viii, section 2b.   [5] *Ibid.*, Clause viii, section 2f.

[6] *Ibid.*, clause viii, section 2c.   [7] *Ibid.*, clause viii, section 4.

The National Executive also plays a role of considerable importance in the selection of party candidates. The Constitution of 1947 provides that, 'The selection of Labour Candidates for Parliamentary Elections shall not be regarded as completed until the name of the person selected has been placed before a meeting of the National Executive Committee, and his or her selection has been duly endorsed'.[1] In the case of by-elections, the candidate chosen must also submit 'his or her Election Address to the National Executive Committee for approval'.[2] In regular elections all candidates are required 'to give prominence in their campaigns to the issues for that election as defined by the National Executive Committee in its Manifesto'.[3]

The actual extent to which the Prime Minister shares in the deliberations and activities of the National Executive must depend upon the time which he has available, and the confidence he has in the other members of that organization.[4] The leader of the party, while in opposition, probably has more direct time for participation. At the same time it seems evident that when the leader of the party is Prime Minister his influence will be greater. Whatever may be said about the programme and principles being adopted by the National Executive Committee, it seems more probable that the Prime Minister and his major Cabinet colleagues make the actual determination of policy issues. Certainly this was the case in 1924, but it may be true that in 1929 the situation was somewhat different. The long-run objectives of the party tend to be stated in more imposing form. From 1918 until 1928 the document 'Labour and the New Social Order' served as the basic statement of party principles. Clement Attlee has described it as 'a declaration of faith and aspirations rather than a political programme'.[5] Although other issues might enter into immediate elections, and did, in fact, this remained the basic document until 1928. At that time the party adopted a new document, 'Labour and the Nation'. It was a short document, but it contained a multiplicity of items, seventy-two in all. As Attlee said,

[1] *Ibid.*, clause ix, section 3. [2] *Ibid.*, clause ix, section 6.
[3] *Ibid.*, clause ix, section 5.
[4] The memoirs and biographies of Labour Party statesmen seldom deal with the relationship between the Parliamentary Leader and the National Executive. The impression gained from the memoirs is that the National Executive has little direct influence upon the Parliamentary Party.
[5] Attlee, *op. cit.*, pp. 50–1.

'It gave the Prime Minister an opportunity to select which items suited him. It gave every malcontent unlimited opportunities of charging the party with breaches of faith for not implementing all of these promises.'[1] Actually, since the party is socialist, it is inevitable that the basic principles of all the programmes will remain substantially the same.[2]

The influence of the Parliamentary Labour Party Leader is probably slightly less than that exercised by the Conservative Leader. The division of directing authority in the National Party makes it somewhat more difficult to exercise supreme directing authority. Where the principal officers of the Conservative Party are appointed by, and responsible to, the party leader, this is not true of the Labour Party. There the party leader is but an *ex officio* member of the Executive. The other members are directly elected by their respective groups at the Party Conference. While it is probable that the Parliamentary Leader exercises great influence, it seems likely that the other members, having formal status derived from election, can exercise more independence of action than the Conservative officers. Still, the Parliamentary Leader occupies an important public position and he must derive considerable power from that fact. He is further strengthened by the fact that the National Executive always includes other members of the Parliamentary Party.[3]

The constitutional relationship between the National Labour Party and the Parliamentary Labour Party is not definable. In 1945, Churchill raised the question of whether this 'Socialist Executive Committee possesses power over Socialist Ministers of a far-reaching character'.[4] He even suggested that a Labour Prime Minister might be called before the Executive Committee to defend his actions.[5] Actually the Constitution of the Party is not specific on this relationship and the only way to

---

[1] *Ibid.*, p. 53.

[2] For example, compare 'Socialism and Peace' (1934) with 'Let Us Face the Future' (1945). The basic essentials remain the same although the immediate problems of the moment result in the interjection of other issues as secondary matters. The same can be said of 'Let Us Win Together', the 1950 statement. It differs mainly in the retrospective pride of achievement, but in essence the basic principles stated in the earlier documents are repeated.

[3] Attlee, *op. cit.*, p. 89.   [4] McCallum and Readman, *op. cit.*, p. 173.
[5] *Ibid.*, p. 175.

determine the precise obligations of one to the other is to look at what has happened in practice.

In practice, it seems quite clear that the Parliamentary Labour Party is an independent entity. It derives its financial support from the National Party, but it is not obligated to reveal information, or to accept all of the decisions of the National Party. Attlee has said that 'in its own sphere the Parliamentary Party is supreme'.[1] This follows in part from a recognition of the facts of Cabinet-Parliamentary government. Cabinet government requires that the responsibility of the government is towards the Parliament only. Furthermore, the requirements of Cabinet secrecy make it impossible that the Parliamentary Labour Party should have intimate relations with the National Executive when it is in office. It is, of course, possible that the National Party might propose action which the Parliamentary Party cannot, or will not, accept. In fact, however, such events do not take place. It may be questioned whether there is any serious problem of the domination of the Executive over the Parliamentary Party. An American student has said, 'Indeed, a leading question facing British Labour today is whether the Prime Minister and other Cabinet members do not overly influence the Labour Party programme and policies'.[2]

One problem which has always plagued the Labour Party is the relationship between the party leaders and the rank and file. This problem is not so serious when they are in opposition for then the party meets periodically, usually once a week, and there is a general discussion in caucus.[3] When the party takes power the situation becomes more complicated. The party's leaders take over governmental departments and they tend to become somewhat isolated from the rank and file members unless something is done to bring them together formally. This problem does not seem to bother the leaders of the Conservative Party, and little effort has been made to bring the backbenchers into closer relations with the leaders. The Labour Party, however, prides itself upon its democratic character. Efforts have been made to bring the party leaders into contact

---

[1] Attlee, *op. cit.*, p. 88.

[2] James MacGregor Burns, 'The Parliamentary Labour Party in Great Britain', *American Political Science Review*, xliv (December 1950), 856.

[3] Attlee, *op. cit.*, p. 88.

with the back-benchers or their representatives in each instance
in which the party held office.

In 1924, a special committee of twelve members, plus three
members of the Cabinet, was appointed to deal with the relations between government and back benchers.[1] It has been said
that this group 'more than once asserted their authority over
the Cabinet'.[2] Spender speaks of an impression 'created in
Parliament and in the country . . . that the Labour Government
was in a peculiar sense not its own master'.[3] He cites, as one
instance in which power seemed to be operating behind the
scenes, the withdrawal of the Campbell prosecution.[4] Actually,
it is extremely doubtful that such influences caused that decision, or any other decision taken by the government. It is true
that there was considerable opposition to the action against
Campbell in the Labour Party,[5] but the determination to withdraw the charge was made quite early as a result of the belief
that the prosecution did not have a good case in the first place.[6]
The Prime Minister's maladroit handling of the whole incident
was principally responsible for the false impression created.[7]

A similar body of twelve members, plus three government
officials, was again established in the period 1929–31. In this
case it seems to have been recognized that the government
needed a freer hand than was ordinarily assumed, but the
relations between the back benchers and the government
during this period were not very cordial. Both accused the
other of failing to fulfil their obligations, the government to
inform the party of what it intended to do, the party to follow
the disciplinary rules of the party and vote with the government.[8] The dissidents were primarily members of the I.L.P.,
who always exercised greater independence of action than the
members of the regular party.[9] The fifteen member body con-

---

[1] Burns, *op. cit.*, p. 867.

[2] J. A. Spender, *The Public Life* (New York, Frederick A. Stokes, 1925),
i, 162. See also 'Governing the Government', *The Times*, 27 October 1924.

[3] Spender, *op. cit.*, i, 163.   [4] *Loc. cit.*,

[5] Brockway, *op. cit.*, p. 219. Brockway writes, 'Immediately there was
uproar in the Labour Movement; even those who disliked the Communists
most could not stand for persecution of political opinion by a Labour Government. Under the pressure of the protests the prosecution was withdrawn.'

[6] Snowden, *op. cit.*, ii, 691–3.   [7] *Ibid.*, ii, 693 ff.   [8] Burns, *op. cit.*, p. 857.

[9] Attlee, *op. cit.*, p. 88. Attlee says that the reason for the I.L.P. secession
from the party was the refusal of its members to accept majority rule.

tinued as an integral part of the party apparatus after 1931, with the three leader representatives being chosen from what was obviously the Shadow Cabinet.[1]

The procedure established in the Parliament after the election victory of 1945 seems to have worked more effectively. Again a small committee was established to function as an instrument of liaison between the rank and file and the Prime Minister and his colleagues.[2] In addition, groups, roughly equivalent to the ministries, were also being established to carry on direct liaison with the particular ministers involved.[3] These bodies functioned constantly, although with varying degrees of success. The Parliamentary Labour Party also met in caucus about once a fortnight. It could be called by the Prime Minister at any other time. There was also a trade union group which served as a clearing house for those members who were sponsored and financed by the trade unions. It did not act on behalf of the trade unions on matters of high policy, however. If such issues arose the officials of the Trade Union Congress dealt directly with the Prime Minister or one of his colleagues.[4] Direct contact could be made in the National Council of Labour as well, for both the T.U.C. and the leaders of the Parliamentary Party have representatives in that body.

The attempt to obtain the participation of the rank and file in the formulation of policy, or at least in its prior approval, was sometimes quite effective. In at least one instance the policy of the government on a major issue was affected by the attitude of the Parliamentary Party, and a change was introduced in the government's initial proposal. Professor Burns has described this incident as follows:[5]

'Late in 1946 the Government, disappointed at the low level of voluntary enlistments, decided on an 18-month period of conscription. On November 6 of that year Mr. Attlee announced the proposed bill to a private meeting of the P.L.P. The P.L.P. was divided; according to one report, it voted for the plan by 126–54. Two weeks later 100 Labour M.P.'s abstained in a House vote on a critical amendment attacking the Government's foreign policy. By March 31, 1947, when the

[1] *Ibid.*, p. 88.

[2] *Report* of the 45th Annual Conference of the Labour Party (London, 1946), p. 56.

[3] Burns, *op. cit.*, pp. 858–9.   [4] *Ibid.*, p. 861.   [5] *Ibid.*, p. 865.

Conscription bill was laid before the House, 80 Labour Back-benchers had signed an amendment asking the Party to reject it. Attlee again defended the bill at a meeting of the P.L.P. that was reported to be stormy. Next day 72 Labourites voted against the bill, 20 abstained from voting, and 50 did not show up at the House at all. Two days later the Government suddenly reduced the proposed service from 18 to 12 months. This concession worked, the Government winning passage of the bill the following month by a 368–17 vote and endorsement at the Labour Party conference later in the month.'

One factor in this situation deserves emphasis. Although it is a good example of an incident in which the back-benchers influenced the policy of the government, it develops in unusual circumstances. The bill was one which would not meet with Conservative opposition. It was obvious, therefore, that the government would not fall because of the attitude of the recalcitrant members. Peculiarly enough, it is probable that the government's initial measure would have carried in the House, with the support of nearly all of the Labour members, if the Conservatives had been opposed. The Prime Minister and his colleagues can normally expect a better disciplined party when it is challenged by the opposition, than when it is not. Opposition within the party is more likely to be expressed in the latter circumstances, for the alternative of dissolution or resignation is not present. This is not to say that it is not wise to consider the attitude of the rank and file. A wise Prime Minister never rides rough shod over his back-benchers as it adversely affects their morale.[1] But it is a peculiarity of the British system that to some extent the direct influence of the Prime Minister on all segments of his party is greater when he is challenged by opposition than otherwise. The party closes ranks in the face of a common foe, but it may tend to divide again when the common foe is no longer present. The other great revolt of the 1945–50 period, on foreign policy, also came in a situation in which Conservative support of the government's position was taken

[1] A Conservative Prime Minister has less need to take comparable care in dealing with his backbenchers. A great deal is always made of the strict discipline of the Labour Party, but, in fact, the Conservative Party is a better disciplined organization. Every Labour Government has been plagued by party dissidents, but this has less frequently been true of Conservative Governments.

for granted. After the government's margin was narrowed in the elections of 1950 foreign policy opposition was seldom expressed in formal divisions, although it continued to boil within the party itself.

The Constitution of the National Labour Party provides that 'Any candidate who, after election, fails to accept or act in harmony with the Standing Orders of the Parliamentary Party shall be considered to have violated the terms of this Constitution'.[1] When the Labour Party came to power in 1945 the Standing Orders themselves were quite strict. Members were obligated 'not to vote for any Motion, Amendment or Prayer contrary to the decision of the Party Meeting'.[2] No member could table a motion, amendment or prayer 'without the authorization of the officers of the parliamentary party'.[3] The only loophole left the members was the stipulation that 'on certain matters, for example religion and temperance, Members may have good grounds for conscientious scruples, and in such cases they may abstain from voting'.[4] These Standing Orders had been developed much earlier as means of restraining the I.L.P. By 1945 the I.L.P. no longer constituted a problem and the Labour majority in the Commons was great enough to allow some relaxation in the disciplinary rules of the party. In consequence the Standing Orders were suspended in 1946.

Until 1952 the Standing Orders continued to be suspended by party action at the beginning of each session of the Parliament. Nevertheless, the party had become concerned with disciplinary questions following the election of 1950 in which its majority was almost wiped out. A struggle for actual leadership of the party developed and, in consequence, steps were taken to restore the authority of the Standing Orders. They were, however, modified. The conscience clause, previously restricted by implication, if not explicitly, to matters of religion and temperance was specifically extended to include any matter 'of deeply held personal conscientious conviction'. The only other change of significance seems to empower the parliamentary committee 'to bring before the party meeting persistent

[1] Clause ix, section 8.
[2] *Standing Orders* of the Parliamentary Labour Party (as revised in the session, 1945–6), Standing Order 1.
[3] *Loc. cit.*   [4] *Ibid.*, Standing Order 3.

144

breaches of party discipline outside Parliament'.[1] It is not clear, however, as to whether this was intended.

Even when a strict body of rules exists it does not necessarily follow that it will always be enforced. Some opposition seems to be tolerated when the government has a substantial majority, but this tolerance may rather rapidly be dissipated when the majority is reduced. Actually the Labour Prime Minister starts off with a rather substantial advantage. In the first place there are approximately seventy Ministers in the House. He may expect that each of them will always vote with the government. Furthermore, the professional trade unionists can also be depended upon to vote with the leadership in most circumstances. 'To these M.P.'s loyalty is the central principle of their political lives; most of them grew up in the tradition of industrial unity and discipline, of solidarity as the essential price of survival.'[2] Ministers, even those of second- or third-rate importance, are expected to vote with the government on all issues. In 1949, five parliamentary secretaries voted against the government on the amendments to the bill defining the relations of Great Britain to the Irish Republic. 'The Prime Minister wrote to the Ministers concerned, and dismissals of the errant five followed immediately.'[3]

In 1948–9 two important expulsions took place in the Labour Party. The procedure followed in carrying out an expulsion is rather involved and requires first an action by the National Executive Committee, and later action upholding the Executive, if it is challenged, by the party conference. Two persons, both members of the Parliamentary Party, were subjected to such action. They were Konni Zilliacus and John Platts-Mills.

Zilliacus had been one of the original opponents of the Labour Party's foreign policy. He continued to oppose that policy both within and without the Parliament after many others had ceased their objections. Zilliacus's actions constituted a clear violation of the Standing Orders of the Parliamentary Party, and hence of the Constitution of the National Party.[4] He had been elected originally from the Gateshead (East) Constituency Labour Party and in December 1948 that

---

[1] Ivor Bulmer Thomas, *The Party System in Great Britain* (London, Phoenix House, 1953), p. 127.

[2] Burns, *op. cit.*, p. 866. See also Attlee's comment, *op. cit.*, pp. 61–2.

[3] Burns, *op. cit.*, p. 869.   [4] Clause ix, section 8.

Party proposed to re-adopt him as its candidate for the next election. In January of 1949 the Elections Sub-committee of the National Executive called him to account for his actions. It should be remembered that the Prime Minister is an *ex officio* member of the National Executive, and his attitude must have affected the action of the sub-committee. The Elections Sub-committee is reported, however, to have been prepared to endorse him, but in the interim period the National Executive reached the decision that he should not be stamped as the party candidate.[1] The Gateshead Party was so informed, but continued with its effort to adopt Zilliacus. As it happened, Zilliacus himself brought the issue to a head by attending a Peace Conference in Paris which was purportedly Communist-dominated. As a consequence the National Executive voted to expel him, and the Gateshead Party was informed of their decision. The issue was eventually taken to the annual party conference, and although Zilliacus was not allowed to speak, his defence was conducted by the head of the Gateshead Party. Nevertheless, the conference voted to uphold the action of the Executive. Zilliacus ran as an independent in the ensuing election, but he was defeated.[2] The regular Labour candidate won the election.

The expulsion of Platts-Mills followed the same pattern. He had been responsible for sending a telegram over the signatures of 37 Labour M.P.'s to Nenni, the leader of the Left Socialist Group in Italy, wishing him luck in the coming Italian elections. Nenni's party was allied with the Communist Party. Platts-Mills refused to withdraw from his position, and after a meeting with a sub-committee of the National Executive, his expulsion was recommended. In consequence the Whip was withdrawn from him. The Party Conference in 1948 also endorsed the action of the Executive. The other signatories gave personal guarantees that they would not act against party policy again.[3]

A rather interesting development also took place in Platts-Mills' home constituency. His local party accepted the expulsion, but twenty-four of the members signed a statement in which they expressed their sympathy for Platts-Mills. Sixteen of them eventually retracted their statement, but the remaining eight were expelled from the party. Platts-Mills, like Zilliacus,

[1] Burns, *op. cit.*, p. 868.   [2] *Loc. cit.*,   [3] Burns, *op. cit.*, p. 868.

fought the election as an independent candidate, but was defeated by the Labour Party candidate.[1]

These examples indicate that in exceptional circumstances the rigid disciplinary rules of the Labour Party will be applied to dissident individuals. It is not known how large a role Attlee played in the actions taken, but it is obvious that it must have been one of importance in action of such import. The Prime Minister does have a real weapon at hand with which to control his followers. Even in the case of the members who voted against the amendments to the Irish bill, 'they were warned that if they defied the Government again, they would be reported to the N.E.C'.[2] The power of expulsion is, of course, only of use in dealing with small numbers. There is no effective way to deal with large numbers of internal opponents.

Both of the major British parties, as well as the Liberal Party, follow the practice of holding annual conferences. The method of composition and the powers of the annual conference, however, are quite different.

The Conservative Conference allows equal representation to all organizations. The Labour Conference, on the other hand, allows one voting card, worth one thousand votes, for every one thousand persons or fraction thereof, represented by the delegate. The effect of this rule is to give the trade union representatives a substantial majority in all party conferences. Since the trade union representatives are normally more conservative than the representatives of constituency parties or professional associations this tends to cause the acceptance of a more moderate programme than might otherwise be expected.

There is a more basic difference in the two conferences, however. The conference of the Conservative Party is primarily a meeting place for discussion, speeches, and personal relations. It has no final power. The leader of the party is the man who makes policy as the issue arises. The conference has no direct authority over him. He needs to concern himself with the attitudes expressed by the various members as possible expressions of undercurrents in the party, but there is no formal obligation imposed upon him by the conference. It does not determine the party's programme.

The Labour Party conference, on the other hand, is the

---

[1] *Ibid.*, p. 869.   [2] *Loc. cit.*

highest authority in the party. The Constitution of 1947 provides that 'The work of the Party shall be under the direction and control of the Party Conference which shall itself be subject to the Constitution and Standing Orders of the Party'.[1] The Party Conference, however, may amend the Constitution at any time.[2] The Labour Party Conference is then the highest legal authority in the party. Given such formal status it is likely to be a greater problem to the Parliamentary Labour Party's leader and his colleagues than the Conservative Conference is to the Conservative Party leader.

The Conservative Party leader cannot disregard his conference, and he is always present at the meeting. His speeches are in fact the high point of the conference. The Labour Party leader, however, almost has to be there to maintain his position. If he can retain the support of the conference there is little likelihood that his leadership will be challenged from any other source.

'MacDonald . . . always recognized the supreme importance of attending the Annual Conference of the Labour Party. In the first place, it was the annual and essential confirmation of his leadership. If he retained the support of the Annual Conference, his security in office was assured. Moreover, whoever can win over the support of the Conference can control the Party itself. MacDonald owed a great deal of his standing and prestige in the Labour Party to the uncanny skill with which, year after year, he handled these great gatherings.'[3]

In only one instance was MacDonald subjected to serious challenge at a party conference. This took place in 1930 when he was sharply criticized for the handling of the unemployment problem by Maxton and Sir Oswald Mosley, then a left-wing Labourite. In addition there existed some disillusionment among the rank and file about the inability of the government to proceed with socialist measures. Even in this instance, however, he handled the difficulty with some ease, although his critics 'complained that he . . . made a purely emotional appeal'.[4]

More significant events took place in 1935 when George Lansbury, then the leader of the Parliamentary Labour Party, tried to defend his anti-war position at the conference. He was

[1] Clause vi, section 1.
[2] Clause xiii.
[3] Weir, *op. cit.*, p. 232.
[4] *Ibid.*, pp. 233–45.

defeated, in part as a consequence of the vehemently critical speech made by Ernest Bevin.[1] Lansbury resigned as Parliamentary leader in consequence of the repudiation of his position by the Party Conference. This is the only instance of its kind, but it is significant as an example of the influence which the conference can exercise, even upon the party's leader in the House of Commons. Even so, the action is not likely to be repeated with any frequency. Lansbury's position was an unpopular one in the first place. Further, although he was greatly loved, he does not seem to have been thought of as a permanent leader.

Generally speaking, the Labour Party leader can always expect to face more criticism at the party conference than the Conservative leader. Since the latter deals with a body which has no formal authority over him, he is subjected only to the influence which the expression of divergent principles may exercise. The Labour leader deals with a body, which by adopting different principles, may undermine his position. It does not do so, except in the most unusual circumstances, but as long as it does have the power to do so, it inevitably affects his relations with that body. Some opposition is always expressed at Labour conferences, and it must be dealt with, although it is usually not difficult. In the last resort, however, as Professor Finer has pointed out, Labour Party conferences, like Conservative conferences, 'are demonstrations rather than organizations to think out policy, in spite of the fact that sometimes party conferences achieve success in this sphere, and that their temper may persuade the leaders of the urgency of change'.[2]

As K. B. Smellie has said, 'On the nature and source of party funds the biographies of statesmen are usually discreet'.[3] The word 'discreet' puts it very mildly. In actual fact, there is seldom any mention of the method by which funds are raised or the role which is played by the party leader in the collection of such money. Asquith said, 'As leader, I have never had anything to do with party funds, either with its collection or its

---

[1] Williams, *op. cit.*, p. 352; Strauss, *op. cit.*, p. 228.
[2] Herman Finer, *The Theory and Practice of Modern Government* (New York, Henry Holt, 1949), p. 284.
[3] K. B. Smellie, *op. cit.*, p. 198.

expenditure. In that respect I have followed the example of my predecessor, Sir Henry Campbell-Bannerman.'[1]

Actually there is a basic difference between the Labour Party and the Conservative Party in so far as the collection of finances is concerned. The Labour Party obtains most of its funds by formal procedures, which are applied in all cases. In consequence the party leader has little need to concern himself with such matters. The principal sources of funds are the affiliation fees to the National Party, and the political funds of the trade unions. In both cases the contributions are in pennies, but the number of contributions swells the coffers. The political fund of the trade unions has gone through several stages. Until 1927 trade union members were obliged to contribute to the fund unless they specifically 'contracted-out'. Since such action was not likely to increase the popularity of a worker with the local trade union officers the result was a rather high proportion of contributions. In 1927, approximately three-fourths of the members of trade unions made contributions. The Trades Disputes and Trade Union Act of 1927, however, provided that funds could not be collected from an individual unless he specifically 'contracted-in'.[2] One year later Ramsay MacDonald said, 'It is more difficult for the Labour Party now to get £1 to enable it to fight its election battle than it was two years ago to get £10'.[3] This was an exaggeration, but it is true that the change in the law created a serious financial problem to the party. 'During the first four years of the Act's operation, 1928 to 1932, an average of only fifty-nine per cent of members in "registered" Unions "contracted-in". By 1935 the percentage had dropped to fifty-six.'[4] It is not surprising that one of the first pieces of legislation passed by the Labour Party after 1945 was the repeal of the Act of 1927.

The Conservative Party also has affiliation fees, but they do not provide any significant portion of the political funds available to the party. The Conservatives find it necessary to rely upon large contributions from private individuals. Precisely how much is contributed by various individuals, and what relative proportion of the total of the party's funds is received

[1] James K. Pollock, *Money and Politics Abroad* (New York, Knopf, 1932), p. 30.
[2] McHenry, *op. cit.*, p. 49.   [3] *The Times*, 27 February 1928, p. 16.
[4] McHenry, *op. cit.*, pp. 49–50.

from such individuals it is not possible to say. The parties in Great Britain are not compelled to divulge the source of their funds.[1] The same may also be said of the Liberal Party, although it is obvious that not many persons are likely to make large contributions to that party today. Prior to 1914 it was, of course, the recipient of large sums. At the conclusion of the war Lloyd George himself had substantial sums which he eventually used for the party.

Actually, the Prime Minister's place in this picture is a peculiar one. With the development of the large federations the Prime Minister was not supposed to know anything specific about the funds. The money matters were entirely in the hands of the Chief Whip prior to the First World War and the Party Chairman in the after years.[2] It is rather difficult to believe that the party leader does not know what is going on, but it may be true that the British public traditions operate to keep him in ignorance of such matters. One must never under-estimate the influence of the traditions of British politics.[3]

The problem of funds has an inevitable effect upon the selection of candidates for office. Labour critics have frequently pointed out that the Conservative Party does not necessarily choose its best men as candidates. Instead, they argue, that it chooses those who are personally able to finance their own campaigns. There is unquestionably a great deal of merit in this criticism. Stanley Baldwin himself expressed the same criticism of his party in the mid-twenties.[4]

'An old tradition—and a very bad tradition it was today— still prevailed in too many parts of the country. It was that the first thing a constituency had to do was to look for a member who could carry the association on his back and who would subscribe to everything in the division; and when they had got that, they did not much mind what else they had got.'

It is not surprising that this should seem a bad thing to the party leader, for the quality of the party's representatation in the Parliament is one of the bases on which the public judges it. Baldwin was not the only Conservative to express his opposition

---

[1] The Labour Party does publicize its sources of funds, but it is not required to do so.

[2] J. A. Spender, *The Life of Sir Henry Campbell-Bannerman* (Boston, Houghton Mifflin, 1924), i, 216.

[3] Pollock, *op. cit.*, p. 116.   [4] *Ibid.*, pp. 28–9.

to this situation. Miss Vera Churchill, of the Poulton Women Conservatives, also asked the question, 'How can wealth and political ability go hand-in-hand?' This method of selecting candidates may help to explain the ease with which the Conservative Party leader is able to dominate his party.

The Labour Party is restricted in its choice of candidates by a somewhat comparable situation. The candidate is not expected to supply his campaign funds nor to make additional heavy contributions to the party. But no parliamentary candidate is endorsed by the National Executive unless his campaign costs have been guaranteed by some affiliated organization.[1] This is important for one reason. Whatever be the attitude of the party leader about the desirability of one candidate as against another, the individual who is endorsed by the trade unions in a locality is the most likely candidate. This follows for the trade unions are wealthier, and hence better able to guarantee such expenses than any other organization. At its worst this situation results in the House of Commons serving as a place of retirement for old trade unionists.[2] The party leader may look upon this with some favour, however, if it is remembered that the trade unionists are more likely to follow the leader without question than younger men chosen from the ranks of the constituency parties proper. On the other hand, it does cut into the number of able men who might be able to serve the party advantageously in the Parliament. The zealous young men and the intellectuals, as distinguished from the trade union functionaries who run from safe constituencies, are usually forced to fight difficult seats. Only a landslide victory, as in 1945, is likely to bring them into the House in large numbers.[3]

One method of collecting party funds has been a frequent subject of controversy. This is by sale of honours.[4] A peerage, a baronetcy, or a knighthood, all bring public prestige. It is, therefore, possible to add to the party coffers by granting such

[1] *Constitution of 1947*, clause ix, section 4.

[2] W. I. Jennings, *Parliament* (Cambridge, Cambridge University Press, 1939), p. 49.

[3] Nicholas, *op. cit.*, pp. 61–2. In 1945, 125 out of 140 trade union sponsored candidates were elected. In 1950, 111 out of 140 were successful. In 1951 out of 137 candidates sponsored by the trade unions, 103 were successful.

[4] This is examined at more length in Chapter VI.

honours in return for substantial contributions to the party. In some cases it has even been reported that definite prices were established for particular grants.[1]

The Prime Minister unquestionably plays a role of considerable importance in this area. It is he who makes the final recommendations for honours to the King. As Lord Newton said, 'Who confers these honours? The tout does not. He is not in a position to give them. These honours are distributed by the Government, by means of its Patronage Secretaries, and Party Managers, and finally, the Prime Minister.'[2] The Prime Minister probably does not ask which honours are being granted for contributions to the party, but he must know that some individuals are on the list for that reason, whatever other arguments may be raised in their behalf.

It is true that since the report of the Royal Commission on Honours in 1922 such action is not supposed to take place. On the other hand, it is difficult to believe that it does not in fact. In all probability no Prime Minister since that time has ever used the Honours List as Lloyd George did, as simply a means of extending campaign funds, but there is little reason to believe that such sales have completely disappeared. Great care is taken not to raise the matter in public, nor to discuss the relationship between honours and funds, but it is evident that the relationship still exists. An American student of party financing in Great Britain expressed his opinion of the public statements made about the grants of honours as follows:[3]

'There is a frightful amount of blithering rot in most of the public discussions about the granting of honours. One cannot avoid wondering how so many can speak about this question and its implications without throwing more light upon the realities of politics. The fact of the matter is that the relation between party funds and the granting of honours is so intimate that every informed politician is most anxious to avoid being forced to say anything definite. Let the matter drag along, let there be an abundance of pious talk and moralizing, but be sure to avoid any action which will alter the present convenient system! This just about sums up the attitude of realistic party managers.'

.   .   .

[1] 26 *H.L. Deb*, 5s., 837; 51 *H.L. Deb*, 5s., 509.
[2] 61 *H.L. Deb*. 5s., 823.   [3] Pollock, *op. cit.*, p. 59.

The Labour Party's Parliamentary leader exercises his influence upon the determination of party policy through the National Executive in most instances. This does not mean that he necessarily occupies a position of mere equality with the other members of that body. His predominant public position is likely to give him an influence far greater than that of any other member. In fact, although the official policy statements of the party come from either the National Executive or the Party Conference, it is obvious that the party leader has a great deal to do with the formulation of the issues. He does not, however, have absolute control, and it is possible that the programme contains some items which he does not greatly favour.

At the same time since he is the chief spokesman of the party before the public he has an opportunity to emphasize some issues as against others. Even though the programme may contain items which he does not like, he does not need to emphasize those attributes in his public statements. Since the programmes of the Labour Party are usually rather extensive in content, he has a considerable latitude in his choice of emphasis. It is true, however, that he is not able to issue direct statements of the issues upon his own responsibility, except as they follow the official position. His influence must be felt either through the national organization, or through the exercise of discrimination in the selection of topics for his talks. One does not find any instance in which the election address of the party leader conflicts with the general statement made by the National Party. It is true, of course, that when he is Prime Minister the fact that he is in a position to control the use of dissolution enables him to select the issue, or issues, which he wishes to take to the public. The National Party Organization, as well as many members of the Cabinet, did not wish to fight an election on the Soviet trade agreement in 1924. MacDonald, however, thought it might make an effective campaign issue. Furthermore, he seemed to think that the Campbell case, which was the immediate cause of his defeat in the Commons, would not greatly affect the election outcome. The remainder of the party was stuck with the situation into which MacDonald had led them. The result was a serious electoral defeat.[1]

The Conservative Party leader is in a more effective position to determine the policy of his party. The party conference has

[1] Weir, *op. cit.*, p. 187.

no formal authority over him. The central organizations of the party are directly under his control. The Conservative position seems to be that it is not desirable to draw up a rigid programme ahead of time, but that the party leader should be allowed to deal with problems as they arise. The party leader's statements bind the party as a whole, even in those instances in which it has not been consulted, nor even received prior information as to the content of the statements. Thus, in the election of 1924, Stanley Baldwin expressed the view that it was desirable to extend the suffrage to women on an equal basis.[1] The party had not been consulted on the issue, and later events were to show that many important members were opposed to the reform.[2] Nevertheless, Baldwin's action was held to bind the entire party and the reform was passed in 1928. It should be remembered that it is even difficult for the party adequately to express its dissatisfaction later, for the party leader has control of the party organization.

The existence of opposition was evident, but it had no way to make itself felt effectively. Sir Martin Conway, a party member, felt that Baldwin had frequently led the party into courses it did not like, and protested in the following terms:[3]

'We have been led by him into the wilderness. When he was Prime Minister he imposed upon us measures which we disliked; we only passed them because of the unswerving Party loyalty which is traditional among Tories. . . .

'Mr. Baldwin and the ex-Ministers and others in his immediate entourage have never made any serious attempt to keep in touch with the mass of their followers. We have been treated like sheep, and led or driven according to the whims of our shepherds.'

A challenge to Baldwin's leadership did take place in 1930, but the fact that no other party leader would allow his name to be presented in opposition to Baldwin doomed the challenge

[1] The existing statute allowed women twenty-eight or over the vote. Men were allowed to vote at the age of twenty-one.

[2] Beckhoffer Roberts, *Stanley Baldwin: Man or Miracle?* (New York, Greenburg, 1937), pp. 164–5. Actually Baldwin had not made a direct pledge that the government would lower the voting age for women. He had proposed that the 'matter be referred to a conference of all political parties'. But he had said, 'The Unionist Party are in favour of equal political rights for men and women. . . .'

[3] *Ibid.*, pp. 195–6.

to failure. This was to be expected for should Baldwin be returned that individual's career would be endangered. No one else was put up for nomination. Sir Robert Horne, whom some had thought of as an alternative, spoke in defence of Baldwin.[1] The very meeting at which his leadership was challenged voted to give him a 'free hand' in fiscal matters and only one vote was cast against that proposal.[2]

Winston Churchill in the electoral campaign of 1950 set out upon a line which was almost directly antithetical to the statement of the objectives of the party to be found in either 'The Industrial Charter', or 'Let Us Face the Future'. 'The Industrial Charter', which had been accepted by the party conference in 1947, was a left-wing Tory statement. 'Let Us Face the Future', the official party manifesto, which had Churchill's approval, reflected the same position.

Churchill, however, spoke about the necessity of free enterprise and the undesirability of controls. This conflicted sharply with the other statements which had not only recognized the necessity of controls, but had accepted the nationalization of coal, the bank, etc. Basically, 'Let Us Face the Future' was not drastically different from the Labour Party's statements. But Churchill's speeches were quite different. Whether his statements affected the outcome of the election either favourably or adversely, it is difficult to say.[3] In this instance other Conservative candidates could take their choice of two irreconcilable alternatives, both of which had received Churchill's approval.

The Prime Minister may, of course, always rise on the floor of the House of Commons to accept an amendment which may bind his party to its displeasure. Sir Henry Campbell-Bannerman twice did so in connection with legislation, once in the face of rather strenuous opposition from some members of his Cabinet.[4] Ramsay MacDonald's insistence upon treating even the Liberal amendment to the Conservative motion of censure as the equivalent of a no-confidence vote, forced his party to face an election, which was opposed by the majority of his colleagues.[5] Asquith said that 'he had never known a case

---

[1] *Ibid.*, pp. 198–9. [2] *Ibid.*, p. 197. The one vote was Lord Beaverbrook's.
[3] Nicholas, *op. cit.*, pp. 96–7.
[4] J. A. Spender, *The Life of Sir Henry Campbell-Bannerman* (Boston, Houghton, Mifflin, 1924), ii, 278, 280.   [5] Snowden, *op. cit.*, ii, ch. lii.

where the Government had so wantonly and unnecessarily committed suicide'.[1] Snowden himself described it as 'one of the most ill-considered and tactless decisions in Parliamentary history'.[2] As the party leader and Prime Minister, MacDonald was in a position to enforce his views, and the only method of controlling him would have been to try to remove him as leader. The latter procedure was impossible as it would have split the party, and dimmed its electoral prospects. Divided parties do not win elections as the Unionists discovered in 1905, the Liberals after 1918, and Labour in 1931. The latter instance was somewhat different, but it is probable that Mac-Donald's action in breaking with the party created some internal tensions which made fighting the election a more difficult task. A sense of bewilderment might be expected among the rank and file in such circumstances.

Any party leader must recognize that some pressure and interest groups must be treated with care. This follows not only because they are potential voters, but because some groups of this sort are rather definitely aligned with one party. The trade unions, for example, must be treated with some circumspection by a Labour Prime Minister for they provide the broad basis of the party's strength. Similarly, it is to be expected that a Conservative Premier will consider the interests of the National Farmers' Union. That group nearly always aligns itself with the Conservatives and it delivers a substantial bloc of votes. As a consequence it must receive special consideration.

In fact, whatever the Conservative leader may think of agricultural policy, he is almost forced to take his farm policy from the Farmers' Union. On occasion the Union has gone so far as to threaten to put its own candidates in the field when the programme of the party was not to its liking. This is an impossible position for the Conservative leader. He will realize that should it run separate candidates, the Labour Party might cut into the vote of rural areas and pick up seats that would otherwise be Conservative. The consequence is that the Conservative leader usually accepts a farm policy like that of the Farmers' Union, although it might differ on incidentals.[3]

[1] *Ibid.*, ii, 697.   [2] *Ibid.*, ii, 690.
[3] W. I. Jennings, *The British Constitution* (Cambridge, Cambridge University Press, 1944), p. 46.

The Federation of British Industries is another interest group which normally operates within the ambit of the Conservative Party. Today, it is probable that the Conservative leader can afford to disregard some of its desires, for the only alternative party left is the Labour Party. Since the objectives of the F.B.I. are obviously quite different from those of the Labour Party it is left with little hope outside the Conservative Party. In the earlier days when the Liberals and Conservatives competed for power, the industrialists were able to exercise some discrimination between the two. Today, the party leader needs to consider their interests, for party funds may be derived from them, but the absence of a possible alternative party strengthens him in dealing with them.

To some extent the Labour Prime Minister is in a comparable position in dealing with the trade unions. The trade unions have attached themselves quite closely to the party, and there is not much possibility that they will align themselves with the Conservatives. This is not to say that all trade unions and their officials support Labour; they do not. If they did, Labour would win all of the elections. The influence of the trade unions, however, may make itself felt at the annual conferences, at which they hold predominant power. The Prime Minister is not likely to take action which will antagonize the trade unions for it might result in a reaction against him at the annual conference. It would be difficult for him to remain the party leader if his views were repudiated at the conference.

Actually every Labour Government has had difficulties with the trade unions. The first Labour Government was troubled by strikes, some of them serious. A railway strike took place within a week of MacDonald's accession to office. This was followed by a strike of dock workers. As soon as that was ended there was a strike in the transport services in London.[1] This must inevitably place a Labour Government in an embarrassing position. If the party leader and his colleagues determine to take action to halt the strike, they will antagonize the trade unions. If they do not try to protect the public from the effects of an incident like the dock strike,[2] they will be accused of offering special privileges and protections to the trade

[1] Snowden, *op. cit.*, ii, 633–5.

[2] MacDonald said that meat prices and other prices had risen by as much as fifty per cent during the dock strike. *Ibid.*, p. 634.

unions. The same sort of problem frequently plagued the Attlee government. Strikes which disrupted transport and food distribution even led to the use of troops to carry out the necessary public services. Such a decision must be a hard one for a Labour Prime Minister to make, for to antagonize all trade unionists is to endanger himself. Attlee was successful in maintaining his position, however, even in the face of demands by the T.U.C. for an increase in wages.

The most significant example of trade union pressure took place in the crisis of 1931. The Prime Minister and the Chancellor of the Exchequer were convinced that substantial economies in governmental expenditures were absolutely required. Among the proposed economies was a cut in the unemployment compensation provided for industrial workers. Inevitably, this was adversely received by the leaders of the T.U.C. Snowden, the Chancellor of the Exchequer, met the General Council of the T.U.C. on the 20th August 1931. The National Party Executive Committee and the Consultative Committee of the Parliamentary Party were also present.[1] At the time the Prime Minister and Chancellor had not definitely arrived at the conclusion that a reduction in unemployment benefits was necessary, and it was known that substantial numbers of the Cabinet were not prepared to accept such cuts. Later the same day, the representatives of the T.U.C. made the fall of the government inevitable. The Liberals had already made it known that they would withdraw their support unless substantial economies were made. Yet a Labour Government cut off from trade union support was almost impossible to visualize. MacDonald and Snowden, as a result of their belief in the necessity of the reductions, went into the National Government. The majority of the Labour Cabinet supported the position taken by the trade unions and went into opposition. MacDonald's experience indicates that no man can retain the leadership of the Parliamentary Labour Party who has deeply antagonized the trade unions. [2]

---

[1] *Ibid.*, ii, 940–1. Snowden says, 'I had never recognized the right of the Trade Union Congress Committee to be consulted on matters of Cabinet policy. I went to this meeting, however, because, in addition to the Trade Union Congress Committee, there were present representatives of the Labour Party Executive and of the Parliamentary Labour Party.'

[2] *Ibid.*, ii, 940–2. Cf. Feiling, *op. cit.*, pp. 189–93; Brockway, *op. cit.*, p. 292.

Actually, some difficulties between the government and the trade unions, regardless of who heads the government, must be expected. As Clement Attlee has said:[1]

'It is . . . inevitable that there should from time to time be misunderstandings between the industrial and political sides of the movement. The Trade Union leaders do not always understand the exigencies of political warfare, but equally there is sometimes a lack of understanding on the part of Parliamentarians of the necessary conditions of Trade Union action. They are apt to consider that Trade Union leaders have more power than is actually the case. For instance, when the first Labour Government was in office there were a number of industrial disputes which embarrassed it. There were those among the political leaders of Labour who seemed to think that by a word the Trade Union leaders could have stopped industrial action. They were quite wrong. The Trade Union leader, like the political leader, has only a certain amount of power. He derives it from his supporters, and he cannot flout their wishes.'

One recurring area of conflict between politicians and trade union representatives has turned around the question of worker representation in the management of nationalized industries. The trade union position, which was for some time the official position of the party, emphasized such participation.[2] The superior influence of the party leader and his colleagues is indicated, however, by the fact that the industries nationalized since 1945 do not provide for such representation.[3] The exponents of 'efficiency' have won out. There was grumbling from the trade unions, but Attlee was able to ride out such criticisms. Actually it is doubtful that the desire for participation in management ever went very deep into the rank and file members of the unions.

There are, of course, some institutional procedures for settling difficulties between the Prime Minister and the trade unions. First, is the fact that the trade unions have substantial representation on the National Executive of which the Prime

[1] Attlee, *op. cit.*, pp. 64–5.

[2] Cf. R. Dahl, 'Workers' Control of Industry and the British Labour Party', *American Political Science Review*, xli (October 1947), 875–900.

[3] Cf. D. N. Chester, *The Nationalised Industries, A Statutory Analysis* (London, Published for the Institute of Public Administration by Allen and Unwin, 1948).

Minister is an *ex officio* member. They can, therefore, in the meetings of that body press their case directly upon the Prime Minister. Additionally, as has been pointed out, minor issues affecting the trade unions may be dealt with by direct contact with the trade union M.P.'s in the Parliament who have an informal organization which may be approached. Furthermore, it is also possible to deal directly with the leaders of the T.U.C. as in 1931.

In addition to these techniques the complexity of the National Labour Party's organization made the addition of a co-ordinating body necessary. This body is the National Council of Labour. It has twenty-one members of whom seven are selected by the T.U.C., three from the National Executive, four from the Parliamentary Party, and seven others from the Co-operative Union. This body has no directing authority but its monthly meetings allow an interchange of opinion which keeps the other groups informed of the problems which exist.[1] Thus the Prime Minister and his parliamentary colleagues are kept in touch with the grass roots on which their parliamentary strength, in the last resort, is based.

The party leader in Great Britain occupies a position of great power. It is unlikely that he will have to face serious challenge to his position or authority if he acts with circumspection. He has obligations to the rank and file as well as to the other leaders of the party. Sometimes this forces him to perform tasks which he does not like. Bonar Law complained that he had to speak on many occasions when he had no desire to do so.[2] This type of responsibility cannot be escaped. The party leader has to be prepared to speak on any important topic. He has great powers of leadership, but he may not distort the party's principles and retain his party. He may, temporarily, subvert his party, but in so doing he subverts himself. Lloyd George recognized this and hoped to create a new party, after he had destroyed the Liberal Party as an effective political force.[3] There are reciprocal obligations upon both the leader and his followers. The rank and file are expected to follow and support, but only if the leader serves the interest of the party.

[1] Attlee, *op. cit.*, p. 65.
[2] Lord Oxford and Asquith, *Memories and Reflections* (Boston, Little, Brown and Company, 1928), i, 239–40.
[3] Riddell, *op. cit.*, p. 395.

The party leader's position in election campaigns is one of considerable magnitude. Since the elections are now, to a considerable extent, plebiscites in which a Prime Minister and a government are chosen, his personality affects the electoral outcome. If he is popular the public may throw their weight behind the party, although they may not be entirely satisfied with its principles or actions. In the springtime of 1951 only thirty-one per cent of the persons sampled by the Gallup Poll were satisfied with the government. At the same, forty-four per cent approved of Attlee as Prime Minister.[1] This situation must have inevitably affected Attlee's position *vis-a-vis* the rest of the party, including other Cabinet ministers, to his advantage. In some circumstances, as with the Conservatives in 1945, all the party has is the person of its leader, and its entire hopes must be gathered together into the public appeal of that individual.

Both of the party leaders always campaign widely in efforts to influence the voters in general elections.[2] When by-elections are held they send letters in support of the local party candidate. Should such a letter be withheld by the party leader, the local candidate will face extreme difficulty, for the failure to receive a letter of support indicates that the candidate does not have the support of the party.[3] Some individuals, of course, cannot be opposed by the party leader whatever he may think of them. Stanley Baldwin might have felt unhappy at the attitude expressed by Winston Churchill in the House of Commons between 1931 and 1935, but intervention would certainly have been ineffective in this case. It is not possible to repudiate a man who is a major public figure in his own right, even though he may be a party rebel.

The national tours, and the national election addresses tend to emphasize the personality of the party leader over that of the local candidates. The subordination of the local candidate is further accentuated by the parliamentary system itself. Since the British people cannot vote directly for a Prime Minister they must make their choice felt through their elected representatives. If they wish Attlee as Prime Minister they vote

---

[1] Louisville *Courier Journal*, 23 March 1951.   [2] *Ante*, ch. iv.

[3] In the campaign of 1945 nearly all of the election addresses of Conservative candidates contained endorsements from Churchill. However, in 1950, only one-eighth of the addresses quoted from his letter of endorsement. Nicholas, *op. cir.*, p. 215.

Labour. The local candidate knows that he is being chosen, not for his own personal abilities, but in order that Attlee may become the Prime Minister. Only in exceptional cases does the personality of the local candidate play an important role in the election. Normally he is only the representative of a particular party and a particular party leader. The choice of the electorate is made in favour of the latter. The increasing tendency to reject independent candidates, as revealed in the election of 1950, emphasizes this situation.[1]

The development of the radio also provides another instrument which serves to elevate the power of the party leader. He, and his major colleagues, now makes national appeals. He is able to enter the home of every British citizen who is interested in hearing him speak. He is no longer limited to access through the newspapers or tours alone. The consequence of this is that inevitably the person of the local candidate carries even less weight. The direct appeal by the party leader further removes the elements of localism from the elections. The ardent party workers in a particular locality might conceivably be highly embarrassed with their local candidate, but the floating vote, the vote which determines an election, will pay attention to the party leader. They must, for is he not a possible Prime Minister?

The British central organizations maintain tight and direct controls over the local parties. Inevitably, the party leader as the principal spokesman of the party, is left in a position of pre-eminence in dealing with the rank and file. As has been indicated this is perhaps less true of a Labour Party leader than of a Conservative leader. But even in the case of the Labour Party leader the effective limiting forces upon him are located in the central organizations of the affiliated groups. Other leaders may force him to modify his position, and his actions, but the ordinary party member is able to touch him effectively only through the officers of his organization. The British party leader is thus in a position in which he heads a disciplined organization, and in which his own personal power is substantial. He need not worry about the divisions and particu-

---

[1] Cf. *Ibid.*, pp. 251–63, for an examination of what happened to the independents in the election of 1950. For similar information with respect to the 1951 election see D. E. Butler, *The British General Election of 1951* (London, Macmillan, 1952), pp. 240–1.

larisms which plague the American party system and which weaken the authority of the President.[1] The party leader in Great Britain can always depend upon his party following him if he acts reasonably. Only if he flouts a powerful affiliated group is he likely to lose his position. His position enables him to exercise an authority as great as a reasonable man might desire. If he tries to exceed that limit he has only himself to blame.

[1] The titular leader of the opposition party in the United States quite frequently has no authority at all. Since he is usually the defeated presidential candidate, and since he is seldom in the Congress, he faces great difficulties in asserting himself. Sometimes, by virtue of holding a major governorship, he has limited opportunities for influencing his party's public policies. It is notable, however, that while Thomas E. Dewey remained Governor of New York it was Senator Taft who was rightfully known as Mr. Republican. At the present time Adlai Stevenson faces an even more difficult task as he holds no elective office. He has, however, been somewhat successful in focusing public attention and party attention upon his pronouncements.

V

The Prime Minister and the Formation of a Government

T he formation of a government is one of the most crucial and difficult tasks to face a Prime Minister. Upon taking office he is faced with the necessity of filling a large number of ministerial positions in order to carry on the operations of the government. There are approximately thirty-five ministerial positions, but this does not complete the offices to be filled. There are also approximately forty other positions as undersecretaries or whips for which appointments must be made.[1] Such offices are of vital importance to the Prime Minister and of similar interest to the prospective office holders themselves. It is the ambition of a majority of the members of the Parliament to be selected for such a position, for an appointment constitutes recognition of the political and personal worth of the individual selected. It brings with it not only responsibility but also social prestige. In making his selections the Prime Minister has one central objective, that being to create as strong a government as he can, for the stronger the internal composition

[1] Herman Finer, *The Theory and Practice of Modern Government* (New York, Henry Holt, Rev. Ed., 1949), p. 583. It is not possible precisely to determine the degree of control exercised by the Prime Minister over the appointment of subordinate officers. It is likely that a strong minister will insist upon making his own selections for appointments to subordinate positions within his ministry. It may be noted that Herbert Gladstone once spoke of 'the custom' under which he had his way in the appointment of the Under-Secretary in his department. In this particular case, he desired to have Herbert Samuel in that post and the appointment was made, although the Prime Minister, Campbell-Bannerman, opposed his selection. Viscount Herbert Samuel, *Memoirs* (London, Cresset Press, 1945), p. 51.

of the government, the more parliamentary and public support upon which it may rely. Thus the strength of the government, i.e., the character of its composition, influences the stability of the government itself, and it is this strength and stability, consistent with the successful implementation of the party programme, which is the first objective of the Prime Minister.

Formally, the persons holding these positions are appointed by the King. In fact, the primary control rests in the hands of the Prime Minister who nominates individuals for formal appointment by the King.[1] In nearly every case the King will accept the recommendation made by the Prime Minister without question or serious effort at obstruction.

The King may, however, insist upon the consideration of his viewpoint with respect to such appointments if he is in disagreement with the Prime Minister. He has a right to express an opinion as to the merits of any of the proposed appointments with the objective of persuading the Prime Minister of the rectitude of his views.[2] It may be the case that the monarch believes that an individual is not fitted to hold a particular office. Lord Salisbury wrote, 'Her majesty was very anxious that Mr. Matthews should not again be Home Secretary; and I have obeyed her Majesty's wish.'[3] It is not essential that the Prime Minister should accede to the wishes of the monarch. In the same year, 1895, the Queen also objected to the appointment of Goshen and Hamilton. In particular she objected to the appointment of the former as First Lord of the Admiralty. Lord Salisbury, however, insisted upon the appointments in these cases and the Queen gave way.[4]

It is also conceivable that the monarch might have a particular individual in mind for an office. It is reported that in 1886 Victoria recommended that Sir Henry Campbell-

[1] 'Though the Prime Minister nominates, or technically, recommends, it is the King who appoints. Consequently, though a new Prime Minister may recommend that one minister be superseded by another, it is not necessary for him to recommend that an existing minister be re-appointed.' W. I. Jennings, *Cabinet Government* (Cambridge, Cambridge University Press, 1936), p. 49.

[2] Cf. Sir Sidney Lee, *King Edward VII* (New York, Macmillan, 1927), ii, 37–8.

[3] George Buckle (ed.), *Letters of Queen Victoria* (London, J. Murray, 1931), 3s., ii, 529.

[4] *Ibid.*, ii, 526–8.

Bannerman be named Secretary of State for War.[1] Similarly, in the same year, she also recommended that Lord Rosebery be appointed to the Foreign Office.[2] In both cases her advice was followed by Gladstone. In 1892 she exerted pressure on Lord Rosebery which led to his acceptance of the Foreign Office again.[3] She was less successful in gaining acceptance for her proposal that Lord Ripon be named to the War Office and Lord Northbrook to India in 1886.[4]

Such concern with appointments does not seem to have been characteristic of Victoria's successors, although it is admittedly dangerous to generalize given the absence of appropriate materials upon which to base the comment.[5] Sir Sidney Lee stated that at the time of the formation of the Liberal Government in December 1905, the King 'abstained from making any suggestion as to the distribution of the more important ministerial offices.'[6] Edward did, on one occasion, let it be known that he would object to the presence of Winston Churchill in the Cabinet while he was holding the position of Colonial Under-Secretary.[7] This action is not surprising, for while the Prime Minister has considerable discretion as to the offices which shall be included in the Cabinet, it is out of the ordinary to bring a departmental subordinate into the same body as his chief. If he is of Cabinet calibre he will ordinarily be placed at the head of a department or become a Minister without Portfolio.

In the case of disagreement as to the merits of an appointment the Prime Minister will inevitably have his way if he is determined to do so. The monarch has no alternative but to submit. If he does not the Prime Minister may threaten to

---

[1] *Ibid.*, i, 42; J. A. Spender, *The Life of the Right Hon. Sir Henry Campbell-Bannerman* (Boston, Houghton Mifflin, 1924), i, 99.

[2] *Letters of Queen Victoria*, 3s., i, 32.   [3] *Ibid.*, ii, 142.   [4] *Ibid.*, i, 32.

[5] For a more complete discussion of Victoria's concern with appointments see Jennings, *op. cit.*, pp. 49–53; Frank Hardie, *The Political Influence of Queen Victoria, 1861–1901* (London, Oxford University Press, 1935). There have been frequent reports that George VI objected to the appointment of Hugh Dalton as Foreign Secretary in 1945 and that his objection was accepted by the Prime Minister. To date there is no evidence available to determine the veracity of this story.

[6] Lee, *op. cit.*, ii, 445.

[7] J. A. Spender and Cyril Asquith, *The Life of Herbert Henry Asquith, Lord Oxford and Asquith* (London, Hutchinson and Co., 1932), i, 195.

resign and it is inconceivable that the King will not give way in such circumstances. The Prime Minister's real control of appointments is a fundamental principle of the British Constitution and has been recognized as such since the incident of the Ladies of the Bedchamber.

The Prime Minister himself is usually able to select any office which he desires. By law, he is now bound to be First Lord of the Treasury as the offices were made inseparable by an Act of Parliament in 1937.[1] He may, if he wishes, take another office as well, for there is no rule which prevents an individual from holding two or more positions at the same time. Lord Salisbury held the office of Foreign Secretary while Prime Minister in his first short administration and again from 1886 to 1892 and from 1895 to 1900. Upon relinquishing the Foreign Office in 1900 he became Lord Privy Seal. In 1914 Asquith took the War Office for a short time in order to deal with the Irish crisis. Ramsay MacDonald combined the Premiership and Foreign Office in 1924. Winston Churchill became Minister of Defence in 1940 and again in 1951. Clement Attlee similarly held the Ministry of Defence for a short time after 1945. Stanley Baldwin nominally took the office of Chancellor of the Exchequer in 1923, but he did not take over departmental supervision as his action was only a temporary expedient until McKenna had made up his mind whether he would accept the post.[2]

Such action is not always wise. The obligations which already rest upon the Prime Minister are extremely heavy. The addition of departmental labours is likely to lead to either a failure to meet his responsibilities as Premier or inadequate consideration of departmental affairs. Ramsay MacDonald discovered in 1924 that it was an overly burdensome task to try to carry out the responsibilities of the Premiership and those of Foreign Secretary at the same time. It seems fair to say that some of his responsibilities as Premier, particularly the obligation to be available for consultation, suffered in consequence. As a result of his earlier experience he did not combine the two offices in

---

[1] *Ministers of the Crown Act of 1937*, 1 Edw. 8 and 1 Geo. 6, c. 38. This is a sinecure post which carries no specific departmental responsibilities. Originally it was of importance as it provided funds for partisan purposes.

[2] Philip Viscount Snowden, *An Autobiography* (London, J. Nicholson and Watson, 1934), ii, 590.

1929 despite his strong interest in foreign affairs.[1] Lord Salisbury's control of the Foreign Office was carried through with less strain because he did not make a very serious effort to direct and supervise his Cabinet, leaving his colleagues a substantial degree of latitude as to the course of action they might follow.[2] It is also noteworthy that Lord Salisbury was not faced with the obligation of leading the House of Commons, itself an onerous task. Churchill's combination of the Premiership and the Ministry of Defence was carried through in order to concentrate and co-ordinate the military arms under the direction of the Prime Minister.[3] Since the Ministry existed only in name, detailed responsibilities did not necessarily fall upon the Prime Minister.

Asquith considered that his attempt to combine departmental duties with the Premiership was unsatisfactory.[4] Asquith even doubted the desirability of the rule that the Prime Minister should be from the House of Commons upon the grounds that the addition of this responsibility to the already heavy burdens of office was too much for one man to handle. This latter problem has been at least partially solved by the creation of a separate officer who serves as Leader of the House of Commons. Bonar Law served in this capacity under Lloyd George and later Herbert Morrison held the position in Attlee's Cabinet. This means that some of the responsibilities of this office, particularly the task of arranging debates, speakers, questions, etc., through consultation with the Leader of the Opposition are carried out by a separate officer thus relieving the Premier of some of his obligations. The final responsibility, however, still rests with the Prime Minister who must approve of the arrangements reached. It is clear that so long as the Prime Minister is in the House of Commons he must remain the principal

---

[1] MacDonald was tempted to take the office again, but his previous experience with the burden of the dual functions plus Arthur Henderson's insistence upon the post led to the latter's appointment. Mary Agnes Hamilton, *Arthur Henderson* (London, W. Heinemann, 1938), pp. 281–2.

[2] 'It was to his departmental work that the bulk of his time was devoted. The demands of the Prime Ministership were superadded. . . .' Gwendolin Cecil, *The Life of Lord Salisbury* (London, Hodder and Stoughton, 1931) iii, 202.

[3] Winston Churchill, *Their Finest Hour* (Boston, Houghton Mifflin, 1949), p. 16.

[4] *Report from the Select Committee on the Remuneration of Ministers* (1929), p. 9.

government spokesman whatever be the title given to other members of the Cabinet.

Thus normally the Prime Minister does not attempt to take over direct control of a department with all of the concentration upon departmental duties which that entails, although it is probable that he will usually be able to take the office of his choice if he is insistent. In one instance, an attempt was made by other party leaders to stipulate a restrictive rule upon the functions to be undertaken by the Prime Minister as a price of their entrance into the Cabinet. In 1905, Grey, Asquith, and Haldane had entered into an agreement not to enter the Cabinet unless Sir Henry Campbell-Bannerman, the Prime Minister, went to the House of Lords. It was their belief that he would prove to be ineffective as Leader of the House of Commons and that more advantage to the party would be derived if Asquith performed that function. This effort, however, failed and Sir Henry retained his leadership in the Commons until his resignation in April of 1908.[1]

Although it is recognized that the primary responsibility for the selection of the government rests upon the Prime Minister it is obvious that he will consult with personal friends and political colleagues in many instances. Thus in 1895 Lord Salisbury conferred with the Duke of Devonshire and Joseph Chamberlain, the leaders of the Liberal Unionists, prior to forming his Cabinet.[2] Similarly, in 1905, Campbell-Bannerman talked with John Morley about the possible composition of a Liberal Cabinet eleven months prior to taking office.[3] Sir Henry also saw Asquith, who made some recommendations.[4] Naturally Asquith consulted the leaders of the Conservative Party in forming the coalition of 1915.[5] Lloyd George also consulted Conservative and Labour leaders in forming his coalition in December 1916.[6] In 1924 MacDonald consulted with

[1] Richard B. Haldane, *Autobiography* (Garden City, New York, Doubleday Doran and Co., 1929), pp. 180–94; Sir Edward Grey, *Twenty-five Years* (New York, Frederick Stokes, 1925), i, 62; Spender, *op. cit.*, ii, 193–7; J. A. Spender and Cyril Asquith, *op. cit.*, i, 172–4.

[2] *Annual Register* (1895), p. 139.

[3] *The Works of John Morley* (London, Macmillan, 1921), ii, 102–3.

[4] Spender and Asquith, *op. cit.*, i, 172.   [5] *Ibid.*, ii, 165.

[6] Lord Beaverbrook, *Politicians and the War, 1914–1918* (London, T. Butterworth, 1932), ii, 302, 318–25.

Henderson, Webb, Clynes, Thomas, and Snowden over the distribution of government posts.[1] Similarly, he met with the same group, with the exception of Webb, prior to the formation of his second government.[2] It is, of course, obvious that consultations were held between MacDonald, Baldwin, and Samuel in 1931.

In addition to consultation with other leading party figures, it is also desirable that the Prime Minister should consult the Chief Whip of his party. 'The Chief Whip might be in a position to warn his leader that the appointment of particular men, or a particular man, in a particular post, would be risky, dangerous, and inadvisable.'[3] This is to be expected for the Chief Whip through his more frequent contacts with the backbenchers is in a much better position to evaluate their attitudes towards the appointments of particular individuals. He may be able to inform the Prime Minister as to the probable effect of an appointment or an omission upon the rank and file of the party.[4]

Although the Prime Minister's responsibility is primary in the formation of a government, he will very likely consult with friends in the process of selection. As Professor Laski has said, 'In fact, though the Prime Minister's discretion is wide, consultation with his personal colleagues is inevitable. He has not only to form a team; he has also to form a team that will satisfy them. He will have to be an autocrat, indeed, to be able to impose his views upon them against their will, since there is always the danger that they may not serve.'[5]

In addition to making the appointments to the ministry the Prime Minister is also able to determine the size of the Cabinet. He is, therefore, in a position to decide, within limits, what

[1] Snowden, *op. cit.*, ii, 594. J. H. Thomas has said that the principal appointments were actually decided upon in a private meeting between MacDonald and him. Thomas, *My Story* (London, Hutchinson, 1937), p. 75.

[2] Snowden, *op. cit.*, ii, 757; G. D. H. Cole, *A History of the Labour Party from 1914* (London, Routledge and K. Paul, 1948), p. 227.

[3] Viscount Herbert Gladstone, 'The Chief Whip in the British Parliament', *American Political Science Review*, xxi (August 1927), 520.

[4] It is obvious that in some cases the party leaders know the attitude of the backbenchers without such consultation. The appointment of Lansbury to a Cabinet seat in 1929 was made as a result of the substantial support he had among the rank and file. The principal leaders of the party did not think highly of his abilities. Snowden, *op. cit.*, ii, 760.

[5] Harold J. Laski, *Parliamentary Government in England* (New York, Viking Press, 1938), p. 198.

offices shall or shall not be included in the Cabinet. This power has enabled the British to reduce the size of the Cabinet in time of war in order to expedite the decision making process. In normal times, however, some offices are inevitably included in the Cabinet. Among these are the Chancellor of the Exchequer, the Secretary of State for the Home Department, the Secretary of State for Foreign Affairs, the Secretaries of State for Commonwealth Relations, for the Colonies and for Scotland, and the President of the Board of Trade, the Lord Chancellor, the Minister of Defence,[1] the Minister of Labour, the Lord Privy Seal, and the Lord President of the Council. Other offices may be added in case of need, as for example, the Minister of Fuel and Power and the Minister of Health in the Labour Cabinet of 1945.

The Prime Minister is in a position to bring other officers into the Cabinet if he wishes, or to exclude one or more of the above offices if the needs of the moment should make them politically less significant than they might otherwise be. New offices may also be created in time of necessity as in the case of the Minister of Economic Affairs established in 1947 in order to allow Sir Stafford Cripps to exercise general control over British economic policy. The resignation of Hugh Dalton as Chancellor of the Exchequer and his subsequent replacement by Sir Stafford made the other office unnecessary and it was abolished.[2]

While the Prime Minister does not have unlimited discretion in selecting the members of his government, and particularly the Cabinet, there have been some exceptional instances in which the Prime Minister has proposed or made some rather startling appointments. In particular Stanley Baldwin twice, within a year and a half, startled his party and the public by his nominations for the office of Chancellor of the Exchequer, frequently the second highest office in the government. In 1923 he offered the position to McKenna, who was a Liberal. The

---

[1] Until the creation of the Ministry of Defence in 1946 the First Lord of the Admiralty and the Secretary of State for War were nearly always in the Cabinet. Since that time they have dropped from the ranks of the Cabinet proper.

[2] A Ministers of the Crown Transfer Act, 1946, allows a department to be abolished and its functions transferred by order in council instead of by statute.

action was taken despite the fact that Sir Robert Horne, a member of his own party, had previously held the Exchequer and expected to receive it again. Horne was so antagonized by the action that he refused to participate in the Cabinet in any capacity despite McKenna's eventual refusal of the offer. Horne remained outside as a focus of discontent around which others might organize.[1] In spite of the effects of this action in 1923, Baldwin, in 1924, offered the same post to Winston Churchill, who accepted. Churchill, like McKenna, was not even a member of the Conservative Party at the time. He had won his seat as a Constitutionalist and did not formally join the Conservative Party until the next year.[2] Ramsay MacDonald also appointed some officers who were not members of his party in 1924, but this grew out of his belief that the party did not have sufficient men of ministerial calibre to fill all of the offices. One of his appointees, Lord Chelmsford, a Conservative, actually held a seat in the Cabinet as First Lord of the Admiralty.[3]

The Prime Minister's discretion is limited by the necessity of making his selections from the members of the Parliament. Violations of this rule are likely to bring down upon his head the antagonism of the legislature which will jealously defend its privileges. There have, however, been exceptions to this rule.

[1] Snowden, *op. cit.*, ii, 589–90. For the development of a Conservative opposition to Baldwin centring around Sir Robert Horne, see Wickham Steed, *The Real Stanley Baldwin* (London, Nisbet, 1930), pp. 73–4.

[2] Winston Churchill, *The Gathering Storm* (Boston, Houghton Mifflin, 1948), p. 23; Steed, *op. cit.*, p. 76. In this instance there were two former Chancellors of the Exchequer in the Conservative Party, Sir Robert Horne and Neville Chamberlain who had eventually been appointed in 1923. Viscount Snowden tells an amusing story of this appointment: 'It was said that when Mr. Baldwin sent for Mr. Churchill and offered him the Chancellorship, Mr. Churchill had assumed that it was the post of the Chancellor of the Duchy of Lancaster, and it only slowly dawned upon Mr. Churchill during the conversation that Mr. Baldwin was offering him the Chancellorship of the Exchequer.' Snowden, *op. cit.*, ii, 719. Churchill admits he was 'surprised'.

[3] Snowden, *op. cit.*, ii, 607; Cole, *op. cit.*, p. 159; L. M. Weir, *The Tragedy of Ramsay MacDonald* (London, Secker and Warburg, 1938), p. 146. MacDonald also appointed a Conservative Lord Advocate of Scotland. Both of these appointments resulted in considerable criticism in meetings of the Parliamentary Labour Party.

General Smuts served in Lloyd George's War Cabinet in 1917–18 without occasioning parliamentary criticism for obvious reasons.[1] Such criticisms did develop when Baldwin appointed two Scottish Law Lords who did not have seats. The criticism resulted in the resignation of one of them and the appointment of a successor from the House; the other found a seat.[2] Both Ramsay MacDonald and his son, Malcolm, held seats in the Cabinet from the fall of 1935 until early 1936 without seats in the Parliament as a result of electoral defeats. It was necessary in these cases to seek out safe seats for them.[3] The Parliament will accept situations of the latter kind if they do not drag out too long. It is always possible that a major party figure may be upset in an election even while his party is winning nationally. Such a situation may easily be remedied by the resignation of one of the elected members and the candidacy of the minister in the consequent by-election.

The Prime Minister is faced with many other factors which limit his choice. Obviously one of the most important limiting factors is that of party. Normally British government is party government. It will, therefore, be expected that the Prime Minister will confine his appointments to those persons who are members of his party. Ramsay MacDonald's appointment in 1924 of some Conservatives is far from ordinary, and it is noteworthy that the second Labour Government did not grant a post in the Cabinet to anyone not a member of the party.[4]

The limitations of party, however, involve more than the simple restriction that selections be made only from the ranks of one's own party. While the British parties seem homogeneous when compared to the heterogeneous American parties there are actually divergences of opinion of substantial importance within all of them. Such differences must be considered in the formation of a government for the wise Prime Minister will make an effort to include representatives of the various wings of the party in order more effectively to stabilize the government's

[1] F. S. Crafford, *Jan Smuts: A Biography* (Garden City, New York, Doubleday, Doran, 1944), pp. 124–5.

[2] W. I. Jennings, *op. cit.*, p. 48.

[3] Keith Feiling, *The Life of Neville Chamberlain* (London, Macmillan, 1946) p. 270.

[4] Cole, *op. cit.*, p. 228.

control of the party majority in the House of Commons. In 1905 Sir Henry Campbell-Bannerman had to consider the Liberal Imperialists and the Liberal Pacifists in the formation of the Cabinet for no government could exist for any substantial period which did not manage to reconcile representatives of both groups. Inclusion in the Cabinet was an essential prerequisite to such reconciliation.[1] It is also noteworthy that Sir Henry took steps to consolidate the loyalty to his government of trade union representatives in the Parliament through the inclusion of John Burns in his Cabinet.[2] The same characteristic division was continued by Asquith when he became Prime Minister in 1908.

The Labour Government of 1945 also provides an example of the same effort to include representatives of all wings within the Cabinet. The Cabinet included both Herbert Morrison and Ernest Bevin. Bevin could probably best be placed as slightly right of centre while Morrison represented the centre. Additionally Bevin represented the trade unions while Morrison represented the local party organizations to a somewhat greater extent.[3] In addition to these men Aneurin Bevan could be classified as the leader of the left wing of the party. Bevan's inclusion is even more noteworthy as he had nearly been expelled from the party only a year previously because of his extreme socialist views.[4]

The inclusion of all wings, or all of political importance, is obviously an essential course of action. The inclusion of potentially dissentient groups in the Cabinet through the presence of their leader enables the Prime Minister to place them in a position in which they must accept their share of the responsibility for the government's action. So long as the faction leader remains in the Cabinet he must act in accordance with the principle of collective responsibility and speak and act on behalf

---

[1] J. A. Spender, *The Life of Sir Henry Campbell-Bannerman* (New York, Houghton Mifflin, 1924), ii, 193–204.

[2] *Ibid.*, ii, 201. The appointment originated with Morley. *The Works of John Morley* (London, Macmillan, 1921), ii, 102–3.

[3] Francis Williams, *Socialist Britain* (New York, Viking Press, 1949), ch. vi; J. T. Murphy, *Labour's Big Three* (London, Bodley Head, 1948). As a matter of distribution there were nine trade unionists in a Cabinet of twenty. Cole, *op. cit.*, p. 473. Seven of the ministers were ex-miners. *Annual Register* (1945), pp. 54–5.

[4] *Annual Register* (1945), pp. 54–5.

of the programme of the government. Such individuals are not likely to give up office unless pressed too far for once outside they are not in such an effective position to affect the course of action determined upon by the government. In addition, it is also true that in some instances responsibilities temper the more extreme views of the faction leaders.[1]

The Prime Minister who does not include representatives of all wings must be prepared to face criticism from the dissatisfied wing of the party in the Parliament itself. Experience indicates that such criticism is more hazardous than the same sort of criticism within the Cabinet, for since the latter is not public the opposition does not find it as easy to seize upon it for purposes of political advantage. Ramsay MacDonald discovered this lesson for himself when he excluded John Wheatley from his second government, after including him in the government of 1924, and had to face the vitriolic attacks of the brilliant Scot in the Commons. Wheatley's early death prevented the development of the consequences inherent in MacDonald's action.[2]

Should the Prime Minister be faced with the necessity of creating a coalition government it is obvious that the difficulties which must be considered are multiplied. He must be concerned not only with appointments, but with the exclusion of men of ability. He must be concerned not only with the representation of the factions in his party, but with the representation of factional groups in the other parties entering the coalition as

[1] It seems to have had this effect upon John Wheatley. Snowden said that Wheatley 'was a man who, when free from the responsibility of office, would make extreme speeches; but as a Minister I had always found him to be reasonable and practical.' Snowden, *op. cit.*, ii, 760.

[2] Both Henderson and Snowden opposed Wheatley's exclusion, but MacDonald's dislike of the Scotsman led him to reject their advice. Mary Agnes Hamilton, *op. cit.*, pp. 347-8; Snowden, *op. cit.*, ii, 760.

Herman Finer has stated that the second Labour Government excluded the left-wingers. Finer, *op. cit.*, p. 481, n. 18. While it is true that the left wing was under-represented in the Cabinet, the statement that it was excluded is too strong. George Lansbury, who was a favourite of the left wing, was included, although admittedly in an inferior position. Snowden, *op. cit.*, ii, 760. For a comment on Lansbury's 'leftism' see Dean E. McHenry, *His Majesty's Opposition, 1931–1938* (Berkeley, University of California, 1940), p. 143. Trevelyan, the President of the Board of Education, soon acquired a 'reputation for leftism'. Cole, *op. cit.*, p. 228.

well. This problem has been more frequent than one is likely to assume. Coalition governments have governed the United Kingdom for thirty-one out of the last fifty-seven years. Between 1895 and 1905 a coalition of Conservatives and Liberal Unionists held power although it is next door to an absurdity to speak of a coalition in the last five years as the Conservatives had swallowed the Liberal Unionists. Coalitions governed Britain from 1915 to 1922, first under Asquith, later under Lloyd George. The National Government created in 1931 and composed of Conservatives, National Liberals, and National Labourites, technically continued until 1940. In fact, the National Government was a peculiar coalition. The Conservatives from the general election of 1931 until 1945 held a majority of the seats in the House of Commons alone.[1] At the same time it is actually doubtful if there was a National Labour Party in anything but name. The rank and file of the Labour Party had almost unanimously declined to follow the leadership of Ramsay MacDonald in 1931.

Some coalitions involve fewer problems than others. The combination of 1895 between the Liberal Unionists and the Conservatives was not too difficult. The former party was relatively small and agreement had been reached between the two sections led by Joseph Chamberlain and the Duke of Devonshire.[2] The principal question, given these facts, was the precise numerical relationship to be set in the distribution of Cabinet offices between the two parties, and the offices to be given to the Liberal Unionists. The agreement reached gave five Cabinet positions to the smaller group and Joseph Chamberlain, their principal leader, was allowed to choose between the Home Office and the Colonial Office, a choice which he made in favour of the latter.[3]

The first Asquith coalition involved somewhat more complex problems. The coalition in this case was to include Conservatives

---

[1] In the 1931 elections the Conservative Party won 470 seats. In the 1935 election it won 380 seats.

[2] Blanche E. Dugdale, *Arthur James Balfour* (New York, Putnam's Sons, 1937), i, 162.

[3] J. L. Garvin, *The Life of Joseph Chamberlain* (London, Macmillan, 1934), iii, 4–7. Chamberlain's preference created some surprise at the time, but later developments made it one of the most powerful offices in the government and paved the way for his virtual control of the government during the Boer War.

and Labourites, the former a powerful political party. The Cabinet had previously been entirely Liberal and Asquith was faced with the necessity of dropping previous colleagues as well as shuffling offices generally in order to find places for the representatives of other parties. The division was made after consultations with Bonar Law and Arthur Henderson, the leaders of the respective parties.[1] It must be admitted that in retrospect it strikes one as a peculiar coalition for the Liberals retained nearly all of the principal offices of state in the new government.[2] The Conservatives were successful in forcing Asquith to exclude Haldane, one of his closest friends, from the Cabinet, accusing Haldane of undue friendship for the Germans.[3] Similarly, the Conservatives also refused to agree to Asquith's proposal that Churchill be made Secretary of State for the Colonies and the Prime Minister had to be satisfied with naming him Chancellor of the Duchy of Lancaster.[4] Asquith had desired to include representatives of the Irish members of Parliament as well and did make an offer of a Cabinet position to Redmond, their leader, but the latter refused while pledging continued support.[5] Lord Lansdowne, peculiarly enough, was invited to join at the request of Asquith rather than at the request of his own party leader.[6]

Lloyd George's coalition of December 1916 also involved the same consideration of multiple factors. In his case his bargaining position was considerably weaker than Asquith's had been for there was some doubt as to his ability to carry a substantial number of the Liberals with him.[7] Before the leading Conservatives would enter his government it was necessary to meet with them and inform them of the Liberal support expected, the attitude of the Labour Party, and the probable composition of the War Cabinet. Similarly, the Labour Party demanded sub-

---

[1] Spender and Asquith, *op. cit.*, ii, 165 ff.

[2] For a complaint that the Conservatives did not receive their just due, see Lord Beaverbrook, *op. cit.*, i, 124–42. The Liberals held the following major posts, in addition to the Premiership: Secretary of State for Foreign Affairs, Chancellor of the Exchequer, Secretary of State for War, Minister of Munitions. This distribution left only the Admiralty among the first-run war departments for the Conservatives.

[3] Lord Oxford and Asquith, *Memories and Reflections, 1852–1927* (Boston, Little, Brown and Co., 1928), ii, p. 122; Haldane, *op. cit.*, p. 305.

[4] Oxford and Asquith, *op. cit.*, ii, 121.   [5] *Ibid.*, ii, 121.

[6] Spender and Asquith, *op. cit.*, ii, 172.   [7] Beaverbrook, *op. cit.*, ii, 302.

stantial concessions involving both a promise of an increase in the number of positions to be given to representatives of the party and some stipulations with respect to policy, particularly in connection with the coal mines, shipping, and the conscripttion of labour.[1] Throughout the entire period, 'Bonar Law and Lloyd George were in constant communication as to the filling-up of prospective offices'.[2] As Lord Beaverbrook has pointed out, there was nothing strange about this co-operation for no one was sure as to how many Liberals would follow Lloyd George, and to the extent that he failed to obtain such followers the responsibility for filling the government from the ranks of the Conservatives fell upon Bonar Law.[3]

The National Government formed in 1931 also involved a consideration of the interests of the three parties which had combined together to seek a solution to the financial crisis. The division of office in this case resulted in the creation of a ten-man Cabinet, four from the National Labour Party, four from the Conservatives, and two from the National Liberal Party.[4] Following the General Election of 1931 the Cabinet was expanded in size and the allocation of offices somewhat inadequately reflected the established Conservative predominance in the newly elected House of Commons. The Conservatives were given eleven posts, while four went to National Labour and five to the National Liberals.[5]

One of the principal reasons for Churchill's appointment to the Premiership in 1940 was the belief that he could gain the support of Labour and Liberals in the formation of a truly national government, while Chamberlain obviously could not.[6] This view was correct and Churchill proceeded to the formation of such a government. His government, however, as initially constituted, did not include any representatives of the Liberal Party in the War Cabinet proper. The leader of the Liberal Party under the terms of agreement was to be called into sessions of the War Cabinet when any matter arose which affected either 'fundamental political issues or party union'.[7]

---

[1] *Ibid.*, ii, 318–25. [2] *Ibid.*, ii, 302. [3] *Loc. cit.*
[4] Feiling, *op. cit.*, p. 199. [5] *Ibid.*, p. 198.
[6] Winston Churchill, *The Gathering Storm* (Boston, Houghton Mifflin, 1948), p. 665.
[7] Winston Churchill, *Their Finest Hour* (Boston, Houghton Mifflin, 1949), p. 12.

Churchill notes, however, that for the convenient conduct of business it was 'necessary that . . . the leader of the Liberal Party should usually be present'.[1] Nevertheless, the Cabinet proper included three representatives of the Conservatives and two members of the Labour Party.[2] Below the War Cabinet the offices listed as 'Ministers of Cabinet Rank,' were divided, sixteen Conservatives, five Labour, one Liberal, two National Liberal, one National Labour, and five others who did not profess allegiance to any party.[3]

Within any political party there are always a number of men who have acquired public stature and political leadership upon their own merits. It is not conceivably possible for any intelligent Prime Minister to pass over such men in the formation of a government. To do so would be to endanger its prospects at its inception. 'Roughly,' the late Professor Laski wrote, 'it is a fair calculation that about half of the Cabinet nominates itself, by the standing of its members in the eyes of the party; and about half of these will be able to bring great pressure to bear in getting the posts they want. It is only with the other half that the Prime Minister really has a free hand.'[4] There are, of course, substantial differences among even this group. In some cases it is only an oversight or a lack of foresight to pass over an individual; in other cases it would be an act of sheer folly.

The individuals in the latter category we may describe as 'essential men'. They are persons who cannot be passed over whatever the Prime Minister may think of them as individuals.

---

[1] *Ibid.*, p. 13. The wisdom of the initial exclusion was questionable for no one can ever be certain when matters affecting fundamental political issues might arise. In such circumstances, if the terms of the agreement were to be met, it would have been necessary to halt discussion to send for the Liberal leader. Once he had appeared at the meeting time would have to be wasted in briefing him on what had occurred previously. Churchill's comment noted above seems to substantiate this criticism.

[2] *Ibid.*, p. 13. The Conservative representatives were Churchill, Chamberlain, Lord President of the Council, and Halifax, who served as Secretary of State for Foreign Affairs. Clement Attlee held the position of Lord Privy Seal and Arthur Greenwood served as Minister without Portfolio. It is rather interesting that when Halifax became Ambassador to the United States it was agreed that he should 'resume his function as a member of the War Cabinet whenever he came home on leave.' *Ibid.*, p. 570. This was an obvious effort to make a demotion appear more palatable.

[3] *Ibid.*, p. 14.   [4] Laski, *op. cit.*, p. 199.

He may dislike them, he may look forward to the prospect of association with them with the deepest distaste, but he must include them if party and public support is to be maintained for they control substantial segments of both. Their omission would result in substantial and effective discontent among groups whose support is necessary for continuation in office.

Such individuals are frequently in a position to demand more than inclusion in the Cabinet; they may be able to demand their choice of office as well. Thus in 1895 the Duke of Devonshire was offered the Foreign Office, but he insisted upon, and obtained, the position of Lord President of the Council, a sinecure post which would not involve any departmental duties.[1] In the same year Goshen demanded and obtained the Admiralty.[2] Grey stipulated for and received the Foreign Office in 1905.[3] In 1908 John Morley insisted that he be allowed to keep the India Office and further insisted upon a peerage. Asquith granted him both although he had wished to make Morley Colonial Secretary.[4] In 1929 Arthur Henderson was successful in obtaining the office of Foreign Secretary upon which he had been determined.[5] Again, in 1931, Neville Chamberlain got the position of Minister of Health at his own request.[6] There are, of course, instances in which the demands were made but were not satisfied. Haldane wanted the position of Lord Chancellor in 1905, but did not obtain it as Campbell-Bannerman had already determined upon the selection of Reid.[7] In the case of Haldane it is clear that his power was not so much individual as it was a result of the fact that he was a close friend of Grey and Asquith. As mentioned earlier Asquith himself had ambitions upon the position of Leader of the House of Commons, but they were not fulfilled.

Such individuals are also sometimes in a position to demand other terms than their own choice of office. The Asquith-Grey-Haldane demand that Sir Henry Campbell-Bannerman go to the House of Lords has already been mentioned as an

---

[1] Garvin, *op. cit.*, iii, 5; *Letters of Queen Victoria*, 3s., ii, 525.

[2] *Letters of Queen Victoria*, 3s., ii, 526–8.   [3] Haldane, *op. cit.*, p. 169.

[4] *The Works of John Morley* (London, Macmillan, 1921), ii, 211–12; Reginald Viscount Esher, *Journals and Letters* (London, J. Nicholson and Watson, 1934), ii, 303 ff.

[5] Hamilton, *op. cit.*, pp. 281–2; Snowden, *op. cit.*, ii, 764.

[6] Feiling, *op. cit.*, p. 193.

[7] Spender, *op. cit.*, ii, 195; Haldane, *op. cit.*, p. 169.

instance of the failure of essential men to receive what they demanded. Randolph Churchill was more successful in achieving his objectives in 1885. Lord Salisbury offered him the post of Secretary of State for India, but Churchill stipulated that he would not accept the position unless Sir Stafford Northcote was excluded from the leadership of the House of Commons and Richard Cross barred from the ministry. Churchill was strengthened in his demand by the acquiescence of Sir Michael Hicks-Beach and George Hamilton who declared that they would withdraw their previous acceptance of Cabinet positions unless Churchill's terms were met. In the face of this concerted action it is not at all surprising that Lord Salisbury gave way to Churchill's demand with respect to Northcote even though insisting upon the retention of Cross.[1] Joseph Chamberlain was also successful in obtaining a right of 'unlimited liberty of judgment and rejection' on future proposals as to the Irish government before entering Gladstone's Cabinet in 1886.[2] The terms demanded by Goshen in 1895 were also accepted. Goshen demanded that he be allowed to bring some of his friends in the Lords into the government, but surprisingly enough, even though his request was granted, he did not take advantage of it.[3]

The Prime Minister must also be concerned about the distribution of appointments between the House of Lords and the House of Commons. By statute at least two of the Secretaries of State must be from the House of Lords. In addition, the Lord Chancellor must also be from the Lords. This does not mean that the persons appointed to those posts must already be members of the House of Lords; selections may be made from commoners who have signified their willingness to accept a peerage. Even given this somewhat wider area of selection it is nevertheless the case that many individuals will be unwilling to enter the Lords, even in order to obtain such appointments, as

[1] Winston Churchill, *Life of Randolph Churchill* (London, Macmillan, 1906), i, 403–98; Cecil, *op. cit.*, iii, 138; Dugdale, *op. cit.*, i, 55–6. Perhaps one of the most surprising things about this incident is that Churchill had never held even a minor post previously. He had built up an almost fanatical body of supporters, however.

[2] Garvin, *op. cit.*, ii, 172.

[3] Bernard Holland, *The Life of Spencer Compton, Eighth Duke of Devonshire* (London, Longmans, Green and Co., 1911), ii, 180–3.

such action is likely to close the road to further political opportunities. The House of Lords has become a political dead-end street. Once you get in it you cannot get out and it leads nowhere. A dilemma of this sort developed in 1915 when too many of the Secretaries were in the lower chamber. The Prime Minister, therefore, had to find one of them who would go into the House of Lords or release one of them and appoint someone else who would. In this case a solution was reached by Sir Edward Grey's acceptance of a peerage as a prelude to his contemplated complete resignation from politics.[1] As it happened Grey did not resign, but retained his office until the fall of Asquith.

It is equally obvious that other offices must be filled by members of the House of Commons. The Chancellor of the Exchequer inevitably must be in the Lower House for it controls finance. It is also usually desirable that the Foreign Secretary shall be in the Commons. This rule is not absolute as is evidenced by Lord Halifax's tenure at that office under Chamberlain and Churchill, but it was made possible only because both of these Premiers actually exercised effective control over the conduct of foreign affairs themselves and therefore could speak on all aspects of policy in the Lower Chamber. Lord Rosebery's action in appointing Lord Kimberley to that post in 1895 is less defensible for this meant that both of the officers with the most immediate concern for the conduct of foreign affairs were out of reach of the Commons. Harcourt was left with the onus of defending the policy of the government in foreign affairs and he frequently complained that he was not adequately informed of developments by the Foreign Secretary.[2] The lack of wisdom in the action is further indicated in that it antagonized John Morley, whose tacit support had made possible Rosebery's original appointment.[3] Generally speaking it is clearly desirable that the Foreign Secretary should be in the House of Commons unless the Prime Minister is both willing and able to take responsibility for informing the House of the principles upon which foreign policy is conducted.

There is no conventional or statutory rule which requires that

[1] Grey, *op. cit.*, ii, 253–4.
[2] A. G. Gardiner, *The Life of Sir William Harcourt* (New York, Constable, 1923), ii, 313 ff.
[3] Spender and Asquith, *op. cit.*, i, 91.

the heads of the great spending departments, in particular the defence departments, shall be in the House of Commons. It is obvious that it sometimes is advantageous to have them in that House, but there have been many instances in which they have come from the Lords. Lord Lansdowne was at the War Office in 1895. Asquith made Lord Kitchener Secretary of State for War in 1914 and Lord Derby took that post when Lloyd George became Prime Minister. Derby later served in the same capacity under both Law and Baldwin. Similarly, Lord Ripon was First Lord of the Admiralty in 1885, Lord Chelmsford in 1924, and Lord Monsell in 1935–36. It may be added that it is no longer possible to speak of the defence departments as if they were the only great spending departments as many of the other departments now spend large sums of money.

The actual distribution between Lords and Commons, subject to statutory provisions, is in the hands of the Prime Minister. As would be expected, Labour Governments are likely to have fewer peers than Conservative Governments, but even a Labour Premier may find it necessary to strengthen his party in the House of Lords in order more effectively to put the party's case there. Sidney Webb accepted a peerage in 1929 for this reason.[1] Whatever be the party in power, however, it is becoming more and more the case that the Commoners predominate over the Lords in the composition of the Cabinet, although the Churchill Cabinet of 1951 contained six peers out of a total membership of sixteen.[2]

[1] Snowden, *op. cit.*, ii, 766. Webb had a price, namely, that he be given a seat in the Cabinet.

[2] The change in the distribution of Cabinet seats between Lords and Commons may be noted by citing a few figures as to the distribution in selected governments when initially formed.

Government	Lords	Commons
1895 (Salisbury)	10	9
1905 (Campbell-Bannerman)	6	13
1919 (Lloyd George)	5	15
1923 (Baldwin)	7	12
1929 (MacDonald)	3	18
1935 (Baldwin)	4	18
1945 (Attlee)	4	16
1951 (Churchill)	6	10

For a more complete breakdown from 1892 through 1937 see Wangteh Yu, *The English Cabinet System* (London, P. S. King and Son, 1939), pp. 24–6. It is obvious that a Conservative government is more likely to have a high percentage of peers in the Cabinet than a Liberal or Labour Government.

One further consideration should be noted before leaving this problem. It is essential that if the Minister be in the House of Lords, the chief Under-Secretary be in the Commons. This is necessary as the department must have a spokesman in debate and during the question periods. It might be added that the responsibility falling upon the Under-Secretary in such circumstances are obviously greater than is usually the case and therefore calls for greater ability. It is conceivably the case that in such circumstances the Under-Secretary may, if he handles himself well, do much to secure his future career. There is little question but that Sir Edward Grey's experience in this capacity in 1894–5 did much to mark him as a future Foreign Secretary.[1] No similar obligation exists in case the Minister is from the Commons as it is not always possible that a party will have such a plentitude of ability in the Upper Chamber. The ministerial members of the House of Lords are therefore likely to be obligated to participate in explanations and defences of the policies of several departments.

Regional representation has always been one of the considerations which the American President recognizes in the formation of his Cabinet. Even those Presidents whose Cabinets have been predominantly from one section must consider the wisdom of such action. Similarly, in Canada regional considerations are of the first importance. Professor Corry described the allocation of posts between the provinces as 'the first imperative in cabinet making'.[2]

Although geographical considerations have some place in Britain, they are not of comparable importance to the position they occupy in the United States or Canada. The United Kingdom is itself limited in size and although there are national and traditional distinctions between the various peoples who comprise the political community, nevertheless the population is relatively homogeneous, the country less divided sectionally than in the case of the North American states. Additionally, the parties are more tightly knit, more disciplined, less susceptible to the influence of local interests. The consequence is that

[1] G. M. Trevelyan, *Grey of Fallodon* (Boston, Houghton Mifflin, 1937), p. 67.

[2] J. A. Corry, *Elements of Democratic Government* (New York, Oxford University Press, 1947), p. 99.

geographical considerations are not fundamental. The Secretary of State for Scotland is normally a Scotsman, but no comparable situation exists for either Wales or Northern Ireland. The Prime Minister may, if he believes it will strengthen his government, make a deliberate effort to include representatives from Scotland, Wales, or Northern Ireland, but it is not absolutely imperative that this be done.[1] It was ordinarily the custom so long as Ireland was under British rule to include one or two representatives from Ireland in the Cabinet, but this was not done in 1880.[2]

The Prime Minister must also recognize that special qualifications are needed for some positions. The Lord Chancellor, the Attorney-General, and other law officers, must be members of the legal profession. Once outside the legal positions, however, special qualifications are not essential although the Prime Minister will naturally consider the known competence of potential appointees in the various areas of governmental affairs. The ability required in most cases, however, is not professional ability or skill, for that is always present in the permanent civil servants attached to the departments. The Ministers remain, in most cases, merely amateurs who may, because they are amateurs rather than technicians, be able to shed new light on an old problem or produce new ideas which undue specialization has caused the professionals to overlook. At the very least 'political heads of department are necessary', as Sir William Harcourt said, 'to tell the civil service what the public will not stand'.[3]

It is also sometimes pointed out that the Prime Minister is expected to select as his Chancellor of the Exchequer someone capable of holding the confidence of the City. This may be of considerable importance as a failure to consider the attitude of

[1] It has been said that MacDonald named Wheatley to the first Labour Cabinet to placate the Scots as well as the left-wingers in the party. Weir, *op. cit.*, pp. 145–6.

[2] Wangteh Yu, *op. cit.*, p. 29.

[3] Quoted in Harold J. Laski, 'The Limitations of the Expert', in William Ebenstein (ed.), *Man and the State* (New York, Rinehart, 1947), p. 165. The one exception to the rule is the Minister of Agriculture. The Minister of Agriculture is always a farmer or one who is cognizant of the problems of agriculture. The *expertise* of this individual, however, corresponds to that of the Secretary of Agriculture in the United States.

the City may conceivably result in a financial crisis growing out of a lack of confidence in the chief financial officer of the government.[1] It is, of course, clear that such a consideration is more likely to affect a Conservative Government than a Labour Government.[2] The Labour Party is pledged to basic reforms in the economic system; it is not to be expected that any Labour Government can obtain the degree of support which a Conservative government will receive from private financial interests. Upon the other hand, it is noteworthy that all of the Labour Chancellors of the Exchequer, with the possible exception of Hugh Dalton, have been men of orthodox financial views. In any case the Chancellor will have to be a man of strong convictions not to be persuaded to take the 'Treasury outlook' by his permanent civil servants.

Another limiting factor which is likely to be overlooked is prior membership in a government, and particularly in a Cabinet. Gladstone once said, 'The next most serious thing to admitting a man into the Cabinet is to leave a man out who has once been in'.[3] Such action may result in the destruction of personal friendship which has developed over a period of decades and may even lead to political opposition itself. Certainly such exclusion cannot be carried out unless a very substantial reason can be given for doing so, although there are notable instances of the exclusion of major figures. Among these examples is the exclusion of Lord Rosebery, the last Liberal Prime Minister, from the Liberal Cabinet of 1905. In this case, however, he had excluded himself by his public statement disagreeing with Campbell-Bannerman's explanation of what the policy of the Liberals would be with respect to Home Rule.[4]

---

[1] Finer, *op. cit.*, p. 581. As Finer comments, 'the confidence of the City is necessary, even if, as since 1946, the Cabinet's intentions are radically to reform the economic institutions of the country when City popularity, of course, could hardly be expected. But active hostility must be averted.' It is reported that Gladstone did not appoint Joseph Chamberlain as Chancellor of the Exchequer in 1885 as he feared that it would arouse the anger of the city. Sir Algernon West, *Recollections* (London, Smith, Elder, 1899), ii, 261.

[2] It has been alleged, however, that Philip Snowden, Chancellor of the Exchequer in the first two Labour Cabinets, turned to the Governor of the Bank of England for financial advice with great frequency. John Hargrave, *Montagu Norman* (New York, The Greystone Press, 1942), p. 104.

[3] Quoted in Wangteh Yu, *op. cit.*, p. 40.

[4] Spender and Asquith, *op. cit.*, i, 169; J. A. Spender, *op. cit.*, ii, 183–5.

Stanley Baldwin did not propose the inclusion of Winston Churchill in the National Government of 1931 although he had been Chancellor of the Exchequer in the last Conservative Government,[1] nor did Baldwin add him to the government in 1935 when he became Premier, despite rumours that such action might be taken. Churchill's overt opposition to the foreign policy of the government undoubtedly explains the omission in this case.[2] Other instances of omission which might be cited include Asquith's failure to reappoint Lord Elgin in 1908 upon the grounds that Elgin, while a good administrator, had not made any contribution to the collective enterprises of the Cabinet.[3]

Despite these instances of omission it is nevertheless the case that such individuals are normally included in later Cabinets under the same Prime Minister or the same party. Even the Liberal Government of 1905 contained seven former Cabinet members out of a total Cabinet of eighteen despite the fact that many Liberals had retired from politics in the interim. This conventional limitation may have undesirable consequences in itself for it may result in the exclusion of younger men who have already proven some ability. The Prime Minister is always faced with the necessity of striking a balance between the old and the new and almost any course he pursues is likely to involve unpleasantness of one sort or another. Should he include too many of the older members of the party he runs the risk of antagonizing the younger men. Should he exclude some of the former ministers, he runs the risk of creating a focus for internal party opposition.

In evaluating the merits and demerits of prospective appointees, the Prime Minister must always consider one factor which is not of basic importance in the selection of the American Cabinet. That is the parliamentary ability of the person under consideration, in particular his forensic ability. Since the Cabinet is an integral part of the legislature and since its members are expected to participate in leading roles in the debates

[1] Feiling, *op. cit.*, p. 199. The reason was probably Churchill's opposition to the Indian settlement, upon which Baldwin and Chamberlain were determined.

[2] Winston Churchill, *The Gathering Storm* (Boston, Houghton Mifflin, 1948), p. 181; Feiling, *op. cit.*, p. 270.

[3] Spender and Asquith, *op. cit.*, i, 198; Sir Almeric Fitzroy, *Memoirs* (London, Hutchinson, 3rd ed., 1925), i, 348.

in that body it is obvious that a poor speaker constitutes a parliamentary deadweight to the government.[1] A strong speaker, on the other hand, obviously strengthens the government. In 1929 Ramsay MacDonald appointed Wedgwood Benn, a new recruit to the party, to the India Office because he had already proved to be extremely effective in debate.[2]

Obviously, prior administrative experience is always considered in the selection of Cabinet members. Gladstone always insisted that no one should be appointed to the Cabinet who had not previously had experience in a junior ministerial position, thus proving his ability to deal with departmental problems. Gladstone did have to appoint Joseph Chamberlain to his Cabinet in 1880 despite Chamberlain's lack of administrative experience. He did it with considerable misgivings, but Chamberlain's public following made it impossible to exclude him from the Cabinet.[3] Naturally, there are other instances in which the obvious merits of a particular individual, revealed while in opposition, mark him off for Cabinet appointment even though he has never held a junior ministerial post.[4] Circumstances may, in a few cases, also make such consideration impossible. Ramsay MacDonald could not stress this factor too strongly in 1924 simply because his party had never held power previously. On the other hand, his appointment of non-party members who had had such experience indicates that it was one of the more important considerations in the formation of his government. Similarly, no party which has been out of power for a long period of time can be sure of having a large number of persons with previous administrative experience in its parliamentary ranks.

All of these considerations then enter into the Prime Minister's selection of his government. He may overlook some of

---

[1] Disraeli did not include Lord Chelmsford in his reconstructed Cabinet in 1868 as he did not consider him a 'very skilful debater'. Wangteh Yu, *op. cit.*, pp. 40–1.

[2] Snowden, *op. cit.*, ii, 765.

[3] J. A. Spender, *The Public Life* (New York, Frederick A. Stokes, 1925) i, 82–3.

[4] As in the case of Herbert Asquith whose first appointment was to the office of Home Secretary. It has been said that from the first moment Asquith spoke in the House, he was recognized as being a front-bencher. Spender and Asquith, *op. cit.*, i, 56.

them, but he cannot overlook all. Obviously the statutory rules must be met. He must include 'essential men', and sometimes meet their demands as to posts or the inclusion or exclusion of particular individuals. There is still some leeway for personal preferences in his remaining selections. Other considerations being equal, such matters as personal loyalty and personal friendship may enter into his decisions. Even such peculiar inclinations as Baldwin's desire to have the largest number of old Harrow boys in his Cabinet of any Prime Minister may play their role.[1] It is clear, however, that the Prime Minister's discretion is far from absolute. It is easy to exaggerate his power of appointment and consequently his position *vis-a-vis* the Cabinet as a whole.[2] The fact that it is the Prime Minister who makes the appointments is an element of his power, but some appointments dictate themselves whatever his attitude may be and multiple considerations influence his selections in the case of many of the others. In addition, it must be recognized that the formation of a government is not a pleasant task; it necessarily involves injured feelings and broken careers as well as the exclamations of triumph and exaltation occasioned by the recognition of 'true worth'. J. A. Spender's description of the formation of the government of Sir Henry Campbell-Bannerman acutely pictures the effect such action has upon the anxious politicians who see their whole future determined in this one process.[3]

'Small wonder if many were "on the door-step" of 29 Belgrave Square during these days. It is customary to laugh at politicians in the throes of office-seeking, but men of other professions may ask themselves what they would feel and how they would conduct themselves if at a given moment their entire career were at stake on the will or whim, as it might seem, of an inscrutable power which can neither be approached nor pleaded with, and whose decision when given is blasting and irretrievable. To be obliged to keep a perfect dignity and

---

[1] Beckhofer Roberts, *Stanley Baldwin: Man or Miracle?* (New York, Greenburg, 1937), pp. 17–18.

[2] Thus Ramsay Muir implies that the Prime Minister has almost unlimited discretion in both the selection and the removal of Cabinet officers. Ramsay Muir, *How Britain is Governed* (New York, R. R. Smith, 1930), p. 82.

[3] J. A. Spender, *Life of Sir Henry Campbell-Bannerman* (Boston, Houghton Mifflin, 1924), ii, 201–2.

reticence when others may be intriguing, to spend miserable hours waiting for a summons which may never come, to be fearful of going out lest it may come in your absence or of returning home to find it not there, to see the days passing and offices filled and yourself forgotten—to be conscious that a large audience is watching your discomfiture—that is the fate of even distinguished men, let alone the scores of others who at this moment are feeling for their footing on the first rung of the ladder. Who shall cast stones if a Prime Minister's letterbag at such times reveals some of the secrets of human nature? One man is taking an untimely holiday at Cairo, and sends a forlorn telegram to say that a cabled word will bring him by the next boat. Alas for him, he is not indispensable, and there are a dozen candidates on the spot for the place that he desires. Another rashly attaches conditions to his acceptance of the offer made to him, and to his dismay the Prime Minister answers blandly regretting that he should have "declined". . . . One receives his appointment on the last day, but too late to recall a letter to his constituents publicly expressing his feelings at having been overlooked, and this quaintly appears in the newspapers together with the announcement of his appointment. Yet another passed the week in intimate association with the Prime Minister without being told what place he is to have, and learns for the first time from a friend of his appointment to a considerable office. The wives, meanwhile, are not negligible. Some of them boldly break through the rules which are binding on husbands and son, and even rush the inner sanctum where the Prime Minister sits guarded by his secretaries. All the time the Press must be at the door seeking intelligent anticipations of facts officially withheld.'

When all of these factors are considered, it is easy to understand why so many Prime Ministers have classed the formation of a government among the most unpleasant aspects of the office. Its difficulties led Ramsay MacDonald to say, 'It is easier to create a revolution than to make a Cabinet, and if I have a second shot I would rather have a revolution than the responsibility of making a new Cabinet. . . .'[1]

[1] H. Hessell Tiltman, *J. Ramsay MacDonald, Labor's Man of Destiny* (New York, Frederick A. Stokes, 1929), p. 207.

VI

The Prime Minister
and the Cabinet

'A cabinet', wrote Walter Bagehot, 'is a combining committee—a *hyphen* which joins, a *buckle* which fastens, the legislative part of the state to the executive part of the state.'[1] Adequate as this description might have been at the time it was first written,[2] it is now difficult to conceive of the Cabinet as a mere hyphen or buckle for such terms do not adequately signify the enormous power of the Cabinet *vis a vis* the Parliament. In 1918 the Machinery of Government Committee stated that the principal functions of the Cabinet were:[3]

(a) The final determination of the policy to be submitted to Parliament;

(b) The supreme control of the national executive in accordance with the policy prescribed by Parliament; and

(c) The continuous co-ordination and delimitation of the activities of the several Departments of State.

This enumeration, helpful as it is, does not provide a comprehensive picture of the real nature of the British cabinet system. The comment that one of the principal functions of the Cabinet is 'the final determination of the policy to be submitted to Parliament' is too prosaic and too lacking in political dynamics to do more than scratch the surface of the actual relationship between the two bodies. One would not realize from the statement that the Cabinet actually exercises effective

[1] Walter Bagehot, *The English Constitution* (New York, World Classics Edition, 1942), p. 12.

[2] 1867.

[3] *Report of the Machinery of Government Committee*, Cmd. 9230 (1918), p. 5.

192

control over the Parliament and that nearly every measure of major importance is of Cabinet origin. No modern government is likely to lose a vote of confidence. The theory of parliamentary control of the Cabinet is only an illusion behind which is hidden the reality of Cabinet control of the Parliament. The Parliament is normally but the institution through which Cabinet policy goes in order to meet the prescribed procedural tests for the issuance of a statute. Debates take place, bills are sent to committee, but they seldom substantially affect the fate of a bill which is deemed a 'must' by the government. Lloyd George in 1931 told the Select Committee on Procedure on Public Business that 'Parliament has really no control over the Executive; it is a pure fiction'.[1] If we accept Lloyd George's comment, as it seems we must except upon extraordinary occasions, it is obvious that the Prime Minister's relations with the Cabinet proper constitute one of the most important aspects of his position, perhaps the most important single aspect, if it is possible to separate the manifold characteristics of the office.

John Morley described the Prime Minister as the 'keystone of the Cabinet arch. Although in Cabinet all its members stand on an equal footing, speak with equal voice, and, on the rare occasions when a division is taken, are counted on the fraternal principle of one man, one vote, yet the head of the Cabinet is *primus inter pares*, and occupies a position which, so long as it lasts, is one of exceptional and peculiar authority.'[2] Sir William Harcourt commented, 'though in theory *primus inter pares* the Prime Minister should really be *inter stellas luna minores*.'[3] Lord

---

[1] Don K. Price in commenting upon this development says, 'Its control has become so general, it is exercised through so rarefied a medium, that the Commons seems to be following the Lords into the status of one of the "theatrical elements" of the British constitution.' 'The Parliamentary and Presidential Systems', *Public Administration Review* (1943), iii, 323. See the same periodical, vol. iv, pp. 347–60, 360–4, for a reply to Price by Harold Laski and Price's comment thereon. This problem is pursued at greater length in the following chapter.

[2] John Morley, *Walpole* (New York, Macmillan, 1889), p. 157. Lord Oxford and Asquith says that the section of the book from which this quotation was drawn was written by Gladstone rather than Morley. *Fifty Years of British Parliament* (Boston, Little, Brown and Co., 1926), ii, 240.

[3] A. G. Gardiner, *The Life of Sir William Harcourt* (New York, Constable, n.d.), ii, 612. Harcourt expressed his opinion that 'on a question of policy there can be no doubt that the most successful administrations are those in which there is a strong Prime Minister and a subordinate Cabinet.'

Rosebery described the Prime Minister as being similar to the foreman of a jury; his influence depending upon his own personal qualities and beliefs.[1]

All such attempts to specifically categorize the office of the Prime Minister must inevitably fail. All of them are partially true, but clearly the Prime Minister is usually more than *primus inter pares* and certainly he is more than the equivalent of a foreman of a jury. Both of these descriptions reveal insufficient consideration of the influence which he derives from being the party leader, and the chief spokesman of the party in so far as the public is concerned. Nor do they involve recognition of the advantages which are derived from the fact that the initiative in appointment inheres in his office. It is really impossible to provide a precise description. We are forced to accept the conclusion stated by Lord Oxford and Asquith: 'There is not, and cannot be, from the nature of the case, any authoritative definition of the precise relation of the Prime Minister to his colleagues. "In practice," as Sir William Harcourt says, "the thing depends very much upon the character of the man." What was true of the Cabinet of Peel and Palmerston would not be true of other Ministers. . . . The office of Prime Minister is what its holder chooses and is able to make of it.'[2]

To a considerable extent the modern office of Prime Minister has developed out of the conception of that office held by Sir Robert Peel.[3] It was possible justifiably to describe the Cabinet of his predecessor, Melbourne, as a republic without a head,[4] but this was far from being apropos to the Cabinet of Peel. Peel insisted upon exercising detailed supervision over the operation of all governmental departments.[5] No measures were brought before the Cabinet without his prior authorization. Once Gladstone is reported to have said to Peel, 'Your government has not

[1] Lord Rosebery, *Peel* (London, Cassell and Co., 1899).

[2] Oxford and Asquith, *op. cit.*, ii, 207.

[3] Gladstone's admiration for Peel's administration may be gathered from his comment in his *Gleanings of Past Years* (New York, Scribner, n.d.), i, 242–3, where he speaks of a 'perfectly organized administration' like that of Peel in 1841–46.

[4] Charles Greville, *Journal* (New York, D. Appleton and Co., 1885), August 1840.

[5] For a description of Peel's handling of the office see W. I. Jennings, *Cabinet Government* (Cambridge, Cambridge University Press, 1936), pp. 140–1.

been carried on by a Cabinet, but by the heads of department each in communication with you.'[1] In fact, it is obvious that Peel exercised a degree of supervision and control which was not possible for his successors. The expansion of governmental functions made such action impossible and even Gladstone made no attempt to accept such comprehensive obligations despite his admiration for Peel's administration.[2]

The office of Prime Minister has differed according to the personal ability of the Prime Minister, the circumstances of the time, and the character and ability of his colleagues.[3] It is obvious, for example, that more can be made of the office in time of war than in periods of peace. The semi-autocratic control of Lloyd George and Winston Churchill depended upon the existence of an external crisis which involved the very life of the British Empire. War requires rapid decisions and a willingness to accept great personal responsibility. In peace time it is possible to use slower methods of compromise, concession and discussion, and any attempt to dictate decisions is likely to be resisted. It might be argued that the times give rise to the type of Prime Minister who fits the need although it would not be wise to depend upon the automatic operation of such a rule in periods of crisis or insecurity.[4]

---

[1] John Morley, *Life of Gladstone* (New York, Macmillan, 1911), i, 298.

[2] Gladstone's own description of the office is as follows: 'The head of the British government is not a Grand Vizier. He has no powers, properly so called, over his colleagues: on the rare occasions, when a Cabinet determines its course by the votes of its members, his vote counts only as one of theirs. But they are appointed and dismissed by the Sovereign on his advice. In a perfectly organized administration, such for example, as was that of Sir Robert Peel in 1841–6, nothing of great importance is matured, or would even be projected, in any department without his personal cognizance; and any weighty business would commonly go to him before being submitted to the Cabinet.' Gladstone, *op. cit.*, i, 242–3.

[3] The Machinery of Government Committee noted that the constitution and the methods of Cabinet procedure depended on the circumstances of the time, the personality of the Prime Minister and the capacities of his principal colleagues. Cmd. 9230, p. 4.

[4] The British system obviously provides a superior means of insuring that the best available person shall rise to the top in times of crisis when compared to the United States. The replacement of Chamberlain by Churchill in 1940 may serve as an example. The fixed terms, and the general inflexibility of the American system, makes it less certain in the case of the United States. Thus from 1857 to 1861 the United States was forced to put up with a man of obvious incapacity in the presidency.

The Prime Minister and the Cabinet

It is also necessary to recognize that the abilities of the Prime Minister's colleagues will have a very considerable effect on the extent to which he is able to exercise personal control and direction. Arthur Balfour has been described as one of the ablest of the British Prime Ministers of this century,[1] but his chief task throughout the first year of his administration was to hold together a Cabinet composed of such irreconcilable colleagues as Chamberlain and the Free Traders. After their resignation his Cabinet was not a patricularly strong one and it was much easier to provide firm direction. Sir Henry Campbell-Bannerman has been criticized for lack of direction in his Cabinet,[2] but, although there is considerable merit in the criticism, it is also necessary to remember that Sir Henry dealt with a Cabinet already divided with respect to foreign affairs and empire. Furthermore, there were men of exceptional ability, particularly Asquith, Haldane, and Grey, in the Cabinet. Any attempt at autocratic control in such circumstances must inevitably have failed.

While it is impossible to provide a precise description of the position of the Prime Minister relative to his Cabinet it is usually the case that he is not stronger than his whole Cabinet as with the American President.[3] Even here, however, it is necessary to add that in the case of Winston Churchill, and to a lesser extent, Lloyd George, it is almost impossible to think of anyone succeeding them in office whatever might be the character of their disputes with the Cabinet. Winston Churchill's personal position as war leader, his strong public support, his symbolic representation to the world of Britain's will to fight, made his position unchallengeable and therefore made united Cabinet opposition to his continuation as leader unthinkable.[4]

Assertions have frequently been made to the effect that the Prime Minister verges upon being a dictator. Ramsay Muir wrote, 'The Cabinet is, in short, the steering-wheel of the ship

[1] W. I. Jennings, *op. cit.*, pp. 146–7.

[2] Reginald Viscount Esher, *Journals and Letters* (London, J. Nicolson and Watson, 1934), ii, 160–1.

[3] Herman Finer, *The Theory and Practice of Modern Government* (New York, Henry Holt, 1949, p. 593.

[4] The evidence available on Churchill's relations with his Cabinet is still quite limited. To date the only memoirs of any importance in this connection are Churchill's own. It is obvious that such materials are insufficient for realistic assessment of his handling of the Cabinet.

of State. But the steersman is the Prime Minister. He not only assigns them to their offices, he can dismiss any of them, or transfer them from one office to another; and within certain limits he can determine the size of the Cabinet . . . it is certainly within his power, if he so desires, to reduce the size of the Cabinet by entrusting two or even more offices to the same man.'[1] Sidney and Beatrice Webb have brought similar charges against the Prime Minister and the Cabinet.[2]

'Today practically all the functions of political government and all the powers of the State, enormously widened in penetration and scope, are concentrated in the House of Commons and the executive it is assumed to create. Further, owing to the obsolete internal machinery of the House of Commons and to the immense variety and complexity of the issues with which it nowadays purports to deal, the power which it is incapable of exercising has been virtually transferred to the Prime Minister and his co-opted group of colleagues in the Cabinet and by them to the Civil Service acting in conjunction with powerful outside interests, The result is that, under the guise of government by a majority of the people acting through its elected representatives, we now have the dictatorship of one man, or of a small group of men, exercised through a subservient party majority of more or less tied members, and an obedient official hierarchy of unparalleled magnitude—a dictatorship tempered on the one hand, by a continual watchfulness against explosions of popular feeling, and on the other by the necessity of privately securing the acquiescence, or at least preventing the revolt, of powerful capitalist or other interests.'

There are elements of truth in the strictures of the Webbs and of Professor Muir, but in each case they have used an extremely powerful miscroscope to look at one aspect of the British political system. In consequence it has been magnified to disproportionate size. The Webbs wrote, it must be remembered, in 1920, during the administration of Lloyd George, who exercised more personal authority than any of his predecessors. This may, in part, explain the somewhat exaggerated picture

---

[1] Ramsay Muir, *How Britain is Governed* (New York, R. R. Smith, 1930), p. 82. See also Muir's testimony in the *Special Report from the Select Committee on Procedure on Public Business* (1931).

[2] Sidney and Beatrice Webb, *A Constitution for the Socialist Commonwealth of Great Britain* (New York, Longmans, Green, 1920), p. 72.

they have drawn. Both the Webbs and Muir are correct in asserting that the Cabinet dominates the Parliament in most cases. It is also true, although less frequently, that the Prime Minister sometimes exercises extremely broad control over the Cabinet, but the term 'dictatorship' is too extreme.

The House of Commons while governmentally controlled nevertheless has a latent reserve power of action which may embarrass the government if it does not respect the privileges of the House.[1] The House creates or produces the Cabinet and it still can, in the last resort, withdraw its support, although it is not likely to do so. Behind the House stands the public, for the ultimate sanction of the British Constitution is found in public opinion. It is always possible that discussion in the House of Commons may affect such a change in public attitudes as to bring about a change in the policy of a government which has actual control of the House.[2] There are still 'rules of the game' which have become a part of the outlook of the British public and equally of British political leaders, including the Prime Minister and his Cabinet. There is no reason to think political leaders are not affected by the same conceptions of political right and wrong as those who are not participants, and this may mean that the recognition of certain principles is part of their personality make-up.

The Webbs themselves admit that the 'dictatorship' is tempered by caution in the face of both popular feelings or possible group or associational protests. All dictatorships, of course, are tempered to some extent by these forces,[3] but it is obvious that the institutional methods for the expression of those antagonisms and the conventional rules of fair play as developed in Great Britain are far more effective checks than the haphazard systems of the one-party state. It is even possible that a convention requiring consultation with interested groups before the introduction of legislation affecting them has been added to

[1] The Savidge incident of 1927 provides the most dramatic example of the sudden rise of the House against the government. 217 *H.C. Deb.*, 5s., 1216 ff.

[2] Professor Finer contends that the opposition's constant criticisms of the government's economic policy in 1947 eventually resulted in a change of government policy brought about through a change in public attitudes consequent upon the criticisms. Finer, *op. cit.*, p. 590.

[3] Stalin's action in calling a halt to enforced collectivization of agriculture may be cited as an example in point.

the British Constitution.[1] If not a constitutional rule, it is at least a common administrative procedure, and provides another example of a method by which the public may restrain the government.

Muir's statement is equally untenable. It is clearly a grotesque parody of the facts to say that Stanley Baldwin was 'the steersman' of his government while the Cabinet was merely the 'steering-wheel'. It was Baldwin himself who once insisted, 'His Majesty's Ministers are *co-equal*'.[2] This description is equally invalid for almost every Prime Minister who may be mentioned, for the Cabinet is not an inanimate mechanism; its role in the formulation of policy is of vital importance in most cases. Muir's thesis tends to exaggerate the power of the Prime Minister as a result of the initial exaggeration of his power of appointment and dismissal. His comment would lead one to believe that the Prime Minister has an unlimited power in these respects, but this is obviously erroneous as was indicated in the preceding chapter. The Prime Minister has a free hand in some appointments, but he does not in others; in all cases he exercises his discretion within the framework of legal and conventional necessities. Similarly, it is also true that though he has substantial powers of dismissal they do not extend to the members of the Inner Cabinet except in the most extraordinary of circumstances. The charge of dictatorship must, therefore, be rejected as over-simplified and exaggerated. We are again left with Asquith's comment that the office 'is what its holder chooses and is able to make of it.'

The consequence is that the characteristics of the office have varied considerably during the period since 1894. There have been strong Prime Ministers who exercised personal direction and control. Lloyd George, Churchill, Chamberlain, and MacDonald, prior to 1931, belong in this category. Others have provided effective leadership without attempting to initiate basic policies. Asquith and Attlee belong in this category. Others have been weaker. Lord Salisbury made no real effort to control his Cabinet; Lord Rosebery made the effort, but his position in the Lords, when added to the personal bitterness of

---

[1] W. I. Jennings, *The Law and the Constitution* (London, University of London Press, 1933), pp. 88–9.

[2] G. M. Young, *Stanley Baldwin* (London, Rupert Hart-Davis, 1952), p. 40. (Italics mine.)

his relations with Harcourt, made success impossible; Stanley Baldwin, while occasionally prone to surprising and somewhat arbitrary actions, was, upon the whole, satisfied to let matters run on without excessively asserting himself. He did, however, in the crisis over Edward VIII's proposed marriage, act with great firmness. The only conclusion possible is that the office cannot be defined; it can only be described in terms of the use to which it was put by different individuals of varying abilities, who faced different problems and dealt with different colleagues.

The control of the agenda for all Cabinet sessions is vested in the Prime Minister. This is not an absolute power; he may not exclude items merely because he does not like them. There are political limits which make such actions impractical. An individual minister with high political status may always be certain that if he is insistent upon the necessity of discussing a particular item it will be added to the agenda.

Prior to 1916, while the Prime Minister made the determination as to what went on the agenda, the method of selection was rather haphazard. It was equally difficult to be sure of the precise content of the decision taken by the Cabinet in many cases for no official record of such decisions was kept. If a minister desired to bring a measure before the Cabinet he sought the direct permission of the Prime Minister. Often when such permission was granted only the Prime Minister and the minister making the request knew that it would be on the agenda. The Prime Minister was sometimes the only person who knew everything which would be on the agenda. This meant that the ministers were frequently not in a position to discuss intelligently an issue raised in the Cabinet meetings, for they were not always informed as to what would be considered. Previous information would have assisted them in making a better contribution to the discussion.

The absence of records also constituted another equally unpleasant evil in the procedure of the Cabinet. Only the Prime Minister was allowed to take notes in order that he might use them as the basis for his letter to the King; the other ministers were forced to rely upon their memories. Lord Curzon commented, 'The Cabinet often had the very haziest notion of what its decisions were; . . . cases frequently arose when the matter was left so much in doubt that a Minister went away and acted upon what he thought was a decision which subsequently turned out to be no decision at all, or was repudiated by his colleagues.'[1] To this stricture Curzon added, 'the civil servants often found difficulty in ascertaining from Ministers what decisions had been taken which affected their Departments, either because the Minister (especially if new to office) did not always know that his Department was concerned or what was the decision. In the early part of the war of 1914–1918 I was frequently approached by senior civil servants as to whether I had or could obtain any information.'[2]

It was obvious before the First World War that this situation resulted in inefficiency; in time of war it became intolerable. The war made it evident that more efficient procedures involving the circulation of the proposed agenda and other memoranda, as well as the keeping of records, were an absolute necessity. The institutional mechanism was already at hand in the Secretariat of the Committee of Imperial Defence. This body had functioned during the first years of the war in conjunction with the War Council and had later been attached to the Dardenelles Committee. One of the first actions taken by Lloyd George after he became Prime Minister was to attach the Secretariat to the War Cabinet. Lt.-Col. Hankey, the secretary, became the Secretary of the Cabinet.

The innovation proved successful in expediting the workings of the Cabinet. The Machinery of Government Committee recommended its continuance, 'for the purpose of collecting and putting into shape the agenda, or providing information and the material necessary for its deliberations, and of drawing up the results for communication to the departments concerned'.[3] The efficiency consequent upon the use of the Secretariat in time of war led to its continuation in the post-war period although some thought it infringed upon the functions of the political departments.

---

[1] 30 *H.L. Deb.*, 5s., 265. See also the comments of Robert Cecil in 155 *H.C. Deb.*, 5s., 246–7. For a contrary view see Asquith's statement at 155 *H.C. Deb.*, 5s., 227 ff.

[2] 30 *H.L. Deb.*, 5s., 265.

[3] Cmd. 9230 (1918), p. 6. However, the Committee inclined towards the idea that the Secretary be excluded from sessions in which policy matters, as distinguished from executive acts, were under consideration.

There was some continued criticism of the Secretariat and in 1922 Bonar Law stated in his election programme that he would abolish it. He was later persuaded, however, that the record proved its usefulness. The criticisms primarily grew out of the fact that the attachment of the Secretariat to the Cabinet had been carried out by Lloyd George and that he had then tied that body to his own person, thus effectively increasing his own power *vis-a-vis* the other members of the Cabinet. In particular it was argued that the Secretariat had interfered with the conduct of foreign affairs.[1] This charge was, to a considerable extent, valid. Lloyd George had taken advantage of its permanent staff to further advance his own control over the conduct of foreign affairs, a control which often involved bypassing the Foreign Secretary.[2] Actually it was not that portion of the Secretariat over which Hankey presided which Lloyd George used to assist in the formulation and execution of his personal foreign policy. Instead, he relied upon his technical secretaries, members of what has been called the Prime Minister's Secretariat. The members of this body were directly and immediately responsible to the Prime Minister personally, rather than to the head of the Cabinet Secretariat.[3] The Cabinet Secretariat has, nevertheless, remained a permanent institution and a very useful one.[4]

[1] 155 *H.C. Deb.*, 5s., 234–49.

[2] See Lord Curzon's statement in the Earl of Ronaldshay, *The Life of Lord Curzon* (New York, Boni and Liveright, n.d.), iii, 316–7. The letter was never delivered to Lloyd George, however, as the government resigned at that moment.

Another criticism was inherently trivial although it was frequently repeated. This criticism was that the presence of the Secretary at Cabinet meetings necessarily involved a restriction of discussion since the Secretary took no oath of secrecy. Bonar Law solved this by appointing Hankey to the post of Clerk of the Privy Council, an office which required an oath similar to that taken by the Privy Councillors themselves. Maurice Lord Hankey, *Diplomacy by Conference* (London, E. Benn, 1946), p. 74.

[3] For a description of the functions of the statistical section of the Prime Minister's Secretariat see Joseph Davies, *The Prime Minister's Secretariat, 1916–1920* (Newport, R. H. Jones, Ltd., 1951).

[4] It should be noted, however, that the size of the Secretarial establishment was sharply curtailed by Lloyd George's successors. In 1922 the Secretariat included a total of 144 persons (including charwomen); in 1923 it had been cut to 38.

The Secretariat has also made an impression upon American observers. There was some dispute before the final report on Administrative Manage-

Professor Jennings has listed the functions of the Cabinet Secretariat as follows:[1]

(a) To circulate the memoranda and other documents required for the business of the Cabinet and its committees;

(b) To compile under the direction of the Prime Minister the agenda of the Cabinet, and, under the direction of the chairman, the agenda of a Cabinet committee;

(c) To issue summons of meetings of the Cabinet and its committees;

(d) To take down and circulate the conclusions of the Cabinet and its committees and to prepare the reports of Cabinet committees; and

(e) To keep, subject to the instructions of the Cabinet, the Cabinet papers and conclusions.

It is not the intention here to argue that the position of Cabinet Secretary is not an office of some power. The Secretariat may influence the making of policy for it does deal with circumstances which affect the making of a decision, but in this respect the position of the Secretary is no different from that occupied by the regular permanent civil servants. The distinction often made between the heads of the departments and the permanent civil servants, on the grounds that the former makes policy and the other executes it, is an obvious oversimplification of the political process. The permanent civil servants often have technical knowledge to bring to bear upon a policy issue and such knowledge may obviously affect the decision made. The permanent civil service through long

---

ment in the United States in 1937 as to whether such a body should be recommended, for the President himself was chiefly responsible for the decision not to include such a recommendation. Louis Brownlow, *The President and the Presidency* (New York, Public Administration Services, 1949), pp. 105–6.

For a criticism of the suggestion that such a system be adopted in the United States see Jonathan Daniels, *Frontier on the Potomac* (New York, Macmillan, 1946), pp. 47–8.

[1] W. I. Jennings, *Cabinet Government* (Cambridge, Cambridge University Press, 1936), p. 189. The earlier practice of the Secretariat was to record discussions of issues as well as of conclusions. This is no longer the case. A. B. Keith, *The British Cabinet System* (London, Stevens and Sons, 1939), p. 134. See also the comments in the debate on the estimates for the Secretariat in 155 *H.. Deb.*, 5s., 213 ff.

experience comes to have an attitude of its own so that it is not incorrect to say that there is a 'Treasury attitude'[1] or an 'Admiralty attitude'. The character of the department head is of fundamental importance in deciding who has the most influence. As Lord Hankey points out, 'The objection that a Secretary of the Cabinet may become too powerful is one that in theory applies to the permanent head of every Government Department with much greater force. It can only happen in a Department if a Minister is either deplorably weak or grossly incompetent. In the case of the Cabinet there are many safeguards against it. The Secretary is under the immediate control of the Prime Minister, who is *ex officio* Chairman of the Cabinet, and a man does not become Prime Minister if he is deplorably weak or grossly incompetent. Further, there are a score of Ministers each with a great Department at his back, to see that the Secretary does not overstep his position. Any trespass by the Secretary on the responsibilities of a Minister of his Department would bring speedy retribution.'[2]

It has been contended that the Secretariat provides the Prime Minister with a more effective means of strengthening his control over his colleagues. E. C. Wade has said that the Secretariat increased 'the power of the Cabinet, and particularly of the Prime Minister.'[3] Similarly Sir D. McLean[4] and Lt.-Col. Guinness[5] also charged that it effectively concentrated more authority in the hands of the Prime Minister. Sir Austen Chamberlain, on the other hand, in speaking for the government, said, 'So far from the effect of having this record taken being to increase the power of any individual Minister, be it the Prime Minister himself, it is an essential feature for the preservation of control by the Cabinet as a whole over the general affairs of

---

[1] Asquith states that when he prepared his first budget and proposed to distinguish between earned and unearned income for purpose of taxation his Treasury experts insisted that it could not be done, arguing that Gladstone had considered it impracticable. Asquith tried to fortify his position through an investigation of the issue by a Select Committee of the House of Commons. The Committee supported him against the experts and in consequence the distinction was made. Lord Oxford and Asquith, *Memoirs and Reflections, 1852–1927* (Boston, Little, Brown and Company, 1928), i, 302.

[2] Lord Hankey, *op. cit.*, p. 77.

[3] E. C. Wade, Introduction to A. V. Dicey's *Law of the Constitution* (London, Macmillan, 9th edition, 1948), p. cxviii.

[4] 155 *H.C. Deb.*, 5s., 215–19.   [5] 155 *H.C. Deb.*, 5s., 254.

the nation.'[1] Lord Hankey has similarly argued that, 'If anything, the Secretariat would seem to act as a check on independent action, as it is its duty to communicate the decision to
the Minister who is called upon to act. When the decision is
written, it must be written clearly. It must be difficult for the
Prime Minister to overstep it.'[2]

The weight of the evidence seems to be upon the side of
Chamberlain and Hankey. It would be difficult for a Prime
Minister to censure an action taken by a Minister if the conclusion upon which it was taken is on the record. It is very
difficult to see how this restricts the freedom of the minister
unless it is argued that the minister should have the discretion
to act against the Cabinet decision. This is an obviously intolerable idea. Both the Prime Minister and the individual
minister exercise individual initiative at the mercy of the
record. The Secretariat, through the records maintained, provides a basis for appeals which must inevitably make acts of
discretion more dangerous to the individual executing them.
It is unlikely that any future Prime Minister can take advantage
of the Secretariat as a means of increasing his power *vis-a-vis*
the Cabinet.[3] The Secretariat has increased the power of the
Cabinet, as any increase in efficiency must increase the power
of any institutional body in the absence of concomitant im-
provements in the institutions with which it has relationships.
But it is difficult to see how it strengthens the Prime Minister
against his colleagues who share its advantages.

The Secretariat has thus provided a means by which the
agenda may be prepared and circulated beforehand, thus improving the possibility of effective discussion. Ministers are now
in a position to inform themselves before the Cabinet meetings
as to the various items to be discussed.[4] Normally such circulation takes place five days before the Cabinet meeting itself.[5]

[1] 155 *H.C. Deb.*, 5s., 223.   [2] Hankey, *op. cit.*, p. 78.

[3] It is, of course, beyond question that Lloyd George used his personal
Secretariat as a means of increasing his control of foreign affairs, but it does
not seem to have been used in this fashion by his successors. Lloyd George
had a compliant Foreign Secretary in Balfour and a Secretary who was not
especially interested in European affairs in Curzon. Cf. Harold Nicolson,
Curzon: The Last Phase (New York, Houghton, 1934), pp. 58–9.

[4] K. B. Smellie, *A Hundred Years of English Government* (New York, Macmillan, 1937), p. 374.

[5] W. I. Jennings, *Cabinet Government* (Cambridge, Cambridge University
Press, 1936), p. 191.

Similarly the records of conclusions are now much clearer than they were under the old system. In consequence there is less possibility of unauthorized action or failure to act when such is required.

It should be added in the case of the circulation of memoranda for the agenda that the Exchequer and the Law Offices usually see such materials before they are sent to other Cabinet officers.[1] Similarly, if another department is concerned it must also see the memoranda prior to circulation. It is not difficult to understand why the Exchequer and Law Offices always see such memoranda, for any proposal is likely to embody sections with obvious financial and legal implications. The two departments most concerned need to be able to make an early examination of such proposals in order to analyse their possible effects. This could conceivably lead to attempts to block further circulation, but the Prime Minister may always be appealed to by the initiator of the proposal, and if he is willing to authorize its inclusion on the agenda the Exchequer and the Law Offices must give way. The Prime Minister still exercises the final control over the agenda, limited only by what is politically practicable. The Secretariat has only provided a more effective method of circulating such documents; it has never managed to absorb the Prime Minister's power to determine what will or will not be put on the list for discussion. In one sense it has made it easier for him to control the discussions, for with a formal agenda prepared beforehand he is in a better position to put off consideration of an item which a minister may wish to raise at the last minute. He may, however, if he wishes, add such an item even after the Cabinet has begun its meeting.[2]

[1] *Ibid.*, p. 191; cf. Sir Thomas W. Heath, *The Treasury* (New York, G. P. Putnam's Sons, 1927), pp. 57–8.

[2] Merely because an item is on the agenda does not necessarily mean that it will be discussed. That depends, in part, upon the inclination of the Prime Minister who may concentrate discussion upon one item to the disadvantage of the other issues.

It has been said of Lloyd George, 'If there were half a dozen items on a prepared agenda he was just as likely to select the last as the first, or to dilate on either one to the exclusion of the other others.' George N. Barnes, *From Workshop to War Cabinet* (New York, Appleton, 1923), pp. 169–70. Arthur Balfour also once commented upon Lloyd George, 'We all unfortunately suffer from the Prime Minister's method—or lack of method—of doing business.' Blanche Dugdale, *Arthur James Balfour* (New York, G. P. Putnam's Sons, 1937), ii, 175.

The Cabinet is a collective executive and a collective instrument for the determination of legislative proposals. Therefore, it is important to acquire some understanding of its method of operations and the precise position and functions of the Prime Minister in the Cabinet. Since it is a collective body the question of whether or not votes are taken is frequently asked. We know that there have been instances of votes. In 1881 the decision to arrest Dillon was carried by one vote.[1] The Education Bill of 1901 also resulted in several Cabinet divisions and the final decision to restrict the bill to secondary education was carried by a vote of ten to eight.[2] It is evident, therefore, that votes are sometimes taken. The size of the Cabinet itself would lead one to the conclusion that such votes would be necessary in certain circumstances.[3]

Lord Oxford and Asquith has stated, 'It is not, or was not in any other Cabinets in which I have sat, the custom (unless exceptional cases not always of the first importance) to take a division.'[4] This is not, of course, an assertion that divisions are never taken, but only that they are unusual. Gladstone spoke of 'the rare occasions, when a Cabinet determines its course by the votes of its members.'[5] The evidence available from an examination of the memoirs of statesmen of the last half-century leads to the conclusion that such formal divisions are very infrequent. Since the Cabinet is a collective body which is required to present a united front to the public, it is essential that the members should be in agreement whenever possible. The normal procedure is to continue discussion until a point has been reached at which mutual compromises have resulted

---

[1] Stephen Gwynn and Gertrude M. Tuckwell, *The Life of the Rt. Hon. Sir Charles W. Dilke* (New York, Macmillan, 1917), i, 370.

[2] Sir Almeric Fitzroy, *Memoirs* (London, Hutchinson, 1925), i, 63–7.

[3] Professor Keith has commented, 'For some obscure reasons there seems reluctance to admit the fact that votes are quite normally taken when requisite.' Keith, *op. cit.*, p. 126.

It may be noted that an argument upon the basis of the size of the Cabinet is not entirely adequate. In fact, there is always a smaller body within the Cabinet which provides the real power of the government. If agreement can be reached within this 'Inner Cabinet' the rest of the members will usually fall into line without difficulty.

[4] Lord Oxford and Asquith, *Fifty Years of British Parliament* (Boston, Little, Brown and Co., 1926), ii, 220.

[5] Gladstone, *op. cit.*, i, 242.

in a final meeting point of agreement.[1] The final policy decision is frequently not the policy enunciated by any individual or group at the inception of the discussion, but a compromise among differing viewpoints.

In most cases compromise is possible. The members of the Cabinet are usually members of the same party. The parties themselves are tightly disciplined organizations. Starting from this common shared background, agreement can usually be reached without the necessity of a formal vote. Sir Edward Grey described the process in the following words:[2]

'The difference of opinion is disclosed, stated, and stoutly maintained on each side at a Cabinet. If it is so important and acute as to make resignations seem certain or probable, individual Ministers of different views seek private talks with each other outside the Cabinet. In this way the strength of their respective arguments is tested; the amount of concession that each feels he can make is ascertained. Finally, a Cabinet again meets with the knowledge that it is going to agree. This presupposes that the difference of opinion is really about the merits of the question, and is not a protest put forward for a personal or political object. When it is a pretext for either of these things, the procedure is much less pleasant and prognosis less favourable.'

Even should the discussion joined reveal continued conflicting viewpoints upon minor issues, it is not always necessary to take a formal vote, for the sense of the Cabinet can be obtained from the discussion itself.

In some cases the Cabinet is divided over matters which are of fundamental importance. In such cases a vote might be necessary, but a vote does not necessarily solve the problem. The imposition of the majority will upon the recalcitrant minority does not necessarily solve the division. It may simply widen the breach and make it unbridgeable. In some cases of this sort action must be taken. Thus in the summer of 1914 there was a sharp internal disagreement in the Cabinet as to

[1] Since Cabinet government depends upon compromise it is an essential prerequisite for membership that the individual should willingly subscribe to the idea of contributing to a common pool of ideas. This involves the possibility that his own viewpoint might be submerged in the final determination.

[2] Sir Edward Grey, *Twenty-five Years* (New York, Frederick Stokes, 1925), i, 194.

the course the British Government should take with respect to the war. There is no record of a formal vote, but some of the Cabinet members resigned.[1] In other cases of importance, it is not immediately necessary to arrive at a decision. It is time which is required as the healing instrument.

The foregoing discussion may seem to be unnecessary to the central focus of this chapter, but it is essential if we are to evaluate the role of the Prime Minister and the responsibilities which fall upon him in his capacity of chairman of the Cabinet. It is in these latter, sharp divisions, that the Prime Minister must show his own mettle. He must be able to bridge over the difficulties which exist within his Cabinet; he must be able to find possible points of agreements between the individuals on each side. Also he must try to keep the disagreement from reaching the boiling point, thus endangering the government itself.

One procedure which may be used will not be approved of by those who think of political leadership in terms of decisive decisions—it is to handle the internal disagreement by the expedient of not taking any action with respect to the area of conflict. The Prime Minister is in a position to carry out this policy as he may adjourn the meeting, or he may postpone the final determination of an issue in the hope that tempers will cool. In 1913, in consequence of sharp differences of opinion, the Naval Estimates were on the agenda of fourteen consecutive Cabinet meetings. Asquith's procedure was simply to adjourn the meeting when tempers got too high and agreement was obviously impossible. Such adjournment was successful in preventing the immediate ill-temper and personal acrimony from becoming permanent. Once the session is adjourned more informal consultations may be carried out. The Prime Minister, unless he has taken a strong position on one side or the other, is in the position to act as an arbitrator or at worst, a mediator, between the ministers of differing viewpoint.

It is not always the case that it is desirable to have a Prime Minister who is a man of dynamic energy with strong views of his own. 'Indeed a Prime Minister in peace time ought not to have a policy. If he has able ministers he ought to rely on them, and policies should come from departmental ministers, assisted

[1] Oxford and Asquith, *Memories and Reflections* (Boston, Little, Brown and Co., 1928), ii, 12–14.

as they are by all the knowledge and experience that their Departments can offer. The qualities which made Lloyd George a great Prime Minister in war time made him a disastrous Prime Minister in peace time....'[1] It must be remembered that the Prime Minister is a chairman of a committee, and it is always possible that the committee as a collective unit will include men of initiative and originality. The problem may be one of co-ordinating them, of providing a judicious weighing of the proposals made, rather than initiating them. Strong leadership in the sense of originality and initiative may be a prerequisite of the individual executive, but this is not necessarily true of a collective executive. In normal times a strong Prime Minister may create friction rather than harmony. A Prime Minister who splits the middle may be in a better position to hold his government together, for the Cabinet's effectiveness depends upon a mutual forbearance which may require that the chairman act as a neutralizer, rather than as an active agent.

The Labour Government of 1945 provides an example of a Premier who lacked the drive and colour of his colleagues. Ernest Bevin and Herbert Morrison were both more colourful than Attlee. Patricia Strauss, in commenting upon Attlee prior to his accession to the Premiership, wrote 'Politically he is always the middle man in Party controversies. He will never give a lead. He seems to think that being a leader of a Political Party is like being an impartial chairman of a committee. He feels it is his duty to be neither on the left nor right, but in the centre, so that he can be a sort of common denominator of the party.'[2] Mrs. Strauss was so depressed by her description of Attlee's characteristics that she insisted he should resign his position as party leader in favour of Bevin or Morrison.

Even if we accept her assessment of Attlee as accurate, and it it was not, it does not follow that he should have resigned. It might be argued that he was the ideal man to head a Labour Government for he could manage to hold together the conflicting personalities and factions within the party. The supporters of Morrison and Bevin had little love for one another.[3]

---

[1] W. I. Jennings, *The British Constitution* (Cambridge, Cambridge University Press, 1944), pp. 160–1.

[2] Patricia Strauss, *Bevin and Co.* (New York, G. P. Putnams' Sons, 1941), pp. 92–3.

[3] Francis Williams, *Socialist Britain* (New York, Viking Press, 1949), ch. vi.

In the long run Aneurin Bevan's group broke with both of the earlier groups. The fact that Attlee considered himself a representative of the centre was advantageous for this meant that none of the prima donnas would lump the Prime Minister with the opposition. In the centre he could act in a mediating capacity with respect to the factions which made up the party. All in all, Attlee was probably the most desirable Prime Minister Labour could have had in 1945, for in normal times it is better to have a Prime Minister who is adept in maintaining Cabinet unity and co-operation rather than a more controversial figure who attempts to lay down the law.

In time of war the situation is quite obviously different. Rapid decisions are required. The Prime Minister must, in many cases, make decisions upon his own initiative rather than waiting for a meeting of the Cabinet and the process of discussion. A Prime Minister like Asquith, who served with real distinction in times of peace, may become inadequate in time of war.[1] Similarly, a Prime Minister who is great in time of war may be inadequate in times of peace as Lloyd George was from 1919 to 1922.[2]

There have, of course, been strong Prime Ministers in time of peace. Both Disraeli and Gladstone provided direct personal leadership, although their techniques differed. Disraeli was something of a gadfly. He was likely to pronounce his opinion and hold it in the face of Cabinet opposition, cognizant that his hold over the public, plus his personal favour with the Queen, made his position as leader virtually beyond challenge. Gladstone, on the other hand, was as successful as Disraeli in gaining

---

[1] Balfour's comment on Asquith is particularly relevant here: 'He is an arbitrator, an eminently fair-minded judge—the best-tempered man I ever knew—a splendid chairman of a committee, and after all a Cabinet is only a committee; but I never heard him originate or suggest. If he were in this room now and heard us talk, he would still be incapable of understanding that more is required of him than the admirable balance he can give. But these are admirable qualities.' Dugdale, *op. cit.*, ii, 110–11.

Winston Churchill has also written, 'Mr. Asquith was probably one of the greatest peace-time Prime Ministers we have ever had. His intellect, his sagacity, his broad outlook and civic courage maintained him at the highest eminence in public life. But in the war he had not those qualities of resource and energy, of prevision and assiduous management, which ought to reside in the executive.' Winston Churchill, *Great Contemporaries* (New York, G. P. Putnam's Sons, 1937), p. 126.

[2] The role of the Prime Minister in war is examined in Chapter VIII.

his own way, but his technique was one of persuasion and conciliation rather than domination. Stansfield described his technique in Cabinet meetings as follows: 'He was always profuse in his professions of respect for the Cabinet. There was a wonderful combination in Mr. Gladstone of imperiousness and of deference. In the Cabinet he would assume that he was nothing. I thought he should have said, "This is my policy. What do you think of it?" and then have fought it out until they had come to an agreement. He always tried to lead them on by unconscious steps to his own conclusions.'[1]

David Lloyd George has similarly stated that Asquith never attempted to crush his colleagues, preferring to allow them to repress their own views and arrive at an eventual compromise. He functioned as a judge who weighted the evidence presented by the various parties prior to presenting his own considered opinion as to the desirable solution.[2] J. A. Spender has emphasized the length to which this moderation and conciliation went with Asquith by his comment that 'after five years of his Prime Ministership he was still in doubt whether he was a partisan of right wing or left.'[3]

To some persons this will seem a picture of a rather inadequate man, but Asquith's administration was a successful one. He held his government together through the crisis of the Lloyd George Budget, the Naval Estimates quarrels, the reform of the House of Lords, the Ulster crisis, and entrance into the First World War. It is not an exaggeration to say that Asquith was one of the most successful peace-time Premiers of this century.[4]

It is rather surprising to be informed that Lloyd George 'never overrode the Cabinet on any decision, and especially where matters of major importance were under consideration

---

[1] John Morley, *Life of Gladstone* (New York, Macmillan, 1903), ii, 415.

[2] Lloyd George described Asquith as 'essentially the judge'. David Lloyd George, *War Memoirs* (Boston, Little, Brown and Co., 1933), ii, 409.

[3] J. A. Spender, *Life, Journalism and Politics* (New York, Frederick Stokes, n.d.), ii, 156.

[4] Austen Chamberlain, of course, contended that he was inept in leading the Cabinet after 1915, and reports that Asquith frequently wrote letters during the Cabinet meetings, paying little attention to the discussion. Austen Chamberlain, *Down the Years* (London, Cassell, 1935), p. 11. Chamberlain's experience with Asquith was confined to the first Coalition and Asquith had been deeply affected by the death of his eldest son.

he invited comment and discussion hoping that this would lead to real agreement.'[1] This is not the usual picture of Lloyd George and it does not square with his inclination toward individual action which by-passed the appropriate minister. In particular his entrance into foreign affairs frequently involved by-passing the Foreign Secretary.[2] Lord Beaverbrook tells us that while Lloyd George was fractious and difficult to get along with in a subordinate position, 'his team play became perfect the moment he was made a captain, and the original source of every disturbance, the target of every mistrust, became a unifying influence in the Cabinet and an object of unbounded confidence.'[3]

It is obvious that the efficiency of the Prime Minister in the conduct of Cabinet discussions varies from man to man. Balfour is reported to have been particularly adept at keeping matters moving, and his memory for detail made him eminently successful in introducing salient information at the appropriate moment.[4] Sir Henry Campbell-Bannerman was far less adept. Lord Esher thought he had no real control over the departments.[5] This view was supported by Viscount Haldane, who said, 'The Prime Minister knew too little of the details of what had to be got through to be able to apportion the time required for discussion. Consequently instead of ruling the Cabinet and regulating the length of the conversations he left things much to themselves.'[6] In fairness it must be remembered that Sir Henry dealt with a potentially divided Cabinet throughout his term of office.[7]

It is more difficult to speak of the Prime Ministers of the inter-war years, but it is generally agreed that Ramsay MacDonald and Neville Chamberlain were the most able in directing Cabinet discussions, although this was not true of Mac-

---

[1] Barnes, *op. cit.*, p. 107.

[2] Cf. Nicolson, *op. cit.*,; Ronaldshay, *op. cit.*, iii.

[3] Lord Beaverbrook, *Politicians and the War, 1914–1916* (New York, Doubleday, Doran, 1928), i, 230.

[4] W. I. Jennings, *Cabinet Government* (Cambridge, Cambridge University Press, 1936), pp. 146–7.

[5] Esher, *op. cit.*, ii, 160–1.

[6] Richard Haldane, *Autobiography* (New York, Doubleday, Doran and Co., 1929), p. 231.

[7] Esher, *op. cit.*, ii, 290.

Donald during his tenure as head of the National Government.[1] Neville Chamberlain exercised firm control over discussions and provided direct initiative for foreign policy discussions.[2] Law's capacities as chairman of the Cabinet remain a mystery due to lack of evidence. Baldwin was not particularly able at handling the Cabinet. Neville Chamberlain is reported to have sometimes 'asked himself where is the lead?' while serving under Baldwin.[3]

It seems evident that Churchill provided real and very effective leadership during the war years, although we must wait for the memoirs and papers of other members of the Cabinet before we are really able to assess his abilities. There are some stories to the effect that Churchill was prone to delivering long monologues at Cabinet meetings. Others have said that while one got a sense of history in the making when Churchill presided over the Cabinet, it was often realized later that very little had actually been done. Comments on Attlee's chairmanship of the Cabinet during Churchill's absences indicated that while the proceedings were systematic and business-like, the chairman rather dry and pedantic, it was often realized in retrospect that a great deal of business had actually been completed.[4]

.   .   .

[1] Two contrasting pictures of MacDonald's position in the National Government are to be found in the characterizations of Neville Chamberlain and Viscount Samuel. It is reported of Chamberlain that 'as he sat beside him on the bench he wrote with pity of MacDonald's nervous trembling, yet would complain he was only interested in problems as they affected himself. . . . MacDonald, says an acid line, reports he has converted Rothermere from opposition by a threat to resign: "I have always heard that Rothermere was easily frightened, but I find it difficult to believe that the thing was done as simply as that".' Feiling, *op. cit.*, p. 228.

Samuel, on the other hand, writes, 'He was a good chairman of the Cabinet, carefully preparing his material beforehand, conciliatory in manner and resourceful. In the conduct of a Cabinet when a knot or tangle begins to appear, the important thing is for the Prime Minister not to let it be drawn tight. . . . MacDonald was skilful in such situations—and there were many.' Viscount Samuel, *Memoirs* (London, Cresset Press, 1945), pp. 214–15.

[2] Winston Churchill, *The Gathering Storm* (Boston, Houghton Mifflin, 1948), pp. 221–2; Feiling, *op. cit.*, pp. 303 ff.; Derek Walker-Smith, *Neville Chamberlain* (London, R. Hale, n.d.) ch. xv–xvii.

[3] Feiling, *op. cit.*, p. 165.

[4] Virginia Cowles, *No Cause for Alarm* (New York, Harper, 1949), p. 47.

The Prime Minister and the Cabinet

Evidence of the relative strength of the Prime Minister as compared with other Cabinet members may be seen in those instances in which he has acted either without authorization by the Cabinet or even against previously determined Cabinet policy. While such events occur it is nevertheless true that they are infrequent. The Prime Minister may, upon occasion, declare a governmental policy which has not yet been approved by the Cabinet. In such circumstances the Cabinet is in a difficult position for it must either follow the policy enunciated by the Prime Minister or run the risk of losing its leader, unless it is possible to find a compromise which will save the prestige of both. Lloyd George, for example, decided upon his own initiative to call a session of the Imperial War Conference and announced it in the Parliament without receiving the prior authorization of the Cabinet. The other members of the Cabinet were displeased and in the end a compromise was reached by which the meetings were held, but not as a formal conference; instead, they took place as an enlarged meeting of the War Cabinet.[1]

Stanley Baldwin took a more drastic step in 1923 when he raised the issue of protection without previously consulting his Cabinet. This eventually brought about the fall of the government.[2] In the same year he also determined on dissolution at an earlier date than his colleagues had thought desirable.[3] In his last administration Baldwin also took the initial steps in the action which led to the abdication of Edward VIII without previously consulting his Cabinet. However, he had consulted his senior colleagues.[4] Some time later the issue was taken to the Cabinet and Baldwin received the support of all of the members with the exception of Duff-Cooper.[5]

[1] David Lloyd George, *War Memoirs* (Boston, Little, Brown and Co., 1934), IV, ch. i.

[2] Wickham Steed, *The Real Stanley Baldwin* (London, Nisbet, 1930), pp. 63–8; Beckhoffer Roberts, *Stanley Baldwin: Man or Miracle?* (New York, Greenburg, 1936), p. 114; Feiling, *op. cit.*, pp. 108–9; Sir Charles Mallet, *Lord Cave: A Memoir* (London, J. Murray, 1931), p. 264.

[3] Steed, *op. cit.*, pp. 63–68; Roberts, *op. cit.*, pp. 117–18. A Cabinet majority had agreed upon January, but Baldwin determined to dissolve in November. Feiling, *op. cit.*, pp. 109–10; Young. *op. cit.*, pp. 66–7.

[4] Duke of Windsor, *A King's Story* (New York, G. P. Putnam's Sons, 1951), pp. 351 ff.; W. I. Jennings, 'The Abdication of King Edward VIII', *Politica*, ii, 292 ff.; Young, *op. cit.*, pp. 232 ff.

[5] Duke of Windsor, *op. cit.*, p. 346; Feiling, *op. cit.*, pp. 288–290.

Sir Henry Campbell-Bannerman on two occasions exercised his own initiative with respect to changes in policy. On one occasion he rose on the floor of the Commons to express the willingness of his government to exempt trade unions from liability for torts. This involved a change in a previously agreed upon Cabinet policy.[1] On another occasion he rose in the House to announce that his government was willing to include domestic servants within the scope of the Workmen's Compensation Bill. In this case his position was contrary to the intention which already had been expressed by the minister in charge of the bill.[2]

As would be expected more instances may be found of action taken by the Prime Minister and Foreign Secretary without previous consultation with other members of the Cabinet. One of the most important examples of this is to be found in the French–English military conversations prior to the First World War.[3] In the Second World War, Winston Churchill made a speech on the 22nd of June 1941 offering all possible assistance to the Soviet Union without consulting the Cabinet and he adds, 'nor was it necessary.'[4] Many military decisions were made without consulting the Cabinet, but this was clearly necessary and no claims of arbitrary action may ensue from such actions.

Of the independent actions taken in time of peace only Baldwin's were of basic importance if we exclude decisions made in the sphere of foreign affairs. Campbell-Bannerman's actions were not such as to strain the ties that bound the Cabinet together, although the exemption of unions from liability for torts was of political importance. Only Baldwin's action with respect to the King compares in magnitude with Lord John Russell's letter on the Corn Laws, written while in opposition, but pledging his party to definite course of action should it take office, or to Russell's later denunciation of the Catholic hierarchy.[5]

[1] J. A. Spender, *The Life of Sir Henry Campbell-Bannerman* (Boston, Houghton Mifflin, 1924), ii, 278.

[2] *Ibid.*, ii, 280.   [3] Grey, *op. cit.*, i, 91–7; Trevelyan, *op. cit.*, p. 152.

[4] Winston Churchill, *The Grand Alliance* (Boston, Houghton Mifflin, 1950), p. 370. Eden, Beaverbrook, and Cripps saw him during the day and were informed of his intentions. It might be noted, on the other hand, that prior to signing the Atlantic Charter he submitted it to the War Cabinet for approval. *Ibid.*, pp. 441–2.

[5] W. I. Jennings, *Cabinet Government* (Cambridge, Cambridge University Press, 1936), pp. 172–3.

As against these examples of independent action by the Prime Minister it is perhaps worth noting that Gladstone both spoke and voted for the secret ballot although he was not persuaded of its merit. The fact that his party was pledged to it was sufficient to cause him to support the measure in Parliament.

While these instances indicate that upon occasion the Prime Minister may act without authorization it is still true that it is unusual and not without danger. This follows because such action endangers Cabinet unity. A Prime Minister who has such proclivities will do well to restrain them. Each incident further intensifies the strain on the thread which holds the Cabinet together, thus endangering its stability and the security of the Prime Minister in his place.

Should the Prime Minister be determined upon a specific course of action, and should that action be opposed by a majority of the Cabinet, the Prime Minister does have at hand the weapon of threatened resignation. This unquestionably creates tension, but it does not create such high-tension as would develop if he publicly expressed his policy without authorization. The threat of resignation is more acceptable, although it is itself a two-edged weapon, for it is always conceivable that it may be accepted.[1] Lord Salisbury sometimes met Cabinet opposition with the comment, 'I shall tell them that if they insist on such-and-such, they must find another Prime Minister.'[2] Asquith also used this technique on occasion,[3] and Disraeli met the crisis over the Eastern question by threatening resignation. It is a weapon of the last resort, however. The Prime Minister must mean it and his colleagues must recognize that he means it or it is of no value.

One of the most important conventions of the British Constitution is that which decrees that the Cabinet is collectively responsible to the Parliament. The Cabinet goes in and out of

[1] Gladstone's threat of resignation in 1894 was received with some satisfaction by many members of the Cabinet who believed that the time had come for the 'old man' to go. Spender and Asquith, *op. cit.*, i, 87–8. Eventually Gladstone did resign as a result of the disagreement. John Morley, *Recollections* (London, Macmillan, 1921), i, 257–9.

[2] Lady Gwendolin Cecil, *Life of Lord Salisbury* (London, Hodder and Stoughton, 1931), iii, 174.

[3] Margot Asquith, *Autobiography* (New York, George H. Doran, 1920), ii, 208.

office together. Membership in the Cabinet entails an obligation to accept responsibility for the collective actions of the
Cabinet, whatever may be the individual minister's own personal predilections with respect to particular policies. As an
auxiliary aspect of the collective responsibility of the Cabinet,
the principle of Cabinet solidarity was developed. Whatever be
the personal views of the Cabinet minister he must publicly
support the policy of the government or he must submit his
resignation, leave the Cabinet, and thus leave the onus of
obligation to his colleagues behind him.[1]

Professor Freidrich has said that 'the resignation of a Cabinet
member such as Anthony Eden showed that the policy of
appeasement was Chamberlain's personal policy rather than
the policy of the Cabinet.'[2] This, however, is an unreal charac-
terization of the incident. It only indicates that there was
opposition to Chamberlain's foreign policy and that Anthony
Eden had found it impossible to continue to serve in a government dedicated to that policy. It would be as valid to say that
John Morley's resignation in 1914 indicated that the declaration of war was the personal policy of the Prime Minister rather
than the policy of the Cabinet, but any such statement is a gross
distortion of the facts. Similarly, it seems evident that while the
initiative for the policy of appeasement came from the Prime
Minister it was nevertheless accepted as Cabinet policy. It is
unrealistic to argue that a policy developed over a two-year
period was carried entirely against the wishes of the Cabinet.
Chamberlain had to have the support of the majority whatever
the reasons for such support might have been. A Cabinet
decision need not be unanimous for a policy to be a Cabinet
policy, for those who disagree may have decided that it is

---

[1] 'The convention of what Harcourt calls Cabinet "solidarity"—that is,
of such an appearance of unity as compels a dissentient to resign his office
before he openly speaks and votes against the policy of his Administration,
may be said to date from the Duke of Wellington's Government in 1828. In
its most extreme form it found expression in Melbourne's cynical dictum
some years later, that "it doesn't matter much what we say, but we must
all say the same thing".' Oxford and Asquith, *Fifty Years of British Parliament*
(Boston, Little, Brown and Co., 1926), ii, 215.

Walpole, however, had insisted upon unanimity in public expression
nearly one hundred years earlier. *Ante*, Chapter I.

[2] Carl Friedrich, *Constitutional Government and Democracy* (Boston, Little,
Brown and Co., 1941), p. 362.

better to publicly support the policy than to resign. Eden's resignation is an example of the operation of the principle of Cabinet solidarity. Eden faced the alternative of either keeping his opinion to himself or resigning. He chose the course of resignation in order to disassociate himself from the government.[1]

There have been other instances in which a policy was considered sufficiently important and erroneous to lead men to give up office. John Morley was joined by John Burns in 1914 in the submission of their resignations as a result of a Cabinet decision that it would not allow the German fleet to bombard the northern French coast.[2] Sir Edward Carson later resigned when the government refused to accept his policy of coercion in Greece.[3] Simon resigned on the issue of compulsory military service in 1915.[4] Philip Snowden and several of the Liberals eventually resigned from the National Government as a consequence of their opposition to the government's acceptance of a 'protection' programme.[5] In all of these cases the Prime Minister had a right to expect such resignations. In the absences of resignation he might have resorted to dismissal.

This does not mean that the Prime Minister is always able to control all expressions of opinion by each and every member of the Cabinet upon all policy matters. Arthur Balfour once said, 'What we require is common action and common responsibility. Nobody asks for uniformity of speech. Nobody who knows how human nature is constituted, nobody who knows how Cabinets are constituted will expect among members of a Cabinet absolute uniformity of opinion.'[6] Balfour's comment must be recognized as a defence of the indefensible. He was faced with the fact that his Colonial Secretary, Joseph Chamberlain, had been making speeches in favour of an elaborate system of Imperial Preference, while other members of the Cabinet had been making Free Trade speeches.

Balfour's argument is not completely acceptable. Normally

[1] Cf. 332 *H.C. Deb.*, 5s., 45 ff., for the debate which followed Eden's resignation. See also Feiling, *op. cit.*, pp. 337–9; Walker-Smith, *op. cit.*, ch. xvi.

[2] Oxford and Asquith, *Memories and Reflections* (Boston, Little, Brown and Co., 1928), ii, 35 ff.; Samuel, *op. cit.*, p. 104; J. Hugh Edwards, *David Lloyd George* (New York, J. H. Sears, 1929), ii, 382–3.

[3] Edwards, *op. cit.*, ii, 475.

[4] Lloyd George, *op. cit.*, ii, 173; Samuel, *op. cit.*, pp. 112–13.

[5] Samuel, *op. cit.*, pp. 226–35; Snowden, *op. cit.*, ii, 1018–30.

[6] 123 *H.C. Deb.*, 4s., 564.

where there is a Cabinet policy it is expected that the members of that body shall publicly express the same views. In the absence of a declared Cabinet policy there is a considerably wider latitude of possible expressions. In this connection it might be noted that there is more control in the field of foreign affairs, even in the absence of a Cabinet policy, than in other areas. It is recognized that the Secretary of State for Foreign Affairs may develop a policy with little Cabinet control so long as the Prime Minister approves. Thus Arthur Balfour cleared his speech on South Africa in 1896 with the Prime Minister (who was also Foreign Secretary) before delivering it. Lloyd George's famous speech in 1911, in which he warned Germany that Britain would not stand idly by in case of German aggression, also received the prior approval of the Prime Minister and Foreign Secretary.[1]

One outstanding example of ministerial disagreement publicly expressed took place in this century. This was the famous 'agreement to disagree'. It was a product of the formation of the National Government in 1931. The Government included representatives of the Conservative, Liberal, and National Labour parties. The Conservatives, who held a majority of the seats in the House of Commons by themselves, proposed to introduce a system of protection. Snowden and some of the Liberals were in disagreement with this policy and it was realized that if ordinary practices were followed the result would be an immediate split in the Cabinet and the resignation of the anti-protectionist members. In order to hold the government together it was therefore decided to allow disagreement on this one issue only and the public was treated to the sight of ministers bitterly disagreeing with one another in the Parliament and in other public speeches.[2]

Stanley Baldwin defended the arrangement on the grounds that no precedents as to what was constitutional or unconstitutional existed for a National Government. The Government itself was a precedent.[3] At the same time he admitted that 'had the precedent been made for a party Government it would

---

[1] Lloyd George, *op. cit.*, i, 43–4; Grey, *op. cit.*, i, 216–17. The idea of making the statement, however, was Lloyd George's. He submitted his proposal to Asquith and Grey who were pleased with the proposition.

[2] Samuel, *op. cit.*, p. 218; Snowden, *op. cit.*, ii, 1010–12.

[3] 261 *H.C. Deb.*, 5s., 535.

have been quite new and it would have been absolutely dangerous for that party.'[1] It is now generally agreed that the action
was not wise,[2] but it is necessary to note that even in this case
it was the policy of the Cabinet which made the innovation
possible. As Stanley Baldwin said, 'We have collective responsibility for the departure from collective action.'[3] No minister
could have taken such action upon his own initiative. It was
further an agreement limited to one specific issue. With respect
to all other matters the usual requirement of unanimity of
expression still applied. Its inadequacy was revealed by the
resignation of the dissident ministers after a brief time.[4]

The Prime Minister may, therefore, expect his colleagues to
vote as deemed desirable by the Cabinet and to speak on behalf
of the programme of the government. Naturally the former is
the more important of the two obligations and it may be the
case that a minister will be allowed to be silent as to a policy
he opposes so long as he casts his vote in its favour. The Prime
Minister may enforce this obligation by the dismissal of a
minister who violates it, although such action has not been
necessary in this century.[5]

While unanimity of expression has been the rule, with the
exception of the 'agreement to disagree', the full spirit of the
principle of collective responsibility has not always been fulfilled. The last term of office of Baldwin offers an instance in

---

[1] 261 *H.C. Deb.*, 5s., 534.

[2] Professor Jennings has commented, 'An "agreement to differ" in order
to maintain a coalition is an attempt to break down the party system and
to substitute Government by individuals for Government by political principles. No harm was done by the precedent of 1932 provided that it is not
regarded as a precedent.' *Cabinet Government* (Cambridge, Cambridge
University Press, 1936), p. 221. See also Harold J. Laski, *Parliamentary
Government in England* (New York, Viking Press, 1938), p. 214.

Leopold Amery, from the other side of the political spectrum, describes
the arrangement as 'fantastic'. *Thoughts on the Constitution* (New York,
Oxford University Press, 1947), p. 27.

[3] Samuel, *op. cit.*, p. 218. For parliamentary debates on the constitutionality of the action see the debates in the Commons at the above citations and
following. For the House of Lords discussion see 83 *H.L. Deb.*, 5s., 551 ff.

[4] Snowden, *op. cit.*, ii, 1018–30; Samuel, *op. cit.*, pp. 226–35.

[5] The Government does, on occasion, allow a free vote. This was done in
the case of the divorce bill and later on the proposal to abolish the death
penalty. In the case of the latter, members of the Cabinet were required to
either vote against the abolition of the death penalty or to abstain.

which the spirit of the rule was violated. Sir Samuel Hoare entered into negotiations with the French Government concerning the position to be taken by the two governments upon the Italo-Ethiopian War. Out of their conversations came the Hoare-Laval Pact. The Cabinet agreed to accept responsibility for it, 'although with much dissatisfaction; as Chamberlain later emphasized in debate, they had not expected final proposals.'[1] Immediate, deep-rooted public dissatisfaction with the Pact was expressed. The Cabinet did not defend the policy as one unit; instead Sir Samuel Hoare resigned, thus taking upon his own shoulders the full responsibility for the Pact. It is clear, despite his action, that the policy was Cabinet policy and had received the support of the Prime Minister. Hoare was thrown to the wolves in order to save the Cabinet.[2] One thing is quite clear—the principle of collective responsibility was violated by the Prime Minister and his colleagues.

While examples have already been cited in which the Prime Minister has taken a course of action not authorized by the Cabinet, it is evident that he is normally the only member of the Cabinet who dares to so act and even in his case he must proceed with caution. Other ministers must not act in such a fashion because all of the members of the Cabinet are expected to accept a collective responsibility for the actions of individual ministers. A minister who acts independently thus involves the fortunes of others with his own and is not likely to achieve a high degree of popularity. There have been instances, however, in which such action was taken.

Winston Churchill sent out an order to keep the fleet in its North Sea stations in 1914 without Cabinet authorization or the knowledge of the Prime Minister, but it was approved *ex post facto*.[3] In 1922, Montagu, the Secretary of State for India,

---

[1] Feiling, *op. cit.*, p. 274.

[2] *Loc. cit.* Feiling speaks of a Prime Minister 'who had been forced to jettison a principal colleague, together with a policy which he had himself accepted'. While Feiling purports to be defending the Prime Minister it is doubtful if he could have written more condemnatory words. A. B. Keith has commented, 'The Cabinet had approved, and the acceptance of his resignation was merely an ingenious device for avoiding the force of public resentment of the complete deviation from the pledges on which the election of 1935 had been fought.' A. B. Keith, *The British Cabinet System, 1830–1938* (London, Stevens and Son, Ltd., 1939), p. 106.

[3] Spender and Asquith, *op. cit.*, ii, 80–1.

authorized the publication of a statement to the effect that the British were not engaged in furnishing assistance to the Greeks for another campaign against the Turks. This action, taken without the authorization of either the Cabinet or the Prime Minister, resulted in a bitter Cabinet session and ended with Montagu's resignation.[1] On another occasion Baldwin, while Chancellor of the Exchequer, entered into an agreement with the United States on the repayment of the war debt which was contrary to specific Cabinet policy. Baldwin was not dismissed because he had made his action public and the Prime Minister, although he thought seriously of resignation, had to accept it in order to secure his government.[2] Independent, unauthorized action is risky and may bring an end to the political career of a minister should the Prime Minister feel strong enough to dismiss him.

One of the most important evidences of the relative superiority of the Prime Minister to his colleagues is found in his power to dismiss them, or transfer them from one post to another, even from a superior to an inferior office. Technically, of course, any dismissal of a minister is carried out by the King, but, in fact, the King acts only upon the advice of the Prime Minister. Since the minister holds office at the pleasure of the Crown he may be dismissed at any moment.

It is of some interest that Gladstone did not believe that the Prime Minister had the power to remove a minister. 'He certainly is disposed,' wrote Sir William Harcourt, 'to regard the heads of Departments like Secretaries of State as to a great degree autonomous in their own province—regarding the Prime Minister as only *primus inter pares*. I know that he entertains great doubts as to the right of the Prime Minister to require a Cabinet minister to resign.'[3] In 1880 Gladstone asked Lord Carlingford to resign his position, but the latter refused.

---

[1] Nicolson, *op. cit.*, pp. 267–8; Ronaldshay, *op. cit.*, iii, 285–6.

[2] Steed, *op. cit.*, pp. 51–5; Roberts, *op. cit.*, pp. 95–6. It is reported that the Prime Minister 'wanted passionately to resign rather than set his hand to the document, and he was only restrained with the greatest difficulty by the arguments of his friends and his sense of duty to the country'. Lord Beaverbrook, *Politicians and the Press* (London, Hutchinson, n.d.), p. 61, Cf. H. A. Taylor, *The Strange Case of Bonar Law* (S. Paul and Co., n.d.) pp. 270–2 ; Young, *op. cit.*, pp. 44–7.

[3] Gardiner, *op. cit.*, ii, 610.

Gladstone's disbelief in his own power led him to drop his action and Lord Carlingford served for the rest of the year.[1]

Whatever Gladstone may have thought of the power of the Prime Minister in this respect it is evident that that officer does have the power to request the resignations of his colleagues and to dismiss them if such resignations are not forthcoming. Lord George Hamilton, who resigned as a result of pressure applied by Balfour, said, 'A Prime Minister has an undoubted right to request any of his colleagues, whose presence in his Cabinet is, in his opinion or judgement, prejudicial to the efficiency or policy of the Government, to resign his office.'[2] The same attitude as to the power of the Prime Minister is implicit in Asquith's comment that 'the first essential for a Prime Minister is to be a good butcher.'[3]

Despite Hamilton's categorical assertion and Asquith's description of the essential requirement of the Premiership it is nevertheless true that dismissals are very infrequent. In fact, overt dismissal has not occurred in this century.[4] The normal procedure is resignation, but it is obvious that some resignations are made at the request of the Prime Minister, an action which is dismissal in everything but name.[5] Normally the Prime Minister need not fear that the minister who is requested to submit his resignation will fail to do so. 'There is a tradition—a kind of public school fiction—that no minister desires office, but that he is prepared to carry on for the public good. That tradition implies a duty to resign when a hint is given.'[6]

Some resignations are obviously dismissals. Among the better-known examples of such actions are those which involved Balfour in 1903. At that time he summarily dismissed Balfour of

---

[1] *Loc. cit.*   [2] Holland, *op. cit.*, ii, 351.

[3] Winston Churchill, *Great Contemporaries* (New York, G. P. Putnam's Sons, 1937), p. 117.

[4] 'Technically, formal dismissal is hardly known, since Pitt gave the King the choice between him and Thurlow in 1792.' A. B. Keith, *The British Cabinet System, 1830–1938* (Stevens and Sons, Ltd., 1939), p. 101.

[5] For an example see Francis Williams, *Socialist Britain* (New York, Viking Press, 1949), p. 53.

[6] W. I. Jennings, *Cabinet Government* (Cambridge, Cambridge University Press, 1936), p. 163.

Attlee, speaking of persons he had dismissed or demoted, says, 'with the exception of one person who was clearly unfit, all of my colleagues took my decision with complete loyalty and never displayed the least resentment.' *As It Happened* (London, William Heinemann Ltd., 1954), p. 155.

Burleigh and Ritchie from his Cabinet by the simple expedient of pointing out that given their opinions they could not remain members of his Government.[1] The Duke of Devonshire said of this action, 'I never heard anything more summary and decisive than the dismissal of the two Ministers.'[2] Other examples which might be cited include Asquith's removal of Lord Elgin in 1908,[3] and a similarly enforced resignation in the case of Lord Tweedmouth, who was First Lord of the Admiralty, in the same year.[4] In 1935 Baldwin removed both Lord Londonderry and Lord Sankey.[5] The resignation of Montagu in 1922, after he had acted without Cabinet authorization, was clearly a case of dismissal and was so described by the Prime Minister.[6]

The power to transfer ministers from one post to another also inheres in the Prime Minister. In 1911 Asquith exchanged offices between McKenna and Churchill, the former going to the Home Office, the latter to the Admiralty.[7] In 1938 Chamberlain transferred Sir Thomas Inskip from the post of Minister for the Co-ordination of Defence to the position of Secretary of State for the Dominions. Chatfield replaced him at the other post.[8] In 1917 Lloyd George removed Sir Edward Carson from the Admiralty, as he believed Carson to be an inefficient administrator. Lloyd George made him a Minister without Portfolio.[9] The same 'public school fiction' which leads to the acceptance of dismissal also results in the acceptance of demotion to an inferior position.

There are, of course, some occasions when these powers are more likely to be used than others. The accession to the Premiership upon the resignation of the Premier as a result of ill-health will leave the new Prime Minister with the right to reconstruct the government, to transfer some officers, and to remove others. It is recognized that the new Prime Minister has a right to reshuffle offices if he thinks it necessary, although it is still a government composed, on the whole, of the same

[1] Dugdale, *op. cit.*, i, 267.　　[2] Holland, *op. cit.*, ii, 340.

[3] Spender and Asquith, *op. cit.*, i, 198.　　[4] *Ibid.*, i, 198.

[5] Feiling, *op. cit.*, p. 243.　　[6] Nicolson, *op. cit.*, pp. 267–8.

[7] Oxford and Asquith, *Fifty Years of British Parliament* (Boston, Little, Brown and Co., 1926), ii, 125.

[8] Feiling, *op. cit.*, p. 387.

[9] Major-General Sir C. E. Callwell, *Field-Marshal Sir Henry Wilson, His Life and Diaries* (London, Cassell, 1927), ii, 6.

party representatives. The other members of the ministery will always submit their resignations upon the appointment of the new Prime Minister, who may then select those whom he wishes to accept and those whom he wishes to drop. Such reconstruction can normally be carried out without much fear of possible political repercussions. Similarly, it is also true that it is usually possible to carry through ministerial reforms after a successful general election.[1] The Prime Minister need not fear possible attacks from the opposition in the latter case for there is no immediate prospect of an election.

Few ministers are dismissed; more are transferred from one position to another, but even in the latter case such occurrences are surprisingly infrequent. Among the factors which lead to this situation is the possibility that such action may weaken the political position of the government. The Prime Minister must realize that if he dismisses a minister or transfers him to an inferior position the opposition will take advantage of this to attempt to impress the electorate with the government's internal weakness. A dismissal frequently constitutes an admission of error in the original appointment; a man not of ministerial calibre, or at least one not capable of handling the particular department he has occupied, has been appointed. The opposition is in a position to use such events to bring strictures against the Prime Minister, and to raise the cry that he is an inept judge of men and hence equally untrustworthy as a leader.[2]

A Prime Minister with a substantial majority in the House of Commons can probably dismiss a minister or transfer him to a subordinate post in the early or middle years of the legal term of the Parliament with safety. It was probably advantageous, rather than disadvantageous, to Attlee and his government when the former transferred Shinwell away from the Ministry of Fuel and Power.[3] Since the Parliament had two years remaining to its legal term of office it was likely that the public would not weigh the alleged inadquacies of Shinwell too

---

[1] It is a great deal easier to transfer or dismiss a minister in time of war as the opposition is not likely to take advantage of it. In usual circumstances there is no opposition, for the major parties enter into coalition arrangement for the conduct of the war.

[2] W. I. Jennings, *Cabinet Government* (Cambridge, Cambridge University Press, 1936), p. 156.

[3] It might be possible to consider this incident as one in which the Minister served as a scapegoat for a governmental failure.

heavily in the election proper. It is unlikely, however, that it would have been safe for Attlee to have so acted if the term of the Parliament had been near its conclusion, for such a procedure would have given the opposition an additional, and advantageous, debating point.

While the Prime Minister does have the power to transfer or dismiss officers it is greater with respect to some members of the government than with others. Some ministers are in a stronger defensive position than those who lack substantial outside support. The latter are more likely to feel the sting of dismissal or demotion in case of maladministration.[1] The situation is very much like that which exists at the initial formation of the government. Certain individuals are so strong as to be almost beyond the reach of the disciplinary powers of the Prime Minister so long as they maintain minimal observance of the niceties of Cabinet etiquette and responsibilities.

'There are two persons with whom a minister ought to be able to toss his thoughts and policy. One is his chief private secretary, and the other is the Prime Minister.'[2] This statement reflects one of the principal obligations incumbent upon the Prime Minister—that he make himself available to his colleagues for purposes of consultation, advice and assistance. It is, of course, obvious that not every matter is to be brought to him by the minister. Only those matters which are of basic importance should be the subject of such consultation. One of the tests of the good minister is whether he is or is not able to distinguish matters of sufficient importance to require consultation with the Prime Minister or the Cabinet prior to making a decision from those which he himself should settle. A Prime Minister must, however, be accessible if he is to be fully effective. One of the most frequent complaints made against

---

[1] While most dismissals or demotions are the result of dissatisfaction with the way a particular department has been operated, as with Colonel Seeley in 1914, this is not always the case. Lord Elgin's removal in 1908 was occasioned by Asquith's belief that Elgin did not contribute much to Cabinet discussions and that he did not adequately assist the government in its parliamentary functions. Asquith was satisfied with his handling of purely administrative matters. Spender and Asquith, *op. cit.*, i, 198.

[2] Grey, *op. cit.*, i, 119.

Ramsay MacDonald was that he was not available to his colleagues when they sought advice.[1]

Consultation not only benefits the minister, but is also advantageous to the Prime Minister, for it brings him into contact with those operating problems of the various departments which frequently impinge upon the efficiency of the government as a whole. This is itself of basic importance for the general supervision of administration and the overall co-ordination of governmental action are responsibilities which inhere in the office of the Prime Minister. This does not mean that he interferes with all aspects of departmental affairs for this is physically impossible. The contemporary Prime Minister is normally concerned with policy.[2] Details are of importance only in so far as they impinge upon an issue of policy, although this is less true of the departments of defence and the Foreign Office than in the case of the other departments.

The degree to which the Prime Minister keeps himself informed on the progress of the departments naturally varies from department to department, and in accordance with the important political problems of the day. It is also true that the degree of supervision varies according to the personality and inclinations of the particular individuals who hold the Premiership. Lord Salisbury, in his last administration, made little effort to maintain systematic supervision of the operations of the subordinate departments. He 'left his colleagues very much to themselves unless they consulted him.'[3] Winston Churchill, on the other hand, seems to have had his hand in almost every department of the government although he was primarily concerned with the conduct of foreign affairs and war in the narrow sense of those terms.[4]

[1] In consequence of MacDonald's inaccessibility many ministers are reported to have turned to Arthur Henderson for advice during the Second Labour Government. Hamilton, *op. cit.*, p. 310.

[2] Weir, *op. cit.*, pp. 218–19.

[3] Lady Victoria Hicks-Beach, *op. cit.*, ii, 363; Cecil, *op. cit*, iii, 153. In 1896 Queen Victoria protested that he had not informed her that the Government intended to mobilize a Flying Squadron. Salisbury replied, 'I was as much surprised as your Majesty to see in *The Times* the account of the intention to send a flying squadron and troops to the Cape. I first heard of the project yesterday, but I did not understand it to be mature.' *Letters of Queen Victoria*, 3rd series (London, J. Murray, 1932), iii, 12.

[4] A cursory examination of the telegrams and memoranda in the appen-

Some departments which deal with a particularly ticklish or important problem are expected to keep the Prime Minister up to date on developments. Under the reigns of both Victoria and Edward VII, Ireland was a continuous trouble spot for the British Government, and in consequence it was customary for the Secretary of State for Ireland to keep the Prime Minister fully informed as to developments there. This was necessary for the Prime Minister was always likely to have to face a situation in which the Irish members of the Commons might begin an attack upon governmental policy in Ireland. In such circumstances it was necessary that the Prime Minister know what was taking place in order to explain or defend the government's conduct.[1]

As would be expected the Prime Minister is normally in close contact with the defence departments. This becomes particularly true in time of external crisis. In such circumstances the service departments are obliged to keep in close contact with the Prime Minister. Thus Asquith stated, 'From that day [when Kitchener became Secretary of State for War] Lord Kitchener and I were in the closest and most intimate contact. Except during his few and brief absences in France and the Dardanelles he came to see me every day, generally more than once, often three and four times.'[2] In the first year of World War II, Winston Churchill, as First Lord of the Admiralty, made a deliberate effort to maintain close relationships with the Prime Minister.[3]

In more normal circumstances the Prime Minister was in a position to have complete information as to defence problems through the Committee of Imperial Defence. This Committee

dices of Churchill's war memoirs indicates that he constantly made suggestions or asked questions of department heads, often on minor matters.

It has been said that 'Only in certain Departmental matters, such as that of the Ministry of Labour, was policy determined by a Minister other than the Prime Minister.' Francis Williams, *Press, Parliament and People* (Toronto, W. Heinemann, Ltd., 1946), p. 90.

[1] For examples of such reports see G. W. Mackail and Guy Wyndham, *The Life and Letters of George Wyndham* (London, Hutchinson, n.d.), ii, 409, 426, 495. Wyndham was Chief Secretary for Ireland from 1900 to 1905.

[2] Oxford and Asquith, *Memories and Reflections* (Boston, Little, Brown and Co., 1928), ii, 81.

[3] Winston Churchill, *The Gathering Storm* (Boston, Houghton Mifflin, 1948), p. 452.

served as an advisory body to the Cabinet on all problems of defence, including long-range strategy. 'Constitutionally," as Ramsay MacDonald said, 'it consists of one member, who is the Prime Minister.'[1] The Prime Minister in his capacity of chairman of the committee[2] could and did ask others to serve on the body. The heads of the defence departments and the chief professional officers of each of the services were permanent members in everything but name.[3] It was also within the power of the Prime Minister to increase or diminish the number of persons who normally served on the body or to call in any outside specialists whom he might wish to add to the organization in order more effectively to handle a specific problem.[4] The Prime Minister also served as chairman of the Chiefs of Staff Committee, a subcommittee of the Committee of Imperial Defence, when the problems they were discussing impinged upon political issues.[5]

The method of co-ordinating the service departments and the prosecution of war under the general supervision of the Prime Minister received a more effective institutional form when Churchill became Prime Minister, for he also took the

[1] 287 *H.C. Deb.* 5s., 1230.

[2] It is reported that from the end of the war until 1924 the Prime Minister did not always act as chairman of the Committee, frequently selecting another individual to perform that function. Baldwin is reported to have taken the chairmanship back in 1924. Herman Finer, 'The British Cabinet, the House of Commons and the War'. *Political Science Quarterly*, lvi, 325.

[3] The composition of the Committee from 1905 to 1909, in addition to the Prime Minister, was: the four Secretaries of State, the First Lord of the Admiralty, the Chancellor of the Exchequer, the First Sea Lord, the Director of Naval Intelligence, the Inspector-General of the Forces, the Admiral of the Fleet, and Lord Esher, who had served on many committees as an adviser on military organization and defence problems. 8 *H.C. Deb.*, 5s., 1382-3.

In 1934 the Committee included the Lord President of the Council, heads of the three service departments, the Secretary for India, the Foreign Secretary, the Chancellor of the Exchequer, and the Chiefs of Staff of the three services. 287 *H.C. Deb.*, 5s., 1230.

[4] 8 *H.C. Deb.*, 5s., 1382. 'On November 12 1936, Mr. Baldwin said that 29 Ministers, 179 officers of the fighting forces, 283 civil servants, 11 Dominion representatives, and 30 outside experts had worked on defence problems of all kinds stimulated by the Committee of Imperial Defence in the preceding year.' Herman Finer, 'The British Cabinet, the House of Commons, and the War', *Political Science Quarterly*, lvi, p. 327, n. 2.

[5] 215 *H.C. Deb.*, 5s., 1030.

office of Minister of Defence, He described the reasons for his action in the following words: 'The key-change which occurred on taking over was, of course, the supervision and direction of the Chiefs of Staff Committee by a Minister with undefined powers. As this Minister was also the Prime Minister, he had all the rights inherent in that office, including very wide powers of selection and removal of all professional and political personages. Thus for the first time the Chiefs of Staff Committee assumed its due and proper place in direct daily contact with the executive Head of the Government, and in accord with him had full control over the conduct of war and the armed forces.'[1]

Churchill's experiment worked so well that a variant of it was continued after the war. Instead of reverting to the Committee of Imperial Defence, the Minister of Defence became a permanent part of the machinery of government and a member of the Cabinet, superseding his subordinates at the War, Air, and Admiralty offices. Additionally, a Defence Committee, first established under Churchill, was continued under the chairmanship of the Prime Minister, although the Minister of Defence frequently deputized for him.[2]

The Minister of Defence, however, is still clearly inferior in position and responsibility to the Prime Minister who must accept the final responsibility for the determination of defence decisions. As Prime Minister Attlee said, 'the Prime Minister presides over the Defence Committee precisely because the wider aspects of defence . . . must be dealt with by the authority of the Prime Minister who has to take full account of not only [*sic*] the claims of defence, but also of the claims of all the other activities of the nation, and obviously that could not be handed over completely to the Minister of Defence.'[3] The new organization would seem to offer the advantage of placing a substantial portion of the more specialized problems upon the shoulders of the Minister of Defence while clearly establishing the superior authority of the Prime Minister.

[1] Winston Churchill, *Their Finest Hour* (Boston, Houghton Mifflin, 1949), p. 16. Cf. *Central Organisation for Defence*, Cmd. 6923 (1946), p. 3. Although the Prime Minister became Minister of Defence there was no Ministry of Defence. For administrative assistance Churchill used the military secretariat of the War Cabinet. *Ibid.*, p. 4.

[2] Cmd. 6923 (1946), p. 6.   [3] 426 *H.C. Deb.*, 5s., 625.

At other times economic problems have been of fundamental importance and it has been necessary for the Prime Minister to assert his over-riding authority in those fields, in recognition of the fact that it is his responsibility to see that decisions in the economic and financial fields are co-ordinated with governmental policy in other areas. In 1919 Lloyd George established a Financial Committee in the Cabinet over which he presided. It contained four other permanent members, the Lord Privy Seal, the Secretary of State for the Colonies, the President of the Board of Trade, and the Chancellor of the Exchequer.[1] Like the Committee of Imperial Defence the Financial Committee was empowered to call other ministers or permanent officials, as well as outside experts.[2] The Financial Committee was not continued by Lloyd George's successors.

Upon the establishment of the second Labour Government, Ramsay MacDonald, the Prime Minister, established an Economic Advisory Council to assist him in executing his responsibilities.[3] As its name implies it was an advisory body, its functions being described as follows:[4]

'To advise his Majesty's Government in economic matters. To make continuous study of developments in trade and industry and in the use of national and imperial resources, of the effect of legislation and fiscal policy at home and abroad, and of all aspects of national, imperial, and international economy with a bearing on the prosperity of the country.'

This body was subject to the general direction of the Prime Minister who served as its chairman. It was provided with a permanent administrative staff and the principal economic ministers served with the Prime Minister.[5] Through the reports received from this body and the special studies made by its sub-committees the Prime Minister was in a better position to supervise the financial and economic policies of the government and thus to provide a more sensible system of economic planning. Gradually, however, the Economic Advisory Council

---

[1] 120 *H.C. Deb.*, 5s., 744.   [2] *Ibid.*, 745.

[3] The roots of this body are found in the Committee of Civil Research established by Baldwin in 1925. See Cmd. 2440 (1925).

[4] *Economic Advisory Council*, Cmd. 3478 (1930), p. 2.

[5] The permanent members in 1930 were, in addition to the Prime Minister, the Chancellor of the Exchequer, the Lord Privy Seal, the President of the Board of Trade, and the Minister of Agriculture and Fisheries. *Ibid.*, pp. 2–3.

became inoperative. It was still functioning as late as 1934,[1] but the indications are that it did not meet in 1935.[2] There is no record of later meetings of the full Council. It is clear that MacDonald's successors did not have his high opinion of the efficacy of the organization.[3] The growing concern with foreign affairs and the fact that Chamberlain, in particular, concentrated most of his attention on international problems probably explains its gradual demise.[4]

When the economic crisis became acute in post-war Britain, the Prime Minister had to concentrate much of his attention upon that problem. A Policy Committee was created in 1947 under the chairmanship of the Prime Minister.[5] The other members of the committee were the Minister of Economics,[6] the Chancellor of the Exchequer, the Lord President of the Council,[7] the Foreign Secretary, and the Minister of Labour. Thus all of the principal economic officers, under the direction and supervision of the Prime Minister, were concentrated upon the solution of the economic problem. It seems evident, however, that while the Prime Minister was in a position to co-ordinate economic decisions with governmental policy elsewhere, the principal responsibility for economic decisions, organizations, and policy was actually undertaken by Sir Stafford Cripps and Herbert Morrison.

As would be expected another department with which the Prime Minister is in close contact is the Foreign Office.[8] In ordinary circumstances the Foreign Office is in daily contact with the Prime Minister. In times of external crisis the association between the department and the Premier becomes par-

---

[1] 304 *H.C. Deb.*, 5s., 1177–8.   [2] 308 *H.C. Deb.*, 5s., 1954.

[3] Attlee, who served on the Committee in the second Labour Government, has said, 'There were interesting discussions but nothing constructive ever emerged'. Clement Attlee, *As It Happened* (London, William Heinemann Ltd., 1954), p. 69.

[4] Some of its sub-committees continued to function as late as 1939. W. K. Hancock and M. M. Gowing, *British War Economy* (London, H.M. Stationery Office, 1949), p. 47.

[5] A similar committee had been created during the war, but it was chaired by the Chancellor of the Exchequer. *Ibid.*, p. 93.

[6] This office was later abolished.

[7] The Lord President of the Council, Herbert Morrison, was recognized as the chief planning officer in the government.

[8] The relations of the Prime Minister and the Foreign Secretary are examined at more length in Chapter VIII.

ticularly close. It is probable that the Prime Minister normally has much closer contact with the Foreign Office than with any other single department. The general responsibility which the Prime Minister has for the functions of all departments becomes more specific in the case of the Foreign Office because of the continuously important considerations with which that department deals.

This does not mean that the Prime Minister is always informed of all details of operation, but he must be consulted on all major matters arising in the province of the Foreign Secretary.[1] Gladstone once said, 'that the First Minister, as well as the Foreign Secretary, is bound to advise the Crown on questions of foreign policy.'[2] Normally the Prime Minister will also see all important correspondence of the Foreign Office.[3] Similarly he is informed of the content of conversations with foreign representatives.[4] In some cases the Prime Minister himself may talk to the diplomatic representatives of a foreign state.[5] In such cases the Prime Minister has an obligation to inform the Foreign Secretary as to what passed in the discussion in the same way that he is expected to inform that officer of the content of telegrams or letters which he may receive from foreign representatives.[6]

Close relations between the Prime Minister and the Foreign Secretary are almost a necessity for the effective prosecution of foreign affairs. In fact, the other members of the Cabinet may be quite concerned that such a relationship exists as otherwise the Foreign Office is subject to little in the way of Cabinet control.[7] Frequently it is necessary to make decisions in the

[1] For examples, see Lord Crewe, *Lord Rosebery* (London, Harpers and Brothers, 1931), i, 277; Austen Chamberlain, *Down the Years* (London, Cassell, 1935), p. 209; Grey, *op. cit.*, i, 78, 165; J. A. Spender, *The Life of Sir Henry Campbell-Bannerman* (New York, Houghton Mifflin, 1924), ii, 265–7; Dugdale, *op. cit.*, i, 278.

[2] *Church Quarterly Review* (1877), iii, 480–1.

[3] Chamberlain, *op. cit.*, p. 209; J. A. Spender, *The Life of Sir Henry Campbell-Bannerman* (New York, Houghton Mifflin, 1924), ii, 248 ff., 265–7.

[4] *Ibid.*, ii, 248–58; Grey, *op. cit.*, i, 91–4, 159–60.

[5] Spender and Asquith, *op. cit.*, i, 245.

[6] In 1938 Chamberlain had a telegram from Count Grandi which he did not show to Eden, although the latter had determined upon resignation as a consequence of the progress of the negotiations with Italy. 332 *H.C. Deb.*, 5s., 257–9.

[7] Sir Algernon West, *Recollections* (London, Smith, Elder, 1899), p. 409.

field of foreign affairs immediately—there is not time for consultation with the Cabinet. The Prime Minister, in such cases, must be in a position to act conjointly with the Foreign Secretary, thus providing at least a possibility of a degree of restraint should the Secretary attempt to act too arbitrarily or unwisely.[1]

The Prime Minister may, if he has strong inclinations, take over the primary initiative in that area even though he does not take the office of Foreign Secretary. Both Lord Salisbury and Ramsay MacDonald, of course, handled the problem of their interest in foreign policy by combining the offices of Foreign Secretary and Prime Minister. On the other hand, Lloyd George, Neville Chamberlain, and Winston Churchill dominated the formulation of foreign policy without heading the responsible department. In the case of Lloyd George and Neville Chamberlain this resulted in some friction with their Foreign Secretaries. Lloyd George, in particular, had difficulty with Lord Curzon,[2] while Neville Chamberlain's views as to policy led to the resignation of Anthony Eden. In both cases the need for unity between the Foreign Secretary and the Prime Minister was clearly indicated by its breakdown and the embarrassments consequent upon those disagreements.[3]

Other Prime Ministers have taken less interest in active participation in the formulation of foreign policy. Asquith generally allowed Sir Edward Grey to take the initiative.[4] Baldwin seems to have had little interest in foreign affairs which

---

[1] The Anglo-French military conversations preceding the First World War provide the most dramatic example of an important decision in foreign affairs made without consultation with the Cabinet. Grey, *op. cit.*, i, 91–2.

The recognition of Franco in 1939 was also made without prior Cabinet consultation although the Cabinet seems to have specifically granted the right to make the decision to the Prime Minister and Foreign Secretary. 344 *H.C. Deb.*, 5s., 874, 876.

[2] Nicolson, *op. cit.*; Ronaldshay, *op. cit.*, iii.

[3] Attlee's comment in the House of Commons, 'We have not had one Foreign Office operating but two Foreign Offices', was clearly true. 332 *H.C. Deb.*, 5s., 65.

For a statement as to the necessity of unity of outlook, see Anthony Eden's statement explaining his reasons for resignation. *Ibid.*, 45–50.

[4] There was no difference of opinion between Asquith and Grey. Asquith wrote, 'Between him and myself there was daily intimacy and unbroken confidence. I can hardly recall any occasion on which we had a difference of opinion which lasted for more than half an hour.' *The Genesis of the War* (New York, George H. Doran, 1923), p. 17.

makes him a singularly unusual Premier for the period 1919–1939.[1] Ernest Bevin, the Foreign Secretary after 1945, seems to have had a relatively free hand in the formulation of British foreign policy although it is not yet possible to ascertain precisely to what extent Attlee influenced the direction of affairs.[2]

In addition to his concern with the operations of individual departments the Prime Minister is expected to act in a mediating capacity between ministers. The role of the Prime Minister as a mediator in Cabinet discussions over policy has already been mentioned. But the possible area of conflict is wider than this. In the conduct of their departmental duties ministers may come into conflict with one another. In particular, the relations between the Treasury and the other departments in the formulation of the budget are likely to be acrimonious.[3] In many cases the disagreements can be smoothed out by letters or conversations; the conversations in some cases being carried on by the permanent officers of the departments. Sometimes, however, disputes cannot be settled so expeditiously and it is necessary to turn to other sources for a satisfactory adjustment of the difficulties. The Prime Minister stands in the forefront as the person most likely to be called into the process of settlement, for it is recognized that he has the obligation to provide effective co-ordination of the governmental process.

A multiplicity of examples might be cited to show the types of disputes with which the Prime Minister is faced. It is always

[1] There were rumours in 1935 when Baldwin became Prime Minister for the third time, that he would become active in foreign affairs. The experience of the following years indicates that this was not true, however.

[2] Bevin's priority in this sphere may be indicated, however, by the fact that it was Bevin, rather than Attlee, who answered Churchill's 'Big Three' proposal in the election campaign of 1950.

[3] The budget is not approved by the Cabinet as a body. The final budget is drawn up by the Prime Minister and the Chancellor of the Exchequer. The Cabinet may, however, and usually does receive an oral report of its content prior to its submission to the House of Commons. Additionally, many of the items, if they have been the subject of a dispute, are brought before the Cabinet for final determination. W. I. Jennings, *Cabinet Government* (Cambridge, Cambridge University Press, 1936), pp. 182–3.

Professor Jennings states that on the average such oral disclosure was made five days prior to submission. Asquith is reported to have warned Snowden not to divulge the contents to his colleagues until the morning of the day it was to be presented, saying, 'If you do it will all be in the newspapers in a few hours.' Snowden, *op. cit.*, ii, 617.

possible that some one minister may be unable to confine himself to the responsibilities of his department. He may become a perpetual source of friction within the Cabinet. McKenna, who was prejudiced, described Lloyd George as a 'pest in council' and insisted that he continually interfered with the other departments.[1] Even in the absence of such an individual it is only to be expected that disputes should develop between men who head great departments and who are forced to attempt to co-ordinate policy and action between those departments. The Prime Minister in dealing with these difficulties must handle each of them on its own internal merits. There is no cut and dried formula which may be applied in all circumstances. In 1909 the Cabinet was sharply divided over the expenditures for naval construction. The First Lord of the Admiralty, McKenna, pressed for six capital ships. An economy bloc led by Lloyd George and Winston Churchill insisted upon a maximum of four. Asquith himself after a period of consultation and discussion with the principals in the dispute finally came up with a compromise which all were able to accept.[2]

Where compromise was possible in 1909 Asquith did not believe that agreement could be reached in the case of the Haldane-McKenna dispute in 1911. The disagreement in this case centred around two basic propositions: (1) a dispute over questions of strategy in case of a German attack upon France; and (2) Haldane's demand that the internal administration for planning in the Admiralty be reformed to provide for more effective co-ordination with the Staff of the War Office. Asquith, who supported Haldane's outlook, feared that the consequence of the dispute would be to damage severely the possibility of effective inter-service collaboration. In consequence he took the drastic step of transferring McKenna to another office and replacing him with Churchill.[3] In the first period of World War I Asquith also had to intervene to settle a dispute between the War Office and the Ministry of Munitions over shell design. He made his determination in favour of the latter while he himself was temporarily serving as War Secretary during Kitchener's absence in Egypt.[4]

[1] Lord Beaverbrook, *Politicians and the War* (New York, Doubleday Doran, 1932), ii, 73. [2] Spender and Asquith, *op. cit.*, i, 253.
[3] Spender and Asquith, *op. cit.*, i, 346–7; Haldane, *op. cit.*, pp. 240 ff.
[4] David Lloyd George, *op. cit.*, ii, 91–2.

In all of the cases mentioned above the settlement was carried through by the Prime Minister acting in his individual capacity. In other instances the Prime Minister has appointed special committees to look into the difficulties and make recommendations for their solution. A dispute occurred in 1916 between the war offices on the one hand, and the Exchequer and industrial mobilization officers on the other. The disagreement was so intense that McKenna, the Chancellor of the Exchequer, and Runciman, who was in charge of industrial mobilization, threatened to resign if the proposed expansion of the troops was carried through. Asquith managed to smooth over the difficulties by appointing a special committee, including representatives of both viewpoints, and headed by himself.[1] Similarly, the special committee technique was used in settling a Cabinet disagreement over the proposal to establish an Irish Parliament in the same year.[2]

While such specially constituted committees serve as an effective method of settling differences of opinion, they are not always successful. During the First World War the War Office and the Admiralty were in frequent dispute over the control of the new weapon, air power. Even the Prime Minister could not settle the disagreement through personal intervention and in consequence a special Air Board was created. The two disputants proved unwilling to accept the recommendations of the Board and the issue eventually had to be appealed to the Cabinet as a whole. The Cabinet decision proved to be mutually unacceptable to both parties. Attempts were made to reopen the controversy when Lloyd George became Prime Minister, but without immediate success, although eventually a separate Air Ministry was established.[3]

The Prime Minister need not wait for the overt expression of disagreement between the heads of the departments. He may intervene before the pot has reached the boiling point. It is more advantageous to the government if he is able to do so, but not all disputes can be seen until they have boiled over. In all cases in which the Prime Minister intervenes it is understood that the ministers have a right to appeal his decision to the Cabinet as a unit. The extent to which such action takes place is consequent upon a multiplicity of factors including the strength

---

[1] Spender and Asquith, *op. cit.*, ii, 203–4. [2] *Ibid.*, ii, 219, 221.
[3] Ronaldshay, *op. cit.*, ii, 142–7.

of the Prime Minister, the political position of the respective ministers, the nature of the disagreement, and the characteristics of the issue over which the dispute has developed. The Prime Minister in proposing a solution needs to be fairly confident that he will have the support of the Cabinet in the particular case at hand. In most cases such support is forthcoming.

One fact of some importance follows from the mediating function. The Prime Minister must have access to appropriate papers. This means that he must be able to write to subordinate officials within the departments in order to obtain the necessary information, for otherwise his decision in a particular case is likely to be inadequate.

All of the examples cited above involved disputes between heads of departments. In these cases it was clear that the Prime Minister had not only a right, but an obligation to attempt to find a way to solve the disagreements. A question may be asked, however, as to whether he has comparable rights in case a dispute develops between a department head and a member of the permanent civil service. Gladstone once stated, 'While it is my duty to deal with all difficulties arising between members of the government, it is wholly beyond my power, and in no way belongs to my province, to examine and settle the controversies which may arise between them and civil servants who are employed under them.'[1] In all probability this is the correct attitude in most cases, but sometimes an intra-departmental dispute is of major importance. In particular, a dispute between the head of one of the service departments and one of his principal professional subordinates may involve matters of even greater importance than disputes between department heads themselves.

The dispute between Winston Churchill, First Lord of the Admiralty, and Lord Fisher, the First Sea Lord, in 1915, over the former's proposed action at Gallipoli involved fundamental questions in military strategy. Fisher was bitterly opposed to the action and his opposition was reflected in the planning stages of the operation. Asquith tried to act as an arbitrator as he wished to keep Fisher in his position.[2] For a short time he was successful in keeping the bellicose First Sea Lord in his position,

[1] John Morley, *Life of Gladstone* (New York, Macmillan, 1911), ii, 420.
[2] Reginald Viscount Esher, *The Captains and the Kings Depart* (New York, C. Scribner's Sons, 1938), i, 212.

but eventually the latter, in a fit of pique, sent Churchill a letter of resignation and fled to Scotland, leaving Britain without a First Sea Lord. Asquith immediately ordered him back to his position, but accepted his resignation as the Prime Minister supported Churchill's proposed action.[1] This particular controversy was quite unsettling to the Prime Minister as Fisher was a favourite of both the press and the Conservative opposition. Asquith therefore made all efforts to hold him in his position short of submitting to his strategic arguments.[2] Although Fisher's resignation was eventually accepted the importance of this intra-departmental dispute was so great that it was one of the principal immediate causes of the formation of the first Coalition.[3]

A somewhat similar dispute developed early in 1916 between Lloyd George, then Minister of Munitions, and Sir William Robertson, the Chief of the Imperial General Staff. Lloyd George, who was always an advocate of an eastern front, urged immediate assistance to Rumania when that state was attacked by Bulgaria. Robertson intimated that if this was done he would resign his position. Asquith decided in favour of the Field-Marshal.[4]

In another instance the First Sea Lord, Lord Fisher, faced a serious cut in the Naval Estimates initially proposed for the budget of 1908. He appealed first to a committee of the Cabinet which had been specifically constituted to deal with this problem, but his effort to persuade them to restore the sum cut from the appropriations failed. He therefore carried his appeal to the Prime Minister who was persuaded by his arguments and restored the expenditures to their initial level, stating that Haldane would 'take £300,000 off his instead'.[5]

It is of some importance, however, that all of the examples given involved the military. In some ways the professional heads of those branches occupy a position vastly superior to

---

[1] Oxford and Asquith, *Memories and Reflections* (Boston, Little, Brown and Co., 1928), ii, 109–11.

[2] Spender and Asquith, *op. cit.*, ii, 164; Beaverbrook, *Politicians and the War* (Doubleday Doran, 1928), i, 115.

[3] *Ibid.*, i, 115–16.   [4] J. H. Edwards, *op. cit.*, ii, 469–72.

[5] Reginald Viscount Esher, *Journals and Letters* (London, J. Nicolson and Watson, 1934), ii, 283; J. A. Spender, *The Life of Sir Henry Campbell-Bannerman* (Boston, Houghton Mifflin, 1924, ii), 377–8.

the professional civil servants in other departments. Since war is reputed to be a science, and its successful prosecution to require a long and arduous apprenticeship, the position of such officers *vis-a-vis* the civilian heads of their departments is unquestionably superior to that occupied by other permanent government employees. The position of the Chief of the Imperial General Staff is a position of greater prestige than the position of permanent secretary of a department. A disagreement between an individual holding that office and his department head is actually the equivalent of a dispute between department heads.

The Prime Minister's responsibilities for the co-ordination of administration are further indicated by the fact that he heads the civil service establishment. This position is derived from the fact that the office of Prime Minister is combined with that of First Lord of the Treasury.[1] Since 1920 the Prime Minister's consent has been required for the appointment of the highest staff officers, including permanent heads, deputy heads, principal financial officers, and principal establishment officers of the respective departments. The head of the Establishment Division is the Permanent Secretary of the Treasury who may recommend the appointment of a particular individual to such positions, but the approval of the Prime Minister is required before any appointment is made.[2] Similarly, the Prime Minister

---

[1] 'It is not entirely an accident of history that the Prime Minister is First Lord of the Treasury. The employment of personnel is, in the first instance, a financial question. The administration of patronage was one of the means for securing a Government majority both in the House of Commons and in the country. Patronage, therefore, was a question for the Treasury and for the political leader. If the Prime Minister became First Lord of the Treasury, the power of patronage was placed in his hands. The reforms of the late eighteenth and early nineteenth centuries, culminating in the creation of the Civil Service Commission in 1855, converted the distribution of patronage into the control of a permanent civil service. The civil service is therefore controlled by the Treasury under the direction of the Prime Minister.' W. I. Jennings, *Cabinet Government* (Cambridge, Cambridge University Press, 1936), p. 114.

[2] *Report of the Royal Commission on the Civil Service*, Cmd. 3099 (1931), p. 7. This report is commonly referred to as the Tomlin Report. The practice has developed of filling such positions 'by transferring officers, with or without promotion, from the Treasury or other departments rather than by internal promotion.' *Sixteenth Report from the Select Committee on National Expenditure* (1941-42), p. 25.

may remove such officials, once appointed, in order to provide for the more effective operation of the government.[1]

Sir Warren Fisher, former Permanent Secretary of the Treasury, described the process of appointment in the following terms: 'It should . . . be made clear that this officer (the Permanent Secretary) gives advice on appointments after discussion with the minister concerned and after consulting his wisest colleagues throughout the service, and that the Prime Minister, of course, can, and sometimes does, reject his advice.'[2] It should be noted that the advice is given to the Prime Minister not to the minister concerned, although the latter is always consulted prior to the recommendation. The crux of the problem lies in the possibility of disagreement between the Permanent Secretary and the political head of the department concerned. In such a case whose recommendation is likely to carry the greatest weight with the Prime Minister? No real evidence is available in this respect although the triumph of the Cabinet minister is probable in most instances.[3] This must follow for the Cabinet minister carries the twin guns of administrative and political authority which must overpower the Permanent Secretary, unless he has made a recommendation which the Prime Minister considers as of such superior worth as to make even the overriding of the Cabinet minister desirable.

The Permanent Secretary of the Treasury and his subordinates also serve as a staff of advisers and technical assistants for the Prime Ministers.[4] They must be ready with advice in case an emergency requires that the Prime Minister find an immediate solution to a problem of importance. They must assist him in keeping up to date on developments in the departments which may bear upon his general responsibilities.[5]

In addition to the multiple responsibilities incumbent upon him as chairman of the Cabinet and as the highest officer in

---

[1] H. R. G. Greaves, *The Civil Service in the Changing State* (Toronto, Oxford University Press, 1947), p. 178.

[2] *Manchester Guardian*, 28 November 1942.

[3] Sir Warren Fisher does not state this overtly, but it is implicit in his discussion.

[4] The Prime Minister may, of course, set up other bodies such as the Economic Advisory Council to assist him in his work. In particular such bodies are likely to be established in time of war.

[5] Greaves, *op. cit.*, p. 180.

the administrative hierarchy, the Prime Minister is also required to maintain relations with the Sovereign. First, he is required to see that the King is adequately informed of what has transpired in the meetings of the Cabinet. The old procedure involved the obligation of writing a letter to the monarch setting forth the main points discussed, and the decisions reached, by the Cabinet.[1]

The question as to whether the Prime Minister was obliged to state the full facts in case of internal Cabinet disagreement, and in particular the question of whether those upon each side in the controversy should be included in the information submitted to the King was a matter of some controversy. Different Prime Ministers answered in different fashions. Gladstone took the position that the Prime Minister was morally obliged to his colleagues not to provide the Sovereign with such information.[2] Other Prime Ministers did not always feel the necessity of such secrecy. Disraeli usually gave the Queen the information, as did Lord Salisbury.[3] Asquith gave the King the names of the disputants in the controversy over the Naval Estimates of 1909,[4] but this was not his usual practice. Little evidence exists for the later Premiers although it is known that MacDonald kept George V fully informed of the internal division in his Cabinet in 1931.[5]

In part, however, the question of whether such information should be supplied was solved by the fact that the minutes kept by the Cabinet Secretary do not include the names of those who propose the various points of view stated in the Cabinet.[6] The Prime Minister might, of course, inform the Sovereign upon his own initiative or at the request of the monarch, but it is also

---

[1] The scope of the reports varied according to the inclinations of the Prime Minister. Edward VII frequently protested that Campbell-Bannerman's letters were inadequate. Sir Sidney Lee, *King Edward VII* (New York, Macmillan, 1927), pp. 454-5, 466-7; Esher, *Journals and Letters* (London, J. Nicolson and Watson, 1934), ii, 265-6.

In 1893 Gladstone turned this responsibility over to Sir William Harcourt.

[2] Gladstone, *op. cit.*, i, 74-5. 'The Sovereign is to know no more of any differing views of different ministers than they are to know of any collateral of the monarchical office; they are an unity before the Sovereign; and the Sovereign is an unity before them.'

[3] *Letters of Queen Victoria* (London, J. Murray, 1933), 3s., iii, 685.

[4] Spender and Asquith, *op. cit.*, ii, 81-3.   [5] Snowden, *op. cit.*, ii, 950.

[6] 155 *H.C. Deb.*, 5s., 213 ff.

within his power to withhold the information. There is no clear-cut rule which establishes one practice or the other as definitive. The Prime Minister may pursue either course.

In addition to the formal communications, either through letters or the Cabinet minutes, the Prime Minister will also frequently see the Sovereign personally. It is difficult to obtain information as to the frequency of such personal contacts, but during the Second World War Winston Churchill saw the King once a week if he was within the country.[1] At such meetings he informed the King of the conduct and problems of the war, but no precise information as to what was discussed at any one meeting may be found in his memoirs. It is also, of course, possible that communications may be carried out by telephone if the King finds such a method desirable.[2]

The Prime Minister also has an obligation to make sure that the King is supplied with important state documents for 'the Sovereign has a right to be made acquainted with everything for which his Ministers are responsible. . . .'[3] It is obvious that the King cannot be expected to master all papers, but, if he desires, he has a right to receive copies of the important papers. It is particularly likely that he will see the important papers in the field of foreign relations although the degree to which this is true depends upon the personal inclinations of the monarch.

In addition to the right to be consulted the King also has the 'right to encourage, the right to warn.'[4] These obviously require the prior existence of the right to be consulted for without the latter he can neither encourage nor warn.

Should the Sovereign disagree with a policy he has a right to express his disagreement and to attempt to persuade the Prime Minister of the error of his ways. Edward VII made such an effort when it was proposed to establish a Royal Commission of Inquiry to look into the prosecution of the South African War, but without success.[5] He also frequently warned Sir Henry Campbell-Bannerman of the possible undesirable consequences which might follow attempts radically to disregard the views of the House of Lords on educational reform.[6]

---

[1] Winston Churchill, *Their Finest Hour* (Boston, Houghton Mifflin, 1949), p. 379.

[2] Lee, *op. cit.*, ii, 48–9.   [3] Churchill, *op. cit.*, p. 379.

[4] Bagehot, *op. cit.*, p. 67.   [5] Lee, *op. cit.*, ii, 91–2.

[6] J. A. Spender, *Life of Campbell-Bannerman* (Boston, Houghton Mifflin, 1924), ii, 301–2, 306.

The Prime Minister and the Cabinet

The Prime Minister may disregard the warnings or the advice of the monarch if he wishes to do so, but he is expected to allow the monarch to express his opinion upon the particular matter, and it is wiser to attempt rationally to defend the initial position than to attempt to overpower the monarch by superior political power. It is to be expected that the monarch will always be informed and allowed to express an opinion before a new policy is discussed in the Cabinet itself. A similar obligation does not necessarily exist in those instances in which a Prime Minister states a new policy in public speech,[1] but it would be an unwise course both because it involves damages to relations with the monarch and because it involves a policy determination made by the Prime Minister without the knowledge of the Cabinet. However deeply the Sovereign may disagree with the policy of the Prime Minister and his Cabinet he must not enter into conversations with members of the Opposition in the hope of subverting the government. He is limited to consultation with members of the government unless specifically authorized to see representatives of other parties by the Prime Minister.[2] He himself may, however, advise the Prime Minister to consult with persons outside of his government before continuing a particular course of action.[3]

In the nineteenth century the Sovereign had one recourse against the decision of the Prime Minister—that was an appeal to the Cabinet. In the foreign crisis of 1859–61 some of the despatches were 'referred back by the sovereign from the Foreign Secretary and the Prime Minister to the Cabinet as a whole, and were there constantly modified in the sense desired.'[4] Such an appeal is probably still possible, but the increase in the

[1] Lord Crewe, *Lord Rosebery* (New York, Harpers and Brothers, 1931), ii, 378. Rosebery admitted that he had no right to place a new policy before the Cabinet without previously informing the Sovereign. Yet he held that this was not necessary when a new policy was expressed in a public speech. It is rather difficult to understand this particular distinction.

[2] Queen Victoria saw Lord Salisbury in 1893 and 1894 in an attempt to find some way to get rid of the Liberal Government. Her action, however, was clearly unconstitutional. Cf. J. A. R. Marriott, *Queen Victoria and Her Ministers* (London, J. Murray, n.d.), pp. 181 ff.

[3] Edward VII advised Campbell-Bannerman to consult with the Archbishop of Canterbury on the education bill. The Archbishop was one of the leaders of the opposition to the bill. Spender, *Life of Campbell-Bannerman* (Boston, Houghton Mifflin, 1924), ii, 302.

[4] John Morley, *Walpole* (New York, Macmillan, 1889), p. 159.

power of the Prime Minister and the tightening of party discipline, make it unlikely that it would lead to a great deal of success.[1]

Not only may the monarch advise or warn the Prime Minister, he may also offer him words of sympathy, encouragement, and support. Psychologically this may be of some importance, for the Prime Minister is raised and conditioned within the framework of the British political myth,[2] and the myth exalts not only the institution, but the person, of the monarch. An expression of personal support may be of some importance in intensifying the Prime Minister's belief in the programme or issue under consideration.[3]

In the last resort the degree of influence exercised by the Sovereign depends upon his own ability and the inclinations and abilities of the Prime Minister. Frequently the monarch holds his position for a long period of time; this means that he gradually accumulates a body of information which may be of substantial advantage in handling a particular matter. If the Sovereign is a person of ability and has worked to keep himself informed he may serve as something of an 'expert' in his relations with the Prime Minister.[4] The Sovereign, for example, who has diligently applied himself to a study of the despatches of the foreign office, may be able to advise the Prime Minister as to how a similar problem has been handled in the past. Britain has been fortunate in the character of her monarchs in this century. With the exception of Edward VII, who was more interested in ceremonial than state affairs,[5] the evidence

---

[1] As has been said of this right of appeal, 'if there chanced to be a strong Cabinet, the use of such a power might result in a considerable reduction of the Prime Minister's normal authority, and its transfer to the general body of his colleagues.' *Ibid.*, p. 159. It is extraordinary, however, to find a Cabinet in which the view of the Prime Minister and the Foreign Secretary are so contrary to the view of the Cabinet.

[2] The best statement of the monarchy as social myth is in Bagehot, *op, cit.* For a modern statement of the thesis see Kingsley Martin, *The Magic of Monarchy* (New York, Knopf., 1937).

[3] For examples see Feiling, *op. cit.*, pp. 378–9, 400–1; Churchill, *Their Finest Hour* (Boston, Houghton Mifflin, 1949), p. 627.

[4] Asquith, in commenting upon advice received from the King, said, 'such intimations are always received by ministers with the utmost respect and considered with more respect and deference than if they proceeded from any other quarter.' Spender and Asquith, *op. cit.*, ii, 30.

[5] Cf. Lee, *op. cit.*, ii, 448; also note the rather acid comment in D. W. Brogan, *The English People* (New York, Knopf, 1943), p. 127.

indicates that the other monarchs worked extremely hard at keeping themselves informed of the problems of government.[1]

The Prime Minister may find that his relations with the monarch are not particularly pleasant but he is obliged to carry out his responsibilities however unpleasant the personal relationship may be. No Prime Minister of today is likely to suffer the treatment Gladstone received from Victoria,[2] and he may be sure that in the last resort he will have his way.[3] The argument of Lord Lansdowne that the King has a power of veto over the government since the passage of the Parliament Act of 1911[4] is clearly erroneous. The King is a constitutional monarch. He acts upon advice; he exercises influence, but he does not wield direct power.

In the United States patronage has often been described as the life blood of party politics.[5] If this is true one would expect considerably less vigour in party activities in Great Britain than is actually to be found. The British political parties and their leaders operate in a situation in which nearly all of the positions in the government are filled through merit examination. Only a limited number of officers, or special marks of prestige, can be awarded to persons who have contributed to the party's welfare. The primary control over these awards is in the hands of the Prime Minister who has the chief voice as to appointments to high judicial positions, church offices, and the granting of titles and honours.

Formally, all appointments and all titles and honours are derived from the monarch, but, in fact, 'in the selection of the recipients of these grants, as in other things, he is in use not to act upon his own initiative, but on the advice of his Ministers. The Minister responsible for advising is the Prime Minister

---

[1] J. H. Thomas, *My Story* (London, Hutchinson, 1937), p. 154; Winston Churchill, *Their Finest Hour* (Boston, Houghton Mifflin, 1949), p. 379.

[2] Michael MacDonagh, *The English King* (London, E. Benn, 1929), pp. 201–22.

[3] There is one possible area of action in which this may be questioned— that is the dissolution of the Parliament. The relation of King, Prime Minister and Cabinet to dissolution is considered in the following chapter.

[4] Spender and Asquith, *op. cit.*, ii, 25–6.

[5] For a classic expression of this thesis see William Riordan, *Plunkitt of Tammany Hall* (New York, Knopf, 1948), pp. 20–1.

except in certain special cases . . .'[1] Even in those cases in which some other minister recommends, the Prime Minister is previously consulted.[2]

At one time the control of patronage was a matter of fundamental importance, for the control of the Parliament often rested upon an efficient use of patronage. In the eighteenth century Sir Robert Walpole made effective use of patronage as a means of stabilizing and maintaining his control of the majority in the House of Commons. George III took advantage of the same opportunities in his struggle to reassert royal authority. The younger Pitt also used the same techniques to maintain his position. The fact that the Prime Minister usually took the office of First Lord of the Treasury enabled him to gain control of patronage and all Prime Ministers took advantage of their opportunities to reward the party faithful or to offer concessions to the powerful who needed to be coaxed into supporting the government.

The progress of reform legislation led to a decline in the political importance of patronage. Even prior to the introduction of the merit system Sir Robert Peel had rejected the worst abuses of the old system, and had commented that 'the party interests of a Government are in the long run much better promoted by the honest exercise of patronage than by the perversion of it for the purpose of satisfying individual supporters.'[3] The gradual improvement by which the merit system was adopted, first in individual departments, later as a method of recruitment in all departments, obviously made it impossible to rely upon any broad use of the appointing power to serve party advantage. There are, however, still a few areas in which the Prime Minister may, through appointments, reward those who have contributed to the party or who might contribute to its future welfare.

There are, at the present time, three main areas in which the Prime Minister exercises a considerable amount of control over appointments: some of the judicial offices; the honours list; and certain other public offices, mainly diplomatic in character. Ecclesiastical patronage is still in the hands of the Prime Minister, but it is not particularly useful for political purposes

---

[1] *Report of the Royal Commission on Honours*, Cmd. 1789 (1922), p. 99.
[2] *Ibid.*, p. 6.
[3] *Peel Papers* (London, 1899), iii, 414.

and normally its exercise is extremely distasteful to the Prime Minister. It has been said of Lord Salisbury, 'The making of Bishops was, indeed, the one of his public duties which cost him most heavily in labour and anxiety. "I declare they die to spite me," he groaned when vacancies were piling up.'[1]

The Sovereign at one time exercised a considerable amount of influence in ecclesiastical appointments, but since the reign of Edward VII this interest has been on the decline.[2] It is evident that today the Prime Minister relies primarily upon advice from church authorities. Randall Davidson said that none of the Prime Ministers from Balfour to MacDonald made any appointments which were objectionable to the Archbishop, although they did not always follow his advice.[3] This would seem to indicate considerably less interest in such appointments than was shown by Gladstone,[4] but it also indicates the declining political importance of the Church. In the nineteenth century the Church was an important political force, whereas today it verges upon political impotency.[5]

The Prime Minister also plays a major role in the selection of the diplomatic representatives of Great Britain. This does not, of course, mean that he initiates every appointment, but, on the other hand, no important appointment will be made without consultation with the Prime Minister.[6] Similarly, until

---

[1] Cecil, *op. cit.*, iii, 194. Asquith described this situation as 'indefensible'. Oxford and Asquith, *Fifty Years of British Parliament* (Boston, Little, Brown and Co., 1926), ii, 242–3.

[2] Lee, *op. cit.*, ii, 53.

[3] W. I. Jennings, *Cabinet Government* (Cambridge, Cambridge University Press, 1936), p. 350.

[4] Gladstone took Church appointments with the utmost seriousness. Sir Henry Campbell-Bannerman also approached ecclesiastical appointments with great care and sought the best available advice. Spender, *Life of Campbell-Bannerman* (New York, Houghton Mifflin, 1924), ii, 359.

[5] But, as Professor Jennings says, 'Even now political considerations are not always absent. It was probably not entirely a coincidence that Bishop Barnes and Archbishop Temple were promoted on the recommendation of a Labour Prime Minister.' *Cabinet Government* (Cambridge, Cambridge University Press, 1936), p. 342, n. 2.

[6] A peculiar situation existed when Churchill named Lord Halifax Ambassador to the United States for Halifax himself was Foreign Secretary. The appointment might be interpreted as either a demotion or a recognition of the tremendous importance of the ambassadorial post. Churchill gives the latter reason, but admits it was not a promotion. *Their Finest Hour* (Boston, Houghton Mifflin, 1949), p. 570. Lloyd George was first offered the post.

the grant of independence to India the Prime Minister also appointed the Viceroy of India. This would be expected for the office was of greater importance, and carried greater prestige, than many positions in the Cabinet itself. In some cases the Prime Minister seems to have consulted the Cabinet prior to naming the Viceroy.[1]

Judicial appointments would seem to offer more prospect for use as political rewards. Many of the judges, in particular the *puisne* judges of the High Court, are appointed by the Lord Chancellor, but it is probable that such appointments are made only after consultation with the Prime Minister.[2] Other judicial officers are appointed directly by the Prime Minister. 'The appointments of the three great titled judges and of their humbler brother the President, of the seven Law Lords, and of the five Lord Justices, are by long-established practice, in the hands of the Prime Minister; who is, therefore, the supreme source of judicial promotion.'[3] In the case of the Lord Chief Justice a tradition has developed that the Attorney-General in office at the death or resignation of that officer is entitled to the appointment.[4]

It is quite possible that the Prime Minister in the exercise of his appointing power may use it to reward a member of his own party who is also a barrister of some ability.[5] Upon the other hand, it is sometimes argued that the weight of tradition is such as to cause him to select the more able man, whatever be his party background, in such cases.[6] Nevertheless, it would seem evident that political considerations will always be of influence in such appointments although they are not of comparable importance to such considerations in the United States due to the absence of any power to pass upon the constitionality of acts of the Parliament.

[1] Oxford and Asquith, *Fifty Years of British Parliament* (Boston, Little, Brown and Co., 1926), ii, 218.

[2] At least this was true as long ago as 1850. Henry Brougham, *Life and Times* (New York, Harper and Brothers, 1872), iii, 86–8.

[3] R. C. K. Ensor, *Courts and Judges in France, Germany and England* (London, Oxford University Press, 1933), pp. 5–6.

[4] H. G. Hanbury, *English Courts of Law* (New York, Oxford University Press, 1944), p. 165, n. 2.

[5] The appointment of Slesser as Lord Justice in 1929 probably resulted from the fact that he had argued the General Strike was legal.

[6] Hanbury, *op. cit.*, pp. 165–6.

While the judicial offices may be used as a technique of advancing men who have contributed to the interests of the party, it is unquestionably true that the more fruitful source of patronage for party purposes in this century has been the honours list. Formally, as noted earlier, the Sovereign makes such grants, but he acts upon the advice of the Prime Minister in nearly all cases. In a few instances, he acts upon the advice of other ministers who have, in all probability, previously consulted the Prime Minister. The Sovereign maintains a few honours as his private grant, the most important of which is the Royal Victorian Chain.[1] Under the Premiership of Lord Salisbury an agreement was reached between the Prime Minister and the King whereby the latter also controlled the Order of Merit.[2]

While titles and honours obviously provide a method of rewarding individuals for their contributions to the party, not all Prime Ministers have been pleased with the necessity of spending time upon such appointments. Asquith once stated, 'Of the many classes of Patronage which come within the Province of the Prime Minister, the grants of honours for political and the public services is the most irksome and the most thankless. I suspect that there are few holders of the office (since the days of the Duke of Newcastle and Lord North) who would not have been heartily glad to be relieved of it.'[3] It is doubtful if Lloyd George would have associated himself with this statement for he found the honours list an effective means of raising party funds.

It is difficult to delineate the degree to which the King may influence the grant of honours or to answer the question as to whether he may veto a nomination made by the Prime Minister. Professor Jennings states, 'The King is able to resist the grant of honours of which he does not approve.'[4] Nearly all of the examples cited to substantiate this statement are prior to

[1] Cmd. 1789 (1922), p. 99; Sir Sidney Lee, *op. cit.*, ii, 99 ff.

[2] *Ibid.*, ii, 99. Professor Jennings states that today this order seems to be awarded on the advice of the Prime Minister. *Cabinet Government* (Cambridge, Cambridge University Press, 1936), p. 351.

[3] Oxford and Asquith, *Fifty Years of British Parliament* (Boston, Little, Brown and Co., 1926), ii, 235. See also his comments at 156 *H.C. Deb.*, 5s. 1770.

[4] W. I. Jennings, *Cabinet Government* (Cambridge, Cambridge University Press, 1936), p. 352.

the beginning of this century and he admits that in the case of Edward VII in 1906 the King gave way upon being pressed.[1] We have no direct evidence as to the authority possessed by twentieth-century monarchs. One may seriously question the existence of the veto power, however, given the use of such grants made by Lloyd George. It seems improbable that George V approved of his Prime Minister's use of the honours list, and even more improbable that he did not know what was happening since the matter was frequently debated in both houses of the Parliament.[2]

The Sovereign may propose the names of persons in addition to those recommended by the Prime Minister, but in such cases the latter's control is even more specifically indicated by the fact that the names the King wishes to add appear on the Prime Minister's list.[3] Normally the Prime Minister will raise no objection to the addition of such names but will consider it a pleasure to be of service to the King in this respect.[4]

From the standpoint of the political party the chief importance of the honours list lies in the possibility of using it as a means of providing recognition for party service. One of the first essentials of any political party is that it have money. In consequence it has frequently been the case that charges have been levied against the Prime Minister on the grounds that honours were sold. In 1914[5] and again in 1917[6] the House of Lords passed resolutions censuring grants made upon such a basis. Reverberations were heard in the chamber of the Commons as well, and Bonar Law, the Leader of the House of Commons, stated in 1919, 'The Prime Minister has made, and

[1] *Ibid.*, p. 353.

[2] Cf. *H.L. Deb.*, 5s., 252–96; 26 *H.L. Deb.*, 5s., 172–212; 50 *H.L. Deb.*, 5s., 1126–40; 51 *H.L. Deb.*, 5s., 103–8; 116 *H.C. Deb.*, 5s., 1334–83; 156 *H.C. Deb.*, 5s., 1745–1862.

[3] Cmd. 1789 (1922), p. 99.

[4] An untoward incident occurred in 1908 in which this was not the case. Edward VII made the Tsar of Russia an honorary Admiral of the Fleet without ministerial authorization. Asquith informed the King's Secretary, 'it would have been more in accord with constitutional practice and with the accepted condition of ministerial responsibility, if before his Majesty's departure, some intimation had been given to me and my colleagues that it was in contemplation.' Spender and Asquith, *op. cit.*, i, 249–50.

[5] 15 *H.L. Deb.*, 5s., 252–96.

[6] 26 *H.L. Deb.*, 5s., 172–212.

will make, no recommendations to his Majesty as a reward for contributions to party coffers.'

Although such charges had been heard prior to the administration of Lloyd George[1] they became a great deal more intense at that time. The charges became extremely specific in some instances and definite price tags were reputed to have been placed upon different levels of honours.[2] Similarly, questions were raised as to whether it was accidental that papers which supported the Prime Minister usually received consideration on the honours list either through their proprietors or through their editors.[3] In consequence of this criticism, and the public reaction which followed it, the Government eventually set up a Royal Commission of Inquiry, 'not to investigate the degree of truth in the allegations that peerages were frequently awarded for contributions to the party funds, but to propose remedies and a procedure for the future.'[4]

The report of the Royal Commission, made in 1922, clearly recognized that party service was of importance in granting honours. 'The practice of giving honours for purely political service has been continuously followed ever since the growth and development of the Party System of Government.'[5] It was recognized that so long as party government exists such grants are essential. What the Royal Commission proposed was not the abolition of awards made for party services, but the prevention of the abuse of such grants involved in using them for increasing party funds. The Commission therefore made the following recommendations:[1]

'(i) That a Committee of the Privy Council, of not more than three members, be appointed of persons not being mem-

---

[1] 15 *H.C. Deb.*, 5s., 252–96; see Lloyd George's comments at 156 *H.C. Deb.*, 5s., 1761 ff.

[2] In 1917 Earl Loreburn put the price at £25,000 for a baronetcy and £15,000 for a knighthood with an outside chance of the latter for only £10,000. 26 *H.L. Deb.*, 5s., 837. Inflation had hit the baronetcies by 1922 when the Duke of Northumberland quoted a price of £35,000 while quoting £12,000 for a knighthood. 51 *H.L. Deb.*, 5s., 509.

[3] 116 *H.C. Deb.*, 5s., 1341, 1786.

[4] Hugh McDowall Clokie and J. William Robinson, *Royal Commissions of Inquiry* (Stanford University, Stanford University Press, 1937), p. 129. No effort was made to interrogate the touts. An interesting description of his efforts to work as a tout for a baronetcy may be found in the statement of Lord Willoughby de Broke at 15 *H.L. Deb.*, 5s., 269.

[5] Cmd. 1789 (1922), p. 6.   [6] *Ibid.*, pp. 11–12.

bers of the Government to serve for the period of the duration of office of the Government; the Committee to have a Secretary taken from the ranks of the Civil Service:

'(ii) That before submission to His Majesty of the names of persons for appointment to any dignity or honour on account of political service, the names of such persons should be submitted to the Committee with, appended to each name, the following particulars:

(*a*) A statement of the service in respect of which, and the reasons for which, the recommendation is proposed to be made;

(*b*) A statement by the Patronage Secretary or the Party manager that no payment, or expectation of payment to any Party or political fund is directly or indirectly associated with the recommendation;

(*c*) The name and address of the person who the Prime Minister considers was the original suggester of the name of the proposed recipient.[1]

'(iii) That the Committee, after such enquiry as they think fit, should report to the Prime Minister whether, so far as they believe, the person is, in the whole circumstances, a fit and proper person to be recommended.

'(iv) That in the event of the Committee reporting against any name and the Prime Minister determining still to recommend such name, the King should be informed of the report of the Committee.

'(v) That an Act be passed imposing a penalty on anyone promising to secure, or to endeavour to secure, an honour in respect to any particular payment or other valuable consideration, and on any person promising such payment or consideration in order to receive an honour.'

The report and recommendations made by the Royal Commission were accepted and seem to have been followed in most cases. It would be too much to expect that awards made upon

---

[1] The problem of who first recommended appointments had been raised on several occasions, notably in connection with the controversy which arose over the inclusion of Sir Joseph Robinson's name on the honours list. See 50 *H.L. Deb.*, 5s., 1126–40; 51 *H.L. Deb.*, 5s., 103–38. The importance of such knowledge is implicit in Sir Samuel Hoare's comment, 'There was the case of a man who was made a Knight, and the people who recommended him did not even know his Christian name.' 156 *H.C. Deb.*, 5s., 1750.

this basis should completely disappear, but there have been no outbursts comparable to the series of debates in both houses, which led to the establishment of the Commission.[1]

It should be stressed that even in the case of Lloyd George there was no belief upon the part of the critics that every one on the list had made such contributions, or even the most considerable portion of them. It was recognized that most of the persons granted honours were deserving recipients. Lloyd George himself, in defending his actions, stated quite correctly that the 'political Honours List is a minority.'[2] He pointed out that there are many other reasons for granting honours than political services and specified seven distinct categories: (1) civil servants, including naval and military men, who had rendered special service; (2) persons who had made contributions in science, art or literature; (3) persons who had rendered special service locally; (4) persons who had shown munificence in charitable matters; (5) outstanding figures in commerce, industry, and finance; (6) persons who had made notable contributions during a national emergency such as war; and (7) political service.[3]

The Prime Minister does not himself determine precisely who shall be nominated without the participation of other persons. In fact, the primary initiative in the preparation of the lists comes from other quarters. The departments submit names of individuals they believe worthy of such grants as does the Patronage Secretary to the Treasury who is more specifically concerned with the political grants. In addition it seems evident that private individuals also submit names to the Prime Minister.[4] In the last resort the Prime Minister weighs the individual

---

[1] In 1924, the Prime Minister, Ramsay MacDonald, accepted a gift of an automobile and some shares in a biscuit concern from Mr. Alexander Grant, an acquaintance from boyhood days. Shortly thereafter Grant's name appeared on the Honours List and there were immediate outcries that the Prime Minister had been trafficking in honours for personal advantage. Weir, *op. cit.*, ch. xx.

It is noteworthy that both Canada and South Africa have abolished honours on the grounds that they have a corrupting effect. A. B. Keith, *The British Cabinet System* (London, Stevens and Son, 1938), p. 548.

[2] 156 *H.C. Deb.*, 5s., 1765.

[3] *Ibid.*, 1762–63.

[4] 155 *H.C. Deb.*, 5s., 1841–2 (Lloyd George). He stated that lists were submitted 'from every quarter'.

nominations and determines which ones should be made. It is also the case that the Prime Minister customarily asks the opposition to submit names in case a special list is prepared for an occasion like the Jubilee or a Coronation.[1]

[1] Asquith commented that the opposition had been asked to submit names on the occasion of the Coronation of George V in 1911. 156 *H.C. Deb.*, 5s., 1771. It seems probable that this is the usual rule.

VII

The Prime Minister
and the Parliament

The supremacy of the Parliament is one of the basic principles of the British Constitution. Legally, the authority of the Parliament is both transcendent and absolute. The term Parliament, however, must be understood in its full meaning rather than the ordinarily accepted conception of the two houses of the legislature, or sometimes as merely the House of Commons. Technically Parliament, as used in such statements, means the King in Parliament and when it is said that its authority is absolute, what is meant is that when the House of Commons, the House of Lords, and the King formally approve a bill, thus making it law, there is no other body which may void this statute. 'The principle of Parliamentary sovereignty means neither more nor less than this, namely, that Parliament thus defined has, under the English constitution, the right to make or unmake any law whatever; and further no person or body is recognized by the law of England as having a right to override or set aside the legislation of Parliament.'[1]

Although the approval of the King is required before it may be said that the Parliament has approved a bill, it must be recognized that, in fact, the King always approves any bill

[1] A. V. Dicey, *Introduction to the Law of the Constitution* (London, Macmillan, 9th edition, 1939), pp. 39–40. Cf. W. I. Jennings, *Parliament* (Cambridge, Cambridge University Press, 1939), ch. i; A. B. Keith, *The Constitution of England from Queen Victoria to George VI* (London, Macmillan, 1940), p. 8. The classic statement by the courts on parliamentary supremacy may be found in *Lee v. Bude and Torrington Junction Railway Co.*, L.R. 6 C.P. 582 (1871).

which is passed by the two houses of the legislature.[1] Further, although the House of Lords participates in the formal process by which law is made, its role is far inferior to that of the House of Commons. Under the terms of the Parliament Act of 1911, the Lords held a suspensive veto of two years over all bills with the exception of finance bills.[2] In 1949 this was further reduced to one year.[3] Even this does not adequately reflect the real power relationship between the two houses for the Lords seldom exercised the suspensive veto which they held.

It must be recognized that this picture of the power of the Parliament is fundamentally unrealistic. In the first place, it is merely a description of the 'legal authority' of the Parliament. Its practical authority is, obviously, considerably less. While it may be true that legally the Parliament could pass legislation providing for the seizure of all property belonging to persons with red hair, in fact it will not so act.[4] The conception of Parliamentary sovereignty does, however, provide a basis for law, and it does enable one to recognize and distinguish law which is enforceable in courts from other rules of individual or social behaviour.

Further, the description of the powers of the Parliament is misleading in another respect. It tends to produce a distorted picture of the actual relationship which exists between the Parliament and the Cabinet. Many persons have thought that the Parliament dominates and controls the executive in Great Britain.[5] In legal theory this is true, but at the same time, in practice, the executive tends to dominate the legislature. Technically, the Parliament may bring down any government by the simple expedient of withdrawing its support, either through the passage of an outright vote of no confidence or through the defeat of a major proposal made by the government. This power does exist, but it is seldom used. In the period with which this study is most immediately concerned, 1894 to 1953, only two governments resigned as a consequence of adverse votes in the

[1] Jennings, *op. cit.*, p. 3; Jennings, *Cabinet Government* (Cambridge, Cambridge University Press, 1936), pp. 296–7.

[2] 1 & 2 *Geo. V.*, Cap. 13.

[3] 12, 13 & 14 *Geo. VI.*, c. 103.

[4] Cf. W. I. Jennings, *Law and the Constitution* (London, University of London Press, 1933).

[5] For an example of this argument see Henry Hazlitt, *A New Constitution Now* (New York, McGraw-Hill, 1942).

House of Commons. The first instance was the fall of the Rosebery government in 1895 when it was defeated by seven votes on the cordite issue. In this case it is possible that Rosebery, tired of his continuous conflict with Harcourt, seized upon the defeat as an excuse to rid himself of the increasingly unpleasant function of heading a divided Cabinet. A substantial number of the members of the Cabinet were opposed to resignation on the issue.[1]

The second incident was the resignation of the Baldwin government in 1924. The government was defeated on an amendment, moved by the Labour Party, to the Speech from the Throne. The circumstances, however, were unusual. Baldwin had had a majority in the House of Commons prior to the election. After the election he no longer had a majority, but he headed the largest party in the House of Commons. It was not clear what party should be in power and he determined to meet the House of Commons and let the decision lie with the House. The support given by the Liberals to the Labour amendment brought Baldwin and his government down immediately.[2]

In one other instance defeat in the House of Commons led to the government's eventual defeat. In 1924, the government of Ramsay MacDonald was defeated upon a measure which they had specified a confidence issue. The government did not resign, but it asked for and obtained a dissolution of the Parliament. In the general election consequent upon the dissolution it was defeated.[3]

The resignation of Neville Chamberlain in 1940 may properly be traced to a loss of confidence in the House of Commons. Even so, he received the overwhelming support of those who did vote. The lack of confidence felt in his leadership was seen in the enormous number of abstentions, which made it evident that he was no longer satisfactory to the House. Thirty-three Con-

[1] Lord Oxford and Asquith, *Fifty Years of British Parliament* (Boston, Little, Brown and Co., 1926), i, 262; ii, 219.

[2] Beckhofer Roberts, *Stanley Baldwin: Man or Miracle?* (New York, Greenburg, 1937), pp. 124–5. Philip Viscount Snowden, *An Autobiography* (London, J. Nicholson and Watson, 1934), ii, 601–5. The vote against Baldwin was 328 to 256.

[3] Snowden, *op. cit.*, ii, 697–8, 707–18. MacDonald was defeated in the House by 166 votes.

servatives voted against him and sixty more showed their displeasure by abstaining.[1]

All of this leads to the conclusion that the Parliament's control over the Cabinet is more fiction than reality. Even should the government be defeated, it is up to the Prime Minister and his colleagues to make the decision as to whether the issue upon which they were defeated was of sufficient importance to entail either resignation or dissolution. Some issues are of such obvious importance that defeat would inevitably require one of the drastic alternatives. Other issues are not so important, and it is up to the Prime Minister to decide whether they require resignation or dissolution. It is probable that an issue such as the 'peanut vote' of February 1951 would not be considered sufficiently important to require such action.[2] Further, when the government is a minority government it is likely that it may suffer defeats without resignation which might lead to the fall of a stronger government. In 1924, MacDonald said, 'I propose to introduce my business knowing that I am in a minority, accepting the responsibilities of a minority, and claiming the privileges that attach to those responsibilities. And if the House on matters non-essential, matters that do not strike at the root of the proposals that we make—and do not destroy fundamentally the general intention of the Government in introducing legislation—if the House wish to vary our proposition, then the House must take the responsibility of this variation—then a division on such amendments and questions as those will not be regarded as a vote of no confidence.'[3] When he was defeated in the House in 1931 on the Education Bill, a measure of considerable importance, he did not resign or ask for a dissolution.[4]

The Prime Minister may then expect that he will be able to

---

[1] Keith Feiling, *Life of Neville Chamberlain* (London, Macmillan, 1946), p. 440; Winston Churchill, *The Gathering Storm* (Boston, Houghton Mifflin, 1948), pp. 660–1.

[2] On the 22nd of February 1951 the Government was defeated in the House. The House gave its approval to a bill which gave small private truck operators a share of the business done by the State-owned truck lines. The vote was 242 to 234. The Government did not consider it sufficiently important to resign or request a dissolution.

[3] Snowden, *op. cit.*, ii, 627–8; K. B. Smellie, *A Hundred Years of English Government* (New York, Macmillan, 1937), p. 366.

[4] L. M. Weir, *The Tragedy of Ramsay MacDonald* (Plymouth, Secker and Warburg, 1938), pp. 256–7.

control the Parliament so long as his actions and proposals are within the bounds of reason. Party discipline is extremely strong in the case of the two major British parties, and the discipline is further enforced by the whiphand of the threat of dissolution. An additional factor, which leads to a further curtailment of the members' independence, is the near certainty that the local party will not renominate a member who does not follow the party's leader.[1] Furthermore, dissatisfaction is most likely to develop among the extremist wings of the parties, but a left-wing Labour reaction is not likely to lead to a vote cast with the Conservatives. Similarly, one does not expect Conservatives of the Sir Waldron Smithers variety to show their objection to a Conservative position by voting with Labour.

Should the Prime Minister wish to make a vote a confidence issue, he can almost be completely assured that he will be victorious. In 1944, after the House had carried an amendment providing for equal pay for women in the teaching profession, Churchill rose to say that he would consider this result the equivalent of a vote of no confidence. In consequence, the House quickly reversed itself.[2] A similar occurrence, upon an almost identical issue, equal pay for women in the civil service, had arisen in April, 1936 when Baldwin asked for a reversal of the previous vote, stating that the government would consider any other action equivalent to a no-confidence vote. The vote was reversed.[3]

This description might lead to the mistaken conclusion that the Cabinet and Prime Minister act in a completely autocratic fashion. This is not true. It should be noted, for example, that the procedure in committees is less controlled than that in the House. The government is not likely to 'put on its whips' in votes taken in committee, and it is quite possible that concessions may be made upon some matters.[4] 'But no serious concessions of principle are made.'[5] In case there is a serious threat

---

[1] W. I. Jennings, *Parliament* (Cambridge, Cambridge University Press, 1939), p. 123. See *Ante*, ch. iv, for a more extensive examination of this point.

[2] 398 *H.C. Deb.*, 5s., 1356–92, 1617–18, 1646.

[3] 310 *H.C. Deb.*, 5s., 2021–85, 2450 ff., particularly 2477.

[4] W. I. Jennings, *Parliament* (Cambridge, Cambridge University Press, 1939), p. 271.

[5] Herman Finer, *The Theory and Practice of Modern Government* (New York, Henry Holt, 1949), p. 491.

of defeat in committee on a matter of importance, it is always possible that the government may send out for supporters in order to carry the day, but this is an unusual situation.[1]

The Prime Minister and his colleagues are also restrained by the necessity of not taking action which is clearly unpalatable to large numbers of their party supporters in the House of Commons. The whips are expected to keep the Prime Minister informed of the attitudes of the back-benchers so that legislation which is likely to be ill-received may be toned down before submission. The Prime Minister must not only be concerned with formal divisions, but with the attitudes of the members as they may be expressed outside the walls of the House of Commons.[1]

So long as he pays attention to these factors, however, the Prime Minister may be secure in the knowledge that he has command of the House of Commons. It has been said that a party requires a forty- to fifty-vote majority if it is to be secure. It is probably true that such a majority is necessary, if the Prime Minister and his colleagues are not to feel the pressure of parliamentary necessity in an extreme form. A smaller majority means that it will be necessary for the Prime Minister, and other ministers, to spend time in the House of Commons which might otherwise be used for other purposes. On the other hand, the experience of the Labour Government in 1950–1 indicates that a party with a six- to ten-vote majority can effectively control the House. The slim margin by which the party held the House seems to have led to an intensification of discipline. It is also noticeable that the radical wing of the party was not so vocal in criticizing the government as in the past, nor were there many instances of deliberate abstentions, for abstentions could have led to the fall of the government. The conclusion seems inescapable, that the government can expect to complete its legal term of office unless it is advantageous to dissolve earlier, or unless it is necessary to seek a public mandate upon a new controversial issue.[1]

[1] W. I. Jennings, *Parliament* (Cambridge, Cambridge University Press, 1939), pp. 271–2.

[2] *Ibid.*, pp. 121–2; cf. David Lloyd George, *War Memoirs* (Boston, Little, Brown and Co., 1933), ii, 184–5.

[3] The theory of the 'mandate' and its relationship to dissolution is examined later in this chapter.

Although the Parliament is more frequently the tool, rather than the master of the Cabinet, it is, nevertheless, a jealous body. The Prime Minister cannot afford to disregard or antagonize the Parliament, and, in particular, he must take care to satisfy the members of the House of Commons of his high respect for that institution. However certain he may be of the support of the House, the wise Prime Minister will act as if the Commons might decide to bring his government down at any time. The House can and will explode into righteous anger if it thinks it is being disregarded or taken for granted.[1] As Lloyd George said, in speaking of the House of Commons, 'It is a wild and savage animal! This minute it will stroke and fondle you. The next it may rend you in pieces. You must always be watching it. . . .'[2]

If the Prime Minister is in the House of Commons he is inevitably the chief spokesman for the chamber. He serves as the Leader of the House and his position and responsibilities are recognized by the House as a whole, despite the fact that no mention of a leader of the House of Commons appears in the Standing Orders of that Chamber.[3] He functions as an important part of the extra-legal, informal machinery of the House, through which the formal procedural rules become operative and effective. As the leader of the House he 'suggests, and in a great degree fixes, the course of all principal matters of business, supervises and keeps in harmony the action of his colleagues, takes the initiative in matters of ceremonial procedure and advises the House in every difficulty as it arises.'[4]

The function of fixing the business of the House is of basic importance, for government business has precedence over all other matters. Excluding the periods allotted to questions, it has been estimated that the time devoted to government business in a normal parliamentary session amounts to seven-

---

[1] For an example see 344 *H.C. Deb.*, 5s., 874 ff. This exchange developed out of the House's feeling that it had been inadequately informed on relations with Spain.

[2] Lord Riddell, *Intimate Diary of the Peace Conference and After, 1918–1923* (New York, Reynal and Hitchcock, 1934), p. 142.

[3] It is of some interest that only one reference to the Prime Minister appears in the index of Sir Erskine May's *Parliamentary Procedure*. See the 14th edition (London, Butterworth, n.d.), pp. 334–5.

[4] W. E. Gladstone, *Gleanings of Past Years* (New York, Scribner, n.d.), i, 241.

eighths of the time of the House.[1] Even this domination of the time of the legislative chamber has frequently been surpassed. Between 1939 and 1949 the government took all the time of the House. The exigencies of war and the sweeping character of the Labour Party's legislative programme explain this development.[2]

The Prime Minister, or the Leader of the House of Commons if the Prime Minister is a peer,[3] or if another minister is delegated that function, does not fix the business of the Commons in an arbitrary fashion. The Leader of the Opposition is always consulted in preparing the calendar for future debate. In most cases the actual contact with the opposition is made by the Chief Whip for the government, who sees his opposite number in the ranks of the opposition. It is obvious, however, that the Chief Whip must previously be briefed by the Prime Minister as to arrangements which he desires to make with the opposition. The arrangements are then made by the two whips subject to the concurrence of their superiors.[4] This means that, in the last resort, the business of the House is arranged by informal consultation and agreement between the representatives of the government and the opposition. This involves the making of material concessions. The government may agree to a debate on an issue which the opposition wishes to raise; in return they may receive a promise from the latter to expedite the handling of a particular bill on which the government desires early action. A failure to consider the rights of the opposition may lead the latter to deliberate acts of obstruction. Although infrequent, such obstructive tactics are sometimes used to show the opposition's dislike for what it interprets as a government attempt to exercise steam-roller tactics.[5]

[1] W. I. Jennings, *Parliament* (Cambridge, Cambridge University Press, 1939), p. 66. For a breakdown which includes private member days, opposition time, and specifically government time, see *Third Report of the Select Committee on Procedure*, 189 H.C.R., 30–1 (1946).

[2] It is of some interest, however, to note that in 1931 Ramsay MacDonald, then the Prime Minister, thought it desirable to give the Government more time. *Report of the Select Committee on Public Procedure*, H.C. 161 (1931), p. 135.

[3] The specific office of Leader of the House of Commons is discussed later in this chapter.

[4] W. I. Jennings, *Parliament* (Cambridge, Cambridge University Press, 1939), p. 137.

[5] Obstruction is a product of the failure to operate through 'the usual channels'. *Ibid.*, pp. 138–9.

Although the actual arrangement of the business of the House is made in this informal fashion, the members of the House receive their information as to the content of the next week's business in a more formal fashion. The Leader of the Opposition, or one of his lieutenants, will raise the question of the arrangement of business during the question period in the House. The Prime Minister will then reply, stating the programme already agreed to by the opposition, but previously unknown to the rank and file members of both groups. Normally, the question on the arrangement of business is raised on Thursdays.

In addition to his participation in the determination of the order of the business of the House as it concerns government legislation, the Prime Minister must also participate in the determination of the government's attitude toward some private member legislation.[1] Should he decide that the private member's proposal is not in harmony with the government's programme, he may send down word that the government wishes its supporters to oppose the particular measure. This is normally enough to assure the defeat of the measure.

The question period, with which the daily sittings of the House of Commons open, has been described as 'perhaps the readiest and most effective method of parliamentary control over the action of the executive.'[2] During this time the private member of the House of Commons becomes an important, rather than a minor, part of the House. He may ask questions which are mainly concerned with the elicitation of information, but he may also ask questions with the deliberate intent of embarrassing the government. Similarly, the opposition may prepare a series of questions aimed precisely at this latter objective. The questions make it necessary for the government to explain and defend policies, which, in some instances, might not be brought directly to the floor of the Commons through any other procedure.

All members of the Cabinet must go through the question period. The Prime Minister, naturally, falls heir to the same responsibilities. The questions with which he deals are likely to be of a somewhat different character than those asked of the department heads. The latter will frequently be called upon to

[1] *Ibid.*, p. 69.
[2] *Second Report of the Select Committee of Procedure*, H.C. 58 (1946), p. iii.

answer questions which are quite specific. The Prime Minister, on the other hand, is expected to answer questions in which general issues are raised, or in which inter-relationships between the various departments constitute the basic issue raised by the question. Questions as to future policy of the government, as distinguished from the future policy of a specific department, will also be asked of the Prime Minister.[1]

As with other ministers most of the questions directed to the Prime Minister are placed on paper and the Prime Minister has three days within which to answer the question.[2] Some questions may be answered in writing, but these are usually specific questions for particular information, and the Prime Minister is not likely to receive many questions of this kind. Other questions require an oral answer and are subject to the consequent 'supplementary questions' which may embarrass the unprepared minister.

In some cases the Prime Minister has accepted the chief obligation of replying to questions on foreign affairs. Ramsay MacDonald, of course, answered many of the questions raised on foreign policy issues in his first term, as he had combined the office of Prime Minister with that of Foreign Secretary. Neville Chamberlain also answered questions on foreign affairs, even while Eden held the office, however. When Lord Halifax became Foreign Secretary, it was necessary for the Prime Minister to answer such questions as Halifax was not in the House of Commons. All Prime Ministers must expect to participate to some extent in replies to questions in the foreign policy area, and, similarly, they must expect to participate frequently in responses to queries on military organization and policy. When other areas of governmental activity become controversial the Prime Minister acquires similar responsibilities with respect to them.

Some questions may not be asked of the Prime Minister. He may not be asked to answer a question about statements made by some other minister in a public speech. He may, however, be asked whether such statements constitute the policy of

---

[1] Cf. Finer, *op. cit.*, p. 531.

[2] It has been recommended that the time allowed to the Prime Minister be extended to five days. *Second Report of the Select Committee on Procedure*, H.C. 58 (1946), p. 36.

the government.[1] The Prime Minister is also exempted from questions which attempt to elicit the advice he has given to the Sovereign with regard to honours or ecclesiastical patronage.[2]

The extent to which the Prime Minister is expected to appear for questions cannot be stated definitively. He must take care not to antagonize the House by too obviously neglecting the interrogation, but it is not expected that he will always be present. One of the chief criticisms levelled against Ramsay MacDonald was that he did not appear very frequently in the House for either questions or debate.[3] In time of war, it is recognized that his appearances must, of necessity, be somewhat infrequent. In both wars other individuals have exercised the chief responsibility for acting as the government's spkesman in the House of Commons, including the question period. Bonar Law served in that capacity in the First World War, while Clement Attlee, Sir Stafford Cripps and Anthony Eden, all performed comparable functions in the Second World War.

As would be expected one of the most obvious requirements in the way of parliamentary functions is that the Prime Minister should participate in debate. This is important not only because the House will ill-receive a failure to participate, but, additionally, because the debates are one of the ways in which the government reaches the public. Debate is not likely to change the outcome of a division, but it serves as a means of explaining and defending the government's policy to the public at large, while the opposition states its objections and alternatives with the same objective in mind. Both are attempting to mould public opinion in preparation for the next election, whenever it may come. The Prime Minister, as the government's leading officer, is bound to participate by virtue of the office which he holds. The office itself means that his comments will receive wide publicity. This fact also means that it is necessary to exercise some care as to the content of the speech for a poor speech may have adverse effects upon the public. It is probable that MacDonald's ineffectual defence of his government's

[1] Sir Erskine May, *Parliamentary Procedure* (London, Butterworth, 14th edition, n.d.), p. 334.
[2] *Ibid.*, p. 335.
[3] Weir, *op. cit.*, pp. 555–6.

policy in the debates on the Campbell issue had much to do with its defeat, both in the House and in the country.[1]

This does not mean that the Prime Minister must participate in all debates, but he must shoulder part of the responsibility of speaking on behalf of important measures or policies. Furthermore, he plays a leading role in the selection of other government spokesmen. The agreements which are made 'behind the Speaker's chair' quite frequently include stipulations as to who shall speak for each side. The Speaker is informed of the individuals chosen by both sides so that he will be able to recognize them when debate is under way.[2] The Prime Minister is expected to line up strong speakers if a major piece of legislation is involved, for a series of able presentations of the government's programme will help to create a favourable climate of opinion outside the Parliament.

All major statements of governmental policy will involve the participation of the Prime Minister if any important innovation is proposed. This applies not only to substantive decisions in which new policy objectives are elaborated, but to changes in governmental institutions or procedures which are of basic importance. It is noteworthy that it was Attlee who carried out the principal task of explaining to the House of Commons the changes which had been made in the organization for defence and the reasons which were behind the change.[3] Similarly, he spoke on behalf of major nationalization measures as Asquith had in the past spoken in support of the social service proposals made by his government.[4] In addition the Prime Minister is sometimes faced with the necessity of explaining developments, either domestic or foreign, which involve crisis possibilities. Naturally he makes the major statement when such events as declarations of war or the conclusion of war take place. He also speaks for the House of Commons when it is necessary to extend either the congratulations or condolences of that body to the

[1] Snowden, *op. cit.*, ii, 693–8. The Zinovief letter also contributed to the defeat of the government, although Snowden did not think it was one of the basic causes of the country's repudiation of MacDonald. *Ibid.*, ii, 716–17.

[2] W. I. Jennings, *Parliament* (Cambridge, Cambridge University Press, 1936), p. 68.

[3] 426 *H.C. Deb.*, 5s., 624 ff.

[4] Lloyd George later contended that Asquith had never participated to the extent necessary and that he had left the rough work to his colleagues. Riddell, *op. cit.*, pp. 201–2.

government of some other state, as with the death of President Roosevelt.[1] Similarly, he usually makes a statement when an eminent British statesmen dies. He is also expected to speak for the House on great ceremonial occasions, as he is expected to represent the House when participation in ceremonial events is required.[2]

Such requirements make it evident that it is desirable that the Prime Minister be an effective speaker. The question of what constitutes an effective speaker, however, involves a distinction between parliamentary oratory and the techniques used in addressing large gatherings. The fact that a man is an effective crowd pleaser is not a guarantee that he will be able equally to impress the members of the Parliament. There have been men who had the ability to impress their personalities upon a crowd, but who, at the same time, proved somewhat less effective in the House of Commons. Lloyd George was not a bad parliamentary orator; he was a good one, but his parliamentary ability was inferior to his ability to sway great crowds. In the latter respect he was the finest speaker of his day. However, the very qualities which made him a great public orator worked against him in the House of Commons. Exaggeration, emphasis, and emotional appeal enabled him to capture a crowd, but the same glibness seemed to have displeased the House.[3] The result was that while the House was always anxious to hear him, it did not hold him in the same high respect as some less powerful, but more temperate speakers.[4]

The House of Commons seems to have preferred Asquith and Balfour to Lloyd George. In neither case did these men carry comparable weight upon the public platform. Asquith was not an effective platform speaker, nor was Balfour. On the other hand, both were exceptionally popular speakers in the House of Commons. Lord Samuel, who was probably prejudiced,

---

[1] 409 *H.C. Deb.*, 5s., 2120; 410 *H.C. Deb.*, 5s., 73–7.

[2] Gladstone, *op. cit.*, i, 241.

[3] J. A. Spender has commented, 'To be clever or glib is one of the most dangerous reputations a public man can earn, and he who is either of these things may consider himself fortunate if he is not deemed also to be dishonest. The presumption is that keen wits are not with solid worth allied, and Parliament is for ever on guard against the too accomplished speaker.' *The Public Life* (New York, Frederick A. Stokes, 1925), p. 133.

[4] Herbert Viscount Samuel, *Memoirs* (London, Cresset Press, 1945), pp. 88–9.

considered Asquith, 'the most impressive speaker of his day'.[1] He does not classify Balfour far below him.[2] Balfour was not the polished speaker Asquith was. He sometimes stopped in the midst of a flowing sentence to seek the word which best suited the idea he had in mind. 'At such times the assembly joined him sympathetically in the search. It was as if he had dropped his eyeglasses when reading an important despatch. Everyone, friend and foe, was anxious to recover them for him. All were delighted when he found them himself in his top right-hand waistcoat pocket. Out came the right word, amid loud cheers or loud howls and general satisfaction. This faculty of enlisting the whole audience, both sides alike, in the delivering of his speech was a potent gift; and as far as speech can influence opinion or votes, he swayed the House of Commons.'[3] It is not difficult to understand that while the House of Commons and its members might appreciate the quest for the *bon mot*, the public might not have the same response.

Churchill, of course, must rate among the greatest parliamentary speakers of all time, but even his sonorous prose and his flights into Gibbonesque phrases did not impress the House of Commons between 1929 and 1939. Lloyd George, while recognizing Churchill's oratorical gifts, once said of him, 'he sometimes ends by blowing up his guns. You never feel quite safe until he sits down.'[4] Perhaps Churchill lost influence in the House because he was too glib, too effective, as well as because of the Cassandra-like content of his speeches. In times of crisis, however, when his prose style exactly fitted the character of his times his reputation as a parliamentary speaker rose to phenomenal heights.

The techniques to be used by speakers must vary from one individual to another. Lloyd George thought it necessary to speak directly to the opposition, phrasing and modifying his speech as he noted its effects upon his opponents.[5] Bonar Law thought it wise to begin a speech in a low voice for that demanded the attention of the House and gave the speaker an initial advantage.[6] Balfour used the same technique, and it was from him that Law learned the lesson.[7]

---

[1] *Ibid.*, p. 87.   [2] *Ibid.*, p. 47.

[3] Winston Churchill, *Great Contemporaries* (New York, G. P. Putnam's Sons, 1937), pp. 216–17.

[4] Riddell, *op. cit.*, p. 189.   [5] *Ibid.*, p. 158.   [6] *Ibid.*, p. 88.   [7] *Loc cit.*

Other factors will play upon the speaker, causing his effectiveness to increase or decrease. Lloyd George thought Asquith's first speech, after his election in 1920, ineffective. He gave as the principal reason for the failure of the speech that Asquith, 'had been accustomed to rise with a burst of applause from his supporters. Now there were but few cheers and he had to address a huge unfriendly mass of opponents.'[1] It is certainly probable that such a situation might tend to lower the effectiveness of the speaker. Any man is likely to deliver a better speech if he has a substantial body of vocal supporters behind him.[2]

As the functions of government have become more extensive, and the subject matter of those functions more complex, the drain on the time of the Prime Minister which follows from his parliamentary duties has sometimes been excessive. Asquith arrived at the conviction that the work of the Prime Minister, excluding his parliamentary functions proper, was so onerous that it was undesirable to plague him with the additional burden of leading the House of Commons.[3] That this is a problem of import is beyond question, but it cannot be solved by making the Prime Minister a peer, as Asquith implied, for to do so would cut him off from the major machinery of government.

J. A. Spender has said, 'experience . . . goes far to suggest that the Prime Minister can only undertake the duty of leading the House of Commons if he is permitted to absent himself from a large part of its proceedings.'[4] This problem has been handled informally in that fashion, and more formally through the development of deputy leaders, or even officers specifically titled Leader of the House of Commons. Even in the absence of

[1] *Ibid.*, pp. 201–2.

[2] The party leader always has an advantage as a consequence of this fact. Even a great orator, like Sir Charles Dilke, was unable to draw a large audience, but 'a leader is always sure of a goodly number of members to listen to him even if he be a mere driveller.' George N. Barnes, *From Workshop to War Cabinet* (New York, Appleton, 1924), p. 92.

[3] J. A. Spender and Cyril Asquith, *The Life of Lord Oxford and Asquith* (London, Hutchinson and Co., 1932), i, 176. Stanley Baldwin indicated the difficulties occasioned by parliamentary duties in his comment, 'it is an immense relief when the House is up, because you can get on with your own work; you have more time in the evenings, but there is plenty of work to do all the year round.' *Report from the Select Committee on Ministers' Remuneration*, H.C. 170 (1930), p. 16.

[4] Spender and Asquith, *op. cit.*, i, 176.

such an officer it is generally recognized that the Chancellor of the Exchequer acts as the deputy leader of the House.[1] This. does not constitute a hard and fast rule, and the Prime Minister may, if he wishes, choose some other officer to act as his principal deputy in the Commons. Sir John Simon served as deputy leader in 1935 while holding the office of Home Secretary. Herbert Morrison served as Leader of the House while Lord President of the Council, and later while Foreign Secretary.

The specific development of an officer with recognized responsibilities as Leader of the House took place during the First World War. In 1915 Asquith made Lloyd George the equivalent of Deputy Prime Minister, although the specific term was not used.[2] Later, under Lloyd George's premiership, Bonar Law took over the functions of the Leader of the House of Commons and was so recognized by that body. While Winston Churchill held to the position of Leader of the House during the first years of his administration, it was nevertheless the case that Attlee, the Lord Privy Seal, handled day-to-day parliamentary relations.[3] Later Sir Stafford Cripps took the specific office of Leader of the House.[4] When Cripps resigned his post Anthony Eden took over.[5]

It was not hard to gain parliamentary acceptance of this practice during times of war. The strain of other duties, and the enormous expenditure of time involved, led to a general recognition that the Prime Minister could not fulfil his normal parliamentary functions. Bonar Law, however, believed 'that after the Peace the House would not submit to anyone leading it except the Prime Minister.'[6] In this expectation Law proved to be incorrect. He himself continued to serve as Leader of the House of Commons for two years after the conclusion of the war. Upon his resignation, Austen Chamberlain took over the same function. Later, when MacDonald combined the offices of Prime Minister and Foreign Secretary, Clynes became the Deputy

[1] W. I. Jennings, *Parliament* (Cambridge, Cambridge University Press, 1939), p. 65.

[2] Lord Beaverbrook, *Politicians and the War, 1914–1916* (New York, Doubleday, Doran and Co., 1928), i, 156–7.

[3] Winston Churchill, *Their Finest Hour* (Boston, Houghton Mifflin, 1949), p. 9.

[4] Winston Churchill, *The Hinge of Fate* (Boston, Houghton Mifflin, 1950), pp. 79–80.

[5] *Ibid.*, p. 561.　　　　　[6] Riddell, *op. cit.*, p. 67.

Leader of the House of Commons, and normally acted as the government's chief spokesman, since it was obvious MacDonald would not have the time to fulfil all the normal requirements.[1]

Even though the development of this practice tends to subtract from the total load carried by the Prime Minister it is, nevertheless true, that the Prime Minister is still the most important member of the Commons. Many of the detailed functions, including handling questions, arranging the business of the House, and even dealing with rank and file party members,[2] may be undertaken by the Leader of the House of Commons, but the Prime Minister still must keep himself available, if not in the House itself, in his work room, in case a new issue of importance arises. An able Leader of the House may do much to relieve him of excessive concerns with details, but he cannot relieve the Prime Minister of the fact that he remains the real leader of the House. No decision as to government business, who shall speak, what modifications shall be made as a consequence of criticism, or any of the other manifold difficulties which may arise, can be completely removed from the purview of his office.

Upon its face the subject of the dissolution of Parliament would seem to be relatively simple. Ordinarily, it is handled in text books on the government of Great Britain as if the subject were one lacking in complexities. In reality, any adequate examination of the dissolution of Parliament is likely to lead one into labyrinths of confusion, and, in some of the dark caverns of disagreement no path which leads inexorably to one definite conclusion may be found.

The discussion of dissolution inevitably involves an examination of both practical and constitutional ramifications of considerable import. It is, in the realm of political techniques, a method of enforcing and maintaining discipline upon the government's supporters in the House of Commons. In the same realm its use involves the study of political advantage, in the sense that the Prime Minister and his colleagues must try

---

[1] Snowden, *op. cit.*, ii, 611.

[2] Herbert Morrison took over the responsibility for the largest portion of party work in the House after 1945. He presided over party meetings and served as the principal contact between the Government and the party. John Parker, *Labour Marches On* (Penguin Books, 1947), p. 48.

to discover the appropriate moment for dissolution, the moment and the issue which are likely to lead to the return of the government in the ensuing general election. Constitutionally, several problems arise. One of the most significant, and at the same time one of the most troublesome issues, is the precise place and power of the King with respect to dissolution. May he refuse a dissolution? If so, under what circumstances? May he force a dissolution? If so, how may he do so? The last two questions actually lead into another problem. May the King dismiss a government? If so, under what circumstances? Other constitutional issues also arise. Who advises a dissolution? The Cabinet? The Prime Minister alone? Is it obligatory to dissolve the Parliament if it is proposed to introduce a new policy which was not an issue in the last election? If the government suffers a continuous series of defeats in by-elections, is it obliged to dissolve in order that the seeming change in public will may be reflected in the Parliament?

These questions involve complexities and complexities within complexities. Some, it is true, may be answered quickly. Others require more intensive examination. Some may not be answered in a definitive fashion, but must remain subjects of controversy. It is not the task of an American student to settle disputes between British constitutional lawyers.

The earlier discussion of the relations of Cabinet and Parliament in Great Britain emphasized the extent to which the government tends to dominate the legislature. The reasons for this are several in number, but the power of dissolution is unquestionably one of the government's stronger weapons. For the moment, leaving aside the constitutional complexities of the subject, we may notice that normally the government may be secure in the knowledge that it will receive a grant of dissolution from the King when it is requested.

The effect of such a weapon is obvious. The members of the House of Commons hold their seats at the mercy of the government's use of this terrifying power, which may force them to return to their constituencies and go through the process of campaigning over again. Men do not like to run the risks which are involved in this process if little is to be gained from incurring the dangers. Of course, the members of the opposition party may seek to force the government to dissolve the Parliament. Their objective is to successfully wrest the control of the government from the party which holds power. On the other hand, the members of the government party will realize that if they cross the lines in such a fashion as to defeat the government, they run risks with little possibility of advantage. Any minority which aligns itself with the opposition on a specific vote risks political destruction. It may very easily mean the loss of the party's endorsement in the ensuing election. Given the nature of British politics this is equivalent to the kiss of death.[1]

The threat of dissolution thus hangs over their heads, restraining them, restricting their independence, leading them into the government's lobby. The power of dissolution leaves little room for the independent legislator, and it secures to the government the almost absolute certainty that its majority will not be shaken. If no power of dissolution existed, minority groups within a party might do much more to limit and restrain the Cabinet, but in its presence dissent dies. Even in those circumstances in which there are three parties and the government does not have the absolute support of a majority, it is noticeable that the third party, the party which made power possible, walks warily in the face of a possibility of dissolution.[2]

It has been pointed out earlier in the text of this study that normally the King accepts and acts upon the advice of his ministers. His power is limited to warning, encouraging, and advising. It does not extend to the negativing of measures passed by the two houses of the Parliament. Even so, a question exists about the precise extent of the power of the King with respect to dissolution.

In the first place, it is necessary to note that constitutionally

---

[1] British elections turn around the parties with very little interjection of such personal considerations as the character of the individual candidate. The only constituencies in which independents have had much strength in recent years were the university constituencies. These have now been abolished. For a statement as to the universities' preference for independents, see R. B. MacCallum and Alison Readman, *The British General Election of 1945* (New York, Oxford University Press, 1947), p. 124. In the elections of 1950 and 1951 the independent candidates were subjected to overwhelming defeats.

[2] The Liberals in 1924 and again between 1929 and 1931 did not look forward to the fall of the Labour Government. Although it was a Liberal motion which led to the dissolution of 1924 it does not seem that the Liberals desired the dissolution. MacDonald could have accepted their motion, which was offered in part, to protect the Government against more extreme criticism.

it is the King who dissolves the Parliament.[1] Similarly, however, it is the King who constitutionally makes treaties with foreign states, whereas in fact, the Cabinet makes the agreements in the name of the King. Does a comparable situation exist with respect to the dissolution of Parliament? Does the King act only upon the advice of his ministers? Is he required to accept that advice?

It would seem that his power with respect to dissolution is considerably greater than in the case of the treaty-making prerogative. In the first place, it is beyond question that in certain circumstances he may refuse a request for dissolution. Should the government have already had a dissolution and suffered an electoral defeat, he is not obliged to grant another dissolution in consequence of that defeat. This would seem to be a self-evident limitation although the last years of the Weimar Republic provide an example of contrary practice. The problem becomes more complex, however, if we posit a situation in which the result of the earlier election had given the government a slight majority, but one which is too small to guarantee control of the House over a considerable period of time. In those circumstances is he obliged to give them a dissolution should they request it?

While no situation of this sort has developed in recent British history, one very similar did take place in Canada in 1926. In 1925, the Liberal Government, under MacKenzie King, which had the support of the Progressives, advised and received a dissolution. At that time the Liberals had a parliamentary strength of 117 members to 50 Conservatives and 68 Progressives and others. In the ensuing election the results were: 101 Liberals, 116 Conservatives, and 28 Progressives.[2] The Prime Minister determined to meet the new Parlimaent relying upon the support of the Progressives to maintain his government.

Initially his expectations proved to be justified and the government won a series of votes by very narrow margins. Six months after the new Parliament had met, the government was defeated. The Prime Minister then sought a dissolution, but the

[1] A. B. Keith, *The Constitution of England from Victoria to George VI* (London, Macmillan, 1940), i, 50, 85–7.

[2] Eugene A. Forsey, *The Royal Power of Dissolution of Parliament in the British Commonwealth* (Toronto, Oxford University Press, 1943), p. 131.

Governor-General refused to grant his request. The Prime Minister resigned, insisting that the Governor-General had no right to refuse his advice. The Conservative leader was called upon to form a government and did so, having received some guarantees of Progressive support in completing the work of the session. The situation, however, was complicated by the fact that under existing statutory rules any member of the Parliament who accepted a ministerial post had to resign and seek re-election. This would inevitably lead to the destruction of the government's majority. After an attempt to escape from this limitation, the government eventually had to face it, and in consequence it wsa defeated. The Conservative leader asked for and obtained a dissolution. An immediate outcry followed, for the Conservative leader had been granted a dissolution whereas the Liberal leader had been refused the same grant.

There is little point in continuing an examination of this particular issue. It has been argued, by Professor Keith, that the action of the Governor-General in refusing the grant of dissolution to the Liberal Prime Minister was unconstitutional *per se*. This follows as the Conservative Prime Minister 'was unable to carry on . . . without a dissolution proving the soundness of 'Mr. King's' opinion . . . that the time had come when the electorate must be given an opportunity to cast a decisive vote.'[1] The results, it should be added, restored the Liberals to power. Evatt, on the other hand, has argued that the refusal of dissolution was justified as no party had a majority and the only way in which it could be ascertained that the Conservatives could not control the House was by an actual test vote on the issue.[2]

It would seem the greatest merit must, in this particular case, lie with Evatt's position. Additional factors tended to further complicate the immediate issue, but they are extraneous to the basic principle involved. However, a different situation might have existed had the Liberal Government been in power three years, rather than six months. In such circumstances the use of dissolution might have been extended to the Liberal Prime Minister with less question than in the case of the shorter period. The latter point further complicates the issue, as it

[1] Keith, *op. cit.*, i, 86–7.
[2] H. V. Evatt, *The King and His Dominion Governors* (Oxford, Oxford University Press, 1936), p. 60.

introduces the question of what is a 'short period' and what is a 'long period'. Dissolution is more likely to be granted in the latter case than the former, but the problem of who determines whether it is long or short remains to be solved.

A situation which was somewhat comparable to the Canadian incident did take place in 1924, but the dissimilarities must also be noted. The Labour Government of Ramsay MacDonald held a minority of the seats in the House of Commons. The government was sustained by the support given by the Liberal Party. Eventually defeat was suffered on a confidence issue. MacDonald sought and obtained a grant of dissolution. Asquith, the Liberal leader, seems to have thought that in such circumstances the King should first see if it were possible to obtain a parliamentary majority under some other Prime Minister and from some other party.[1] Since the defeat took place within less than a year of the opening of the Parliament it is probably safe to consider it as a 'short period' since the last dissolution.

There were, however, dissimilarities which explain the grant of dissolution. First, the previous grant of dissolution had been to a Conservative Government, not to a Labour Government. This was the first grant given to the Labourites. In all probability this was the most important reason for granting MacDonald's request, although it is likely that the desire to show the impartiality of the Crown, even to Socialists, influenced the King. He might also have thought it unlikely that any other government could have obtained the support of the House of Commons. It would be expected that the Labourites would take vengeance on the Liberals should they take power, and there was no indication that Asquith visualized the possibility that Baldwin, who had already been defeated in the House, would again become Prime Minister. The attitude of the Conservatives towards the Liberals was also likely to be very hostile as they had been defeated by the Liberal support of the Labour motion of censure. Practically speaking, the possibility of the Liberals gaining the support of the House was unlikely, although this argument is subject to the principle stated by Evatt with respect to the Canadian crisis.

Outside of circumstances of this unusual character, a refusal of dissolution would seem to be extraordinary. Although it is at least possible that a dissolution might be refused a short time

[1] *The Times*, 19 December 1923.

after a successful election, it is improbable. Baldwin's request for dissolution in 1923 was granted although the last election had occurred less than a year previously.

A second question arises as to the power of the King. May he force a dissolution? Professor Keith has said, 'The prerogative of the Crown to dissolve Parliament is undoubted. The manner of dissolution does not, as often said, strictly speaking, involve the aid of ministers, for the King could still present himself in the House of Lords, and by word of mouth, dissolve the Parliament.'[1] As Professor Keith admits, 'in practice dissolution takes place by a proclamation under the great seal, which is based on the advice of the Privy Council, and which refers to an Order in Council requiring the issue of the writs for the meeting of Parliament.'[2] Rather surprisingly, given his initial statement, Keith concludes that 'no ministry which did not wish to dissolve would give the necessary aid, and therefore a forced dissolution is impossible, though one induced by royal pressure is perfectly in order'.[3] It is rather difficult to understand the logic which allows Professor Keith to say the King could still personally dissolve the Parliament, but that a 'forced dissolution is impossible'. It would seem to be more nearly true to say that while the King might once have had the power personally to dissolve the Parliament, it has atrophied by long disuse.

Forgiving Professor Keith his momentary lapse into illogic, his conclusion is important. While a forced dissolution is impossible, 'one induced by royal pressure is perfectly in order'. Various questions must immediately rise to mind in the face of such a statement, in particular, the question of when such pressure is justified. What circumstances must exist before the King may try to pressure his government into a dissolution? What takes place if the government refuses? Professor Keith has continued his thesis with the following statement:[4]

'The power to force a dissolution undoubtedly exists, but it means the dismissal of a ministry and the power to find a ministry which will take office and bear the responsibility for dismissal. This necessarily involves bringing under the con-

---

[1] A. B. Keith, *The British Cabinet System* (London, Stevens and Son, 1939), p. 391.
[2] *Loc. cit.*   [3] *Ibid.*, pp. 391–2.
[4] A. B. Keith, *The King and the Imperial Crown* (New York, Longmans, Green, 1936), pp. 177–8.

sideration of the electorate the action of the king, and must create the impression that the king is capable of partisanship in politics. It is of such high importance to prevent any such impression that in the great majority of cases this mere possibility rules out any action of the kind, leaving the possible use of this final power for the gravest occasions. But the fact that a power exists only for wise employment in grave crises, does not mean that it is obsolete, as is sometimes suggested. The mere fact that a safeguard exists is often and perhaps always will be a sufficient preventive of such unrestrained action as would bring the safeguard into operation. The issue is of special importance in regard to the maintenance of the constitution . . . the conduct of foreign policy on which decisions may be taken of vital and irreparable consequence, and the preservation of law and order against domestic strife of a serious character menacing the public security.'

Keith's argument amounts to an assertion that the King is the guardian of the Constitution. He has written, 'The Crown remains in fact an authority charged with the final duty of preserving the essentials of the constitution. The passing of the Parliament Act, 1911, has weakened enormously the potency of resistance to change of the Lords; it has only enhanced the importance thus left to the action in emergency of the king.'[1] Such powers, as he writes, are 'not to be lightly used, but their use is justifiable if they are necessary for the purpose of giving the will of the people its just course, though such a criterion of action is plainly difficult to formulate or apply.'[2] As an example of its application he defends the action of the King in 1931 on the grounds that 'the dissolution which shortly afterwards was resolved on gave a decisive majority of 559 to 56 votes and was followed by a reconstruction of the ministry to normal size. The result of the election forms the complete justification of the

---

[1] *Ibid.*, p. 183. The similarity between this argument and the view propounded by Lord Lansdowne in 1913 is rather striking. Lansdowne argued that since the Parliament Act had destroyed the power inherent in the House of Lords to kill a bill and compel an election, that power now belonged to the King alone. Spender and Asquith, *op. cit.*, ii, 25–6. Considering what had just happened to the House of Lords as a consequence of its use of that power, it is not necessarily true that Lansdowne's position would have strengthened the King over the long run.

[2] A. B. Keith, *The King and the Imperial Crown* (New York, Longmans, Green, 1936), p. 140.

royal action. The King had correctly adjudged the wishes of his people, and his action conformed to the supreme test of conformity to the popular will.'[1] One is tempted to ask what might have been said had the election results been reversed? In that case would the King's action have been unconstitutional? The King is left in a difficult position if the constitutionality of his action is determined by future results, rather than by immediate, known principles.

Professor Keith's position leads to the conclusion that in certain circumstances the King may refuse to follow the advice of his ministers if the basic principles of the constitution are endangered by their policy. The difficulty with this thesis lies in the problem of defining the 'basic principles' or determining what constitutes 'a drastic change' which requires public authorization. Such matters, as Professor Laski has said, turn 'on the premises of judgment from which we start'.[2] The basic principles are not so clear as Professor Keith seems to assume. 'Not only do they change in time; even in any given time there is no agreement about their content.'[3] Professor Laski, fearing the consequences for socialist legislation, said of Keith's argument, 'The volume of actual and active power it would transfer to the King's hand would be enormous. For, clearly, it would give him at once a pre-natal and post-natal control of all government legislation which would arouse deep feelings of hostility in the country; and the House of Lords, that is, the Conservative Party, would be made aware that it has only to use its veto under the Parliament Act to compel either the postponement of government measures or their submission to the electorate.'[4]

The basic reason for denying the desirability of the thesis elaborated by Keith would seem to lie in a slightly different direction, although it is implicit in Laski's criticisms. Keith has proposed an argument which amounts to an assertion that the King may force a dissolution, through the dismissal of his government, when he believes that the government's policy does not have public support, although it has the support of the House of Commons. Professor Jennings has asked the right

[1] *Ibid.*, p. 137.
[2] Harold J. Laski, *Parliamentary Government in England* (New York, Viking Press, 1938), p. 364.
[3] *Ibid.*, p. 364.   [4] *Ibid.*, p. 365.

question, 'Is he sufficiently in touch with public opinion to be able to form a judgment?'[1] His answer also hits the centre of the problem. 'It is suggested that the answer to the . . . question is in the negative. Though his "splendid isolation" makes him more impartial than most, it also keeps him away from the movements of opinion. He can judge only from newspapers, from by-elections, and from his own entourage. Of the first, it is enough to say that even the unanimous opposition of London newspapers would be no criterion. Of the second it can be said that by-elections . . . are apt to prove deceptive, especially to one far removed from them. Of the third it must be asserted that it is always more biased and less well-informed than the King himself.'[2] It seems highly questionable that the King should attempt to interpret the pulse of the public for he is in no position to obtain adequate, objective information as to its beat. It is furthermore obvious that any conclusion he reaches must be a subjective conclusion, 'which it is his duty, as an impartial Sovereign, to ignore'.[3]

Certainly it is evident that the King's intervention in this fashion would do much to undermine the confidence of the British electorate, or significant portions thereof, in the neutrality of the King. How can a King be neutral if he enforces the wishes of one party upon another, although the first party is not in power? The monarchy itself might well become a matter of controversy in future elections, and the legacy of mistrust occasioned by the incident would remain to plague the future of British politics.

Upon the whole the above discussion, while fundamental, has dealt with possibilities rather than actualities. In fact, in the period under study, no request for dissolution has been refused. On the other hand, it must be added that a degree of royal pressure was applied in the case of the disolution of 1910, although the Prime Minister seems to have thought the King's reasons valid. The government proposed the passage of a bill limiting the veto of the House of Lords. The King insisted that an election must be held before he would promise to create a sufficient number of peers to insure a government majority should the Lords reject the bill. What he wanted was a public

[1] W. I. Jennings, *Cabinet Government* (Cambridge, Cambridge University Press, 1936), p. 306.
[2] *Ibid.*, p. 306.   [3] *Loc. cit.*

mandate on a particular issue. The election, which returned a house divided exactly as before, satisfied the King's desire for an expression of the public will upon the particular issue.[1] The other dissolutions of the last fifty-five years have been ordinary from the standpoint of the constitutional power of the monarch, although other problems deserve some consideration.

The King's desire for an expression of public opinion on the government's proposal for a change in the constitutional status of the House of Lords leads logically into a discussion of the mandate. The doctrine of the 'mandate' seems to have first developed 'to justify the opposition of the House of Lords to Liberal measures. It is, however, based upon an important principle. A government exists only because it has secured a majority at an election, or is likely to secure such a majority when an election takes place. But it secures that majority by appealing to the electorate to support a policy. The electorate expects that the policy will be carried to fruition. It does not expect that radical changes will be made unless they were part of the party policy or are the necessary consequences of that policy. The Government must, of course, meet emergencies if and when they arise, but emergencies apart, major develop-ments of policy should not be entered upon without that approval of the electorate which is secured by the return of a party to power.'[2] There are difficulties to this doctrine, even as Professor Jennings has stated it, for the phrase 'necessary consequences of that policy' is not precise and may, and has led to controversy, as with the Liberal Home Rule measure of 1913–14.

This is not the place to examine all of the aspects of the doc-trine of the mandate.[3] It becomes important in the context of a discussion of dissolution as it raises the question of whether the Prime Minister is obliged to dissolve the Parliament, if he pro-poses to introduce a new major policy which was not at issue in the last election. It has been argued that the theory of the mandate is undesirable upon the grounds that it created two separate centres of authority—the Parliament, on the one hand,

[1] Lord Oxford and Asquith, *Fifty Years of British Parliament* (Boston, Little, Brown and Co., 1926), ii, 102–7.
[2] W. I. Jennings, *Cabinet Government* (Cambridge, Cambridge University Press, 1936), p. 388.
[3] Cf. *Ante*, ch. iii.

and the plebiscite upon the other.[1] Whatever be the merit of this argument, it is clear that the mandate theory is here to stay.

There have been a number of instances in which a 'mandate' has been sought, and in which a dissolution of the Parliament has served as a preliminary to the taking of the public pulse. The dissolution of 1910 on the issue of a change in the status in the House of Lords was one. In 1909, Asquith sought and obtained a dissolution as a consequence of the action of the House of Lords in rejecting the Lloyd George budget. The consequent victory of the government was interpreted as a public mandate for the budget and the House of Lords passed it when it was again sent up from the House of Commons.[2]

Again in 1918, the government dissolved, purportedly to obtain a mandate in support of its prosecution of the peace conference, although it seems more probably that the argument of a mandate, in this instance, was a façade behind which was hidden the reality of the desire for a 'khaki election' like that of 1900.[3]

A more significant incident emphasizing the importance of the mandate took place in 1923. The election of 1922 had brought a Conservative majority, but 'protection' had not been a part of the Conservative programme. Stanley Baldwin, the Prime Minister in 1923, thought it necessary to adopt a protectionist system, but he did not think the government had the power to do so in the absence of a specific mandate from the public on the issue. In consequence he sought and obtained a dissolution in order to place the issue before the public.[4]

Thus in both of the elections of 1910, and in the election of 1923, the public was asked to pass upon a specific policy issue. The principle which Anson had considered doubtful had become operative as a part of British constitutional practice.

Some care needs to be taken, however, in discussing the extent of its adoption. Some mandates are particular and specific, as with the dissolutions of 1910 and 1923. Others are phrased in much more general terms. Thus it was argued that the National Government received a 'doctor's mandate' from

[1] Sir William Anson, *The Law and Custom of the Constitution* (Oxford, Clarendon Press, 4th edition, 1909), i, 308.

[2] Oxford and Asquith, *op. cit.*, ii, 88–95.

[3] But see Lloyd George's statement in *The Times*, 18 November 1918, p. 9.

[4] Roberts, *op. cit.*, pp. 115–17; 168 *H.C. Deb.*, 5s., 39–40.

the dissolution of 1931. Upon that basis they felt free to introduce protectionist measures although these measures had not been an integral part of the election issues.[1]

Again, criticisms have sometimes been levelled against governments on the ground that they did not have a mandate for a particular policy. The Conservatives between 1945 and 1950 criticized the Labour Government's steel nationalization bill on the grounds that the public had not authorized the measure. The nationalization of steel, however, had been an integral part of the Labour Party's election programme of 1945.[2] The Conservative argument amounted to an insistence that the nationalization measure was so important that a specific expression of the public will was required prior to its implementation. In part, the Attlee Government seems to have accepted the argument, as its nationalization statute did not become operative immediately upon passage. An election was required in the period before the legislation became effective. Arguments continued as to whether the public did or did not authorize the measure since the election results gave the Labour Party a slim majority in the House, but only a minority of the total vote cast.

Criticism was also directed at the Asquith Government's proposal of Home Rule in 1913. The Conservatives contended that no specific authorization existed for the measure. The Liberals contended that it had been recognized as one of the principal issues of the election of 1910. It was true, they admitted, that the immediate issue was the Parliament Act. The public, however, knew that the basic reason for the proposal to limit the power of the House of Lords was to make it impossible for that body to impose a veto upon Home Rule legislation.[3]

Later Neville Chamberlain was subjected to criticism on the ground that no public mandate existed for his foreign policy. It is true, in this case, that the foreign policy adopted by the Prime Minister did not correspond to the emphasis on 'collective security' which had been integral to the Conservative

---

[1] Cf. MacDonald's speech requesting a free hand to deal with the economic crisis. *The Times*, 8 October 1931, p. 10.

[2] Cf. Labour Party, *Let Us Face the Future* (London, 1945).

[3] Oxford and Asquith, *op. cit.*, ii, 148–9, 158–9; Spender and Asquith, *op. cit.*, ii, 32.

election programme of 1935.[1] In general it should be noted that a strict application of the mandate theory to the sphere of foreign policy is unworkable. New issues develop rapidly in the relations between states, and frequently immediate responses are required. The deterioration of relations between the Western states and the Soviet Union following 1945 made the foreign policy statements of the campaign of that year inapplicable. The necessary readjustment in British policy, including rearmament, however, would certainly not be considered unjustified upon the grounds that the policy was not at issue in 1945.

The practical difficulties of determining when a mandate is necessary are obvious, but it seems evident that the doctrine is accepted, although its application in particular cases is not always simple. 'In general, the position taken by the British statesmen since the beginning of the present century as regards the theory of the mandate has been that, while maintaining an unyielding attitude in regard to the legal omnipotency of Parliament, they were not unaware of the constitutional propriety and practical expediency of asking for fresh authority in dealing with some novel and important measure or some unusual situations.'[2]

It has sometimes been argued that, where the government suffers a series of losses in by-elections, it should dissolve the Parliament in order to obtain an accurate representation of the public's immediate attitude. This argument is a post-1867 development. This is a consequence of the fact that, 'from that time on, the contests at by-elections naturally assumed greater practical significance, since they were waged more and more by candidates chosen from the two big political camps rather than by people who cherished independent beliefs or who meant, if elected, to take independent action.'[3]

It is obvious that from a constitutional standpoint the government is not obligated to dissolve merely because it has lost a series of by-elections. Upon the other hand it is possible that a

---

[1] W. I. Jennings, *The British Constitution* (Cambridge, Cambridge University Press, 1944), p. 47.

[2] Chia Kao Wang, *Dissolution of the British Parliament, 1832–1931* (New York, Columbia University Press, 1934), p. 108. See Neville Chamberlain's statement at 339 *H.C. Deb.*, 5s., 548.

[3] Wang, *op. cit.*, p. 94.

moral argument in favour of dissolution might be adduced in certain circumstances. It is also possible that a series of defeats in by-elections might make it impossible for a government with a slender majority to maintain its control, thus necessitating another election. The tenuous majority by which the Labour Party held control of the Commons in 1950–1 could have been shaken by as few as three defeats in by-elections.

A series of defeats in by-elections was the reason given by Gladstone for his decision to dissolve in 1874. In 1868 Gladstone and his party had received a majority of one hundred seats. In the next five years twenty-four seats were lost to the Conservatives in by-elections. Gladstone himself said:[1]

'I conceived it was a peculiarity of which I knew no parallel within the Parliamentary experience of the present century. . . . I have never known a Parliament . . . in which single elections of themselves went so far towards establishing a presumption that the opinion of the country had changed with reference to the politics of those whom it desired to conduct public affairs as that of the last, and the consequence was that from time to time it was a matter of inquiry to us whether our position gave us the strength to enable us to conduct with dignity and with credit the affairs of the country.'

This may be an accurate description of the causes of the dissolution of 1874, but it should be noted that Gladstone was in serious disagreement with a portion of his Cabinet over the army and navy estimates for 1874–5. It is possible that the series of defeats in by-elections may have served as a method of escaping from the difficulty created by that internal disagreement.[2]

Another instance of a rather similar kind developed between 1900 and 1905. The Conservatives had a substantial majority gained in 1900, but in the next five years the results of by-elections diminished that margin by twenty-one seats.[3] Sir Henry Campbell-Bannerman, the Liberal leader, raised the issue of whether the government should continue in office in the face of such defeats.[4] In the summer of 1905 he again raised the

---

[1] 218 Hansard (Commons), 3s., 1121–1122.
[2] This is the position taken by John Morley. See his Life of Gladstone (New York, Macmillan, 1903), ii, 478–90.
[3] Wang, op. cit., p. 100, n. 100.
[4] 141 Hansard (Commons), 4s., 123 ff.

argument, stating, 'it is common for us to say, and it is true constitutionally, that the Minister of the Crown in this country is selected and appointed because he is the man who commands a majority in the House of Commons. But what does that mean? It means that the command of the majority represents the feeling of the country. The moment the House of Commons gets out of touch and harmony with the country then that plea for retaining office dissolves. . . .'[1]

Balfour, the Conservative Prime Minister, refused to accept this line of argument. He insisted that 'there is one plain test whether the Government can carry on the business of the country, and that plain test is whether the House of Commons support them. . . . Those who are defeated at by-elections are always rich in explanations why that particular disaster should have happened. The conditions under which a by-election is taken are very different from those which obtain at a general election and necessarily different.'[2]

It is also possible that by-elections in 1921–22 led to the fall of the Lloyd George Government. The government suffered a defeat in 1922 at the hands of a Conservative who did not have the support of the Conservatives in the coalition. This did much to lead to the Conservative conclusion to withdraw from the coalition. The latter action led inevitably to Lloyd George's resignation and the dissolution of Parliament.[3]

It is probable that no general requirement exists for the Prime Minister to dissolve as a consequence of by-election defeats. As Balfour pointed out, the conditions under which a by-election is fought are quite different from the conditions of a general election. Between 1945 and 1950 the Labour Government did not lose a single seat in a by-election although their majority in the constituencies was sometimes reduced. The general election of 1950, however, brought a result far more adverse to the Attlee Government.

Any historical examination of the question of who dissolves the Parliament is likely to lead to confusion multiplied. It is not intended here to trace all of the instances of dissolution over the period since 1832, but merely to describe the relations between Prime Minister and Cabinet in the determination of this action.

[1] 150 *Hansard* (*Commons*), 4s., 70–5.
[2] 151 *Hansard* (*Commons*), 4s., 975–8.
[3] Roberts, *op. cit.*, pp. 71 ff.

Asquith wrote, 'such a question as the Dissolution of Parliament is always submitted to the Cabinet for tultimate decision.'[1] Professor Keith has also said, 'There is no case on record where action [dissolution] has really occurred without the assent of a Cabinet majority . . .'[2] Dr. Wang has also said, 'Parliament is dissolved by the Prime Minister with the approval of the Cabinet and the sanction of the sovereign . . .'[3] On the other hand, Professor Jennings says, 'The decision now rests with the Prime Minister'.[4]

Professor Jennings' statement seems to be more accurate as a description of present practice. Asquith's statement, of course, was correct as a description of the practice of his Cabinet and its predecessors. The only possible exception was the dissolution of 1868. In 1868 Disraeli requested and received a dissolution without calling a Cabinet. He had, however, received Cabinet sanction for a dissolution ten days earlier. It is probable that he did not again call them together for fear that they had changed their minds.[5] Today, the Prime Minister seems to have absorbed this power, although it is evident that the extent to which he acts independently depends upon his own strength and the attitude which his colleagues are likely to take.

Professor Jennings has said, 'Probably the change was due to the hiatus during the war, but there is some suggestion that it was Mr. Baldwin . . . in 1923 . . .'.[6] The circumstances surrounding Baldwin's decision to dissolve in 1923 are not completely clear, but it seems probable that at least the date of dissolution was determined by the Prime Minister. Baldwin seems to have carried the day with his Cabinet and have gained their support for dissolution, although many opposed it. The date of the dissolution was to be January 1924. Baldwin later selected an earlier date, and requested and obtained a dissolution for November 1923. This would seem to indicate not an instance of the Prime Minister's individual determination to

[1] Oxford and Asquith, *op. cit.*, ii, 218.

[2] A. B. Keith, *The King and the Imperial Crown* (New York, Longmans, Green, 1936), p. 176.

[3] Wang, *op. cit.*, p. 68.

[4] W. I. Jennings, *Cabinet Government* (Cambridge, Cambridge University Press, 1936), p. 312.

[5] Wang, *op. cit.*, pp. 29–30.

[6] W. I. Jennings, *Cabinet Government* (Cambridge, Cambridge University Press, 1936), p. 313, n. 2.

dissolve so much as the Prime Minister's determination of the date at which the dissolution should occur.[1]

Some evidence exists which tends to indicate that the Prime Minister's control of dissolution had developed somewhat earlier. In 1918, Bonar Law, the Leader of the House of Commons, was asked about the possibility of an early dissolution. He replied, 'Nothing is more clearly recognized by our constitution than that these things are the subject, not of any written rule, but they are governed by custom, and in my belief there is no custom more clearly defined than that what advice in this matter should be given the Sovereign is a question not for the Cabinet but for the Prime Minister.'[2] It is interesting to note Law's definite belief that the decision as to whether a dissolution should be requested lies with the Prime Minister. It is very obvious that his knowledge of the constitution, on the other hand, is more questionable.

The Prime Minister's control over dissolution was again expressed in 1929. On this occasion the speaker was the Marquess of Salisbury, the Lord Privy Seal, and Leader of the House of Lords. He said, 'The responsibility for advising as to the date of the Dissolution of Parliament I believe rests constitutionally not with the Government but with the Prime Minister alone.'[3] This primacy is also implicit in Chamberlain's statement in answer to a question about a possible election in the fall of 1938. He replied, 'There are only two conditions which I can see that would lead me to change my mind. One is if some new issue arose which I felt required a new mandate from the country, and the other would be, of course, if I felt I had lost the confidence of my supporters.'[4] Implicit in Chamberlain's reply is the belief that the determination was the Prime Minister's alone. A similar position had been expressed earlier, in 1935, by Sir John Simon, who wrote, 'The decision whether there shall be an immediate general election, and, if so, on what date the country shall go to the polls, rests with the Prime Minister, and until the Prime Minister has decided all anticipations are without authority.'[5] In 1945 Churchill, at a

[1] Roberts, *op. cit.*, pp. 117–19; Wickham Steed, *The Real Stanley Baldwin* (London, Nisbet, 1930); G. M. Young, *Stanley Baldwin* (London, Rupert Hart-Davis, 1952), pp. 66–7.

[2] 110 *H.C. Deb.*, 5s., 2425.   [3] 74 *H.L. Deb.*, 5s., 5–6.
[4] 339 *H.C. Deb.*, 5s., 548.   [5] *The Times*, 18 October 1935.

meeting of the Conservative Ministers, asked each of them to write his choice as between a June or October dissolution. Only two opposed the June date. But, as Churchill continues, 'This, of course, did not govern. The right of recommending a dissolution to the Crown rests solely with the Prime Minister.'[1]

The evidence, therefore, indicates that while the Cabinet made the determination as to whether a dissolution should be requested prior to the First World War, it is now the case that the Prime Minister alone may make the decision. It is, of course, evident that he will probably consult with other important government officials, but it is not necessary to go to the Cabinet as a body. As noted above, Churchill did approach the Conservative Ministers in 1945, but no one would have expected that he had approached the Cabinet as a whole, including representatives of the Labour and Liberal Parties, both of which opposed dissolution at the time. Similarly, no one would expect to find that Lloyd George had acted solely upon his own initiative in dissolving in 1918. In fact, he talked with Bonar Law and other important figures, as well as eventually taking it to the entire Cabinet.

It has been pointed out previously that the threat of dissolution provides a weapon by which the government is able to control its followers. It must also be recognized that the fact that the Prime Minister is the officer who requests a dissolution gives his party an advantage over the opposition party or parties. Except in those cases in which dissolution or resignation is forced by defeat in the House of Commons, the fixing of the date of dissolution, within the limits of the law, gives the Prime Minister an initial political advantage.

It is possible for the Prime Minister to seize upon an issue which is likely to bring the government greater advantage than might otherwise be expected, and to seek dissolution in order to gain the benefits of the extension of power offered by the public's immediately favourable attitude. The dissolutions of 1900 and 1918 provide examples of this type of action. Lord Salisbury decided upon dissolution in 1900, despite his substantial majority in the House of Commons, because he believed, and rightly so, that his party would be able to gain another endorsement from the public at that time. The Liberal Party was

[1] Winston Churchill, *Triumph and Tragedy* (Boston, Houghton Mifflin, 1953), p. 589.

divided over the Boer War; the public thought that the victory had been won, and these factors contributed to an overwhelming Unionist victory in the ensuing election.[1]

The election of 1918 was of the same character, despite the excuses made that it was an old Parliament. The most obvious reason for Lloyd George's decision to dissolve was that the public would be expected to reward a victorious war leader with a continuation of its confidence at the moment of victory, where delay might lead to repudiation at a later date. It is probable that a similar consideration underlay Churchill's request for dissolution in 1945, although he was repudiated at the polls.

It is of interest that this kind of action was once deemed not only immoral, but unconstitutional. In 1880 Disraeli made the following statement:[2]

'People insisted that I should have dissolved Parliament when I came home from Berlin. To have done so would have been one of the most unconstitutional acts of the century. A minister with a large majority in the House of Commons has no business to dissolve merely with the object of gaining an advantage at the polls due to transitory circumstances.'

Disraeli's statement is of interest as reflecting nineteenth-century constitutional attitudes, but dissolution for partisan political advantage is now an integral part of British political practice. We have noted earlier that only one dissolution has taken place as a direct consequence of defeat in the House of Commons. If we add to this a consideration of the number of Parliaments, excluding the war Parliaments, which have sat for their full legal term it becomes even more evident that dissolution has frequently occurred as part of an effort to take advantage of what are conceived to be immediately advantageous political circumstances. Since 1895 there have been twelve parliaments elected, excluding the war parliaments. Since it is obviously impossible to expect that dissolution shall be put off until the precise week or date of initial election we

---

[1] Salisbury used the argument that the legal term of the Parliament had nearly run out, but it was obviously not justified since it had approximately two more years to go. *Letters of Queen Victoria*, 3s. (London, J. Murray, 1932), iii, 586.

[2] Henry W. Lucy, *A Diary of the Unionist Parliament, 1895–1900* (Bristol, J. W. Arrowsmith, 1901), pp. 349–50.

shall consider that any Parliament which has entered its last year is dissolved because of the nearness of its legal expiration date. Even so, eight of the twelve Parliaments were dissolved with more than one year of their legal term yet remaining.[1]

In addition to such matters as the doctrine of the mandate, partisan political advantage is clearly one of the important reasons for early dissolution. If the Prime Minister believes he is more likely to gain the assent of the public at the end of four years than at the end of five, he is able to find other excuses to justify a dissolution. The opposition may criticize and complain, but this does not alter the fact that the Prime Minister is in a position to take such action. Attlee could have held off dissolution in 1950 until the summer, but preferred to hold the election at an earlier date, probably because of a fear that the consequences of devaluation might become more noticeable by summer than at the earlier date. In the winter of 1950 the British economic position was improving but there was some reason to expect difficulty in the summer. It should be added, however, that in 1950 Attlee 'allowed four weeks and in 1951 two and a half weeks to elapse between making known his intention of going to the country and the actual dissolution of the Parliament'.[2] Such tactics gave the opposition a more favourable opportunity for the election fight and sacrificed, to some extent, the government's initial advantage in the choice of time and issue upon which the election might be fought.

The dissolution of 1931 also provides another example of the use of the power for partisan advantage. The National Government was formed to deal with a specific crisis situation, but dissolution was determined upon to justify the radical innovation implicit in the formation of the coalition, and to take advantage of the public attitude, which was held to be quite adverse to the Labour Party.

The tightly disciplined character of the House of Commons makes it possible for the Prime Minister to feel secure in his ability to choose the time and the issue over which dissolution will take place. Even in a House as closely divided as the one elected in 1950, the Prime Minister occupies a position of greater power over the selection of the date of dissolution than

[1] Seven years prior to 1911, five years since that date.
[2] D. E. Butler, *The British General Election of 1951* (London, Macmillan, 1952), p. 85.

does the Leader of the Opposition. Churchill attempted, on many occasions, to carry a vote against the government, but the Prime Minister was able to carry the day on all important issues. Generally speaking, the Prime Minister is nearly always in a position to dictate and control the time and issue of dissolution. Through this means he is able to gain partisan political advantage.

VIII

The Prime Minister and the Conduct of Foreign Affairs and War[1]

T he British pride themselves upon the democratic nature of their political system and the manner in which their electoral system secures, more or less adequately, that governmental policy shall be controlled by representatives popularly elected. However, this is less true of foreign than of domestic issues. Foreign affairs are still conducted under the prerogative of the Crown and in consequence treaties, agreements, and other international relationships may be entered into by the British Government without the necessity of prior Parliamentary authorization or even the necessity of legislative ratification.[2]

---

[1] It is recognized that it is not possible to separate the conduct of foreign affairs from war in actuality, but for the sake of analysis it is simpler to handle them in isolation as the major strands can be more easily seen. The discussion of the Prime Minister's relationship to the prosecution of war is confined to such matters as specifically military decisions, questions of internal organization for the purpose of expediting governmental action, and the handling of interrelations between economic, financial and social problems and the specifically military ones.

[2] Treaties which require the cession of British territory may require parliamentary authorization. Cf. Sir Sidney Lee, *Edward VII* (New York, Macmillan, 1927), ii, 251–3. Stanley Baldwin did not seem to consider this an essential rule in 1935. He and his Foreign Secretary proposed a transfer of a part of Somaliland to Italy during the Ethiopian crisis without considering parliamentary authorization necessary. A. B. Keith, *The British Cabinet System, 1830–1938* (London, Stevens and Son, 1939), p. 494. It is worthy of note that the first two Labour Governments followed the rule of

Even declarations of war do not require the authorization of the Parliament.[1]

The Cabinet, as in the case of domestic affairs, has the primary responsibility for the formulation and elaboration of the foreign policy of Great Britain. It is obviously impossible that the Cabinet as a whole should exercise such supervision on a day-to-day basis, while at the same time it is equally evident that the decisions made in that fashion may determine the future prospects of war or peace. The chief responsibility for supervising the work of the Foreign Secretary must inevitably fall upon the Prime Minister. He 'is charged with the responsibility of harmonizing foreign policy with the general policies of the Government, settling serious disputes that arise between the Foreign Office and other Departments, consulting with the Foreign Secretary on the conduct of international relations, and deciding questions too important for the head of the Foreign Office to decide on his own responsibility yet not sufficiently important to deserve discussion in the Cabinet.'[2]

Certain requirements consequent upon the Prime Minister's concern with foreign affairs have already been noted.[3] He must see all important correspondence of the Foreign Office; he must be informed of the content of conversations with important foreign representatives; he must make himself available to his Foreign Secretary should that individual feel that it is necessary to consult with him on a matter. These, however, are but

---

placing all treaties on the table of the House of Commons for twenty-one days prior to ratification. 172 *H.C. Deb.*, 5s., 1677–8; 230 *H.C. Deb*, 5., 408. The Conservatives did not consider these actions a constitutional precedent. 179 *H.C. Deb.*, 5s., 565.

[1] Francis R. Flourney, *Parliament and War* (London, P. S. King and Son, 1927), pp. 7, 8. In both of the great conflicts of this century war followed as a consequence of an ultimatum sent without the prior authorization of the Parliament. In each case the Parliament endorsed the action of the Government by overwhelming vote, but the parliamentary action occurred after, rather than prior to, the issuance of the ultimatum. Parliament is able to exercise a degree of control through debate, criticism, questions, or, in the last resort, the possible withdrawal of support.

[2] R. Victor Langford, *British Foreign Policy: Its Formulation in Recent Years* (Washington D.C., American Council on Public Affairs, 1942), p. 143. See also F. Gosses, *The Management of British Foreign Policy before the First World War* (Leiden, A. W. Sijthoff, 1948), p. 125; John Morley, *Walpole* (New York, Macmillan, 1889), p. 158.

[3] *Ante*, ch. vi.

minimal requirements. They do not adequately portray the precise relationship of the Prime Minister to the conduct of this particular sphere of state activities. In fact, it is impossible to state precisely the role played by the Prime Minister in the conduct of foreign affairs. It depends upon his own inclinations and abilities, the personality and bent of his Foreign Secretary, and the existing international situation.[1]

There is then no consistent pattern of behaviour or of functions which one may say describe the responsibilities of the office of the Prime Minister in the handling of international problems. There are certain minimal requirements which he should meet, but there is no maximum limit set as to the degree of interest or of action which he may take. Some Prime Ministers have felt little inclination to take an active role in the conduct of foreign affairs, either through disinterest, as seems to have been the case with Baldwin[2] and Law,[3] or as a result of a deep confidence in the abilities of the Foreign Secretary as in the case of Asquith.[4] This has not been the characteristic attitude of the Prime Ministers of the last half-century. Most of them have had vigorous inclinations towards establishing their own primacy in foreign affairs, although some have been more successful than others in achieving their objective. Similarly, they have also used different techniques. Two men, Lord Salisbury and Ramsay MacDonald, combined the offices of Prime Minister and Foreign Secretary. Others have appointed Foreign Secretaries, but have nevertheless participated in the formulation of policy either directly by virtue of their office as Prime Minister or through their domination of the Foreign Secretary.

[1] Gosses, *op. cit.*, 126–7. Whatever the inclinations of Neville Chamberlain might have been in the period 1937–39 he would have been forced to concentrate most of his attention on the conduct of international affairs as a result of their overweening importance. The same factors forced Stanley Baldwin to take some interest in 1935–36.

[2] It is reported that Anthony Eden frequently found that Baldwin was of no real assistance in handling foreign policy issues and that his advice was frequently incomprehensible. Derek Walker-Smith, *Neville Chamberlain, Man of Peace* (London, R. Hale, n.d.), p. 287.

[3] At least if not disinterested he had little knowledge of foreign policy and sometimes embarrassed his Foreign Secretary. Cf. Harold Nicolson, *Curzon: The Last Phase* (New York, Houghton, 1934), p. 325.

[4] Herbert Asquith, *The Genesis of the War* (New York, George H. Doran, 1923), p. 17.

The combination of the offices has both advantages and disadvantages. The principal advantage lies in the fact that there is no possibility of a sharp division between the Foreign Secretary and the Prime Minister which may impair the solidity o the government or inhibit the development of an effective foreign policy. Unity between the two offices, whether through combination or through co-operation or domination, is an essential requirement for the effective prosecution of a policy.[1] The two principal disadvantages are probably of greater weight. If the Prime Minister combines the office with his own then there is no officer in a position to exercise day-by-day supervision over the Foreign Secretary's conduct of his office. Since this enterprise is physically impossible for the Cabinet, it is conceivable that foreign policy could be developed and applied without the reality of either Cabinet or parliamentary control restraining the responsible officer.[2] A second disadvantage lies in the fact that the combination of the two offices creates almost insuperable difficulties in consequence of the physical and mental efforts required for effective performance of both functions. Lord Salisbury suffered less from this disadvantage than MacDonald, but this was a consequence of his neglect of the office of Prime Minister for the Foreign Office which he preferred.[3] Even so, it was evident towards the middle of his third administration that the combination of offices was becoming an intolerable burden and he eventually relinquished the Foreign Office.[4] MacDonald attempted to carry out all of the requirements of both positions with debilating physical consequences, although he held them for less than a year. As a consequence of this, as well as other factors, he did not again attempt to combine them when he returned to power in 1929.[5]

[1] See Eden's statement at 332 *H.C. Deb.*, 5s., 45–50.

[2] Langford, *op. cit.*, pp. 145–6.

[3] Gwendolin Cecil, *Life of Lord Salisbury* (London, Hodder and Stoughton, 1932), iii, 137, 202. Salisbury had even expressed his willingness to serve under Northcote if he could be Foreign Secretary. Gosses, *op. cit.*, pp. 134–5.

[4] Lord Esher noted the physical effect of this action as follows: 'Lord Salisbury at the last three Cabinets, in the autumn, when he was Foreign Secretary, sat a crumpled heap—like Granpa Smallweed—evidently wearied out. Since giving up the F.O. he is brisk and attentive. A changed man.' *Journals and Letters* (London, J. Nicholson and Watson, 1934), i, 144.

[5] Philip Viscount Snowden, *An Autobiography* (London, J. Nicholson and Watson, 1934), ii, 760–5; Mary Agnes Hamilton, *Arthur Henderson* (London, W. Heinemann, 1938), pp. 281–2.

Lord Rosebery came to the premiership from the Foreign Office. As he admitted, he had carried on foreign policy with a high hand, frequently in a minority of one, taking advantage of the interest of the Prime Minister in other spheres of activity.[1] This interest in foreign affairs continued after he became Prime Minister, and he appointed a weak minister, Lord Kimberley, to the post of Foreign Secretary. Through this procedure Rosebery was able to dominate the conduct of affairs himself as the Foreign Secretary became 'little more than his instrument'.[2] Rosebery's difficulties did not arise from any conflict with his Foreign Secretary but from the problem created by having both the Prime Minister and the Foreign Secretary in the Upper House. Sir William Harcourt, the Leader of the House of Commons, distrusted Rosebery's attitude towards international problems in the first place,[3] but the chief source of disagreement grew out of the fact that he had to defend the policy of the government in the House of Commons since both the Prime Minister and Foreign Secretary were peers. Frequently Harcourt complained that he was inadequately informed of the content of a decision, and there are even instances in which accusations were made that the Prime Minister and Lord Kimberley had taken action of fundamental importance without informing either the Leader of the Commons or the Cabinet as a whole.[4] In consequence, although Rosebery had a relatively free hand in the conduct of foreign affairs, it became one of the sore spots in his troublesome relations with Harcourt and played a role of some importance in the fall of the Liberal Government.[5]

Sir Henry Campbell-Bannerman exercised little control over his Foreign Secretary. In the first place he chose a man with whom he disagreed on imperial issues as his Foreign Secretary.[6]

---

[1] Lord Crewe, *Lord Rosebery* (New York, Harpers and Bros., 1931), ii, 589.

[2] Langford, *op. cit.*, p. 150.

[3] Lord Oxford and Asquith, *Fifty Years of British Parliament* (Boston, Little, Brown and Co., 1926), i, 252.

[4] A. G. Gardiner, *The Life of Sir William Harcourt* (New York, Constable, n.d.), ii, 331, 332, 337.

[5] *Ibid.*, ii, 306, 307. Harcourt had posed this problem when the Government was first formed. *Ibid.*, ii, 270–2.

[6] 'When Campbell-Bannerman's Cabinet was being constructed in November 1905, Grey at first refused to join it unless Bannerman would go to the House of Lords. . . . Grey was persuaded to withdraw his objections

More significantly, the Prime Minister was chiefly interested in the successful development of his policy toward South Africa. He left the conduct of foreign policy in the hands of his Foreign Secretary although the latter made every effort to keep him up to date on developments in his sphere of activity.[1] On one occasion Campbell-Bannerman acted on his own initiative. This was the instance in which he made his famous statement, 'Le Duma est morte, Vive le Duma', but Grey seems to have thought it relatively unimportant and perhaps even of value in clearing the air.[2] The initiative in continuing the Franco-British military conversations begun by Balfour's Government came from the Foreign Secretary, who was successful in persuading the somewhat reluctant Prime Minister of their necessity and value.[3] Again it was Grey who proposed affirmative British action in the Morocco crisis of 1906 and carried the Prime Minister with him.[4] The Anglo-Russian Agreement of 1907 also was initiated by Grey although he had the complete support of the Prime Minister.[5]

Grey continued to exercise the dominant influence in the conduct of British foreign policy under Asquith, but no difficulty ensued for they were in genuine agreement and so cordial were their relations that no serious dispute ever developed between them.[6] Grey continued the practice he had followed under Campbell-Bannerman of consulting the Prime Minister on all important matters. This unity of outlook between Asquith and Grey made any effective Cabinet opposition to their policies almost impossible, and in consequence even the

on condition that he should be allowed his own way absolutely in foreign affairs, and he had ever since been extremely jealous of Bannerman, a jealousy which had accentuated his obstinacy in pursuing imperialistic lines.' Wilfred Blunt, *My Diaries* (London, Martin Secker, n.d.), ii, 202. This description is quite wrong. No evidence exists to substantiate such an absolute grant of authority, nor, for that matter, did any fundamental differences of opinion crop up between the Prime Minister and Grey.

[1] J. A. Spender, *The Life of Sir Henry Campbell-Bannerman* (Boston, Houghton Mifflin, 1924), ii, 252, 256.

[2] Sir Edward Grey, *Twenty-Five Years* (New York, Frederick Stokes, 1925), i, 150.

[3] *Ibid.*, i, p. 85. G. M. Trevelyan, *Grey of Fallodon* (Boston, Houghton Mifflin, 1937), p. 155.

[4] Trevelyan, *op. cit.*, pp. 139-40.   [5] *Ibid.*, p. 204.

[6] Herbert Asquith, *The Genesis of the War* (New York, George H. Doran, 1923), p. 17.

presence of a majority of Liberal Pacifists in the Cabinet did not prevent the team from successfully controlling all developments. On occasion Asquith himself saw foreign representatives. In 1908 he conferred with Isvolsky when the Russian Foreign Secretary was in London.[1] In 1911 the Austrian Ambassador, Count Mensdorff, interviewed the Prime Minister on the Tripoli question.[2] In all cases, however, Asquith informed the Foreign Secretary of the content of the discussions.

The primacy of the Foreign Secretary ended with the administration of Lloyd George. Lloyd George himself began to participate in the formulation of foreign policy and while he did not take over the office of Foreign Secretary, the actual control of British foreign policy fell into his hands. No real difficulty existed in the first portion of his administration for Arthur Balfour, the Foreign Secretary, was quite willing to allow the Prime Minister to exercise such control. Balfour, formerly Prime Minister himself, recognized that the Prime Minister was almost bound to interfere with the business of the Foreign Office, particularly if he held strong views in such matters and if they were of primary importance in the context of the times.[3] In fact, it seems evident that Balfour subordinated his views to those of the Prime Minister in order that Great Britain might speak with a single voice.

The conclusion of the war resulted in an accentuation of this dominance by the Prime Minister as may be seen from the role he played at the Peace Conference. Lloyd George, Wilson, Clemenceau, and to a lesser extent, Orlando, made the basic decisions while their Foreign Ministers were shunted off into a separate council which dealt with matters of lesser importance than those submitted to the four leaders.[4] Balfour did not raise any objection to this subordination of his office and seems to have been satisfied of the necessity that the Prime Minister should exercise predominant influence.[5]

The cordial relations which had existed between Lloyd

[1] Spender and Asquith, *op. cit.*, i, 245.

[2] G. P. Gooch (ed.), *British Documents on the Origin of the World War* (London, H.M.S.O., 1928), iii, 418–9.

[3] Blanche Dudgale, *Arthur James Balfour* (New York, G. P. Putnam's Sons, 1937), ii, 215.

[4] *Ibid.*, ii, 199; Lord Maurice Hankey, *Diplomacy by Conference* (London, E. Benn, 1946), pp. 28–9.

[5] Dugdale, *op. cit.*, ii, 215.

George and Balfour were not carried over into the tenure of Lord Curzon as Foreign Secretary. Both Lloyd George and Curzon had definite views upon the conduct of foreign policy and frequently their views did not coincide. When Curzon became Foreign Secretary he found himself faced by a situation in which the Prime Minister claimed the right to deal with all major matters. Curzon's personality was not such as to make subordinate status palatable. He made great efforts to assert himself against the Prime Minister. To this difference must also be added the fact that the personalities of the two men grated upon one another, although this was less true in the case of Curzon than of Lloyd George. Curzon, peculiarly enough, at times seemed to have a sneaking sort of admiration for the dynamic Welshman.[1] No similar attitude existed in the case of Lloyd George. Lloyd George was the antithesis of Curzon for where the latter was of aristocratic lineage and personality, Lloyd George was clearly a man of the people and had a deep distaste for aristocrats. In consequence the Prime Minister rather frequently took actions which caused Curzon the deepest mortification, even going so far as to insult him in the presence of representatives of foreign states.[2] Most men would probably have resigned in such circumstances, but Curzon had long had his eye upon the post of Foreign Secretary. He felt that he was eminently qualified to fulfil the requirements of that office. In consequence he clung tenaciously to his office and accepted rebuffs that few men would have taken.[3]

In a very real sense Britain had two foreign policies in some areas of the world. Curzon seems to have been willing to leave most of the major European questions to the Prime Minister in order to more effectively concentrate his attention upon the East and Near East, particularly India, Persia, and Egypt, areas in which he felt the deepest and most abiding interest.[4] The decisions made with respect to Europe were frequently

[1] Nicolson, *op. cit.*, p. 34.

[2] *Ibid.*, pp. 213–14; Langford, *op. cit.*, 171–2. Lord Curzon was not even invited to attend the inter-allied conference at Lympe in April 1921. Lloyd George seems to have thought it a waste of time to send him.

[3] Lloyd George is reputed to have told some of his friends, 'Curzon was always sending me letters of resignation. He would send them by a messenger afflicted with a club-foot. A second and more nimble messenger would thereafter be despatched with a second letter.' Nicolson, *op. cit.*, p. 214.

[4] *Ibid.*, pp. 23, 58–9, 88–9.

made by the Prime Minister without consultation and hence without the knowledge of the Foreign Secretary. Additionally, Lloyd George had his own personal secretariat, which he used for technical advice, thus by-passing the Foreign Office completely.[1] Curzon complained of such action, but it did not affect the Prime Minister who continued in his independent course.

The world cannot be cut into segments and the segments isolated from one another. In consequence, even the fact that Curzon was not particularly interested in Lloyd George's conduct of European affairs did not prevent the latter from reacting upon the policies pursued by Curzon in Asia. Harold Nicolson has pointed out that in one instance Curzon made a masterly analysis of the essential elements of the Turkish problem and proposed a programme of action which later events proved to be of the highest statesmanship, only to have them rejected by Lloyd George. Yet at the same time Nicolson emphasizes that Lloyd George was not acting stupidly; he faced the facts as adequately as Curzon, but they were a different set of facts. Curzon made his analysis and recommendations without thought of the possible attitudes of other allied powers. Lloyd George quite correctly recognized that however able the analysis was, the Allies and the United States would not accept it.[2] Curzon was too tied down by his restricted outlook, his restricted interest; where he saw the solution of the Turkish problem as the most urgent of British problems, Lloyd George thought of the entire Near Eastern area as a source of concessions upon which a general European settlement might be reached.[3] The whole incident points up the inherent undesirability of the division of authority which existed at the time.

It was Lloyd George's insistence upon the control of foreign affairs and his rather high-handed method of conducting that policy which provided the immediate cause of the downfall of his government. In 1922 Lloyd George issued a statement of policy to the press which verged upon being an overt declaration of war against Turkey. The action was taken without the knowledge of Curzon or, for that matter, of the largest number of the members of the Cabinet.[4] The Conservatives hurriedly

---

[1] *Ibid.*, p. 60.   [2] *Ibid.*, p. 82.   [3] *Ibid.*, pp. 89–90.
[4] Wickham Steed, *The Real Stanley Baldwin* (London, Nisbet, 1930), p. 35; Winston Churchill, *Great Contemporaries* (New York, G. P. Putnam's Sons, 1937), p. 243; Earl of Ronaldshay, *The Life of Lord Curzon* (London, Boni and Liveright, n.d.), iii, 314 ff.

decided to withdraw their support from Lloyd George and his government consequently fell.[1]

The wisdom or lack of wisdom revealed in Lloyd George's actions are of no particular importance in the immediate context of this study. The important fact is that his administration made it evident that a powerful Prime Minister could take the control of foreign affairs into his own hands even at a time when the individual holding the Foreign Office had strength in his own right. Lloyd George actually did not trust the conduct of such important affairs in the hands of others, and in particular he did not trust diplomats. He once told the Prince Sixte de Bourbon-Parma, 'I want no diplomats, diplomats were invented simply to waste time.'[2] This dislike of diplomats was an attribute which was to be shared by one of his successors, Neville Chamberlain.

It is probably inevitable that war should result in the transfer of primary control over foreign affairs into the hands of the Prime Minister. Winston Churchill carried out the same type of functions and exercised the same degree of authority, perhaps even greater, over the conduct of British foreign policy. It would seem, however, that no serious friction existed between Churchill and his two Foreign Secretaries, Lord Halifax and Anthony Eden. The evidence available on the relations between the Foreign Office and the Prime Minister is, of necessity, rather limited. That Churchill had the real control of the conduct of affairs is, however, beyond question.[3] It seems to be the case that he had no serious disagreements with Eden; at least no dispute of importance leaked to either the press or the public. Eden cannot be considered a weak Foreign Secretary. He had earlier stood upon principle and resigned from Chamberlain's government. It is probably true that there were no serious disputes between him and the Prime Minister for they were in general agreement on the objectives which ought to be sought.

[1] Beckhoffer Roberts, *Stanley Baldwin: Man or Miracle?* (New York, Greenburg, 1937), ch. v; Ronaldshay, *op. cit.*, iii, 309–321.

[2] Nicolson, *op. cit.*, p. 60, n. 1.

[3] Churchill makes a revealing comment in his memoirs upon his relations with the Cabinet as a whole. 'I did not suffer from any desire to be relieved of my responsibilities. All I wanted was compliance with my wishes after reasonable discussion.' *The Hinge of Fate* (Boston, Houghton Mifflin, 1950), p. 89. Who would wish for more?

Churchill's primacy is indicated by the fact that it was through conferences with the heads of state of the United States and the Soviet Union that the major agreements as to the postwar settlements were reached. In every case the chief British representative was Churchill and in some cases the Foreign Secretary was not even present.[1] Churchill thus accepted the responsibility for stating, defending, and sometimes modifying the British viewpoint in order to achieve a compromise mutually acceptable to the three allies. There is little indication of any actual control being exercised by the Foreign Secretary, the Cabinet, or the Parliament over the agreements which he made. He had an almost completely free hand in all respects. He was, however, extremely careful to keep the Cabinet informed of the progress of conversations and negotiations. He did not give final approval to agreements until the Cabinet had been notified of its content, but there is no evidence to indicate any instance in which the Cabinet seriously modified an agreement.

The most dramatic recent instance of conflict between the Foreign Secretary and the Prime Minister occurred during the government of Neville Chamberlain. Chamberlain had little background in dealing with foreign policy when he became Prime Minister, although it is reported that there had been instances of consultation between him and the Foreign Secretary while Chamberlain was still Chancellor of the Exchequer.[2] Chamberlain, however, clearly had a foreign policy line of his own which he desired to see carried into execution. That policy was one of appeasement. It was not entirely the opposite of the policy line of his Foreign Secretary, but as time passed they fell into serious disagreement. Although Eden insisted that his relations with Chamberlain remained cordial up until the time of the break[3] it is rather difficult to accept this statement in its entirety.

The record of the conduct of British relations with Italy and Germany in 1937–8 indicate that Chamberlain and his Foreign Secretary were in frequent disagreement. Further, they reveal

---

[1] Eden was not present at the Casablanca conference nor did he make the trip to Moscow in 1942 with Churchill. Most of Churchill's trips to Washington were made without Eden. In part this was clearly a result of the necessity to keep a major figure in London to deal with relations with the other major war-time partner. Eden was at both Teheran and Yalta.

[2] Walker-Smith, *op. cit.*, p. 287.   [3] 332 *H.C. Deb.*, 5s., cols. 45–50.

that Chamberlain upon occasion acted without consulting his Foreign Secretary. The Prime Minister even went so far as to enter into correspondence with the Italian Duce without the knowledge of the Foreign Secretary.[1] In a later instance he told Halifax to accept Hitler's invitation to a private meeting without the knowledge of Eden.[2] In both cases it is clear that the Prime Minister acted in this fashion because he feared the opposition of the Foreign Secretary. Even at the moment of Eden's resignation the Prime Minister failed to inform him of the receipt or the contents of a telegram received from Count Grandi which bore directly upon the immediate cause of the Foreign Secretary's action.[3]

The Foreign Office's permanent civil servants were not cordial to the views held by Chamberlain. Chamberlain protested that they were too anti-German in orientation.[4] As a consequence of this situation Chamberlain did not rely upon the Foreign Office experts, but turned instead to Sir Horace Wilson, who had no specific knowledge or background, for the the purpose of gaining 'technical' advice.[5] This in itself led to friction with the Foreign Office, a friction which continued even after Eden's resignation, for Chamberlain continued to by-pass the chief diplomatic officers of the government. When he went to Munich, 'he chose as his companions, not the Parmanent Under Secretary of State or the Chief Diplomatic Adviser to the Government, but officials of much less diplomatic experience, a fact which led to the inevitable conclusion that he did not desire to receive any advice which might be unpalatable.'[6] Inevitably such an attitude increased the tension with the Foreign Office. In January of 1938, the Prime Minister

---

[1] Keith Feiling, *Neville Chamberlain* (London, Macmillan, 1946), p. 330. Chamberlain commented in his diary, 'I did not show my letter to the Foreign Secretary for I had the feeling that he would object to it.'

[2] Walker-Smith, *op. cit.*, pp. 274–5. Eden, who was in Brussels, is reputed to have returned and submitted his resignation but later to have withdrawn it. Langford, *op. cit.*, p. 168.

[3] 332 *H.C. Deb.*, 5s., 257–9.

[4] It must not be assumed that all members of the permanent foreign service disagreed with Chamberlain. Many of the senior advisers are reported to have supported his views. Feiling, *op. cit.*, p. 327.

[5] *Loc. cit.*

[6] A. B. Keith, *The British Cabinet System, 1830–1938* (London, Stevens and Son, 1939), p. 559.

took a step which might be interpreted as an attempt to diminish the strength of his Foreign Secretary. He transferred Sir Robert Vansittart from the position of Permanent Under-Secretary of the Foreign Office to a new post as Chief Diplomatic Adviser. In fact the new post carried no power at all and there are some grounds for suspicion that Chamberlain desired to remove Vansittart, bitterly anti-German in attitude, from a post in which he might adversely affect the policy Chamberlain had determined to pursue.[1]

The constant friction between the Foreign Secretary and the Prime Minister eventually came to a head in February of 1938. Chamberlain proposed to make an effort to restore cordial relations between Great Britain and Italy and to find a means of solving the problem of intervention in Spain. Eden insisted that no such effort should be carried out until the Italians had shown their good intentions by making concessions, including the withdrawal of a substantial portion of their forces in Spain. Chamberlain thought such a demand undesirable and unwise and insisted upon the acceptance of his position. The dispute itself was carried to the Cabinet where Eden made it clear that he would resign over the issue. Chamberlain, however, made the same threat and the members of the Cabinet were thus faced with a situation in which the choice was the resignation of the Foreign Secretary or of the Prime Minister, the latter, of course, bringing with it the fall of the entire government. In these circumstances Chamberlain received the support of the Cabinet.[2]

The dispute in this case was one which had developed over a considerable period of time. As has been indicated above, the relations between the Prime Minister and the Foreign Secretary had not been good for some months. Eden in explaining his resignation stated, 'I should not be frank with the House if I were to pretend that it is an isolated issue as between . . . the Prime Minister and myself. It is not. Within the last few weeks, upon one of the most important decisions of foreign policy which did not concern Italy at all,[3] the difference was funda-

---

[1] Walker-Smith, *op. cit.*, p. 281. Feiling denies any connection between this action and Chamberlain's difficulties with Eden. *Op. cit.*, pp. 326–7.

[2] Feiling, *op. cit.*, p. 338.

[3] The reference is obviously to Halifax's visit to Hitler. It seems probable that Chamberlain's decision to turn to appeasement grew out of the Halifax-Hitler conversations. *Ibid.*, pp. 332 ff.; Walker-Smith, *op. cit.*, p. 276.

mental. . . . The Prime Minister had strong views on foreign policy and I respect him for it. I have strong views, too.'[1] The basic disagreement is perhaps indicated by another statement made by the retiring Foreign Secretary that, 'of late the conviction has steadily grown upon me that there has been too keen a desire on our part to make terms with others rather than that others should make terms with us.'[2]

Eden's resignation restored unity of outlook on foreign policy in so far as the relations between the Prime Minister and the Foreign Secretary were concerned, although another member of the Cabinet, Duff Cooper, later resigned as a consequence of a disagreement with Chamberlain's policy.[3] Attlee's comment in the debate following Eden's resignation speech had clearly summarized the position existing at that time: 'we have not had one Foreign Office operating but two Foreign Offices'.[4] This was no longer to be the case. Chamberlain appointed Lord Halifax as his new Foreign Secretary and Halifax seemed to be satisfied to allow the Prime Minister to conduct foreign affairs and to make the basic decisions while delegating the handling of departmental details to the Foreign Secretary. Halifax did not even go to Munich with Chamberlain in 1938. The Prime Minister's primacy was clear. Even the fact that Halifax was in the House of Lords tended to substantiate Chamberlain's control, for it was hardly likely that the head of the Foreign Office would be from the Upper House unless it was true that the Prime Minister intended to control affairs himself and handle the responsibility of dealing with the Commons in that sphere of activity.

It has been previously mentioned that given fundamental agreement between the Foreign Secretary and the Prime Minister the Cabinet has little actual control over the conduct of foreign relations.[5] This does not mean there are no disagreements in the Cabinet over external policy. Such diasgreement has, in fact, occurred frequently, but if the Prime Minister and the Foreign Secretary remain united in the expression of their viewpoint, the dissident ministers can usually be defeated. Cooper's resignation has already been cited as one instance of

[1] 332 *H.C. Deb.*, 5s., 49. [2] *Loc. cit.*

[3] Winston Churchill, *The Gathering Storm* (Boston, Houghton Mifflin, 1948), pp. 324–5.

[4] 332 *H.C. Deb.*, 5s., col. 65. [5] Cf. Gosses, *op. cit.*, p. 126.

division in the Cabinet. Others have included disagreement with respect to Near Eastern policy in 1922, and even a bitter disagreement over the declaration of war in 1914.

The Prime Minister and the Foreign Secretary do have an obligation to keep the Cabinet informed of problems arising in the conduct of foreign relations. However, in some cases the Prime Minister and Foreign Secretary have even neglected to inform them of agreements or negotiations of importance. It was several years before the members of the Cabinet as a whole knew of the Anglo-French military conversations prior to the First World War.[1] Lord Curzon has said, 'that, of all Government Departments, the Foreign Office was the only one which was never permitted to conduct itself. Interference which would have been strongly resented by the India Office or the Service Departments was assumed by the Cabinet to be legitimate and commendable when applied to the Foreign Office. If things went well, the Cabinet took the credit; if things went badly, it was the Foreign Office who were blamed.'[2]

This may have been true in so far as Curzon was concerned, but it is obviously untrue in many instances. The Liberal Cabinet of 1906–14 frequently found it necessary to deal with problems of international relations, but it is evident that most of the members of the Cabinet considered such matters secondary. The government had instituted a series of domestic reforms and the department heads consequently had to concentrate the greatest portion of their time and interest upon the execution of those reforms. The fact that the military conversations with France could have been undertaken by the Balfour Government and continued by the Liberal Government without the Cabinet as a whole knowing of their existence until 1912 is a clear indication of the rather general lack of interest in foreign affairs which characterized that Cabinet.

Both Lloyd George and Churchill frequently made decisions without consulting the Cabinet. Lloyd George sometimes did not even immediately inform them of the content of the decision. It is true that as time passed he had somewhat greater difficulty in this respect and in one notable instance an agreement negotiated by Curzon with the support of Lloyd George was repudiated by the Cabinet.[3] This, however, was clearly out of the ordinary.

[1] Trevelyan, *op. cit.*, p. 152; Grey, *op. cit.*, i, pp. 91–7.
[2] Nicolson, *op. cit.*, p. 60, n. 3.   [3] Nicolson, *op. cit.*, pp. 111–13.

There is also an obligation to keep the monarch informed of the principal developments in foreign affairs. The monarch may also express his own personal opinion upon such matters. The extent to which such comments may be influential depends upon the character, ability, and knowledge of the monarch himself. It is possible that he may have some influence, and examples might be cited from the nineteenth century in which such influence was exercised. It is noteworthy, however, that the memoirs of the statesmen of the twentieth century do not indicate any appreciable influence upon the part of the monarch. Upon the whole his statements seem to reduce to comments encouraging the Prime Minister or the Foreign Secretary in attempts to handle such matters. It is possible that the exercise of the monarch's right to see important papers might lead to some delay, as it did during the reign of Victoria, but again there is no evidence of such effect in this century.

It is inevitable that the Prime Minister should occupy a position of great importance in the conduct of foreign affairs. He is the head of the government. Realistically speaking he is the most important single political officer in the land. If foreign affairs are important he must concentrate his attention upon such matters. Unfortunately in our world the relations between states are of greater importance than any purely domestic matter. Wars are no longer fought for prestige or for mere territorial acquisitions. Modern wars have become wars between entirely different philosophies; they are religious wars garbed in new clothing, and their results affect not only prestige, but determine even the survival of nations and patterns of life produced by centuries of human endeavour. In the face of such realities no Prime Minister can abdicate his responsibilities in this sphere of activity. He must take an active interest in the external relations of his state. It is, of course, possible that he may exercise only the most general of supervision in those instances in which he has a Foreign Secretary in whom he has complete trust. Even in the latter case it is sometimes necessary that the Prime Minister participate directly in conversations with the principal officers of other states in order to emphasize the importance of a particular matter. An example of this may be seen in Prime Minister Attlee's visit to Washington in December 1950 as a consequence of the crisis which developed out of Chinese intervention in Korea. Attlee's presence did more to emphasize the importance and the gravity of the situation in British eyes than would the visit of the Foreign Secretary. There is little question but that Attlee gave Bevin a relatively free hand and his full confidence in the conduct of British foreign policy after 1945, but the importance of the issue raised in this instance made personal participation absolutely essential. So long as the chief officers of other states play a major role in the formulation and conduct of foreign affairs the British Prime Minister must do the same. Given the condition of the modern world, it is evident that it is the Chamberlains, the Churchills, and the Lloyd Georges who provide the model for the future rather than the Baldwins or the Laws.

The frequency and the nature of twentieth-century war make it necessary to consider, at least briefly, the position which has been occupied by the Prime Minister in the conduct of such conflicts.[1] The Prime Minister as the central figure and the principal officer of the government is forced to extend his attention over the whole gamut of the enterprises and problems which arise in the process of conducting military operations. Asquith stated, 'I had to deal, not only with military and naval operations, the recruiting of the New Army, transport, food supply, and Labour problems, but also with inter-allied finance, and what at that time was a task of supreme difficulty and delicacy, Allied diplomacy.'[2] Such tasks require a concentration of time and effort which make even the frequently excessive peace-time duties of the Prime Minister seem relatively light in comparison. They also require that the Prime Minister have greater initiative and more self-reliance than is necessary in normal times, for it is frequently necessary to make immediate decisions, sometimes upon admittedly inadequate information and without sufficient time to examine all the ramifications of the issue at hand.

In the conduct of war, as in other matters, a great deal depends upon the inclinations and abilities of the Prime Minister.

[1] See Chapter VII for an earlier description of defence organization and the place of the Prime Minister in that institutional system. While institutional matters receive some examination in the following material it is perhaps wise to re-examine the earlier material as the primary concentration here is somewhat different.

[2] Spender and Asquith, *op. cit.*, ii, 194.

The Prime Minister, Foreign Affairs, and War

All Prime Ministers are forced to make greater efforts, to accept more individual responsibility, but there are differences among them as to the extent of the power which they may wish to exercise or are even able to exercise. Much may depend upon the attitude of the particular individual as to his participation in certain of the enterprises which are necessary in the conduct of war. Different individuals may hold different opinions as to what they may do in the direct determination of military objectives and techniques. Asquith held the belief that he should support his military men and not 'play the part of amateur strategist or foist his opinions upon men who had made soldiering the study of their life.'[1] Lloyd George and Winston Churchill, to the contrary, insisted upon playing a role of considerable importance in the determination of military strategy itself and in some cases even tactical decisions involved the participation of Churchill.

Before examining the precise relationships between the Prime Minister and the military in the conduct of the two great wars, it is first necessary to examine briefly the internal organization of the Cabinet itself during those periods. Both of the great wars have resulted in a change in the organization of the Cabinet as a consequence of the evident inefficiency produced by the use of the normal procedure and organization. For the first two years of the First World War Britain continued the struggle with its ordinary, multiple member Cabinet. There was, it is true, a War Committee,[2] but in the last resort it was subordinate in status to the Cabinet. The existence of the War Committee constituted a recognition of the existence of an Inner Cabinet composed of the strongest members of the government as a whole, but it was itself too large to be really effective in handling problems which required rapid decisions. In 1915 it had eleven members, and in addition, experts were frequently called into the meetings.[3] The consequence was that it offered little advantage over the ordinary sized Cabinet. In addition, large as it was, it was still the case that its major decisions did

[1] *Ibid.*, ii, 121.

[2] The Committee was an outgrowth of the Committee of Imperial Defence which was shelved at the outbreak of the war as it was fundamentally a long range planning body. The Committee was known by various names, first as the War Council, later as the Dardenelles Committee, and finally as the War Committee.

[3] Spender and Asquith, *op. cit.*, ii, 180.

not become operative until they received the approval of the Cabinet as a whole.[1] Although the stronger members of the government were in the War Committee it was still frequently necessary to re-argue the same issues in the Cabinet proper, and upon occasion the Cabinet reversed a previous decision or recommendation reached by the War Committee. The result of this organizational division was delay when delay was dangerous.[2]

One other aspect of the organization at the time should be noted. Although the Prime Minister played a role of considerable importance in the determination of military policy, the primary responsibility for day-by-day relationships between the Cabinet and the professional military was exercised by the heads of the defence departments. They acted in constant contact with the Prime Minister,[3] but he did not exercise a general day-by-day supervision of their activities. His most important responsibility arose in case of dispute between or within defence departments which required that the issue be resolved by either appeal to the Prime Minister or the Cabinet. This type of organization did not lend itself to any particularly effective exercise of control by the Prime Minister.

One of the principal criticisms of Asquith as a war Premier was his failure to introduce institutional reforms. Lloyd George and Bonar Law both became convinced that Asquith was incapable of conducting the war and that, furthermore, the existing organizational apparatus made effective prosecution of military enterprises almost impossible.[4] One of their initial demands was for a reorganization of the Cabinet which would place complete control of the military actions in the hands of a small body which would have the power to act without the authorization of the Cabinet, except in those cases in which the Prime Minister thought Cabinet consideration essential.[5]

[1] Lord Oxford and Asquith, *Memories and Reflections, 1852–1927* (Boston, Little, Brown and Co., 1928), ii, 105; Lord Beaverbrook, *Politicians and the War, 1914–1916* (New York, Doubleday Doran and Co., 1932), ii, 114; Lord Maurice Hankey, *Diplomacy by Conference* (London, E. Benn, 1946), pp. 93–4.

[2] David Lloyd George, *War Memoirs* (Boston, Little, Brown and Co. 1933), ii, 389.

[3] Lord Oxford and Asquith, *op. cit.*, ii, 104.

[4] Beaverbrook, *op. cit.*, ii, 114.

[5] Lloyd George, *op. cit.*, ii, 388–9; Beaverbrook, *op. cit.*, ii, 185.

It is difficult to say how such an organization would have functioned, but it was inevitable that Asquith would reject it for the two critics had stipulated that Asquith was not to be a member of the control body.[1] Such a position was obviously intolerable to Asquith and it must be recognized that it was, in fact, an impossible demand—it amounted to an insistence that Asquith accept the title, but repudiate the power of the Prime Minister; that he accept responsibility without any real possibility of actually affecting the making of decisions for which he would be held liable by Parliament and public.[2]

Lloyd George, upon becoming Prime Minister, set out upon a course of action which immediately remedied the clumsy and time-consuming procedure of the prior organization. He established a War Cabinet of five members, only one of whom, Bonar Law, Chancellor of the Exchequer and Leader of the House of Commons, had departmental functions to perform.[3] This five-man Cabinet had full power. It could and did make the final decisions itself. The heads of other departments were called in whenever it was believed necessary to elicit information or advice from them, but the core body held the final authority. In practice, a considerable number of persons always participated in the process of determining policy. Balfour, the Foreign Secretary, was nearly always present, although he was not a member.[4] In the first year of its life, two hundred and forty-eight persons other than the members of the War Cabinet and its secretariat attended the session of the body.[5] Eventually the membership in the War Cabinet rose to seven persons including the notable addition of General Smuts. Upon other occasions the representatives of the dominions sat in on sessions of the War Cabinet.

The heads of the defence departments were not members of the War Cabinet. This created a peculiar situation in which the chief military decisions were made by the War Cabinet as such

---

[1] Beaverbrook, *op. cit.*, ii, 185.

[2] *Ibid.*, ii, 186–7; for Asquith's comment on this demand see Lloyd George, *op. cit.*, ii, 395.

[3] Reginald Viscount Esher, *The Captains and the Kings Depart* (New York, C. Scribner's Sons, 1938), ii, 73–4.

[4] Dugdale, *op. cit.*, ii, 176.

[5] W. I. Jennings, *Cabinet Government* (Cambridge, Cambridge University Press, 1947), p. 237. In 1918 the number of such participants rose to 278.

and in which the department heads were placed in a subordinate status. The professional military was always represented in such instances by the presence of the principal officers of Great Britain who served as expert advisers to the War Cabinet. This relationship meant, among other things, that the Prime Minister dealt much more directly and much more continuously with the military than had been true under Asquith. Still the War Cabinet as a body made the decisions and Lloyd George's influence depended upon his ability and the rather powerful position which he held as a result of the support of the largest portion of the press. Even this position did not always enable him to win his arguments with the professional military advisers.[1]

The principle upon which Lloyd George had based his organization was recognized as essentially sound at the beginning of the Second World War. Neville Chamberlain immediately cut his Cabinet down to nine members, four of whom had no particular departmental duties.[2] Winston Churchill further reduced the numbers to five when he became Prime Minister in May 1940.[3] The number was shortly increased by the addition of the Chancellor of the Exchequer and the Minister of Labour.[4] The precise number of persons who were in Churchill's War Cabinet did not remain constant and by 1943 there were nine members in the War Cabinet, including R. G. Casey, who was Minister Resident in Cairo.[5] Churchill also failed to follow one principle of internal organization which Lloyd George had considered necessary and even vital to the effective operation of the War Cabinet. That was the principle that the members of the body should be free from departmental duties. Churchill seems to have thought it desirable that the

---

[1] Some of his troubles with the professional military men are described later in this chapter.

[2] Feiling, *op. cit.*, p. 421. Chamberlain was criticized because he did not reduce the number even more sharply.

[3] Winston Churchill, *Their Finest Hour* (Boston, Houghton Mifflin, 1949), p. 13.

[4] W. K. Hancock and M. M. Gowing, *British War Economy* (London, H.M. Stationery Office, 1949), pp. 94–5; Claire Nix, 'The Organization of Supply in Great Britain', in W. Y. Elliott and H. Duncan Hall, *The British Commonwealth at War* (New York, A. A. Knopf, 1943), p. 187, n. 42.

[5] Cf. Winston Churchill, *The Hinge of Fate* (Boston, Houghton Mifflin, 1950), Bk. II, Appendix C.

members of the War Cabinet should handle responsible
departmental functions. He wanted them to keep their feet on
the ground. He started with a Cabinet of five members of whom
only one had departmental duties,[1] but all of the changes in
the composition of the War Cabinet were in the direction of
greater and greater concentration of departmental duties upon
the members.[2] It is probable that Churchill's position *vis-a-vis*
his colleagues was strengthened by this development. The
necessity of concentrating a considerable portion of their time
upon departmental functions unquestionably cut into the time
which they had for the determination of general policy. The
consequence was that in the specifically military sphere the
Prime Minister's power was almost beyond challenge from his
colleagues.

Perhaps the most desirable innovation made by Churchill
was made in the sphere of specifically military organization.
Churchill took the title of Minister of Defence.[3] It was an office
with no specific rights and duties, and it must be emphasized
that it was not a department.[4] It enabled him, however, to take
over supervision and direction of the Chiefs of Staff Committee,
thus placing that body in direct daily contact with the Prime
Minister. The organization was such that the position occupied
by the heads of the defence departments declined in importance. They were not members of the War Cabinet, 'nor did they
attend the meetings of the Chiefs of Staff Committee. They
remained entirely responsible for their Departments, but
rapidly and almost imperceptibly ceased to be responsible for
the formulation of strategic plans and the day-to-day conduct
of operations. These were handled by the Chiefs of Staff acting

---

[1] Winston Churchill, *The Finest Hour* (Boston, Houghton Mifflin, 1949),
p. 13.

[2] For example, by the end of 1942, the offices of Minister without Portfolio and Lord Privy Seal had been dropped from the War Cabinet. Both
of these posts were non-departmental. In addition to the inclusion of the
Chancellor of the Exchequer and Minister of Labour, the Minister of
Production, Secretary of State for Dominion Affairs, and the Home Secretary were added. All were departmental posts.

[3] Winston Churchill, *Their Finest Hour* (Boston, Houghton Mifflin, 1949),
p. 16.

[4] The Ministry consisted of General Ismay's Office, Chief of Staff to the
Prime Minister, and a central statistical department. 373 *H.C. Deb.*, 5s.,
1275.

directly under the Minister of Defence and Prime Minister, and thus with the authority of the War Cabinet.'[1] The specific control of all military enterprises was thus concentrated under the direction of the Prime Minister who did not find it necessary to act through intermediaries. The Defence Organization also included a War Cabinet Defence Committee which was composed of the Prime Minister, Chamberlain, Attlee, and the three Service ministers.[2] The Chiefs of Staff Committee was always in attendance at the sessions of this body, but the Defence Committee did not meet very often. Churchill writes, 'As the machine began to work more smoothly, I came to the conclusion that the daily meetings of the War Cabinet with the Chiefs of Staff were no longer necessary.'[3] As time passed the War Cabinet proper intervened less and less frequently in military matters.[4] Churchill did consult it upon all proposals for future operations,[5] but it is evident that the actual control of such enterprises had fallen into the hands of the Prime Minister. He exercised direction over the formulation and execution of military enterprises almost alone, although always careful to keep his Cabinet informed, while at the same time most of the responsibility for home affairs was shuffled onto other shoulders.[6] This organizational arrangement continued throughout the war. There were minor changes, but the basic principles remained the same. It was subjected to vigorous criticism in 1942 from those who believed that the amalgamation of the functions of Prime Minister and Minister of Defence created an insuperable burden. In one case it even led to a resignation from the Cabinet, for Cripp's disagreement with this organizational principle resulted in his withdrawal from the Cabinet.[7]

Both of the wars brought the Prime Minister into close and almost continuous contact with professional military men.

[1] Winston Churchill, *Their Finest Hour* (Boston, Houghton Mifflin, 1949), p. 16.

[2] The Defence Committee later included the Foreign Secretary and the Minister of Aircraft Production. Upon occasion the Minister of Supply also was present. Nix, *op. cit.*, p. 189.

[3] Winston Churchill, *Their Finest Hour* (Boston, Houghton Mifflin, 1949), pp. 18–19.

[4] *Ibid.*, p. 19.   [5] *Loc. cit.*,   [6] *Ibid.*, ch. i.

[7] Winston Churchill, *The Hinge of Fate* (Boston, Houghton Mifflin, 1950), pp. 554–60.

Since war is supposed to be a science and since it is evidently one of those human enterprises which normally requires the expenditure of considerable time and effort to achieve mastery, the members of the profession are considered to be more capable of conducting military enterprises than are non-professionals. It is not at all uncommon for the public, or large segments of it, to think it desirable that the complete control of such matters should be passed over to the military during a war. Yet at the same time it is obvious that Clemenceau was correct when he asserted that war was too serious to be left to soldiers. War is not merely an enterprise in which professionals are able to test their training and capacity upon one another; it involves political and economic matters of the greatest moment. The consideration of strategic objectives involves the recognition of political considerations and the bases in economic, material, and psychological strength which are the prerequisites of successful military action. The Prime Minister is in an excellent position to bring those considerations to bear upon the military problem. He may, however, also attempt to use his political predominance to exert direct influence upon the determination of specific military policy in the narrow sense. If he does so, and it is inevitable, as will be noted, that he must so act in certain circumstances, there is always the possibility of increasingly unpleasant relationships and struggles for power with the professional military.

It is probable that all professional servants of the government are sometimes at sword point with their political minister or ministers, but it is clear that the civil servant does not occupy a position of power comparable to that held by the professional soldier. In time of war the professional soldier moves to a level of equality with the political leader. He asserts a primacy and a superiority within his chosen field, and asserts them with a degree of success which has not been attained by the professional advisers of other departments. He is recognized as an expert whose word should carry great weight by the public, a recognition which other experts have not been able to achieve. Yet the Prime Minister must deal with the conduct of military affairs. How shall he approach them? To what extent shall he attempt to pressure his military advisers to the pursuit of a course of action which they consider unwise or excessively dangerous? To what extent shall he allow his knowledge of other facets of the problem of waging national war to impinge upon specifically military matters?

'It is the common belief that when naval or military questions arise, a Prime Minister has nothing to do but deliver himself into the hands of experts who will decide for him, but much more often he finds himself called upon to decide between rival experts advancing contradictory propositions of equal authority.'[1] This was the situation which Asquith faced when the First World War broke out. Asquith clearly had no desire to make military decisions himself; he would have preferred to follow the advice given him by responsible advisers, but his advisers did not always give the same advice. Additionally, in some cases civilian ministers had conceptions of military strategy which conflicted with the views of the professionals. Asquith had to make decisions in such cases. He found himself immediately in the middle of a dispute between those who advocated the opening of a stronger eastern front and those who insisted that Britain's force must be concentrated in the west. Asquith felt that his military advisers were predominantly in the latter camp and in general he supported the 'westerners' while making a few placating moves in the direction of the 'easterners'.[2] Again he found it necessary to make a decision in a conflict of opinion between Winston Churchill, First Lord of the Admiralty, and the First Sea Lord over Churchill's proposal for a Dardenelles attack. Churchill's position also had the support of the Army. In this case, although Asquith found his principal naval professionals advising against the enterprise, he supported Churchill.[3] It was inevitable that such actions made enemies.

Asquith did attempt to rely upon professional advice whenever he could. His Secretary of State for War was a professional soldier.[4] Yet his Secretary of State did not always agree with what the soldiers in the field were doing and Asquith was drawn into controversy. In particular Asquith made two serious enemies among the generals, Sir John French, the first Com-

---

[1] Spender and Asquith, *op. cit.*, i, 346.
[2] Oxford and Asquith, *Memories and Reflections* (Boston, Little, Brown and Co., 1928), ii, 64 ff.
[3] David Lloyd George, *War Memoirs* (Boston, Little, Brown and Co., 1933), i, 344.
[4] Lord Kitchener.

mander-in-Chief of the British Expeditionary Force in France, and Sir Henry Wilson, French's Assistant Chief of Staff. The enmity first arose over a dispute about munitions,[1] and was intensified when Asquith, with the agreement of Kitchener, removed French as the commander in France and replaced him with Haig.[2]

Constitutionally it was to be expected that both French and Wilson would recognize that they were obligated to obey the orders of the Prime Minister and to limit their efforts to change such orders to normal channels. In fact, they did not do so. French actively worked to subvert the Prime Minister. French himself claimed that he was primarily responsible for the formation of the first coalition, that it was forced on Asquith as a result of the criticism made of his handling of the munitions problem.[3] He went so far as to send some of the officers on his staff to Britain to give information to both the press and the leaders of the Conservative Party which might be used against the Prime Minister.[4] This action amounted to an effort by French to subvert the position of the officer to whom he was responsible. Sir Henry Wilson followed a course of action of the same character. He 'wrote and spoke continually to the Conservative leaders urging them to turn Asquith out. In fact, he devoted much of his energy to fighting the Prime Minister.'[5]

By 1916 Asquith had lost the support of the general's party. The generals had reacted very unfavourably to civilian authority and it is evident that their effort to rid themselves of Asquith amounted to an effort to gain a free hand in the conduct of military affairs.[6] The presence of the generals in the opposition probably weighed very heavily against Asquith when the crisis came, for the military men had influential newspaper support. The whole incident does not reflect particularly well on the military for Asquith was as careful of their interests as any man

[1] Major Gerald French, *The Life of Field-Marshal Sir John French* (London, Cassell, 1931), pp. 301 ff.

[2] *Ibid.*, p. 302; Oxford and Asquith, *op. cit.*, ii, 136–8.

[3] This was not correct, but it was believed to be true at the time.

[4] French, *op. cit.*, p. 302; Spender and Asquith, *op. cit.*, ii, 141. French himself supplied Colonel Repington, the military correspondent of the London *Times*, with material to be used against the government.

[5] Beaverbrook, *op. cit.*, ii, 34–5; Major-General Sir C. E. Callwell, *Field-Marshal Sir Henry Wilson, His Life and Diaries* (London, Cassell, 1927).

[6] Beaverbrook, *op. cit.*, ii, ch. ii.

in his position could have been. Their desire for power must have been insatiable to have made him such a formidable bogeyman. It is ironic that in an attempt to free themselves of civilian control they participated in dumping Asquith, only to have him replaced by Lloyd George, who had far less respect for their opinions than his predecessor and who was to attempt to exercise far more direct personal influence on the conduct of the war. Sir William Robertson, the Chief of the Imperial General Staff, has written, 'The constant aim of the new Prime Minister was to take the military direction of the war more and more into his own hands, and to have carried out military plans of his own devising, which, more often than not, were utterly at variance with the views of his responsible advisers.'[1]

The relations between Lloyd George and his principal military advisers were never very cordial. It was almost inevitable that there should be sharp clashes of personality and opinion when professional soldiers were faced with a man of no military background who nevertheless had views of his own and occupied a position which enabled him effectively to press them forward for adoption. It would be possible to cite many instances of dispute and conflict, but only a few will be mentioned for they characterize adequately enough the relationship of Prime Minister and military. One of the fundamental divisions of opinion, and the most important one, was the dispute over the eastern versus the western front. Lloyd George was of the opinion that no conclusive victory could be won in the west; therefore, he wished to try to open a front in another area.[2] The military advisers, on the other hand, were convinced that the war would have to be won in the west and that the removal of any substantial number of British forces from that front, or the failure to keep them supplied with new manpower, would leave the west open for a German attack. The military men were always able to carry their argument in the last resort, but frequently it was carried only after particularly bitter controversy. On one occasion, after an unsuccessful offensive in 1917, Lloyd George went so far as to call upon Lord Ypres[3] and Sir Henry Wilson, neither of whom had any responsibility

[1] Sir William Robertson, *Soldiers and Statesmen, 1914–1918* (New York, C. Scribner, 1926), ii, 300.
[2] Duff Cooper, *Haig* (London, Faber and Faber, 1936), ii, 163.
[3] The former Sir John French.

for the general management of the war, and to ask them pass judgment upon the opinions of Robertson and Haig.[1] On other occasions Lloyd George also tried to get his advisers to send troops to the Italian front. In 1917 he proposed to send troops to support the Italians, again in the face of opposition from Haig and Robertson. The latter eventually prevailed with the Cabinet,[2] but although beaten for the moment Lloyd George did not give up the proposal and soon urged it again.[3]

It is difficult to say whether it was the disagreement over military policy or the clash of personalities which came first. Both of these factors played a part of some importance in the relationship. Lloyd George never had a very high opinion of Robertson; he thought him 'no strategist, just a good Quarter-master-General'.[4] For Haig he initially had a considerable amount of respect,[5] but as time passed, perhaps as a consequence of disagreement over policy, he lost his confidence in the Field-Marshal.[6] Robertson never had any confidence in Lloyd George and Haig's first reaction to him was that he seemed 'to be astute and cunning with much energy and push; but I should think shifty and unreliable'.[7] As time passed Haig's attitude towards Lloyd George became, if anything, more bitter. Thus he thought of him as a 'thorough imposter', and a 'cur' who could not be trusted.[8] At the end of the war he wrote in his diary, 'The real truth, which history will show, is that the British Army has won the war in France in spite of L.G. . . .'[9]

The tenor of their relationship never improved and the disagreements continued to be frequent. In 1917, Lloyd George's proposal that British troops be placed under French command met the opposition of both Haig and Robertson.[10] Eventually this issue was to result in the resignation of Robertson in 1918.[11]

[1] Cooper, *op. cit.*, ii, 179–80; Robertson, *op. cit.*, ii, 256–7. It is rather unusual for a former commander in the field to be asked to pass upon the actions of his successor, but it should be pointed out that if Lloyd George wanted competent advice by which to judge the opinions of his principal officers he almost had to go to such a source. No subordinate officer would have offered anything contrary to that stated by his commanders.

[2] Cooper, *op. cit.*, ii, 125–6.   [3] *Ibid.*, ii, 129.   [4] Esher, *op. cit.*, ii, 159.
[5] *Loc. cit.*   [6] Cooper, *op. cit.*, ii, 17–18.   [7] *Ibid.*, i, 290–1.
[8] Robert Blake (ed.), *The Private Papers of Douglas Haig, 1914–1919* (London, Eyre and Spottiswoode, 1952), pp. 300, 301.
[9] *Ibid.*, p. 346.   [10] Cooper, *op. cit.*, ii, 46–47.
[11] George N. Barnes, *From Workshop to War Cabinet* (New York, Appleton, 1924), pp. 183–4.

Again in 1917, Lloyd George laid a complete military plan of sweeping character before the French and Italians. No member of the British General Staff had seen the plan previously and the staff officers were opposed to it when they did see it.[1]

Disagreement also developed over manpower policy. In this case it was the soldiers who pressed, the Prime Minister who resisted.[2] Basically the difference in this case grew out of the fact that the soldiers were soldiers and as such recognized only military needs. The Prime Minister, on the other hand, was a politician who had to recognize that any extension of manpower requirements would affect him politically and would at the same time affect both the country's morale and its ability to produce materials of war. The Prime Minister acted precisely as a political leader must act. He weighed and assessed the various demands, evaluating not only immediate military needs, but the more abstruse quality of morale plus the factor of industrial potential. It was a clash upon the very kind of issue which it is essential that the Prime Minister be able to handle. No military man is ever in a position to deal with a matter of this kind. He may only demand what he thinks necessary, but the Prime Minister must consider other requirements and needs as well. The decision is both political and military.

It is more difficult to speak of the relations between Churchill and his soldiers for the available evidence is inadequate. The published memoirs of the British soldiers provide little in the way of information. Field-Marshal Montgomery performed the extremely difficult feat of writing two volumes of memoirs without mentioning a single matter of importance about his relations with Churchill.[3] Churchill himself has said, 'There was no division, as in the previous war, between politicians and soldiers, between the "Frocks" and the "Brass Hats"—odious terms which darken counsel. We came very close together indeed and friendships were formed which I believe were deeply valued.'[4]

---

[1] Robertson, *op. cit.*, ii, 195–6.   [2] Cooper, *op. cit.*, ii, 197.

[3] Viscount Montgomery, *El Alamein to the River Sangro* (New York, E. P. Dutton, 1949). *Normandy to the Baltic* (Boston, Houghton Mifflin, 1948).

[4] Winston Churchill, *Their Finest Hour* (Boston, Houghton Mifflin, 1949), p. 21. Cf. Clement Attlee, *As It Happened* (London, William Heinemann Ltd.), 1954, pp. 118–19.

Churchill maintained the closest contact with all military developments. Through the institutional devices previously described he was in a position to exercise supervision and direction of all enterprises. General Eisenhower has said that Churchill maintained such close contacts with all operations as to make him a virtual member of the British Chiefs of Staff.[1] The Prime Minister even reserved to himself the right to select the code name for military operations.[2] That there were some disagreements is evident. Churchill frequently needled his officers in the field, particularly Wavell and Auchinleck, to take the offensive in Africa.[3] He did, on occasion, remove an officer when he deemed it necessary,[4] but it does seem that there were few, if any, bitter disputes. The Prime Minister was sometimes persuaded that his initial views were incorrect and where his professional advisers were insistent upon a point of view he seems to have generally withdrawn from his position.[5] It is reported that Montgomery, while always respectful towards Churchill, nevertheless would fight him when he was convinced that Churchill was wrong.[6] No information is available, however, on the character of the disputes.[7]

Another aspect of military relations must be noted. Churchill dealt directly and personally with the Allied Commander-in-Chief in Europe, General Eisenhower. In this case it must be recognized first that Churchill did not stand in a relationship of

[1] Dwight Eisenhower, *Crusade in Europe* (New York, Doubleday, Doran and Co., 1948), p. 61. Eisenhower states, 'I cannot remember any major discussion with them in which he did not participate.'

[2] Lt.-General Sir Frederick Morgan, *Overture to Overlord* (New York, Doubleday, Doran and Co., 1950), pp. 1–2.

[3] Winston Churchill, *The Grand Alliance* (Boston, Houghton Mifflin, 1950), pp. 257 ff.; *The Hinge of Fate* (Boston, Houghton Mifflin, 1950), ch. xvii.

[4] Because he felt Wavell had lost his initiative he transferred him in 1942. *The Grand Alliance* (Boston, Houghton Mifflin, 1950), pp. 344–6; Major-General R. J. Collins, *Lord Wavell, 1883–1941* (London, Hodder and Stoughton, 1947), pp. 436–7. Auchinleck was removed for similar causes. *The Hinge of Fate* (Boston, Houghton Mifflin, 1950), pp. 457–62.

[5] In the summer of 1940 Churchill wished to send tanks through the Mediterranean to succour Wavell in Egypt. His professional advisers were strongly opposed and in the last resort the Prime Minister gave way. *Their Finest Hour* (Boston, Houghton Mifflin, 1949), pp. 446–9.

[6] Major-General Sir Francis de Guingand, *Operation Victory* (New York, Scribner, 1947), p. 185. De Guignand was Montgomery's Chief of Staff.

[7] De Guingand gives no reference to any dispute.

direct immediate superiority. Eisenhower's authority was an allied authority, derived from the Combined Chiefs of Staff, and hence he was not under the direct control of the British Prime Minister. At the same time the highest authority in the allied states was located in the Churchill-Roosevelt combination. The Prime Minister, however, could expect to have little success in persuading Roosevelt of the desirability of a course of action opposite to that approved by Eisenhower and supported by the Combined Chiefs of Staff. He tried through argument, but he failed.[1] This does not mean that Churchill was without weapons. He was in close contact with Eisenhower at all times when the General was in London. They usually lunched together on Tuesdays, then met again for dinner at Chequers on Fridays.[2]

The two men did not always agree and Churchill was willing to use all of his charms and ability to persuade Eisenhower to his point of view, usually without too much success. It has become a commonplace to assert that there was a fundamental division of opinion about the assault on the French coast. Unquestionably there was some disagreement, in particular disagreement about timing, but Churchill never proposed the complete rejection of the attack on northern France.[3] The Prime Minister favoured some delay, but not the idea that the attack should be dropped.[4]

There were other disagreements: disagreement over the aerial bombardment of the French railway lines prior to the invasion,[5] disagreement over the attack on southern France. Churchill, in the latter case, wished to drop this attack and concentrate on sending supplies into France through Brittany.[6] In both cases Eisenhower carried the day although it is rather

---

[1] See Robert Sherwood, *Roosevelt and Hopkins* (Bantam edition, 1950), ii, 174–81, 361–2.

[2] Eisenhower, *op. cit.*, p. 85.   [3] *Ibid.*, p. 199.

[4] *Loc. cit.*, Eisenhower says, 'His conviction, so far as I could interpret it, was that at some time in the indefinite future the Allies would have to cross the Channel. But he seemed to believe that our attack should be pushed elsewhere until the day came when the enemy would be forced to withdraw most of his troops from north-west Europe, at which time the Allies could go in easily and safely.' He is also reported to have said, 'We must take care that the tides do not run red with the blood of American and British youths, or the beaches be choked with their bodies.' *Ibid.*, p. 194.

[5] *Ibid.*, pp. 232–3.   [6] *Ibid.*, pp. 281–4.

amusing that in the latter controversy Churchill even hinted that he did not know if he could continue as the King's First Minister should the enterprise be continued despite his objections.[1] In all of these controversies the British soldiers who served on Eisenhower's staff supported him against the Prime Minister and it is to the honour of the Prime Minister that he never attempted to apply pressure to these men. One other disagreement was of more importance, but at the same time developed after the event and hence could not be resolved. Eisenhower was authorized by the Combined Chiefs of Staff to communicate directly with Moscow on matters 'that were exclusively military in character'.[2] Later Eisenhower himself made the decision which allowed the Russians to take Berlin while he turned south. Churchill protested that his action exceeded the terms of his power and that this action involved a political as well as a military decision.[3]

In both of the wars the major determinations of strategy and high policy were made through consultation at the highest level. The procedure in the First World War was at first rather haphazard and not at all cordial. Later, a Supreme War Council was established. The Council consisted of the Prime Ministers of the Allied states in addition to one other colleague. The body was advisory and prepared agreements and recommendations to each of the individual governments so that the constitutional rights of each government were protected. In addition the Council had a body of military representatives who served as advisers.[4] This procedure worked fairly well in the latter portions of the war, but it was overly formal and the personal relationship among the wartime leaders does not seem to have been particularly close. The more informal, personal contacts of the Second World War seem to have brought better results. In particular the friendship which developed between Churchill and Roosevelt enabled the two to come to basic agreements which might otherwise have taken greater time, and the interchange between the two was frequently of the frankest character.[5] Personal contacts were also made with Stalin and

---

[1] Captain Harry C. Butcher, *My Three Years with Eisenhower* (New York, Simon and Schuster, 1946), p. 639.

[2] Eisenhower, *op. cit.*, p. 367.   [3] *Ibid.*, p. 399.   [4] Hankey, *op. cit.*, pp. 22–3.

[5] But Churchill always recognized that his formal status was lower than Roosevelt's. Sherwood, *op. cit.*, i, 426. See also Elliot Roosevelt, *As He Saw It* (New York, Duell, Sloan and Pearce, 1946).

although the relationship was not so cordial as with the American President it is evident that such conversations frequently did much to smooth down relations with that suspicious and demanding ally.[1] It was in such conferences that the major startegic objectives and priorities were established.

The Prime Minister also finds it necessary to exercise tact and consideration in the relations with the Dominions during time of war. In both of the great wars of this century the Dominions entered the conflict upon the side of the British. At the same time it must be remembered that the Dominions are free and independent states. Their troops were frequently under British command, but their governments in the last resort had the final say about the use of their troops. It has been mentioned previously that in the First World War the representatives of the Dominions frequently participated in meetings of the War Cabinet. Similarly, in the second conflict every effort was made to keep the Dominions informed of the conduct of affairs, particularly in those cases in which their armed forces were involved. The second war, however, saw more tension between the British Government and the Dominions than in the case of the first conflict. This was particularly true of the relations with Australia.

Australia provided a substantial number of troops for the operations in the Middle Eastern and North African theatres. They were placed under British command and as it happened a substantial portion of the Australian force was trapped at Tobruk. Churchill had to handle the relations with the Australian Government which insistently pressed for action to relieve the Tobruk garrison. Churchill attempted to persuade them that it was undesirable to attempt the relief action at the time as it would drain resources needed elsewhere, but the Australian government was adamant and the relief action was carried out.[2] Militarily the decision seen in narrow terms was probably undesirable, but more than an immediate military issue was at stake, for there was some criticism in Australia that Australian troops were carrying an undue share of the burden in Africa while British troops stayed at home in

[1] See Winston Churchill, *The Hinge of Fate* (Boston, Houghton Mifflin, 1950), Bk. II, ch. iv, v.

[2] Winston Churchill, *The Grand Alliance* (Boston, Houghton Mifflin, 1950), Bk. II, ch. ii.

England.[1] Churchill, therefore, had to make the decision to relieve the Australian units.

The quarrel over Tobruk was mild when compared to the bitterness which followed the Japanese attack in the Pacific. Churchill found himself almost immediately face to face with Australian demands which impinged very drastically upon the British military position in the North African theatre, and more particularly in Asia. The Australian Government considered that the British had failed to fulfil their obligations in the defence of Malaya and the letters which passed back and forth between the two governments were not cordial. The Australians feared that they would be invaded by the onrushing Japanese. The British thought it necessary to concentrate force in areas which were of secondary importance to the Australian Government.[2] Churchill's attempts to persuade the Australian Government of the necessity of following the strategic views of the British were inevitably foredoomed to failure. One Australian division was trapped and destroyed at Singapore and the British were blamed.[3]

In February of 1942 the Japanese forces began their move into Burma. To the British it seemed of immediate importance to rush troops to that area in order to keep the Japanese away from India. To Australia Burma was of secondary importance. As it happened the force immediately available to the British for reinforcement was very small. One Australian division was the only one near enough to get to Rangoon in time to try to hold the city. Churchill, therefore, asked the Australians to allow the division to be sent there, promising that it would be relieved and sent to Australia as soon as possible.[4] The Australian Government refused the request insisting that it would endanger their own security.[5] The acerbity of the relationship was made even worse by the fact that Churchill had either taken the Australian Government's consent for granted (as he implies) or had attempted to pressure them by turning the convoy with the Australian division towards Burma.[6] The

---

[1] *Loc. cit.* The action was viewed with considerable distaste by the military commanders who wished more time to build up supplies for an offensive, R. J. Collins, *op. cit.*, p. 424.

[2] Winston Churchill, *The Hinge of Fate* (Boston, Houghton Mifflin, 1950), ch. i.

[3] *Ibid.*, p. 155.   [4] *Ibid.*, p. 157.   [5] *Ibid.*, pp. 160–2.   [6] *Ibid.*, p. 163.

Australian Government was insistent that it would not allow its troops to be sent to Burma and Churchill therefore gave in.[1] All of this was not a pretty picture, but it deserves inclusion for it characterized Australian-British relations during the Japanese thrust to the south.[2] The Prime Minister had to deal with the Australians precisely as he would have dealt with another independent state. His authority was not greater than it would have been with any other state and he failed to achieve his own ends.

The relations with the other Dominions never reached anything approaching this character. Care was taken in advising them of all uses made of their troops, but no serious disputes developed with them. The Canadian Government did not engage in recriminations after the Dieppe enterprise ended in very heavy Canadian casualties, and Churchill had to do no more than extend his commiserations and explain the advantages derived from the action.[3]

What the Prime Minister does with respect to the conduct of military affairs depends upon his own inclinations and abilities, but it is evident that he must participate to a greater extent than would have been necessary in the last century. He cannot leave matters entirely to his military advisers even when they are in agreement; he must make decisions when military matters affect political objectives or domestic needs. He is the only official in a position to assimilate all facets of the problem of waging war. No one can substitute for him, no one can take the responsibility off his shoulders. He does not have to participate in all military decisions, but he must participate in the formulation of long-run objectives, and he must understand strategic needs. The extent to which his interference with specifically military matters may be justified depends upon his own abilities and the existing situation. It is probable that Lloyd George's interferences did more harm than good, but Lloyd George had no real knowledge of military matters. Winston Churchill, on the other hand, was an amateur, but an exceptionally gifted amateur who felt quite at home in war, and there is no reason to think that he injured the British military

[1] *Ibid.*, pp. 163–4.
[2] Upon one occasion the Australian Government accused the British of an 'inexcusable betrayal'. *Ibid.*, pp. 57–8.
[3] *Ibid.*, pp. 509–11.

cause, and there is a good deal of evidence to indicate that he was of enormous assistance.

One thing is clear. The Prime Minister in time of war must be willing to act quickly; he must have self-reliance. Asquith was ineffective as a war Premier, because he lacked the initiative and the energy which are called for in time of war.[1] Lloyd George, even if his military contributions in the narrow sense were not advantageous, nevertheless had energy, drive, and foresight which on the whole made him an effective wartime Prime Minister. He would act; he would take responsibility; perhaps he took too much responsibility, but that was infinitely better than a Prime Minister who took too little. War requires that the Prime Minister exercise all his power. It is not possible to rely upon brilliant colleagues, for decisions will not wait for discussion nor will it wait for proposals to go through the 'regular channels'. In peace time the Prime Minister may be an eminently successful leader merely by acting as a mediator and relying upon his colleagues for innovation, but such a Prime Minister is inevitably a failure in time of war. War requires a concentration of power and responsibility. Lloyd George and Winston Churchill made good wartime Premiers because they concentrated power and took responsibility.

[1] Winston Churchill has said, 'Mr. Asquith was probably one of the greatest peacetime Prime Ministers we have ever had. His intellect, his sagacity, his broad outlook and civic courage maintained him at the highest eminence in public life. But in war he had not those qualities of resource and energy, of prevision and assiduous management, which ought to reside in the executive. Mr. Lloyd George had all the qualities which he lacked.' *Great Contemporaries* (New York, G. P. Putnam's Sons, 1937), p. 126. Balfour described Asquith's failure in almost the same terms. Dugdale, *op. cit.,* ii, 132.

IX

Some Concluding Observations

I t is evident from the foregoing descriptive materials that the office of the Prime Minister has been undergoing funda-mental changes. The descriptions of the role of the Prime Minister *vis-à-vis* his Cabinet colleagues with which Chapter VI of this study started have all proved to be inadequate. The Prime Minister clearly cannot be described as *primus inter pares*; he is far more than that. It is true, as Asquith said, that the office depends upon the person who holds it as well as upon the character of his colleagues and the conditions of the time. But even so it is equally obvious that the minimum functions and responsibilities which must be exercised by the con-temporary Prime Minister are substantially more complex and diverse than those performed by Lord Rosebery or Sir Henry Campbell-Bannerman. A changing world has brought greater responsibilities and obligations to the individual who holds the office of Prime Minister. Those tasks and functions which were deemed essential by only the stronger of the nineteenth-century Premiers, are now part and parcel of the duties of even the most ordinary of the modern holders of that office.

The earlier conceptions of the Prime Minister as first among equals do not reflect the real and intrinsic difference in status and responsibility between the person who holds the first position and even his senior colleagues. Winston Churchill expressed this distinction in the following words:[1]

'In any sphere of action there can be no comparison between the positions of number one and number two, three, or four. The duties and the problems of all persons other than number

[1] Winston Churchill, *Their Finest Hour* (Boston, Houghton Mifflin, 1949), p. 15.

331

one are quite different and in many ways more difficult. It is always a misfortune when number two or three has to initiate a dominant plan or policy. He has to consider not only the merits of the policy, but the mind of his chief; not only what to advise, but what it is proper for him in his station to advise; not only what to do, but how to get it agreed, and how to get it done. Moreover, number two or three will have to reckon with numbers four, five, and six, or maybe some bright outsider, number twenty. . . .

'At the top there are great simplifications. An accepted leader has only to be sure of what it is best to do, or at least to have made up his mind about it. The loyalties which centre upon number one are enormous. If he trips, he must be sustained. If he makes mistakes, they must be covered. If he sleeps, he must not be wantonly disturbed. . . .'

It is true, of course, that Churchill as Prime Minister exercised more power than any of his predecessors, even including Lloyd George. But it must not be assumed that his statement is valid only with respect to his own use of the office. It is quite noticeable that all of the later Prime Ministers have been forced to accept greater responsibilities than many of their nineteenth- and early twentieth-century counterparts. Stanley Baldwin did not always exert his pre-eminence, but even so the instances of discretionary personal action in his terms of office were frequently of importance. His determination to make the issue of protection a basis for dissolution and general election in 1923 was opposed by his colleagues, but his insistence led to its adoption. Even more striking is the fact that Baldwin, in conjunction with a few of the senior members of the Cabinet, entered into a controversy which ended with the abdication of the King. Neville Chamberlain was able to pull all of the directing strings of foreign policy into his hands and to follow a course which was opposed by his Foreign Secretary. Ramsay MacDonald while head of two Labour Governments was able to exercise substantial control over his colleagues, and, in fact, destroyed both governments by his own personal actions. Even while head of the National Government, without the support of a real party, his titular position made it necessary that all measures pass through his hands.[1] Stanley Baldwin held the

[1] Keith Feiling, *The Life of Neville Chamberlain* (London, Macmillan, 1946), p. 199.

real political power in the government, but MacDonald could not be disregarded for he was the Prime Minister. Nor did the almost deliberate self-effacement of Clement Attlee suffice to hide his control in the Labour Government. Attlee did not exercise his authority with the verve and sense of destiny which characterized the actions of Churchill, but his authority was real. He was inevitably forced to make major decisions arising out of conflicts between departments; he took over departmental responsibilities in the absence of other ministers; he made the final determinations on such issues as devaluation.

The factors which have contributed to the development of the pre-eminence of the Prime Minister are several in number. Some are minor, while others are of great importance. The Prime Minister is the real source of office and honour. He is, as has been pointed out earlier, limited in the exercise of his appointing power by consideration of party and faction, but this power nevertheless increases his influence. Some appointments must be made, but others are not equally necessary. Those individuals who are selected in the latter instances must feel a degree of personal loyalty and obligation to the Prime Minister which inevitably provides an additional element of power in his relations with his more important followers.

Even so, this situation existed prior to the twentieth century, but the power exercised by the Prime Minister was usually not so extensive as it is today. Other considerations of a more significant kind must be added to explain the growth in power of that officer. One of the most notable single factors has been the change in the character of British political parties. Once loose, ill-disciplined organizations, they have become tightly knit, well-disciplined combinations. The control exercised by the central officers of the party over the rank and file has become increasingly rigid, and the prospects of a grass roots rebellion have become dim and distant. Unlike the American President, who is faced with a party organization in which the actual power is in the States, and hence frequently beyond his effective control, the Prime Minister heads a party which he may control and discipline. There are, of course, limits to his authority. If he is the leader of the Labour Party he must not antagonize the trade unions. If he is the leader of the Conservative Party he must not antagonize the important business, agricultural, and commercial interests upon which his party relies. But within the limits of prudence and commonsense he may exercise a directing authority which is the envy of political leaders of other states.

The primacy of the Prime Minister within the party is itself a product of change in the electoral system. Since the passage of the Suffrage Act of 1867 elections have become more concerned with issues of personality than was true in the past. Many members of the electorate equate the party with its leaders and vote accordingly. This inevitably enables the party leader to extend his power as against that of the rank and file members of the party, and even as against those individuals who exercise substantial intra-party influence themselves. This could be exaggerated, and the experience of the elections of 1945 and 1950 does indicate that the electorate is not always primarily influenced by this consideration. Nevertheless, the person of the party leader is of major importance in the electoral process.

The combination of the tendency towards public judgments upon the basis of the personality of the party leader and the centralized structure of the British parties inevitably elevates the position of the party leader. If he is a dynamic, popular figure it is difficult for his colleagues to oppose him. Even should he be lacking in those attributes his public and party status make it difficult to challenge him effectively. Should he be removed from his position as party leader, or should he be forced to resign because of internal opposition, the consequence might very well be the electoral defeat of the party itself. A party which has rejected its leader is not likely to be looked upon with immediate public favour. This situation enables the leader to handle intra-party opposition with less difficulty than might otherwise be the case. The fact that he is the party leader makes his endorsement almost essential for any party candidate. Opposition to his policies may result in a refusal to offer such support, and hence to the almost inevitable defeat of the recalcitrant individual.

In relation to the House of Commons the position of the Prime Minister is almost beyond challenge. The only governments defeated in the House of Commons on a major issue in this century have been minority governments. The Prime Minister can depend upon the support of his disciplined cohorts so long as he acts reasonably, and even occasional irrational or petulant actions may be accepted. He may even be able to push through legislation which is viewed with disfavour by a substantial number of his own party supporters in the House of Commons, although such action is not necessarily wise. Should intra-party opponents carry their opposition into the division lobbies they face the danger of being subjected to party discipline. Such opposition, if frequent, would inevitably result in their repudiation as party candidates in the following general election, and such repudiation is tantamount to electoral defeat.

The fact that he heads a disciplined party is not the only consideration which tends to elevate the power of the Prime Minister in dealing with the House of Commons. He gains additional influence from his control over dissolution. The evidence indicates that the fundamental decisions as to the dates of dissolution have passed from the hands of the Cabinet as a whole to the Prime Minister, probably acting in conjunction with the senior ministers. The fact that he may request dissolution at any time makes it even more necessary that the rank and file members of his party in the House support the government. The alternative is dissolution and the necessity of seeking re-election. Furthermore, no party member who has been responsible for a situation in which a government of his own party has been defeated in the House of Commons can expect to receive party support in the ensuing election. The central control over the selection of candidates and the necessity of support from the higher officers in the party make it inevitable that the rank and file shall remain under the control of the Prime Minister and his major Cabinet colleagues. The Prime Minister does not exercise single-handed control over the party. The other members of the Cabinet, in particular the 'Inner Cabinet', have status and influence of their own. The tightly knit higher organization, however, is in a position to control the back-benchers, and the Prime Minister is the most important member of the higher organization.

The contrast between this position and that occupied by the American President is obvious. The President has no power of dissolution over the Congress. That body sits for a constitutionally specified period of time. It may, and does, drastically amend proposals which emanate from the administration. The President has weapons with which he may attempt to influence legislation, but they are not comparable in effectiveness to those wielded by the Prime Minister. The President is the head of a party, but it is a party in which the central organization has little control. The real basis of party organization in the United States has historically rested in the States. It is difficult for the central party to exercise effective discipline. Even a President as strong as Franklin Roosevelt learned that he could not defeat men who held control of State party organizations. If the President is popular he may appeal over the heads of the Congress to the public. The fireside chats of Franklin Roosevelt were useful means of bringing about a change in Congressional attitudes, but such appeals to the public in the hands of less able and less popular holders of the office have been considerably less effective. In rare moments of public enthusiasm the President may be able to push through measures which are extensive in scope. But even so, what exists only in rare moments for the President is taken as a matter of course by the British Prime Minister.

Comparisons between unlike systems are always inherently misleading, but it does seem safe to say that the power of the Prime Minister and his senior colleagues is substantially greater than that of the American President. Even in the one area in which assertions are most frequently made of the superior power of the President, namely, the conduct of war, it is doubtful that he exercises any greater authority than the Prime Minister. Woodrow Wilson and Franklin Roosevelt were both able to pull the strings of the war effort and the conduct of foreign affairs directly into their hands during the two great conflicts of this century, but so were Lloyd George and Winston Churchill. In speaking to the Congress of the United States Winston Churchill spoke of 'the chief Executive Power which the President derives from his office, and in respect to which I am the accredited representative of Cabinet and Parliament'.[1] Churchill's control of his military officers, and his role in the determination of long-run strategic objectives, was as great as that exercised by Roosevelt. Furthermore, it is well known that Churchill interfered with details of military operations far more extensively than did the President.[2] It may be said that Roose-

---

[1] Winston Churchill, *Onwards to Victory* (Boston, Little, Brown and Co., 1944), p. 126.

[2] Roosevelt himself seems to have taken pleasure in emphasizing this to British military officers. Cf. Sir Frederick Morgan, *Overture to Overlord* (New York, Double, Doran and Co., 1950), pp. 201–2.

velt was not restricted by the necessity of reporting back to his Cabinet, while Churchill was. In fact, however, with respect to the specific military operations Churchill did not need to worry very greatly over the attitude of the Cabinet, which even went so far as to insist that it not be informed of some prospective military plans.[1]

It is obvious, of course, that the Prime Minister is far stronger than his counterpart across the English Channel. The French Prime Minister faces difficulties which makes it impossible for that office to develop strength and stability. Throughout the history of the Third Republic, following the dissolution by MacMahon in 1878, the French Parliament sat for its full term. Dissolution was equated with a *coup d'état*. The French Premier was thus forced to deal with a legislative body over which he had no effective instrument of control. Since the members of the legislature could not be subjected to dissolution they were able to take drastic steps in dealing with governmentally sponsored legislation.

Even more serious than the lack of control over the legislature was the fact that all French governments were, of necessity, coalitions. Since no party ever received a majority of the seats in the Chamber of Deputies it was necessary to form coalitions among groups with somewhat similar programmes. The French Premier was forced to make concessions on policy and the allocation of office in forming his government. Furthermore, he was forced to spend a large part of his time in holding the coalition together even after the government was formed. Instead of being a powerful leader the French Premier was all too often a suppliant who sought, rather than gave, favours. The constitution-makers of the Fourth Republic tried to take steps to remedy this situation, but the continuation of the multi-party system has made it impossible for any individual to acquire real political authority since 1945.

Other factors have also affected the growth in power of the office of the British Prime Minister. The exigencies of two great wars have resulted in the need for stronger personal direction upon the part of the Prime Minister. Asquith failed as a War Premier because he refused to accept those responsibilities. Lloyd George and Winston Churchill grasped them firmly. The

[1] Winston Churchill, *Their Finest Hour* (Boston, Houghton Mifflin, 1949), p. 19.

Prime Minister has lost some of the powers which he exercised in war after the cessation of hostilities, but even so a residue of the accretion of power seems to remain.

Another factor which has been of basic importance in the elevation of the office of the Prime Minister has been the change in the functions of the modern state. The modern state now performs a multiplicity of functions, some of them extremely complex. The heads of departments have to concentrate an even greater portion of their time upon the activities of the departments than in the past. This restricts the time which they have available for participation in the general formulation of governmental policy. The Prime Minister is inevitably left with somewhat greater responsibilities in the supervision and co-ordination of policy and action. Further, the Prime Minister is sometimes forced to make more final determinations of policy with less assistance.

The aftermath of modern war also results in an increase in the number of problems which require the attention of the heads of the departments. To this must be added the fact that party programmes today are much more extensive than fifty years ago. The economic crisis which followed the Second World War and the introduction and implementation of socialist measures both curtailed the time available for many members of the Cabinet to participate in policy formulation. There is some indication that the Prime Minister was relieved of a portion of the supervisory and co-ordinating responsibilities, but even so an enormous area was left in which such functions had to be performed.

It is possible that the Prime Minister is overworked. Such accusations are frequently made in the British press and by British scholars.[1] There is merit in the accusation as the situation stands today, although certain reforms in the Labour Cabinet, to be discussed below, met the criticism in part. Even so, extensive as are the responsibilities of the Prime Minister, it is obvious that they are not so burdensome as those of the American President. The American President is a 'solitary executive'. His Cabinet does not offer great assistance in either the making of policy or the co-ordination of governmental affairs. His assistants help remove the burden of details, but the

[1] Sir John Anderson, 'The Machinery of Government', *Public Administration*, xxiv, 147–56.

final determinations of policy must still be made by the President.[1]

This does not mean that the Prime Minister is not over-worked; it only indicates that compared to the American President he has greater real assistance and hence is less burdened than the American Chief of State. The concentration of department heads upon departmental affairs does leave the Prime Minister with great responsibilities. It is possible, however, to secure the assistance of others who hold sinecure positions. Herbert Morrison as Lord President of the Council functioned as Leader of the House of Commons, and at the same time conducted most of the daily contact with the Labour Party central organizations. This relieved Attlee of most of the burden of running the House and also provided him with assistance in dealing with the party. It is probable that the office of leader of the House is likely to remain a constant in British practice. It was continued by the Conservatives after 1951.

It has frequently been proposed that the British Cabinet be reorganized so as to distinguish between the planning of broad strategy and the making of detailed decisions.[2] The usual proposals contain two basic recommendations. The first is that the number of members of the Cabinet be reduced. It is obvious, of course, that a committee of twenty to twenty-two members is too large to allow effective deliberative action. Normally the recommendations follow the line of the Haldane Committee Report and settle upon ten members.[3] A reduction in membership is not enough in itself. An additional problem exists as a consequence of the departmental duties of the minister. One critic of existing Cabinet organization has proposed a Cabinet of about six ministers, 'all entirely free from ordinary departmental duties'.[4] This 'Policy Cabinet' would, of course, call departmental ministers into its meetings when matters were being discussed which required precise information or in which the decisions reached directly affected the particular departments.[5]

[1] For an interesting description of the relations of the President and his principal assistants see John Hersey, 'Mr. President', Part II, 'Ten O'Clock Meeting', *The New Yorker Magazine*, 14 April 1951.

[2] *Report of the Machinery of Government Committee*, Cmd. 9230 (1918).

[3] *Ibid.*, p. 3.

[4] L. S. Amery, *Thoughts on the Constitution* (New York, Oxford University Press, 1947), p. 93.

[5] *Ibid.*, p. 93.

This is the extreme view on Cabinet reorganization, and it may be questioned if such reform is desirable. Ministers draw power from the departments which they head, and the small policy committee is likely to have difficulty in dealing with a minister who has the expert knowledge and the technical assistance of the permanent civil service in arguing his case. Further, it may be questioned whether such individuals, cut off from specific, particularized problems, are in an effective position to make intelligent policy determinations. In fact, one may go even further and question the validity of the distinction between broad strategy and the making of detailed decisions as it is stated here. There is a fundamental inter-relationship between the two which may require persons who are forced to deal with both kinds of problems if intelligent conclusions are to be reached.

Generally, the critics of existing Cabinet organization have recognized that some department heads must be in the Cabinet. The Chancellor of the Exchequer, the Foreign Secretary and the Home Secretary occupy positions of such importance that it is essential that they be in the Cabinet. The other officers, however, might more easily be given supervisory functions rather than specific departmental obligations.

There is merit in these criticisms and proposals. The Prime Minister has been forced to extend his activities over too many areas. Furthermore, the Cabinet is perhaps less effective as a policy-formulating body than it might be. The additional administrative burdens which have fallen upon the heads of departments make it difficult for them to contribute as much to the common pool as might otherwise be possible. It also accentuates the tendency towards an 'Inner Cabinet' in which actual control is vested. Actually, it seems to be the case that the Cabinet is in the process of changing somewhat along the lines recommended in 1918. Viscount Samuel has said that the Cabinet 'is apparently now going through a quiet and silent chrysalis stage: later it will emerge into a fully developed and brilliant butterfly of the Haldane species'.[1] Samuel made his statement in 1940, and since that time there is even more indication that such a transition is taking place, although it is not necessarily true that all aspects of the Haldane recommendations will eventually be accepted.

[1] 143 *H.L. Deb.*, 5s., 300.

Some Concluding Observations

Attlee had long been an advocate of internal reorganization in the Cabinet before he took office in 1945. The proposals for reform which he made in 1937[1] were largely implemented after the Labour Government took office. A long step towards relieving the Prime Minister of his excessive supervisory and co-ordinating functions was taken. One of the most notable changes was the development of the specific office of Minister of Defence.[2] The Minister of Defence supervises and co-ordinates the work of the offices of War, Air, and the Admiralty. The Prime Minister's final responsibility for these activities in time of crisis is continued, but in peace time he is able to delegate much of his concern to the Minister of Defence. The Prime Minister continues to serve as Chairman of the Defence Committee of the Cabinet, but the Minister of Defence normally deputizes for him.[3]

Furthermore, under the Attlee Government, other ministers also took over general supervisory responsibilities.[4] The Foreign Secretary had general charge over all external relations, including colonial affairs. The Chancellor of the Exchequer was given the function of co-ordinating all economic affairs, both foreign and domestic. This followed a period of experimentation in which a domestic economic committee under the Lord President and a foreign economic committee under the Prime Minister functioned. The experiment proved abortive and a Ministerial Economic Policy Committee under the chairmanship of the Prime Minister was established in its place.[5] In practice, however, the Chancellor of the Exchequer normally presided over the committee and exercised the basic supervisory and co-ordinating responsibilities under the general control of the Prime Minister. The Lord President of the Council was given the responsibility of exercising general supervision

---

[1] Clement Attlee, *The Labour Party in Perspective—And Twelve Years Later* (London, V. Gollancz, 1949), pp. 128–30. This book was first published in 1937. The only change made in the 1949 edition was the addition of a rather lengthy introduction by Francis Williams.

[2] *Ante*, ch. vi. Cf. Henry D. Jordan, 'The British Cabinet and the Ministry of Defence', *American Political Science Review*, xliii (1949), 73–82.

[3] *Central Organization for Defence*, Cmd. 6923 (1946), p. 6.

[4] D. N. Chester, 'Development of the Cabinet 1914–1949', in Sir Gilbert Campion and others, *British Government Since 1918* (New York, Macmillan, 1950), pp. 50–1.

[5] *Ibid.*, p. 51.

over all non-economic home affairs. So long as Herbert Morrison held that post the Lord President also handled legislative problems and day-to-day contact with the party.[1] In the first years of the Labour Government the Lord Privy Seal was also in charge of all social service.[2]

One authority is of the opinion 'that a system of standing Cabinet committees is now well accepted and that indeed a formal pattern is beginning to emerge'.[3] To this he adds that 'the most obvious grouping is external affairs, defence and internal affairs with a possible sub-division of the latter into production and economic affairs and other home front questions'.[4] This reform is not a total innovation, but it is important that standing committees are now being used in non-military affairs. With the exception of the Home Affairs Committee, established in 1918, this marked the first use of standing committees, as distinguished from *ad hoc* committees, in non-military affairs.

Professor Chester is of the opinion that a new, more formalized relationship is developing within the Cabinet itself.[5]

'There is a kind of hierarchy of Ministers. The Prime Minister and his three senior colleagues—Lord President of the Council, Foreign Secretary, and Chancellor of the Exchequer—take general responsibility for one or other of the main fields of Government activity; the other Ministers who are in the Cabinet and who therefore partake of collective responsibility as well as each being responsible to Parliament for his own department; and the Ministerial heads who are excluded and who are brought only into such Cabinet discussions as are of particular relevance.'

The ministers who headed the Cabinet Committees always functioned in close contact with the Prime Minister, but they relieved him of some of the burdens of his office at the same time. It has been remarked, by a friend of the Labour Government, that this procedure 'greatly increased the efficiency and speed of government and very much reduced the size of the agenda which has to be brought before the full Cabinet at its regular meetings'.[6] Very many matters which would previously have come to the Cabinet were already settled in the functional

---

[1] Francis Williams, 'Introduction' in Attlee, *op. cit.*, pp. 22–3.
[2] Jordan, *op. cit.*, p. 79.   [3] Chester, *op. cit.*, p. 51.   [4] *Loc. cit.*
[5] *Ibid.*, pp. 53–4.   [6] Williams, *op. cit.*, p. 23.

committees over which the ministers presided. This use of committees is not precisely what the Haldane Committee had in mind, but it makes a contribution towards the same objective. It may even be argued that it provides a better solution than the Haldane Report, for the Report treated the Cabinet as if it were only an institutional mechanism and overlooked the fact that it is composed of party men with party responsibilities. The latter attribute may make a larger Cabinet necessary than was proposed by the Haldane Committee, but at the same time the use of functional committees might provide equivalent supervision and co-ordination at a higher level and with less difficulty.

It is not certain that future Prime Ministers will be pleased with the arrangements made by Attlee. Of necessity, internal organization depends, in part, upon the wishes and inclinations of the Prime Minister. Another Prime Minister may find some modifications in organization more congenial to his tastes. The individual who likes to have his finger in the work of all departments may suffer from an organization in which some of the supervisory functions of the Prime Minister are dispersed among other officers. Even so, whatever be the future organization of the Cabinet, even the development of the functional committees does not significantly restrict the strength and power of the Prime Minister. The division of supervisory and co-ordinating functions leaves him free to exercise greater influence in other areas. The imperatives of the modern social order require that the principal officer of state accept greater responsibilities than in the past. The Prime Minister is much more than *primus inter pares*. The change from the status of a Cabinet Minister to the position of Prime Minister is not merely a change of place but a change of dimension.

Appendix One

MINISTERIAL POSITIONS HELD PRIOR TO FIRST APPOINTMENT AS PRIME MINISTER

LORD ROSEBERY (March 1894)
Under-Secretary for the Home Office, 1881–3.
Lord Privy Seal, 1885.
Chief Commissioner of Works, 1885.
Secretary of State for Foreign Affairs, 1886, 1892–94.

LORD SALISBURY (June 1885)
Secretary for India and President of the Indian Council, 1866–67, 1874–78.
Secretary of State for Foreign Affairs, 1878–80.

ARTHUR J. BALFOUR (July 1902)
President of the Local Government Board, 1885–6.
Secretary of State for Scotland, 1886–7.
Chief Secretary for Ireland, 1887–91.
Leader of the House of Commons, 1891–2, 1895–1902.
First Lord of the Treasury, 1891–2, 1895–1902.

SIR HENRY CAMPBELL-BANNERMAN (December 1905)
Financial Secretary to the War Office, 1871–4, 1880–2.
Secretary to the Admiralty, 1882–4.
Chief Secretary for Ireland, 1884–5.
Secretary of State for War, 1886, 1892–5.

HERBERT H. ASQUITH (April 1908)
Secretary of State for Home Affairs, 1892–5.
Chancellor of the Exchequer, 1905–8.

DAVID LLOYD GEORGE (December 1916)
President of the Board of Trade, 1905–8.
Chancellor of the Exchequer, 1908–15.
Minister of Munitions, 1915–16.
Secretary of State for War, 1916.

Appendix

BONAR LAW (October 1922)
Parliamentary Secretary of Board of Trade, 1902–5.
Secretary of State for the Colonies, 1915–16.
Chancellor of the Exchequer, 1916–18.
Lord Privy Seal, 1919–21.
Leader of the House of Commons, 1919–21.

STANLEY BALDWIN (May 1923)
Financial Secretary to the Treasury, 1917–21.
President of the Board of Trade, 1921–2.
Chancellor of the Exchequer, 1922–3.

RAMSAY MACDONALD (January 1924)
No previous ministerial experience.

NEVILLE CHAMBERLAIN (May 1937)
Director-General of National Service, 1916–17 (non-ministerial post).
Postmaster-General, 1922–3.
Paymaster General, 1923.
Minister of Health, 1923, 1924–9, August–November, 1931.
Chancellor of the Exchequer, 1923–4, 1931–7.

WINSTON CHURCHILL (May 1940)
Under-Secretary of State for the Colonies, 1906–8.
President of the Board of Trade, 1908–10.
Secretary of State for Home Affairs, 1910–11.
First Lord of the Admiralty, 1911–15.
Chancellor of the Duchy of Lancaster, 1915.
Minister of Munitions, 1917.
Secretary of State for War, 1918–21.
Secretary of State for Air, 1918–21.
Secretary of State for the Colonies, 1921–2.
Chancellor of the Exchequer, 1924–9.
First Lord of the Admiralty, 1939–40.

CLEMENT ATTLEE (July 1945)
Under-Secretary of State for War, 1924.
Chancellor of the Duchy of Lancaster, 1930–1.
Postmaster-General, 1931.
Lord Privy Seal, 1940–2.
Secretary of State for the Dominions, 1942–3.
Lord President of the Council, 1943–5.
Deputy Prime Minister, 1942–5.

Appendix Two

In April, 1955, Sir Anthony Eden became the twelfth person to hold the office of Prime Minister in this century. In all respects but one he conforms to my analysis of the attributes of a Prime Minister. Eden is the first Prime Minister in British history to have been one of the parties in a divorce. He brought a successful suit against his wife in 1950 on grounds of desertion. There is no indication that the action has had any adverse effects upon his political career. He remarried in 1952.

Eden was fifty-seven years old when he became Prime Minister. This compares to an average of fifty-nine for the Premiers since Lord Rosebery took office in 1894. Eden comes from an upper-class family, his father being a baronet and his mother a Grey. He followed a typical upper-class educational pattern, although it was interrupted by the First World War. After attending Eton, he went to Oxford at the conclusion of the war. At Oxford he won high academic honours, taking a First in Oriental Languages.

In 1922 he entered upon an active political career standing for a seat in the Spennymoor Division of Durham. In a three-cornered election fight he came in second, but the winning candidate had more votes than Eden and the third candidate combined. In 1923, however, Eden was given the opportunity to fight a normally Conservative constituency in Warwick and Leamington. He was successful in his efforts and has remained a Member of Parliament since that time. When he became Prime Minister he had been an M.P. for approximately thirty-two years, as compared to the average of twenty-three years for the Premiers listed in the table on page sixty-three. Only Churchill and Campbell-Bannerman had served longer in the Commons before their appointment.

While most of Eden's prior administrative experience was

Appendix

in offices concerned with foreign affairs, it has been somewhat more varied than is usually assumed. Before his appointment as Prime Minister he had served in the following official positions:

(1) Parliamentary Private Secretary to the Secretary of State for Foreign Affairs, 1926–29.
(2) Parliamentary Under Secretary, Foreign Office, 1931–33.
(3) Lord Privy Seal, 1934–35.
(4) Minister without Portfolio for League of Nations Affairs, 1935.
(5) Secretary of State for Foreign Affairs, 1935–38, 1940–45, 1951–55.
(6) Secretary of State for Dominion Affairs, 1939–40.
(7) Secretary of State for War, 1940.
(8) Leader of the House of Commons, 1942–45.
(9) Deputy Prime Minister, 1951–55.

Of the Prime Ministers of this century, only Winston Churchill has held an equivalent number of governmental offices. It should also be added that Eden served more years as Secretary of State for Foreign Affairs than any other person in British history.

Index

349

z

353

Index

Index